Toward the Setting Sun

Also by Brian Hicks

When the Dancing Stopped

Ghost Ship

Raising the Hunley (with Schuyler Kropf)

Into the Wind (with Tony Bartelme)

Toward the Setting Sun

John Ross, the Cherokees, and the Trail of Tears

Brian Hicks

Grove Press
New York

Printed in the United States of America
Published simultaneously in Canada

ISBN: 978-0-8021-4569-7

Grove Press
an imprint of Grove/Atlantic Inc.
841 Broadway
New York, NY 10003

Distributed by Publishers Group West

www.groveatlantic.com

12 13 14 15   9 8 7 6 5 4 3 2 1

for Beth, who made it all happen

Contents

PART III

Dramatis Personae

The Ross family

John McDonald—A Scottish trader; John Ross's grandfather

Anne Shorey (McDonald)—A mixed-blood Cherokee; marries John McDonald

Mollie McDonald (Ross)—Daughter of John and Anne McDonald; mother of John Ross

Daniel Ross—A Scottish trader; father of John Ross

Daniel and Mollie Ross's children:

Jane Ross	Andrew Ross
Elizabeth Ross	Margaret Ross
John Ross	Margaret Ross
Susan Ross	Maria Ross
Lewis Ross	

Elizabeth (Quatie) Brown Henley (Ross)—Cherokee widow; marries John Ross

John and Quatie Ross's children:

James McDonald Ross—b. 1814	Silas Ross—b. 1829
Allen Ross—b. 1817	George Washington Ross—b. 1830
Jane Ross—b. 1821	

Cherokees

Black Fox—Principal chief of the Cherokee Nation, early 1800s

Elias Boudinot (formerly Buck Watie)—Nephew of Major Ridge; newspaper editor

John Brown—Principal chief of the Western Cherokees, 1839

William Shorey Coodey—John Ross's nephew; marries Ross's stepdaughter, Susan

Doublehead—Influential Cherokee chief of the late eighteenth/early nineteenth centuries

George Guess (Sequoyah)—A mixed-blood Cherokee; invented the tribe's written language

Charles Hicks—Influential Cherokee chief of the early 1800s

Elijah Hicks—John Ross's brother-in-law, second editor of the *Cherokee Phoenix*

William Hicks—Brother of Cherokee chief Charles Hicks; principal chief briefly

George Lowrey—An influential Cherokee chief from Tellico; Ross's assistant chief

Col. Gideon Morgan—Cherokee warrior who led the tribe's unit in the Creek War

Pathkiller—Principal chief of the Cherokee Nation between 1813 and 1827

John Ridge—Son of Major Ridge; a young Cherokee politician

Major Ridge / The Ridge—Cherokee warrior and politician; Ross adviser

James Vann—A Cherokee town chief in the early 1800s

John Walker—A mixed-blood Cherokee with close ties to white politicians

John (Jack) Walker Jr.—Son of Cherokee John Walker; a rebel Indian opposed to John Ross

Stand Watie—Elias Boudinot's brother, rival of John Ross

White Path—Older Cherokee chief; opposed to European customs

U.S. Government officials

Col. William Bishop—Leader of the Georgia Guard

John C. Calhoun—Secretary of War, Monroe and Adams administrations

Duncan Campbell—Georgia Indian commissioner

Lewis Cass—Secretary of War, Jackson administration

Elisha Chester—A U.S. Indian commissioner, Jackson administration

Maj. Gen. John Cocke—Commander of the Eastern Tennessee forces in the Creek War

Gen. John Coffee—Tennessee military leader in the Creek War; Indian commissioner, Jackson administration

William H. Crawford—U.S. Secretary of War, Madison administration

David Crockett—Tennessee congressman, Creek War veteran and friend to John Ross

Benjamin Currey—A U.S. Indian commissioner, Jackson administration

Silas Dinsmore—U.S. Indian agent in the 1820s

John Eaton—U.S. Secretary of War, Jackson administration

George Gilmer—Georgia governor, 1829–1831

Elbert Herring—U.S. Superintendent of the Department of Indian Affairs, Jackson administration

Andrew Jackson—Tennessee general and politician, seventh president of the United States

John Lowrey—An Indian commissioner for President Jackson

Wilson Lumpkin—Georgia congressman and governor, instrumental in Indian Removal Act

John Marshall—Chief Justice of the United States

Thomas L. McKenney—Superintendent of the U.S. Department of Indian Affairs

Joseph McMinn—Tennessee governor; U.S. Indian agent to the Cherokees

Return Jonathan Meigs—U.S. Indian agent to the Cherokees, friend of John Ross

David Meriwether—Georgia Indian commissioner

Hugh Montgomery—U.S. Indian agent to the Cherokees, beginning 1827

J. F. Schermerhorn—A retired pastor hired by President Jackson to negotiate a
    Cherokee removal treaty

Gen. Winfield Scott—Led the roundup of Cherokees prior to removal

Others

Big Warrior—Chief of the Creek Nation in the early nineteenth century

Gen. William McIntosh—A Creek diplomat

Timothy Meigs—Son of Return Jonathan Meigs, John Ross's business partner

Menawa—Leader of the Creek rebels, the Red Sticks, at Horseshoe Bend

George Murrell—A wealthy Virginian and Ross's neighbor in Park Hill

Sarah Northup—John Ridge's white wife, a native of Connecticut

John Howard Payne—A writer, actor, playwright and composer interested in
    Cherokee history, and friend of John Ross

John Golden Ross—A Scottish trader (no relation to John Ross) who settled
    in the Cherokee country and married Ross's sister, Elizabeth

Mary Bryan Stapler—Second wife of John Ross

Sarah Stapler—Ross's sister-in-law and confidante

Tecumseh—A Shawnee warrior and chief; Tenskatawa's brother

Tenskatawa—A Shawnee prophet

William Wirt—Washington attorney; represented Cherokees in two Supreme
    Court cases

Samuel Worcester—American missionary, resident of New Echota, friend of
    Elias Boudinot

Cherokee Time Line

1540: De Soto encounters the Cherokees; first contact with Europeans

1721: First treaty with whites, in South Carolina

1776–83: Cherokees fight with the British during the Revolutionary War

1785: Treaty of Hopewell

1790: John Ross born in Turkeytown (Alabama territory)

1791: Treaty of Holston

1802: President Jefferson agrees to remove Indians from Georgia

1813: Cherokees join the United States against the Creek rebels, the Red Sticks

1814–17: Andrew Jackson twice tries to buy Cherokee land

1816: Cherokees sell their remaining land in South Carolina

1818: John Ross named president of the Cherokee equivalent of a senate

1821: Sequoyah develops a written language for the Cherokee tongue

1822: Georgia begins efforts to remove tribes from its land

1825: Cherokees begin major construction on New Echota, their most modern city, in Georgia

1827: Pathkiller and Charles Hicks, the top Cherokee chiefs, die within weeks of each other

1827: Cherokees adopt a constitution

1828: Gold discovered in the Cherokee country

1828: John Ross elected principal chief

1828: Andrew Jackson elected president of the United States

1828: Georgia's legislature declares its intention to take control of all Cherokee land

1830: U.S. Congress passes the Indian removal bill

1832: The U.S. Supreme Court declares the Cherokees a sovereign nation

1832: Cherokees move their capital from New Echota to Red Clay, in Tennessee

1832: Georgia subdivides Cherokee land and distributes it to settlers

1834: Renegade Cherokees attempt to negotiate a removal treaty with the United States

1835: John Ross arrested by Georgia troops in Tennessee

1835: Renegade Cherokees sign the Treaty of New Echota, selling all tribal land in the East

1838: The Cherokees are sent west; thousands die along the route. Their journey will later come to be called the Trail of Tears

Toward the Setting Sun

The Time of the Fall

A gray dusk settled over the Coosa.

The sun had slipped behind a steep, plum-colored ridge covered with skeletal trees, their branches reaching into the fading sky like outstretched arms. The last of the leaves had fallen weeks ago and now, as he followed the trail beside the river, they crackled like a great fire under his horse's footsteps.

Winter was coming. John Ross could feel its chill in the wind that swept through dormant fields, rustling brown and withered cornstalks like a diamondback's rattle. The harvest had passed and the days had grown shorter. It was November 30, 1831. In another two cycles of the moon a bitter cold would blanket the Cherokee Nation, and there was much to do before then.

Ross loved this land. Perhaps he realized his affection for the red earth was part of what made him a Cherokee, certainly more than his blood. The great majority of his people had no use for material possessions—they could not be bought, like some Indians, with shiny trinkets, guns, or even food. Nothing mattered to them as much as the land of their ancestors, where they had lived and hunted and fought and died for hundreds—perhaps thousands—of years. Now all of the tribe's great history, and its future, rested on him and yet another trip to Washington City. If this final attempt at diplomacy failed, he knew that his people might not see another spring, another summer, another harvest on this land.

That evening Ross rode with his younger brother Andrew. They had spent the day securing provisions for the Washington delegation and now, as the sun set, they followed the river toward the home of William Shorey Coodey, Ross's favorite nephew and the husband of his stepdaughter. Coodey would lead the delegation; Ross would not go this time. Jackson had turned him into a target, blamed him for all the Cherokees' recent troubles. He knew his presence could cost the tribe what small chance it had to reach an accord with the administration and the Congress. Without realizing the great irony of his words, the president of the United States had suggested this entire conflict was caused by the half-breed John Ross grandstanding for political favor.

To be sure, Ross was not a typical Indian chief. He did not wear the tribal garb of his predecessors but a suit and tie like the finest gentleman farmer. A trading post he barely had time to run had made him more prosperous than most white men. Short, slight, and reserved, he carried himself with the air of a well-educated man, which he was. With his pale skin and European features, he did not even look like an Indian. In fact, Ross looked very like the southerners who had become his sworn enemies. Had he chosen a different path, Ross could have lived among the settlers, hidden his heritage, and never had to worry about removal. But if he ever entertained such thoughts he shared them with no one. He had decided at an early age that he was a Cherokee. Their fate would be his.

For this choice he had inherited all of the tribe's troubles. Since he was a boy—he was now forty-one—he had watched white men chip away at the Great Cherokee Nation. Once, his people's land had stretched from the southern Indiana territory to the seacoast, but they now occupied only small areas of Tennessee, Georgia, Alabama, and North Carolina. Their land had been taken slowly, through negotiation and trickery. And when that had not worked white men simply bribed influential chiefs to sell. Ross had seen it happen any number of times in his life, but when he came to be chief he'd put a stop to it. As the Chickasaws, Choctaws, Creeks, and even the mighty Seminoles fell under the pressure of the United States military Ross held his ground. He had accomplished this without violence, in part because he and his people fancied themselves more peaceful than other tribes. In truth, he knew that no matter how strong or how brave the Cherokees were, they would be no match for the white man's army. He had seen the work of Jackson's troops firsthand years ago, and it made a strong impression on him.

His obstinate nature had not won him many allies outside the tribe, but it had earned him the love of his people. Their faith in him had no limit. Indians went out of their way just to touch him, to speak a few words in his presence. They never questioned him; indeed, to the consternation of his detractors, they nearly worshipped him. The Cherokees knew Ross was their last hope, though he was an unlikely savior: only one-eighth Cherokee, a rich trader barely able to speak his tribe's native tongue. But they had not elected him principal chief for his ability to speak Cherokee; they had elected him, at least in part, because of how well he spoke the white man's language.

It was Andrew who decided they should call on Coodey; Ross had not been inclined to go. He was tired and wanted only to return to his house overlooking the headwaters of the three rivers. But he could not let his brother continue alone, could not abide the thought of others doing the tribe's work while he rested. He had proved himself a tireless leader for more than a decade, both as a member of the council and now as chief, and he did not delegate his duties easily. Yet there was more to it than that. There was the man ahead of them on the trail.

The Ross brothers had seen this stranger once too often in a single day for it to be coincidence, most recently at the ferry landing on the other side of the river. The man said that his name was Harris and that he was looking for a stolen horse. He traveled with a local Cherokee named Oonehutty, a harmless, simple man Ross knew well. But something about this Harris seemed sinister, and Ross thought his story rang false. Harris claimed to have information that a thief had carried his animal away on Ross's own ferry. There was accusation in his tone.

Earlier, Ross had assured the man he had not seen a horse of that description or any strange people in the area, but it seemed to make little difference to Harris. He continued to talk about the horse and asked several times if he was really speaking to John Ross, the famous Cherokee chief. The whole incident left Ross unsettled. When the ferry arrived he had told Harris and Oonehutty they could cross first. He and Andrew would wait for the next trip.

As the man named Harris boarded the ferry he had turned to Ross and said, "I hope we shall be better acquainted after this."

Now these same men were once again ahead of Ross on the trail, and another had joined them. Silhouetted in the dusk, the party made a strange sight: Oonehutty riding with a rifle slung over his shoulder, Harris and the other man following behind, whispering to each other. When Ross and Andrew caught up to them the men claimed they were riding to Coodey's house, too, which only made the chief more suspicious. He was sure his nephew did not know them. Ross suggested that since they had the same destination they should ride together.

The third man's horse matched the description of the stolen animal, but when Ross asked about it he got no response. The two white men were jumpy and guarded, glancing back and forth conspiratorially. Harris, who had been talkative earlier, barely said a word. Oonehutty seemed oblivious to the tension but the Ross brothers felt it. The chief kept talking, trying to loosen the third man's tongue, and before long he allowed that his name was Looney. Perhaps it was Ross's questions, or his unmistakable air of authority, but Looney finally broke down.

"Harris, I am now going to tell the whole truth about this business," he said.

"The truth alone is what I want to know," Ross said.

"He is foolish. The horse is not his," Looney said.

"Whose horse is he?"

"My own."

"Do you know Harris?"

"No . . ."

Before Looney could finish speaking Andrew screamed out to his brother: "Take care!"

Ross turned immediately, as if he had expected the warning. He jerked his horse in the direction Andrew was pointing and saw that Harris had fallen behind them and gotten off his horse. By the light of a waning crescent moon Ross could see him crouched behind a tree, and he saw the gun pointed at him before Harris spoke.

"Ross, I have for a long time been wanting to kill you, and I'll be damned if I don't now do it."

John Ross was close enough to hear the cold steel click as Harris cocked his rifle.

He could not count all the men who wanted him dead. Anymore, it seemed they lined up for the opportunity. Besides Jackson—the great Indian killer himself—Ross knew his most dangerous enemy was Wilson Lumpkin, the Georgia governor. As a congressman, Lumpkin had urged the president to make Indian removal one of his top priorities, as if Jackson had not already been so inclined. Ross had known both these men for years, as allies and adversaries, and realized they were playing to the demands of their constituents. Settlers wanted the Cherokee land and were willing to go as far as they must to take it. Jackson and Lumpkin, who had their own prejudices, were more than happy to oblige.

Ross was surprised only that the violence had not come earlier. For more than a year he had stood up to settlers, using his warriors to drive off illegal squatters, a right given to the tribe in any number of treaties with the United States government. The Indians no longer killed these intruders but still intimidated them by burning their homes, their barns. On a few occasions things had gotten out of hand, and this was used as proof that Indians were savages. But Ross argued that white settlers would react no differently if someone tried to take their property.

The gold had made it worse. When a large mine was discovered on Cherokee land two years earlier, the Indians found it harder to fight off the crazed prospectors than they had the settlers. Georgia authorities would not hear the Cherokees' complaints and, in fact, gave gold diggers legal standing for their claims. The state had long tried to whittle away the rights of the Cherokees and other tribes, sending commissioners to bribe compliant chiefs and intimidate Indian families. Georgia law declared the Indians' title to the land temporary, granted its sheriffs jurisdiction over their territories, and made it illegal for Indians to testify against white men in a court of law.

Ross had played by their rules and took his fight against Georgia to the United States Supreme Court. Even though he lost the case Ross won a single point that he believed could drive a wedge between Jackson and the Congress. The Supreme Court had declared the Cherokees a sovereign nation and, with that concession, Ross would settle for nothing short of legal recognition by the United States. The Indians wanted only what had been theirs before, but Ross dreamed that one day Georgia and Tennessee would border the state of Cherokee.

The chief's position was not universally popular, even among his own people, and some Cherokees held a grudge against him. Ross had soured dozens of deals between whites and Indians, stopped or exposed the bribery of several local chiefs who sold out their people for a few hundred dollars or a shiny new gun. Once, in Washington City, another Cherokee had nearly killed him, believing Ross had ruined his deal in order to get a better one for himself. At that point not everyone realized the "White Bird," as they called Ross, could not be bought.

Anyone could have sent this Harris after him. Ross no longer confined his suspicions to town chiefs or rogue Indians; these days, he had detractors in his own inner circle. Some of his closest advisers thought him hopelessly naive, and Ross knew they questioned his judgment behind his back. *Did he think he could reason with white men just because he was right?* A growing number of the council's most respected minds, and perhaps some members of his own family, believed the tribe would be better served to take the money Congress had offered for their land and relocate to the Arkansas territory. Even Ross's mentor and closest adviser, Ca-Nung-Da-Cla-Geh (or Major Ridge, as the white men—and Ross—called him), increasingly felt the Cherokees had little chance of survival in the east.

Ross had visited Ridge earlier that very afternoon. It was not unusual—the two men saw each other so frequently the locals called the path between their homes the Ross-Ridge road. It was there that Ross had first encountered Harris.

To gather supplies for the Washington delegation, Ross and his brother had stopped at the trading post Ridge operated behind his house. It was a popular gathering spot for Cherokees, a place where Indians passed the time together talking. If there were any strangers mingling among the regulars that day Ross didn't notice. He and Andrew bought their provisions and, when they finished, politely called on the old chief.

Ridge met the brothers on the porch of his sprawling two-story mansion, which sat on a steep bank overlooking the Coosa. At sixty, Major Ridge was still as imposing as a young warrior. The chief was fit and strong, although he had thickened around the middle, and he sported a head of white hair that stood in great contrast to his dark, ruddy complexion. He dressed as fashionably as Ross, and may have been even richer—both had amassed considerable wealth through farming and trading posts. Ridge did not have Ross's education, and could not speak English fluently, but he was just as smart as his protégé. Ross was wise enough to realize this.

Ridge invited Ross and his brother inside to sit by the fire. In one of Ridge's comfortable formal rooms the men talked about the upcoming trip, tribe business, the harvest. Over the years, John Ross had learned a great deal from the old man and still listened to everything he had to say, even if they had begun to avoid matters on which they disagreed. Ridge had come of age in a time when Cherokees—himself included—ambushed and killed settlers who claimed tribal land. But he'd learned to distinguish degrees of right and wrong, and the fact that he lived to tell about it said much about how judicious—and how tough—he was. Ross did not doubt the old man's intellect, but he feared Ridge no longer had that fight in him. It was one source of the growing rift between them.

During the conversation Ross heard someone call his name. There was a man standing on Ridge's porch, just outside the room, interrupting their talk with an insistence in his voice that made ignoring him impossible.

"Is John Ross here?"

Ross had stepped out on the porch to face a tall, gaunt man. Harris introduced himself, said that he'd come from North Carolina. He asked about
Ross's ferry, which crossed the river three miles south near Head of Coosa.
That's when Ross first heard the tale of the stolen horse. He was not interested in this man's problems, but when Ross tried to excuse himself Harris
had kept talking, blathering on in a manner that made little sense. By the
time he eventually shut up and wandered off Ross was bored. At the time, he
didn't give the incident much thought.

That was the man pointing the gun at him now.

When Harris cocked his rifle, Ross wheeled his horse around and galloped off, retreating to the sound of the gun's report. As the shot echoed
through the woods, Ross looked back to make sure his brother was following. Andrew was lagging behind but had not been hit.

Ross knew the countryside well, and that knowledge gave him an advantage in the dark. He rode fast, knowing that it was not only himself but the
entire Cherokee Nation he had to save. The tribe depended on him; there
was no one else who could stop Andrew Jackson.

Even though the attack made his blood boil, turning to fight never occurred to Ross. He was not a warrior and he knew it. Ross's only thoughts were
of escape. Although it would have been natural to be afraid, Ross was primarily just annoyed. The attack was merely something else standing in the way of
his business. He knew that he must get away, for he still had much work to do.

Andrew caught up to John within minutes and the two rode quickly
and quietly through the night. After a while they turned off the trail that led
to Coodey's, not wanting to bring this trouble on their nephew.

As his horse sprinted, dodging branches on the narrow trail, John Ross
had little time to wonder who had sent this man Harris. Had it been the
governor of Georgia, the president of the United States, or one of his own
tribesmen? In truth, he knew it mattered very little at that moment, because
he could hear the man gaining.

Then another shot rang out in the dark.

PART I

Major Ridge, c. 1834.
Illustration courtesy of the Oklahoma Historical Society Research Division.

ONE

An Old Prophecy

The sounds of battle echoed through the Tennessee Valley—shrill and staccato war cries, the crescendo of a thousand voices screaming at once.

The noise bounced off rocky mountain faces and washed over the land below, a rumpled quilt of forested hillsides and pastures of high, thick grass that rolled gently toward a wide river. When a breeze came off the water, the meadows swayed as if the very land were breathing. The drought of a few years earlier had given way to a lush summer, and the green fields nearly glowed in contrast to the dark mountains and silver-blue water where the Hiwassee met the Tennessee River.

This land was unspoiled in every direction save for a small collection of buildings that sat behind the walls of a military garrison near the riverbank, a lone outpost on the edge of the American frontier. On this day, hundreds of Cherokees were gathered outside the garrison to watch their warriors compete in a spirited version of ballplay. The object of the game was simple: two teams fought to put a ball about half the size of an apple through the opposing team's goal, two tall poles at either end of an acre of field. Players were given cupped sticks to scoop up and carry the ball, but in truth there were no rules. The men carried the ball—usually a clump of grass tucked into deerskin—any way they could, and took it from the other team in any way possible, no matter how violent.

The pace of the game was relentless; the action stopped only when a pile of players so large and confusing accumulated that it was impossible to continue. When that happened, the men were separated, the ball was thrown into the air, and it all started again. The first team to score twelve goals won.

For the Cherokees the ballplay was serious business. They bet on the outcome in the weeks leading up to it, and talked about it for months afterward. Legend had it the tribe once won half of Georgia from the Creek Indians in a single match (the Creeks, in their version, claimed they won). The players followed strict rules in the days before a game, the most arduous of which dictated that they not lie with their women. But warriors were willing to do anything to gain the slightest advantage, to the point of smearing bear grease on their bodies to slip tackles. It was not a sport for the weak. Players were injured constantly, sometimes even killed. It was with good reason the ballplay was called *anetsa,* a Cherokee word that meant "the little brother of war."

These games were scheduled for all large meetings and celebrations, and this day, August 9, 1807, was supposed to be both. Hundreds of Cherokees had come to Hiwassee Garrison to collect the tribe's annuity from the white men. The money amounted to a yearly mortgage payment on land the Cherokees had deeded to settlers or the United States government in various treaties. There was no payoff date, and the amount changed only when a new treaty was signed or more land was sold. The white men's Congress had promised that these payments would continue forever.

Although the money helped the tribe survive in what had become increasingly a white man's world, the vast majority of Cherokees would have quickly, and gladly, given it all back for what they had lost. In just the past two decades, the Indians had sold nearly half of their vast ancestral lands for a modest sum of a currency that meant little or nothing to them. These annual payments amounted to barely more than a few pennies for each member of the tribe.

The newest treaty was the most troubling of all. In October of 1805, a few chiefs had sold every acre of Cherokee land north of the Tennessee River between the Holston River and Muscle Shoals. The United States would come to call this region the Cumberland Plateau, but most Indians knew it only as their hunting grounds. For those tens of thousands of acres, the Indians received $17,000 in cash and a promise of $3,000 annually—and in the bargain they lost their greatest source of wild game. The sale forced the Cherokees to take up farming, which white men had tried to impose on them for years. When news of the treaty, and the loss of their hunting grounds, first spread through the Cherokee Nation it nearly set off a tribal war. To keep the peace, the tribe's council adopted new laws making it nearly impossible for anyone to sell Cherokee land. But enforcing these rules would prove difficult. It was clear the white men had an insatiable taste for Indian land, and a few powerful Cherokees were always eager to deal.

In recent years, the United States government had begun an aggressive campaign to convince the southern tribes to trade their homes for large tracts of land west of the Mississippi River, where President Jefferson had secured a vast frontier from the French. Indian agents bragged about the "great plains" shamelessly, claiming that this western land held the promise of bountiful hunting and no interference from whites. In truth, the government was merely promoting the interests of its constituents, new settlers who were hungry for land, caught up in the country's great expansion. Since 1790 Tennessee's population alone had grown from thirty-five thousand to nearly a quarter million. These families—drawn to the temperate climate and fertile ground—needed homesteads. And they didn't want to share their new homes with the natives. It was a volatile mix of greed and prejudice.

Some Indians, weary of the endless encroachment by settlers, reluctantly accepted these government land swaps. The great majority of Cherokees, however, swore they would never consider the white man's deal. According to tribal legend, the Creator had made man out of the red clay of the earth, and that meant the red men were the first race, the most pure. The Cherokees felt tied to their land spiritually and saw themselves as a part of its nature. They loved their land as much as the white men coveted it, and most of them would rather die than give it up.

The tension that resulted from these land deals was a cause of great concern for Return Jonathan Meigs, the local U.S. Indian agent. Although he had become accustomed to life among the Cherokees, he wasn't sure it was a good idea for so many members of the tribe—some of them overtly hostile to the United States government—to converge on his office at Hiwassee Garrison. Many of these warriors were the same men who had murdered hundreds of settlers in the Indian wars twenty years earlier. The log walls of the garrison he'd spent $20,000 and a year building were a reminder of that history. There were still Indians who would just as soon kill whites as take their money, and that was trouble Meigs preferred to avoid. Yet despite these private fears, he was a most gracious host.

Meigs served as a diplomat between the tribe and the United States, but his job was much more complex than simply acting as an interpreter or ambassador. He was charged with keeping the peace between Indians and settlers, and with introducing the tribe to more civilized methods of survival, primarily farming and education. He prompted many Cherokees to learn the English language, to read and to write, and encouraged the women to sew and weave. He also served as judge and jury in the conflicts that arose between whites and Indians. Meigs meted out justice without any appearance of favoritism, and that had won him the respect of many Cherokees.

These days, his bosses at the U.S. War Department also frequently urged Meigs to convince the tribe to move west. They told him to bribe any chief he felt could be persuaded with a little money or a new gun. In his time, the Revolutionary War veteran had seen a great many things, and he knew his situation was not ideal. It was a patronage job, easy living for a respected war hero. An Indian agent did not carry the same prestige as an ambassador to, say, France but it was important work. Nonetheless, the problem for Meigs was that, at sixty-seven, he was too old to have his opinions dictated to him.

Living among the Cherokees, Meigs had gained a great deal of respect and sympathy for these Indians. They were a special tribe; he considered them more civilized than most of the other tribes, saw them quickly adapting to modern, European ways. Given time, the Cherokees would live almost exactly like the settlers moving into the area daily. Above all else, Meigs realized the Cherokees had been there first, that it was indeed their home. He also knew that if the United States wanted their land, the tribe's only chance to survive might be to do as they were asked. He had lived through the frontier wars, and the old soldier realized the next time the Indians fought the U.S. Army it would be much worse for both sides.

So Meigs did as he was told and reluctantly offered kickbacks to Indians willing to deal with the government. And he found no one more willing than the old chief who showed up at the ballplay late that afternoon.

Doublehead walked with an unmistakable swagger. He was one of the most feared men in the Cherokee Nation, and he knew it. Over the years, Doublehead had killed more whites and Indians than anyone cared to count, and he had become politically powerful in the process. Few dared to cross him, and most Indians moved out of his way as he passed. But when Doublehead saw Meigs watching the ballplay with James Robertson and Daniel Smith—two U.S. commissioners—and Sam Dale, a trader from Mississippi, he displayed none of his famous temperament. He put on a great show of affection for these white men.

"Sam, you are a great liar," Doublehead said. "You have never kept your promise to come to see me."

He presented the group with a bottle of whiskey and soon they were drinking together, a spectacle nearly as interesting to the Indians as the ballplay. It was only further proof that Doublehead was in the pocket of the white men, and it stirred resentment among the assembled Cherokees. The old chief, it seemed, had no shame.

Doublehead brokered the 1805 treaty almost single-handedly, and the Cherokees had since learned that he'd profited handsomely from it. As a reward for selling off the tribe's hunting grounds, the United States had given Doublehead a cash bonus and two tracts of land for himself and a relative. Instead of hiding his involvement the chief bragged that he had secured a good deal for his people. One story held that after the treaty was completed,

Doublehead even demanded a bottle of whiskey—from a local missionary, no less—for all his hard work.

It had not always been that way. Years earlier, Doublehead had been one of the most loyal protectors of Cherokee land. When the Indians were practically at war with settlers in the final years of the eighteenth century, he fought as tirelessly as the legendary Dragging Canoe, and was perhaps even more relentless. For a time, he had been a hero to some Indians, hailed as their greatest protector. With the passing of those days Doublehead had not grown any less violent. It seemed he still had a taste for blood, and it did not matter whose it was. Now, he mostly fought his own people.

Doublehead was speaker of the council, an important position among the Cherokees, and some Indian agents misinterpreted this as a sign of respect. In truth, he won the job only for his talent as a storyteller and ability to translate English messages from the government, not for any recognition of great wisdom. Doublehead keenly felt this lack of respect, and it weighed on him; perhaps it is what led him to put his own desires ahead of the tribe. Even if Doublehead did not think of it in such terms, many Cherokees believed he no longer cared if the tribe lost land so long as he didn't lose his.

Although he may not have been particularly wise, Doublehead was not stupid. He knew there was talk about the consideration—the bribes—he accepted from white men. But he didn't care. He did as he pleased and it had made him very wealthy. He now believed that he was all powerful, perhaps even more so than the principal chief. Doublehead was confident no one would challenge him. Accordingly, he made no attempt to hide his relationship with the white men.

As the afternoon passed the group cheered on the ballplay and drank until they finished Doublehead's whiskey. Dale offered to refill the bottle from his own supply, but the old chief preferred to play the gracious host, acting as if the entire gathering were his own private party.

"When in white man's country, drink white man's whiskey, but here, you must drink with Doublehead," he said.

* * *

The ballplay ended soon after the sun fell behind the mountains. The crowd slowly wandered off in the dusk. Some Cherokees headed home and others gathered around kegs of whiskey set out by soldiers from the fort, a gesture by Meigs meant to improve relations. The game would turn into a party, Indians lingering outside the garrison walls well into the night. Finally Doublehead rose to leave, saying his good-byes to Meigs and the others, who had gathered around one of the barrels. As the chief was climbing onto his horse a Cherokee named Bone Cracker called out to him. The man had been drinking, and the liquor coursing through his blood gave him the courage to grab the bridle on Doublehead's horse.

"You have betrayed our people," he said. "You have sold our hunting grounds."

Doublehead had heard these charges before, but rarely had any Indian so brazenly confronted him. Trying not to attract attention or embarrass himself in front of the white men, the old chief showed a measure of restraint. He calmly told the man to walk away.

"You have said enough. Go away or I will kill you."

It happened in an instant. Some later said that Bone Cracker stepped toward the chief; others claimed he pulled his tomahawk, maybe even struck Doublehead with it. Either way, Doublehead reacted instantly. He pulled his pistol and shot the Cherokee at near point-blank range. Bone Cracker fell instantly and died within moments.

No one spoke. Doublehead sat there atop his horse, staring at the limp body on the ground with only mild interest. The crowd had grown quiet, but most of the Indians pretended they had not seen the killing. Many simply walked away or turned their attention to the kegs or the distant mountains, as if something else held their attention. Eventually, Doublehead gave a quick kick to his horse and rode off without a word.

Meigs and the others were astonished. Their gregarious friend had killed another man as casually as most would smack at a fly, and he did not seem to give it a thought. They took it as more proof that, in the Cherokee Nation, Doublehead was untouchable.

But he wasn't.

* * *

More than two dozen Cherokees were already deep in their cups at McIntosh's Long Hut tavern when Doublehead walked in that night. Situated on the trail near the tiny outpost of Calhoun, the bar—an oversize cabin, really—was a favorite among the Indians. Doublehead was a friend of the owner, another Cherokee, and the old chief spent many hours entertaining customers with outrageous stories. This evening, however, he brushed by McIntosh and the others without a word, took a seat in the back of the room, and ordered a drink. He appeared mad and most of the men, wise enough to avoid drawing his anger, left him alone.

News of the incident at Hiwassee Garrison had not yet reached the tavern. McIntosh was expecting a crowd later that night, but most Indians leaving the ballplay would travel the five or six miles between the fort and the tavern at a more leisurely—if not drunken—pace, thanks to Meigs's hospitality. Even if they had known about the killing of Bone Cracker, no one at McIntosh's would have said a word to the old chief. And it would not have mattered to the three men watching him from another table.

They did not need another excuse to kill Doublehead.

The men had been sent by a faction of the tribal council to assassinate their own speaker, an almost unprecedented act. James Vann, a local chief, had decided it was time Doublehead paid for his many crimes against the Cherokee Nation, and several other chiefs agreed. But there was more to Vann's plot than simple politics; it was also personal. The trouble between the two men went back years. On a trip to Washington City in 1805, Vann had tried to stop Doublehead from selling the tribe's hunting grounds. When he called the old chief the Cherokee's "betrayer," knives were drawn. The two men nearly killed each other before they were separated. To make matters worse, Doublehead had married the sister of one of Vann's wives and then beat her to death while she was pregnant. Doublehead's family made excuses, claimed the woman was keeping the company of another man. But Vann did not believe them and, spurred on by his wife, wanted revenge.

Vann was no innocent himself. A prosperous trader and tavern owner, he was known to liberally use his own merchandise and, even sober, had a violent temper. There were rumors that he was not above taking a bribe from Indian agents, either. The difference was Vann seemed to have the best interests of the Cherokees at heart. He aligned himself with young, progressive members of the council and was a leading advocate for farming, education, and the other accepted tools of modern civilization. Vann and his allies, including Charles Hicks, a mixed-blood Cherokee who served as Meigs's interpreter, had become influential voices in the nation, so when they agreed it was time to do something about Doublehead it wasn't difficult to recruit volunteers. One of them, a new council member, now sat at a table in McIntosh's watching the old chief hold court with a few drunks. The Ridge had agreed to help Vann, but he had his own reasons. He believed justice demanded that Doublehead must die.

At thirty-six, The Ridge—as the white men called him—already had a considerable reputation for uncommon intelligence and morality. He was the son of a hunter, and his parents had believed he was destined to follow his father's path and named him Nung-noh-hut-tar-hee, or "He who slays the enemy in the path." It was other Cherokee hunters who gave him his adult name. As a young brave he often emerged from the forest unexpectedly, taking hunting parties by surprise. When they asked where he had come from, he would say, "I came along the top of the mountain." The Cherokees began to call him "The man who walks on mountain's top." The white men interpreted this as "The Ridge."

He made an excellent hunter, for it seemed he was always thinking several moves ahead of his prey. Had he been overly religious, some might have believed The Ridge was a prophet. But it was common sense, and not visions, that guided him. He could not read or write but he had the analytical mind of a learned man. The Ridge urged his people to educate their children in the language and ways of the whites. He believed it was the only way the tribe could survive in the changing world. Some Indians ridiculed his ideas, but Ridge knew all too well that the old times had passed.

When he was a child his family had been forced to abandon their home on the Hiwassee, fleeing white settlers in a single canoe. The Ridge never forgot that feeling as he grew up in the Sequatchie Valley, where he heard countless stories of the Indians' sad and unending retreat. By the time he reached his teenage years he had joined the tribe's fight against white settlers. He learned to kill men, and found little respect for the whites, who sometimes seemed more vicious—more uncivilized—than any Indian. But Ridge also learned that many things were more complicated than they first appeared. Riding alongside Doublehead as a young man, Ridge had found that a person could fight for the right thing and still be wrong.

In 1793, Ridge was traveling with a band of Cherokees that overtook a family of settlers outside a Knoxville garrison. The Indians far outnumbered the whites, even after the cornered family managed to shoot five of them. Alexander Cavett had barricaded his family in a blockhouse, one of the fort's outbuildings, but they were trapped with little way to fight. Only three of the thirteen people inside were men, so Cavett asked for a truce. The Cherokee leader, a warrior named Bench, promised Cavett everyone inside would be spared in exchange for Indian prisoners if the fort surrendered. The white man agreed, but when he opened the door to the blockhouse Doublehead attacked. As the surprised Cherokees watched, he killed twelve of the thirteen people inside in a matter of minutes. Bench begged him to stop, but Doublehead was enraged by the death of his brother Pumpkin Boy at the hands of a settler earlier that year. He would not be denied his revenge, even as other warriors urged him to quit, claiming that he had besmirched their honor. Bench could do no more than save one of Cavett's young sons.

That day Ridge had looked away, "unwilling to witness that which I could not prevent," he later said. He would remember the scene for the rest of his life. That was not justice, he knew; it was cold-blooded murder.

The hour grew late. Doublehead continued drinking and Ridge watched, waiting for the right moment. The hunter sat with two men who had accompanied him to Hiwassee: Alex Saunders, a mixed-blood Cherokee, and John

Rogers, a white trader who lived among the tribe. Vann had set out with them, insisting that he deliver the killing blow, but he got sick, or drunk, on the trail and had to be left behind. When Vann bowed out, Ridge knew the killing fell to him.

As the evening wore on the conditions slowly turned to his advantage. McIntosh's was dark, lit only by small candles that left shadows dancing on the dark log walls and a handwritten sign that listed the price of drinks and salted meat. It was loud and crowded, filled with a rowdy bunch of men who could not sit still. The Ridge believed the darkness and noise would add to the confusion when the time came, perhaps give them time to escape. With luck, no one would realize what had happened until they were gone. But they had to time it perfectly. Doublehead was no fool. He was always on guard and, even drunk, was amazingly strong. Ridge realized he could not miss, because there would not be a second chance.

Rogers approached Doublehead first. He stopped in front of the chief's table and made insulting remarks about "any Cherokee who would sell tribal lands." The old chief was by then intoxicated enough to let the remark pass with no more than an angry look and a threat.

"You live among us by our permission," Doublehead told Rogers. "I have never seen you in council or on the war path. Be silent and interfere with me no more."

But Rogers did not move; instead he kept talking. No one heard exactly what he said but his insults eventually hit their mark. Doublehead pulled his pistol.

He would have shot Rogers on the spot but the gun misfired. Still, the trader did not jump out of the way or move to retaliate. He just stood there, confusing the chief. That was the idea, because John Rogers had not been sent to kill Doublehead, only to distract him for a moment.

In the excitement, no one noticed Ridge creeping along the wall, ducking between shadows and Indians. While Rogers taunted Doublehead, Ridge sneaked up from behind and laid the barrel of his gun against the old chief's jaw. In one fluid motion The Ridge blew out the candle on the table and fired.

* * *

The gunshot silenced the crowd momentarily, but soon a confused chorus of voices filled the room. Drunken men yelled "Who did it?" demanding to know who had fired the gun, whether anyone had been hit. They could not see the blood splattered on the wall because the extinguished candle had left the back of the bar dark. A few Indians stumbled around in the shadows until one located the candle and relit it. They found Doublehead bleeding on the dusty plank floor. The Ridge was gone.

As the Cherokees stood in a circle staring at the fallen chief, McIntosh pushed his way through the crowd and checked his old friend. *Still alive.* He then ordered everyone out of the building, and as soon as the last one was outside McIntosh barred the door. He would not give the assassins a chance to finish the job.

Doublehead needed help. He was barely conscious and unable to move. McIntosh realized that whoever had shot the chief would likely return to finish the job, so he sneaked out the back and found a neighbor, a schoolmaster named Black. While the excited Indians stood in front of the tavern discussing the shooting, McIntosh and Black passed Doublehead through a back window and carried him off into the darkness.

The crowd outside McIntosh's grew larger as the night wore on. They built a fire in front of the tavern using newly cut branches that crackled and sent glowing embers floating into the night sky. Wild stories concocted of drink and conspiracy traveled around the bonfire along with bottles of whiskey. Some said Doublehead was dead, while others believed he had been taken to Hiwassee Garrison, where Meigs would protect him. And when Cherokees from the ballplay arrived with news of Bone Cracker's death, many speculated the man's family was behind the shooting. Later, when Bone Cracker's relatives did show up, they were disappointed to hear someone had already shot Doublehead. They had, in fact, been coming to kill him.

After initially making their escape, Ridge, Saunders, and Rogers returned a few hours later. They had gotten no more than a few miles away before hearing a rumor that Doublehead had survived and turned back to find him. At McIntosh's they huddled around the fire, where they blended into the crowd and listened to the drunken speculation, trying to decide what to believe. Soon, Ridge quietly recruited Bone Cracker's family to look for Doublehead, and they spent the rest of the night searching the area. Everywhere they went they got the same answer. No one knew where Doublehead was. He had disappeared.

McIntosh had indeed wanted to take Doublehead to Meigs for protection, but the chief was too weak to travel so many miles. He had lost a lot of blood, was still groggy, and certainly was not fit to ride horseback. Initially, McIntosh hid Doublehead at his house but had decided that was too obvious —and potentially dangerous for him. He had no desire to draw the ire of his friend's assassins. Ultimately, Black offered to hide Doublehead in the loft of his schoolhouse, just a few hundred yards from the tavern. There, the old chief suffered alone into the morning hours.

The Ridge searched all night, but turned up nothing. He was frustrated and worried that he would not get another chance. If Doublehead survived, he would go into hiding and Ridge might become the hunted. Someone would eventually find out who was behind the shooting; keeping a secret among the tribe was nearly impossible. The Ridge knew it must end now, and that it was up to him. Saunders and Rogers had learned nothing from the Indians outside the tavern, and Bone Cracker's relatives had proved useless.

Ridge was about to give up when the first strains of gray morning light filtered into the valley. And then he saw it. Behind the tavern, he found a crimson trail of blood that led him to the school. Doublehead had left a path that any competent hunter could follow.

They stormed the schoolhouse at dawn. The Ridge had decided they should attack quickly, so that anyone guarding Doublehead would have no chance to react. He kicked in the door and ran into the building, followed by Saunders and Bone Cracker's family. But they lost what small element of surprise they had when one of the men let out a loud, screeching war cry.

The noise woke Doublehead and, through sheer will or meanness, he managed to stand up and pull out his knife. When his attackers reached the loft the old chief lunged. The Ridge and Saunders had their pistols drawn, but when they took aim both misfired. Before they could get out of the way Doublehead tackled Ridge.

The two Cherokees struggled on the floor while Saunders fumbled to reprime his pistol. Doublehead was trying to draw back his knife and stab Ridge and he nearly succeeded. Even mortally wounded, the old man seemed as strong as an Indian half his age. But just before Doublehead could plunge his knife into Ridge's heart Saunders fired again and the old man crumpled.

Saunders took out his tomahawk and leaned down to crush the chief's skull. Before he could strike, however, the old man grabbed the tomahawk and knocked Saunders backward. Instead of finishing off the man who had just shot him, Doublehead jumped on Ridge again and wrestled him to the floor. The two men rolled around on the rough plank floors, knocking furniture over as they struggled. Soon Doublehead had the advantage.

Overpowered and unable to fight back, The Ridge thought his end had come. *Could this man not be killed?* His strength was remarkable, his will to live seemingly supernatural. The old warrior never said a word. He raised the tomahawk and prepared to strike. The Ridge had seen the same black look in Doublehead's eyes years earlier. If this was the end, Ridge would accept it silently. He would not satisfy the old man by begging for his life.

And then, suddenly, Doublehead slumped over as quickly as he had risen, falling on top of Ridge, a tomahawk wedged deep in his skull. Saunders had grabbed the ax from one of Bone Cracker's relatives and hit the old chief with it just before he struck. Twice in a minute Saunders had saved his friend's life.

This time there was no doubt. The tomahawk was buried so deep in the chief's head that it took two men to pull it out. When they did, Bone Cracker's family beat Doublehead's skull to a pulp, taking out the frustrations of a thousand Cherokees on his lifeless body. Ridge and Saunders watched the grisly scene, surprised they had survived, and relieved that it was over.

When Doublehead was buried a few days later, several Cherokees noted that no one shed a tear.

In the early days of the nineteenth century, when John Ross was just a boy, some Cherokees still clung to an old prophecy delivered to the council decades earlier. According to legend, it foretold of coming trouble between the red men and white. Prophecies were not uncommon in the old days, when a good number of Indians believed the Great Spirit sent messages through chosen people. These prophets often delivered eloquent sermons at council sessions, dressed in leggings made of unsmoked deerskin and the feathers of great birds. Even those Indians who did not accept these prophecies as gospel would listen politely, perhaps trying to discern some hidden truth within.

This particular Cherokee legend held that, in the late eighteenth century, when the Indians were in their most violent period of fighting white settlers, an old man had a vision of the tribe's end. That man had recalled an even earlier prophecy that told of "our elder brother"—what the Indians called the white men—occupying ancient Cherokee lands. As he recounted the prophecy, the old man claimed he had been shown the misery that would befall the Cherokees long after the old generation passed away.

Your elder brother will settle around you—he will encroach on your lands, and then ask you to sell them to him. When you give him part of your country, he will not be satisfied, but ask for more. In process of time he will ask you to become like him. He will tell you your mode of life is not as good as his. Whereupon you will be induced to make great roads through the nation, by which he can have free access to you. He will learn your women to spin and weave and make clothes and learn you to cultivate the earth. He will even teach you his language and learn you to read and write. But those are but the means to destroy you and eject you from your habitations. He will point you to the west, but you will find no resting place there, for your elder brother will drive you from one place to another until you get to the green western waters. These things will certainly happen, but it will be when we are dead and gone. We shall not live to see and feel the misery which will come upon you.

Many of those things had come to pass already. The white men had encouraged them to learn the language of the English, to farm, to make their clothing through spinning and weaving. And there was no question the white men wanted their land. After Doublehead's death, a divide grew among the Cherokees between those who shunned all modern ways and those who promoted these advances. Men such as James Vann, The Ridge, and Charles Hicks urged their tribesmen to adapt in order to survive. They claimed farming would offset the loss of game, promote education, pay for roads to be built throughout the nation. Many Cherokees resisted their efforts, and the tension would lead to years of internal feuding. It was a turning point for the tribe and set the Indians' course for the next century. But no matter how much the two factions differed they nearly all agreed on one thing. They would not give up their land.

The Cherokee called themselves Yun wiya, the principal people. It may have been a corruption of a word with similar meaning to the Iroquois, and some believed the Cherokee had once been a band of that northern nation of tribes. But that had been centuries earlier, longer than the longest memories and legends had survived. By the nineteenth century the Cherokee spoke of their origins only in parables.

Unlike some tribes, the Cherokee had never believed they were the only people. They had traded and fought and aligned themselves with other Indians for as long as anyone could recall. But they first learned the red men were not alone in the world when the Spaniard Hernando de Soto wandered onto their land in 1540. The Cherokee were hospitable to the explorer, enough so that he remembered them as peaceful savages. The Cheraqui, as he called them, offered de Soto a variety of food—berries, corn, turkeys, small dogs. De Soto accepted everything except the dogs.

Within 150 years of that encounter, the Cherokee began trading with European colonists for firearms, the one invention of the white man they did not shun. Some members of the tribe even traveled to the great water to meet these men in Charles Towne, the busy South Carolina port city. A number of Cherokee were kidnapped and sold as slaves in the West Indies, but by

1721 the tribe had signed its first treaty with these new people, establishing a boundary between the colonies and the Indian territory.

After that, the English colonists courted the Cherokees relentlessly to gain trading rights and, later, land cessions. From time to time there was fighting, but the British tried to maintain good relations, especially as war with the colonists became inevitable. The Cherokees, angry that white settlers had moved onto their land without permission, sided with the British and for a while even fought for King George along the border. The Revolutionary War era was perhaps the bloodiest period in the tribe's history. It went on for a few years until, finally beaten, the Cherokee Indians made peace with the colonists in 1785 at Hopewell, South Carolina.

Some rogue Indians did not give up as easily. One chief, Dragging Canoe, became so incensed by white intrusion on Cherokee land that he broke from the tribe and terrorized the frontier that would soon become Tennessee. Dragging Canoe killed nearly every living relative of the Tennessee governor John Sevier, and his Chickamaugas—the name of his new tribe—wiped out entire settlements. One day, they murdered almost an entire family named Crockett, leaving behind few survivors, among them a small boy named Davy.

The violence continued for several years, in part because settlers and state governors broke treaties as quickly as they were signed. Even then, few respected legal agreements with Indians. But in 1790, when a group of settlers tried to take Muscle Shoals, in Alabama, the new American president issued a proclamation forbidding it. Under George Washington's administration, the fighting subsided and a strained diplomacy took shape. The Cherokees came to admire Washington immensely, and bestowed upon him the title "great father," a name that would be given to succeeding presidents, although with varying degrees of sincerity.

By 1800, years after Washington had left office, the white men had developed a new strategy for besting the tribes: they simply bought the land they wanted. It was an inexpensive, and less violent, way to get new territory. They discovered that they could buy thousands of acres of land for a few hundred dollars, meager supplies, and various trinkets. Indians, it seemed, did not know the value of currency.

The Cherokees had little choice but to go along with these deals, for they no longer had the manpower to fight. By the dawn of the nineteenth century there were only about twenty thousand of them left. Two generations earlier, South Carolina settlers had introduced smallpox to the Cherokees, and the disease killed off nearly half the tribe. As their numbers dwindled, the number of whites in the region increased rapidly. Still, the Cherokees did not face the same pressures as other tribes. In 1800 the tribe still controlled more than fifty thousand square miles of territory. A century of fighting and treaties had cut deep into the nation's population and landholdings, but they were still one of the largest Native American tribes and controlled the most territory. They felt confident they could live peacefully with what they had left.

The Cherokees adapted to the changing world better than many tribes. They gradually allowed some settlers to live among them, befriended a few of their white neighbors, and reluctantly accepted the increasingly common practice of interracial marriage between white men and Cherokee women (white women rarely married Indian men). The men who married into the tribe were expected to live by its laws, and most did so without question. In the late eighteenth century, none of these men was more respected than a kindly Scots trader named John McDonald.

McDonald had traveled a long, circuitous route to the Cherokee Nation. He sailed from Inverness, Scotland, for the new world when he was just nineteen, arriving in Charles Towne in 1766. He migrated south to Savannah, where he took a job as a clerk for a trading company. McDonald worked there little more than a year before his bosses, impressed by his talents, sent him north to manage their growing trade with the Cherokees in the Tennessee territory.

John McDonald felt at home in the mountains of the Cherokee country, a terrain not unlike that of his homeland. He ran a trading post at Fort Loudon, in the northern reaches of the tribe's territory, near Knoxville. McDonald managed to do business with the settlers while maintaining a good relationship with the tribe—no easy balancing act in those days. Even though he had seldom seen an Indian before, he seemed to fit in with them naturally, instinctively showing the proper respect to the Cherokees and their customs. The tribe slowly came to accept his presence, and even his friendship.

Before long McDonald met a young girl named Anne Shorey and he fell in love. She was only half Cherokee—her mother was a full-blooded member of the tribe's Bird Clan but her father, William Shorey, was a Scottish trader like McDonald. The two likely met through Shorey, and their shared heritage may have been the first bond between them. McDonald regaled Anne with stories of her father's native country and she introduced him to Cherokee history. They began a lengthy courtship and, when they finally married, McDonald was accepted as a member of the tribe. Within a year the couple had their only child, a daughter they called Mollie.

Over the years the Cherokees grew to trust John McDonald more than any other white man. His honesty was unquestionable, and he helped the chiefs negotiate with the growing number of squatters and settlers that wandered into their towns. He was more than fair in his dealings with Cherokees, and he offered his advice on dealings with the British, the Spanish, and the colonists. He became a valuable counselor to the tribe. The Tennessee governor William Blount once remarked that McDonald held more sway over the Cherokee council than many if not most full-blooded Indians.

For that reason, McDonald found himself constantly courted by colonists attempting to gain diplomatic ground with the Cherokees as the war approached. It did little good, for his loyalties lay elsewhere. When the Revolution began, McDonald—like most of the Cherokees—fought for the British. By the war's end, when colonists encroached on Loudon, the violence around Knoxville escalated; these new settlers, harboring grudges, fought constantly with the Cherokees and loyalists. McDonald and Anne moved south to avoid trouble, settling near Lookout Mountain, a great sloping landmark on the banks of the Tennessee River.

They may have been attracted to the area for the rolling hills surrounded by steep mountains, which had to remind McDonald in some ways of the

Scottish Highlands. Lookout Mountain rose more than two thousand feet above the river and the Tennessee Valley, and was only the most distinctive of several peaks in the area. Its name came from a Cherokee description of the area, *o-tullee-ton-tanna-ta-kunna-ee,* which meant "the mountains are looking at each other." There, McDonald opened the first of many trading posts he would own. And it was there, in the Tennessee Valley, that McDonald met another young traveling Scot, just as the Cherokees were about to kill him.

In 1785 a man from Baltimore named Mayberry sailed into Sitico, several miles north of Lookout Mountain, with a boatload of furs and big plans to strike it rich by trading with settlers and natives alike. But he and his assistant, a young man named Daniel Ross, had made one mistake. Along the route they picked up an Indian named Mountain Leader, who had asked for a ride. Mayberry thought Mountain Leader would make a good guide as they navigated the Cherokee country but instead he brought nothing but trouble.

When the boat landed at Sitico, some Cherokees recognized Mountain Leader as a hostile Indian suspected of many crimes against the tribe. Bloody Fellow, the local chief, was alerted and he decided the rogue Indian and everyone else in the boat must be executed. This stirred debate among the Cherokees, some of whom thought the penalty too harsh. They could not persuade the chief to change his mind, however, so they sent for McDonald, who lived about fifteen miles south. The trader made the trip quickly and, when he arrived, explained to Bloody Fellow that killing whites would only bring more trouble for the Cherokees.

The chief was reluctant to spare the men, but McDonald insisted. Do what you must with Mountain Leader, McDonald said, but he would consider it a personal insult if the Cherokees killed the white traders.

Bloody Fellow relented, if for no other reason than his respect for McDonald. Fearing the Cherokees might have a change of heart, Mayberry left as soon as possible. But the young Ross was so taken with McDonald that he stayed behind. McDonald did not realize it at the time, but he had saved the life of his future son-in-law.

Like McDonald and Shorey before him, Daniel Ross quickly adopted the Cherokee Nation as his new home, perhaps in part because he had lost his old one. His family had set out for the new world from Sutherlandshire when he was only a boy, but his mother died on the ocean voyage. By the end of the Revolutionary War he had lost his father as well, another casualty of the fighting. Orphaned, Ross managed as best he could. By the time he grew into a young man he had decided that his fortunes lay south, and he took a job with Mayberry.

McDonald gave Ross a job in one of his trading posts, and the young man made a fine partner. The slight, fresh-faced Scot was a quick learner, ambitious, and smart—in his spare time, Ross even collected books. Most likely, he reminded McDonald of his younger self. And within a year Ross had fallen in love with sixteen-year-old Mollie McDonald. No one understood the situation better than McDonald, who may have recognized history repeating itself. McDonald not only gave his blessing; he performed the ceremony using an Episcopal prayer book.

Although Mollie was only a quarter-blood Cherokee, Ross's marriage to her gained him admittance to the tribe's prestigious Bird Clan. He considered it an honor to become a member of the tribe that had once considered killing him. And, like McDonald, he would never act against the wishes of the Cherokees. He finally had found a place where he belonged. Soon, he would become nearly as respected by the Indians as his father-in-law.

Daniel and Mollie Ross became active members of the tribe, attending all the councils and ceremonies. They followed McDonald as he expanded his business, moving from one town to the next, tending to the trading posts as the family grew. Their first daughter, Jennie, was born in 1787, followed two years later by Elizabeth. Their third child, a son, was named after his grandfather. John Ross was born on October 3, 1790, on the banks of the Coosa River near Turkeytown, an important Cherokee village in the Alabama territory, which at the time belonged to Georgia.

Young John Ross, born just as the Indians and white men had reached an uneasy peace, would grow up with a unique understanding of both the white and the Indian heritages, and the strained relationship between the two. From his father and grandfather, however, he would learn to navigate both cultures gracefully.

As the tribe became more integrated, the Cherokee Nation slowly began to accept more modern ways. Soon after Doublehead's death, The Ridge used his new standing to nudge his people away from their most ancient customs, including the tribe's blood laws. The Cherokees had long believed a murderer's fate should be left to the victim's family. They could execute the killer without consequence or extract from him any payment they thought suitable. If the murderer fled, a member of his family became responsible. In many cases, Cherokees had been killed for someone else's crime. Ridge argued that the practice was wrong and must stop. Although some thought he was merely trying to protect himself from Doublehead's heirs, the council agreed with his logic. And they made Ridge responsible for enforcing the law. A new force on the tribal council had arrived.

The Ridge was appointed leader of a traveling police force called the Lighthorse Guard. It was a compliment to his abilities as a warrior and his great sense of justice that he became the Cherokees' ranking lawman. He rode from one village to the next, ruling on disputes and arresting criminals, a task previously performed by U.S. Indian agents. Before long, even white men came to respect his wisdom and morality.

While hunting turkey near his home one day, Ridge watched a South Carolina deputy approach two men watering their horses at a spring. He recognized the two Cherokees but, more important, he knew Wiley Hyde and Tom Phillips were criminals. As the lawman, Colonel James Blair, approached them, Hyde and Phillips raised their rifles. Blair tried to reassure them that he was a friend, but still Hyde cocked his gun and aimed at the deputy. Before Hyde could pull the trigger, however, Ridge shot him. Blair pulled his own rifle and covered Phillips.

It turned out Blair had trailed the men from Oconee Station, where they had stolen the horses from settlers. The incident earned Ridge, and by extension the Cherokees, a measure of respect from whites in the area. It also solidified the perception that the Indian lawman was an impartial judge.

The Ridge still harbored his own biases, and with good reasons. But he had learned that not all white men—or the things they offered—were bad. He had taken to farming and sent his own children to missionary schools to get a better education than they would among the tribe. He believed the differences between Indians and whites were similar to the balances found in nature. At the same time, he recognized the dangers predicted in his tribe's prophecies and, even though he dismissed most of these superstitions, he agreed with their message.

That is why Ridge objected, a year later, when the principal chief seemed to fall under the same spell as Doublehead. At the urging of Return J. Meigs, Black Fox had secretly prepared a treaty party to travel to Washington City to negotiate relocation with the president. Meigs had convinced the old chief that a move west held certain appeal. The Cherokee would live far from any white men, free to do as they pleased, and the land open to them in the foothills of the Ozarks was terrain not so different from their own land. Even if Meigs did not believe this, he would not openly disobey his orders from Washington.

To entice Black Fox further, Meigs had offered the chief a rifle, $1,000, and a $100 annuity for life. Black Fox knew he had the support of the chiefs in several lower Cherokee towns, many of whom were eager to move away from the settlers. The chief surprised the rest of council with this news at the fall 1808 meeting, when he had a prepared statement read aloud to the crowd: "Tell our Great Father, the president, that our game has disappeared, and we wish to follow it to the west. We are his friends, and we hope he will grant our petition, which is to remove our people towards the setting sun. But we shall give up a fine country, fertile in soil, abounding in water courses, and well adapted for the residence of white people. For all this we must have a good price."

Black Fox's message stunned the council into silence—it was not only a surprise; it was an unprecedented show of power. For a long moment no one said a word, although several old chiefs were clearly alarmed. Even though he had no real standing or seniority among the council, and should not have been the one to answer, The Ridge rose to speak. His words would be recorded in the major nineteenth-century histories of Indians as a turning point in the coming trouble.

"My friends, you have heard the talk of the principal chief," he began. "He points to the region of the setting sun as the future habitation of this people. As a man he has a right to give his opinion; but the opinion he has given as the chief of this nation is not binding; it was not formed in council, in the light of day, but was made up in a corner—to drag this people, without their consent, from their own country, to the dark land of the setting sun. I resist it here, in my place, as a man, as a chief, as a Cherokee, having the right to be consulted in a matter of such importance. What are your heads placed on your bodies for, but to think, and if to think, why should you not be consulted?

"I scorn this move of a few men to unsettle the nation," Ridge continued, "and trifle with our attachment to the land of our forefathers! Look abroad over the face of this country—along the rivers, the creeks, and their branches, and you behold the dwellings of the people who repose in content and security. What is this grand scheme projected, to lead away to another country, the people who are happy here? I, for one, abandon my respect for the will of the chief, and regard only the will of thousands of our people. Do I speak with the response of any heart in this assembly, or do I speak as a free man, to men who are free and know their rights? I pause to hear."

The Ridge did not have to wait for an answer. Cheers and acclamations followed his remarks, as if he had spoken the thoughts of everyone assembled. His speech stirred the council into action. They ousted Black Fox as principal chief at once and stacked the Washington City delegation with Cherokees opposed to moving west, including Ridge. The junior member of council had suddenly become a very influential man.

The delegation still reflected a very real split in the tribe, a geographical fault line that threatened to divide the Cherokees. Indians from the upper towns, which were located in the Appalachian Mountains and sparsely populated foothills of eastern Tennessee, wanted to hold their land. But Cherokees in the lower towns inside Georgia's boundaries lived among a growing number of settlers, and they favored a move west to avoid further contact with these new neighbors. It was lower town chiefs who had convinced

Black Fox to seek a deal for removal. But now the delegation had new orders: they were instructed to seek help from the United States government to establish a boundary between the two factions. It appeared the Cherokee Nation, with the help of white men, would be split in two.

The delegation traveled on the tribe's finest horses through South Carolina, North Carolina, and Virginia. The Ridge had never ventured so far from home and was amazed by the changing geography. First the mountains grew taller and then gave way to fields and marshland. It seemed there was more than enough open land in the country for everyone, and this only made Ridge wonder why the whites were so desperate for the Cherokees' homes. It would be years before he realized that it was not entirely about the land.

The changing landscape paled, however, in comparison to the white man's capital, a modern city with streets, public squares, and tall buildings rising out of the marsh. The Ridge was most impressed with the large legislative building, still under construction on a small hill, and with the Executive Mansion of the president, the finest and grandest white house he had ever seen. Ridge was also amazed that such buildings had been constructed so close to a swamp. But he was most surprised to find the delegation greeted as foreign diplomats and invited to meet the president himself. Ridge knew little about the government of the white men but he had heard many stories about the great red-haired father.

Thomas Jefferson met with the Cherokees alone in his office, and Ridge considered it a compliment that the president did not require bodyguards to meet with a group of Indians. The conversation was pleasant; Jefferson was friendly and expansive and lived up to his reputation as a genial and wise man. It seemed he knew a great deal about the Cherokees—he congratulated the Indians on their advances in agriculture and suggested they set up a representative form of government like his own. He even offered to have Meigs help them do it.

"This council can make a law for giving to every head of a family a separate parcel of land, which, when he had built upon and improved it, shall belong to him and his descendants forever, and which the nation shall have no right to sell from under his feet," Jefferson said. "They will determine, too, what punishment shall be inflicted for every crime."

The president treated the Cherokees like allies, but he seemed most interested in their internal conflicts. He expressed some regret for their trouble and quickly offered the services of his own surveyors to establish a boundary between the lower and upper towns. That, he explained, would give the lower Cherokees authority to sell their land and move west if they wished. Jefferson went so far as to promise the lower Cherokees they would never suffer the white man's intrusion again if they chose to move. It was a subtle, but telling, sales pitch.

The upper Cherokees assured the Great Father that his help would not be necessary, and the Indians quickly bade the president farewell. The visit had done little but convince the lower town chiefs to secede from the tribe. The Ridge, for his part, had come away with a sense of the larger world. In his short encounter with Jefferson he was struck by the president's wisdom and intrigued by his ideas for a new Indian government. But he left the meeting convinced that land was what most concerned the white men. Ridge had seen it even in Jefferson's eyes.

The tribe was in even greater turmoil when the delegation returned in January of 1809. Someone had shot James Vann, the outspoken leader of the upper Cherokees, but his killer had not been caught. The lower Cherokees were blamed, but in truth no one could establish a single motive for the crime; it seemed there were endless possibilities.

Vann had grown even more quarrelsome of late. Drunk at his own tavern more often than not, he had killed one white man and seriously wounded another. He had spread rumors about Alex Saunders, driving off his closest friend. In his more lucid moments he claimed to be possessed by demons. One day, as Vann sat with a bottle of whiskey in one hand and a cup in the other, the barrel of a rifle slowly pushed open the tavern door. No one saw who pulled the trigger. Vann was shot just once and then died on the floor of his bar. The Cherokees did not bother making an official inquiry because Vann had crossed so many people that the truth might never be sorted out.

Charles Hicks took Vann's place on the council, and as Ridge's main ally. Hicks had quit his previous job as an interpreter for Meigs when he learned of the Indian agent's bribes to Doublehead and Black Fox. At the age of forty-four, the mixed-blood Cherokee was considered a great intellectual by most of the tribe. He was never a warrior—scrofula had crippled his hip at an early age—but a man who collected books and newspapers and used wisely the information he found in them. On the council Hicks became another strong voice opposed to removal, and his respect among the Cherokees would eventually propel him to the position of second principal chief, the tribe's version of vice president. Years later, Hicks would be hailed as the Cherokee who led the tribe into its renaissance. Vann's death, ironically, cleared a path for the advances he had long championed.

The tribe debated removal for most of the year. The upper Cherokees argued that only a unified tribe could fend off the constant immigration of white settlers, but they won few converts. That spring, some prominent families from the lower towns migrated west and, without the pressure of their constant coercion, the other lower Cherokees soon dropped their insistence on moving. Everyone who wanted to leave had done so, and the remaining Indians were resolved to stay. By the fall Meigs had received official notice from the council that there would be no boundary; the tribe was no longer divided.

To signify this renewed unity, the Cherokees established a new council to manage its affairs, and Ridge was one of the first men appointed. Whether the Indians had taken the advice of Jefferson or simply believed the old council was too large, the change represented a new determination to stand together. Perhaps as a concession to the lower towns, Black Fox was reappointed principal chief. But by then Black Fox was an old man, and he would not last long in the position. He would die in 1811. His time, and his ways, had passed.

For the moment, it seemed the crisis of the preceding decade—and those of suspicious treaties—was over. The Cherokees had agreed they would give up no more land and seemed to have reached a semblance of accommodation with the white men. Yet it would not last. Another prophecy was coming, much like the one the Cherokees had heard years ago. And it would require an entirely different kind of prophet to hold the nation together.

TWO

Little John

They set out at daybreak on a beautiful December morning, a winter sun rising over the mountains behind them. A thick mist blanketed the river and frost covered the ground like fine white powder. Cattle huddled for warmth in the middle of vast fields and an occasional plume of campfire smoke wafted above distant trees. From the deck of their little boat, John Ross watched his homeland drift by from an entirely new perspective, and not even the biting cold wind off the water could make him look away.

Ross was excited; he was going to see the West. He had been hired by the Indian agent Return J. Meigs, a friend of the family, to deliver money and supplies to the Cherokees who had relocated beyond the Mississippi years earlier. For his entire life he had heard stories of the distant land. Indians described it as purgatory, a barren land of exile, while whites claimed it held all the promise of a new Eden, a country where the game was plentiful and settlers were scarce. The Arkansas territory had naturally become a place of myth in the Cherokee Nation, and now Ross would find out which description was actually true.

Of course, there was more to it than curiosity. Now twenty-two, Ross felt he was finally stepping out of the shadow of his father and his grandfather. He had trained to be a merchant, and even apprenticed in a store while he was away at school. Since returning home four years earlier, he had worked for his grandfather, managing some of John McDonald's trading posts. He enjoyed the job and very nearly idolized his grandfather. Even at his age he was wise enough to realize he could still learn much from McDonald. Indian and white men came into the store every day, and the deference these men showed his grandfather astonished Ross. But as much as he wanted that same respect, John Ross was not sure he wanted to follow in his grandfather's—or his father's—footsteps. He wanted desperately to be his own man.

For the past few years Ross had spent his days at the trading post talking with Indians and white men who were traveling west. Their stories of exploration and discovery on the trail left a strong impression. Although he loved the Cherokee land as much as any Indian, he sometimes wanted nothing more than to follow those men, to see what was out there. He was not particularly adventurous but worried he was missing out. Mostly, Ross wanted somehow to distinguish himself. If nothing else, he had inherited his father's and grandfather's ambition.

The offer from Meigs appealed to that ambition. The Indian agent wanted Ross to not only deliver supplies but also gauge the mood of the western Cherokees. Other tribes had begun to talk of a confederation of Indians to fight the settlers, and Meigs needed to know the western Cherokees' intentions. He may not have been entirely candid with Ross, but Meigs allowed at the very least that Ross was not simply delivering supplies; he was on a diplomatic mission.

Ross accepted the assignment graciously but he had larger plans. He hoped to convince Meigs that, once he was in Arkansas, he could establish and manage a large factory there—a trading post for Indians, settlers, and government agents. He was confident enough in his abilities to propose a salary of $1,000 a year and a dollar per day for expenses to perform this service. Meigs had been politely vague in his response. Perhaps he wanted first to see if Ross could even complete the journey. Already, one Indian had been unsuccessful, turning back when he felt earth tremors. For some, the West was a scary place.

If Ross had known any more about boats than he did about the West, he would not have been so confident. The rickety craft Meigs supplied would barely stay afloat, for the Indians accompanying Ross had overloaded it. But he did not notice how low the boat rode in the water that morning in the final weeks of 1812. He simply passed the morning watching the scenery. And as the boat rounded a bend in the river he was thrilled to see the familiar sloping profile of Lookout Mountain, the most recognizable landmark of his childhood. Beyond it, the West waited.

After a "disagreeable voyage" of barely a hundred miles, they stopped to rest at a small outpost in the Alabama territory. The boat was slow and sluggish, and Ross had begun to have his doubts about it. While they were docked Ross met the famous frontiersman Isaac Brownlow. A friendly and sympathetic man, Brownlow examined the boat and confirmed Ross's growing suspicion that it would not make it to Nashville, much less Arkansas. Brownlow took pity on the Indians. He sold them his good keel boat for sixty dollars and agreed to send the bill to Meigs. He then sailed with them for eighty miles before deciding they might make it to Arkansas without killing themselves. Brownlow was not impressed with their nautical skills, and later said Meigs had been careless to send a bunch of inexperienced men on such a long voyage in that rotten boat.

A better boat did not solve Ross's problems, however. He found trouble of one sort or another in nearly every bend of the river. On December 28, a group of white men hailed the boat and tried to lure them to shore. They invented any number of excuses: they wanted news from the east; the local garrison had ordered them to search all vessels for Indians. Finally, they demanded Ross bring the boat ashore or they would swim out to it. One of the men claimed an earlier vessel had reported a boatload of Indians behind them.

"And damn my soul if the two men behind you aren't Indians," the man said, not recognizing that Ross himself—too short and pale to pass for Cherokee—might also be one.

Ross had better sense than to stop and claimed the other men on his boat were Spaniards, going so far as to make one of them say a few unconvincing words. The men on shore continued to make threats, but finally the boat drifted far enough downstream that Ross could no longer hear them. He thought little of it until they reached Fort Massac two days later.

The fort sat on a high bluff overlooking the Ohio River. This was the former site of a French fort; Washington had ordered the structure rebuilt to protect the country's interests in the Ohio valley years earlier, and it had become an important way station for western travelers. When Ross arrived on December 30 soldiers were busy with extensive repairs—the fort had been damaged by a massive earthquake, the same one that had scared away Meigs's last envoy.

Ross and his party bunked at the fort for two days. There they enjoyed dry beds, hot meals, and wood-plank floors in cabins protected by a thick log wall and a company of armed soldiers. It was a pleasant respite from boat travel. In the afternoons, Ross stood on the bluff looking across the wide river at Kentucky, where stands of trees made the rolling hills look like distant mountains. Occasionally, he could still feel the ground shake, residual tremors from the earthquake. But that was the least of his worries.

The soldiers at Fort Massac warned him to watch out for a gang of white men who had plundered a number of homes in the area and blamed their crimes on Indians. In the week before Ross arrived, three Cherokees had been killed in the area. Ross wondered if these criminals were the same men who had tried to stop him and began to question the wisdom of agreeing to the mission. Still, Ross would not think of breaking his word. Turning back was not an option.

On the first day of 1813, Ross's party continued their voyage, but traveling became more troublesome the farther they went. The additional supplies they collected at the fort slowed their progress to a crawl. They were chased by settlers who suspected they were Indians, and by Indians who thought they were white men. Eventually the Cherokees wrecked the keel boat, lost part of their cargo, and had to walk the final two hundred miles—part of it through mud and water up to their knees. They survived by eating whatever game they could kill along the trail. Their situation did not improve when they reached the western Cherokee settlement. Arkansas was wet, treacher-ous, and desolate. Ross decided the Indians back home had offered the bet-ter description of this place.

When he returned home in April Ross had little desire to make the trip again. He had discovered that, outside the Cherokee Nation, whites and Indians still fought, survival was a struggle, and the West was a wild place. When he reported to Meigs, he did not renew his offer to manage a trading post in Arkansas. Ross had decided he belonged with his own people.

John Ross had been raised a Cherokee. Daniel and Mollie Ross faithfully ad-hered to tribal customs, bringing up all their children in a traditional Indian home. The first stories young John heard were the myths of the Cherokees—fables about the earth, fire, and the sun and the role mythical animals played in the creation of his homeland. His mother and grandmother sang Indian lullabies to him, taught him the Cherokee names for animals, dressed him in tribal garb. As a baby he was toted to green corn festivals, celebrations that marked successful harvests, where he played with other Cherokee children and watched traditional dances. When he was old enough to wander out-side, he spent his days with Indian children, hunting, fishing, and searching for interesting rocks in clear-water streams. As a boy, he likely did not realize his tenuous blood link to the tribe, was not overly conscious that his skin was lighter than the other children's.

The Rosses and McDonalds moved often, expanding their trading posts to the outskirts of the Cherokee Nation, places such as Willstown and Tur-keytown in the Alabama territory. Ross spent much of his early years dragged from one village to the next, never staying long enough to make close friends. In most of these towns, five hundred or so Indians lived in rectangular cabins spread over a few dozen acres, the typical Cherokee model. These homes, normally fifty or sixty to a town, were built near streams to provide drinking water and a place to bathe. The cabins—connected by worn, dusty paths—surrounded a square, which usually included a field for ballplay and a council house for meetings and ceremonies. Each village also had a log hut where food from private and common gardens was stored for the poorer Indians.

There were no rules governing this stock; Cherokees provided what they could spare and took only what they needed.

In earlier times the Cherokees had lived in villages of huts covered with grass and protected by a single log wall to keep out intruders and wild animals, much like a government garrison. But by the final years of the eighteenth century, thanks to the influences both tacit and overt of the settlers, the Indians were living much like the whites, in two-room wood cabins that included fireplaces and dinner tables. Their beds lined the walls, which were packed with hardened mud to protect them from the elements. For large families—and most Cherokee families were large—these were cramped but comfortable quarters. A few wealthy Indians had begun to build two-story homes by the time Ross was a boy.

In 1797 Daniel and Mollie Ross built their own cabin near Cha-ta-nu-ga, a little fishing village at the base of Lookout Mountain. Ross opened his own trading post on the road that skirted the mountain, catering to the ever-increasing number of people moving west. Every day, parties from Charleston, Augusta, and Savannah passed through, some herding cattle, horses, or pigs for trade with Indians and settlers alike. Some of these parties included families, and probably the first white children John had ever seen.

Living outside a traditional village for the first time, the Ross children were forced to keep themselves entertained. John's older sisters, Jane and Elizabeth, looked after him while his mother was busy, but he spent most of his time with his younger brother Lewis. The two became close at an early age, out of necessity if nothing else. They had few other friends and grew up playing together on the side of Lookout Mountain. In time, each of the two Ross boys learned to tell what the other was thinking. Lewis was fiercely devoted to his older brother; John would never trust anyone else as much.

John McDonald had built his own house a few miles away in Chickamauga, a two-story log cabin with a breezeway and verandas along both its front and back. On those porches, Ross's grandmother likely told him the history of the Bird Clan and the tribe's great myths: how the buzzard helped to shape the earth, that the redbird was the daughter of the sun. According to Cherokee myth, owls were the living embodiment of witches and ghosts.

A child whose eyes were bathed with water in which an owl's feather had soaked could stay awake all night. Perhaps the most frightening tale concerned a warrior who killed an eagle without the blessings of the gods. The Cherokee dreamed of being attacked by a great flying bird until a shaman exorcised the demon and the gods forgave the warrior his sin against the great bird. Such stories filled young John with wonder.

When he was not visiting his grandmother or playing with his brother, Ross passed his time at the family's trading posts. There, he met both white men and Cherokee chiefs who stopped in to visit his grandfather. The Indian traders talked openly about tribal business with McDonald, and were fond of Ross, who was quieter and more mannerly than most boys. They called him Tsan Usdi, Little John. It made him feel very much a member of the tribe.

Even isolated from a traditional village, the Ross family engaged in Cherokee life. They did not miss a green corn festival or any other gathering. It was during one of these celebrations that John first learned he was different. One day, his mother dressed him in a new nankeen suit, a present his father had probably acquired on a trading trip. The other children mercilessly ridiculed Ross's clothing. For the entire day they taunted him, calling him *unaka*, white man. Little John maintained his composure, even after his friends refused to play with him. He would not show any emotion; it was not the Cherokee way. He endured the torment and humiliation, playing alone and waiting for the day to end.

The next morning Ross refused to wear the suit. When his grandmother set out the new clothes for him to put on he began to cry. It took Anne a long time to persuade her grandson to tell her what was wrong—he was stubborn even as a child. When he finally relented and explained what had happened, she immediately gathered up a hunting shirt, leggings, and moccasins for him to wear. More than anyone else in the family, Anne McDonald understood what John was going through. For the rest of his childhood, John would not dress like a white child around his friends—his grandmother would see to that.

In the last days of the eighteenth century the Cherokees still discouraged members of the tribe from adopting white customs. They did not trust the settlers and their strange ways, and that posed a problem for Daniel Ross. Education was very important to him. One traveler described Ross's home as being filled with so many newspapers, books, and maps that it might have been a country house in England or Scotland rather than the American wilderness. More than anything else, Ross wanted a formal education for John and his other children, who now included Susan and Andrew, with Annie, Margaret, and Maria soon to follow.

Ross did not want to insult the tribe, so he struggled with this problem until younger, progressive Cherokees began to have a voice on the tribal council. When James Vann suggested it would benefit the tribe for their children to be educated as whites, Daniel Ross offered to establish a school in his home and hire a teacher out of his own pocket. The council eventually agreed to the arrangement, and soon the Ross children were attending classes alongside other Cherokees from nearby villages under the tutelage of a man named George Barbee Davis. Perhaps the most important lesson John Ross learned came from his father, who never did anything that might show disrespect for the tribe. Daniel Ross had waited until he was confident the tribe would accept the idea of establishing a school before he even suggested it.

As resistance to the European ways of life began to fade in the early nineteenth century, the tribe openly embraced education. David Vann, James Vann's nephew, and Charles Hicks allowed a group of ministers to build a mission at Spring Place in 1801, so long as book learning—and not religion—was the primary focus. They "had no ears for it," the Cherokees said of the white man's religion. Many Cherokees sent their children to the school, but Daniel Ross instead enrolled John and Lewis in an academy at Kingston, Tennessee, nearly sixty miles north. The Kingston Academy, run by a Presbyterian minister, became the most popular choice for mixed-blood Cherokee children.

By all accounts John Ross was one of the brightest boys ever to attend the school, and he learned as much outside the classroom as in it. Kingston sat on the road that ran to the Cherokee Nation from Kentucky and Virginia, a road built as a result of an early treaty between the tribe and the United States government. The ramifications of that agreement were now clear to the Cherokees: every day a constant stream of emigrants passed through Kingston, heading west.

It was there, living as a white person for the first time, that Ross realized just how closely he identified with his Cherokee heritage. Although he seemed to fit in with the other boys, and did well in his studies, he did not respect the culture he was learning nearly as much as he did the Indian life. Ross realized the hordes of people passing by the school every day were coming to take the land of his people. These were the settlers he had heard Indians complain about at his grandfather's store, and he was surprised to see how many there were. Tens of thousands of whites settled in Tennessee each year Ross was at Kingston, most of them arriving in wagons filled with supplies, leading cattle to graze on Indian fields. Ross knew it was wrong for these people to encroach on Cherokee land, and he would not forget it.

In Kingston, Ross boarded with the family of Thomas Clark, a friend of his father. John was away for months at a time, and his family kept in touch mostly through letters. But when someone in Clark's family contracted smallpox in 1806, Anne McDonald made the trip north alone to make sure her grandson was well; she had bad memories of the disease that had killed scores of Cherokees just a few generations earlier. Daniel Ross considered sending a doctor but feared it would offend the chiefs to introduce European medicine to the tribe. Anne assured him the boy was fine. John Ross never got sick, and rarely ever would.

After he finished school Ross took work in Kingston as a clerk for the trading post of Neilson, King, and Smith. It was much the same way his grandfather had gotten his start, and Ross similarly impressed his employers. He seemed to learn the business quickly. More than possessing any natural talent for the trade, the young Cherokee was simply intelligent. It served him well in most everything he did. During his days in Kingston, Ross may have met another young man working there, a boy named Sam Houston. If they didn't meet then, they soon would.

Ross was still in Kingston when he learned of the assassination of the old chief Doublehead and the turmoil it sparked, and he may even have heard tales of the new generation of powerful Cherokee leaders, men such as Vann and The Ridge. This political intrigue and murder would have seemed as foreign to him as the tales of the West that traveling soldiers swapped while mingling in his store.

He kept his job with Neilson, King, and Smith until he received word that his mother, Mollie Ross, had died unexpectedly on October 5, 1808, just two days after John's eighteenth birthday. Ross was devastated. He had not seen much of his mother in recent years, and he may have blamed himself for putting his own desires ahead of his family. Whatever the reason, Ross quit his job at the trading post and, with Lewis in tow, hurried back to Lookout Mountain.

When he returned to Chickamauga, John Ross moved in with his grandparents. They were getting old and McDonald, now sixty-one, needed help managing his trading post on the federal road between Missionary Ridge and Lookout Mountain. Ross did not mind the work or living in an upstairs room in the relatively spacious cabin. After the death of his mother, he seemed to prefer being with his grandmother. Everything about his old home reminded him of Mollie.

Ross still saw his father often, and they maintained a strong bond, but John would barely ever live with his younger siblings. He would never be particularly close to Andrew, Annie, Margaret, and Maria, although Andrew idolized his older brother. Daniel Ross was left to raise their children with the help of Return J. Meigs's daughter, a family friend whom he had hired as a nanny.

For four years Ross lived quietly and anonymously with his grandparents. He spent his days either at McDonald's store or traveling between Indian villages on business. These trips allowed him to see firsthand how poorly many Cherokees lived, and it saddened him. The Cherokee women in his family had instilled in him a fierce devotion to the tribe and a love of their homeland. It was, for him, a virtue. He realized he had advantages other members of the tribe did not—he had been told that often as a child but it had only recently sunk in—and he wanted to help these people; it was how he was raised. But even as his affection for his tribe grew stronger, it was becoming more apparent that he was not like them.

Cherokee men were almost invariably tall, with rugged, dark complexions. Although his dark eyes were pure Cherokee, Ross's large nose and cheeks were awkwardly European. Cherokee men were practically all strong men, warriors who hunted or worked the land with their hands. Next to them, Ross more closely resembled a settler, and a weak one at that. At Kingston, he had grown into an undistinguished young man, short, slight, and pale. He was a hard worker but would never bulk up—his arms would never bulge with the same muscles as the warriors of his age. He was not a weakling, but John Ross recognized that he did not have the ability to make a man cower with his stare, like other Cherokees. Not yet anyway.

Ross's mannerisms also betrayed his bloodline. Although quiet and stoic like a Cherokee, he did not have the passion for storytelling most Indians did, nor did he drink or carouse at any of the festivals. He could not master the Cherokee language, spoke it "haltingly," as some later said, and was self-conscious about this deficiency.

Instead of a warrior, he had become a dull businessman, like his father and grandfather before him. He made money easily, and few ever got the best of him in a trade. It was hard to read his dark eyes, although it was easy to see he was a young man with much on his mind. Ross could have ignored his Indian heritage, moved to a large city, lived as a white man, and got along well. But he had decided he was Cherokee, even if he did not particularly fit the mold.

It was frustrating. The rest of his family seemed to fall into the traditional, expected roles much more easily. His eldest sister, Jane, had married her distant cousin Joseph Coodey in 1805. Their son William Shorey Coodey became Ross's first—and favorite—nephew. A few years later, Elizabeth married John Golden Ross, another trader from Scotland (with a coincidental surname). It seemed Elizabeth would follow the path of her mother and grandmother by marrying outside the tribe, while Jane conformed to Cherokee custom. But John wasn't sure where, or how, he belonged.

When Return J. Meigs asked Ross to carry supplies to the western Cherokees in 1812, he accepted the job in part out of loyalty. He saw it as a business opportunity, to be sure, but he also felt he owed the Meigs family for
helping to raise his brothers and sisters. And the assignment allowed him to
break out of the increasingly monotonous routine of life in Chickamauga.

Upon his return in the spring of 1813 Ross seemed a changed man. He
had survived the dangers of the trail and learned to fend for himself. It had
matured him, given him confidence. After making another trip at his father's
request, to pick up an aunt in Hagerstown, Maryland, he signed on as partner in a trading business with Timothy Meigs, Return's son. Meigs had established a trading post on an isolated, wooded beachfront on the Tennessee
River. The business did not compete with Ross's grandfather, who now had
Lewis to work for him; their customers traveled the federal road west. Meigs
and Ross catered to those people moving west by boat. It was already a thriving business when Ross joined but he made it more profitable.

Ross immediately expanded the business, establishing a ferry at the trading post to carry Indians and settlers across the deep, wide river. It became
a popular crossing point, although some passengers found the ferry rickety,
unsteady, and downright scary—Ross would never master the arts of water
travel. But he knew how to make money and, for a while, this work seemed
to satisfy his growing ambition.

It was around this time that Ross surprised his family by getting married. Elizabeth Brown Henley—or Quatie, as the Indians called her—was a
kind woman, and she would become a mysterious figure in Ross's life. Some
claimed she was full-blooded Cherokee, but it is more likely she had mixed
heritage. She may have been the daughter of James Brown, the Cherokee
treasurer, and Ross's marriage to her may have strengthened his ties to the
tribe. Subconsciously, he may have been attracted to Quatie for the way she
naturally fit into the Cherokee Nation.

In many ways, the couple seemed very much alike and suited to each
other. One year younger than Ross, Quatie was quiet and unassuming, like
her new husband, but shared none of his ambition. She preferred to spend
her days tending to her family in typical Cherokee fashion. She would

rarely travel with him, and he almost never mentioned her around business associates.

When she married Ross in the summer or fall of 1813, Quatie was recently widowed and had a young daughter named Susan. It is unclear how they met or what first attracted Ross to Quatie, but he took on this instant family without complaint. They wed at her family's house in Ooltewah, about fifteen miles east of Chickamauga, in a ceremony performed by her father. After a brief honeymoon, which may have included a short stay at John Brown's ferry tavern near Lookout Mountain, Ross moved his new bride and her daughter into his grandparents' home.

As Ross built his company and personal wealth, the Cherokees were enjoying one of the most peaceful periods in their history. Young, progressive chiefs were guiding the tribe into what would later be called the Cherokee renaissance. But the peace would not last, and John Ross would soon find new ways to be of use to his tribe. To the south, the Creek Indians were on the verge of an intratribal conflict that threatened all of the tribes in the South. It had been sparked by a conflict that began years earlier, far to the north.

At the turn of the century the United States had embarked on a great expansion north of Tennessee. On surveying missions, white explorers claimed land and bought from local tribes at an amazing rate. In 1809 General William Henry Harrison, governor of the Indiana territory, negotiated with chiefs of the Miami tribe to buy three million acres of land in the northwestern territory for a price that amounted to under a penny for every three acres. With that one sale an entire section of the country was suddenly opened for settlers. Indians from several northern tribes were outraged, but none protested—or used it to further their cause—as much as a band of Shawnees who had built a settlement at the junction of the Tippecanoe and Wabash rivers.

They were led by a man named Tenskwatawa, who for several years had enthralled his followers with tales of his dreamlike visits to the "happy hunting grounds," where he was given instructions by the Great Spirit. His message of shunning the white man's ways was similar to those of Cherokee prophets from the previous century, but it differed significantly in tone. Earlier prophets had issued their warnings as cautionary tales, but Tenskwatawa insisted anyone who ignored his words would anger the Great Spirit. He claimed a great hailstorm was coming to wipe the white men off the earth and return the land to the Indians. The fantastic ramblings of this man, known commonly as "the Prophet," might have been ignored if he had not been the brother of the respected Shawnee warrior Tecumseh. Together, they established Prophet's Town in central Ohio, near the Indiana territory.

Harrison's deal with the Miami tribe gave Tecumseh and the Prophet a great measure of credibility. The Treaty of Fort Wayne, as it was called, was signed by Indians who did not even live on the land. Such blatant disregard for the rights of Indians by the Seventeen Fires—what some tribes called the United States, which at the time numbered seventeen—seemed to corroborate the dire predictions of the Prophet. Tecumseh spent more than a year stirring the ire of neighboring tribes and formulating a plan to unite all the Indian tribes against the white man.

In 1811 Tecumseh met Harrison at Fort Vincennes and asked him to return the Indian land. Although it had not belonged to the Shawnee either, Tecumseh argued the land belonged to all Native Americans, and could not be given to anyone by a willing minority.

"A few chiefs have no right to barter away hunting grounds that belong to all the Indians for a few paltry presents or a keg or two of whiskey," Tecumseh said. "We do not want war with the United States, but there can be no peace until the land is returned."

Tecumseh and Harrison debated for two days. Finally, the Shawnee vowed to unite all the tribes and throw their support to the British, a shrewd threat given the renewed tension between Britain and the Americans. When Harrison ignored his ultimatum, Tecumseh marched south, where he would find other tribes more than willing to hear the great prophecies of Tenskwatawa.

* * *

The Ridge was one of the thousands of Indians gathered in Tukabatchee—the principal Creek town on the banks of the Tallapoosa River—when Tecumseh and his party made their grand entrance in September of 1811. The Shawnee traveled with warriors from various tribes, all of them dressed in hunting shirts, loincloths, and leggings. They adorned themselves with feathers and beads, and a few painted their faces. Upon their arrival they performed the "Dance of the Lakes," a bit of culture from the northern tribes that stirred some of the Creeks—but not stoic Ridge, Cherokee ambassador to the tribe—into a frenzy.

Tecumseh had asked the Creeks to have representatives of all the Five Civilized Tribes at their council. Those southeastern tribes—the Cherokee, Chickasaw, Choctaw, Seminole, and Creek—had been designated the "Five Civilized Tribes" by colonists because they were the most friendly and, by European standards, most advanced of all the Native American tribes. They also were influential and important to Tecumseh's plans.

The Ridge, like a few of the Creek chiefs, knew Tecumseh by reputation and worried about what was coming. When he got the chance to speak after days of waiting, the Shawnee warrior proved as stirring a speaker as his brother. He related a vision from Tenskwatawa that said the Indians should kill their cattle, destroy their spinning wheels, and cast aside their plows, as these were all white customs. The Prophet, he said, had foreseen that when the red men shook their clubs the Americans would become so frightened the rifles would drop from their hands.

"The white people have no right to take the land from the Indians, for it is ours," Tecumseh declared. "The Great Spirit gave it to us. Let all the red men unite in claiming a common and equal right in the land, as it was at first, and should yet be."

Although he struck an aggressive tone, Tecumseh did not openly advocate violence. He preached a message of patience and perseverance and suggested that the time for fighting would come. He spoke favorably of their "friends," the British.

"I do not want war with the Americans, but to be in peace and friendship with them," Tecumseh said. "Do not do any injury to them. Do not steal even a bell from any one of any color. Let the white people of this continent manage their affairs in their own way. Let the red men, too, manage their affairs in their own way."

Tecumseh was not only a fiery speaker; he was a master of symbolism. He delivered to the Creek chief a bundle of red sticks, then took one of them out and snapped it in two. Then he tried to break the entire bundle at once but of course could not. Separately, he suggested, the Indians could be destroyed. Together, they were unbreakable.

Big Warrior, leader of the Creeks, accepted the sticks from Tecumseh but not his message. Although the Shawnee had stirred the blood of many Creeks—and, with his demonstration, given them a new name—Big Warrior was unmoved. The Creek chief believed, like Ridge, that Indians had to become more civilized to survive. Big Warrior could not hide his skepticism, and it riled Tecumseh so much that he criticized the chief in front of his own council.

"Your blood is white! You have taken my talk, and the sticks, and the wampum and hatchet, but you do not mean to fight," Tecumseh said. "I know the reason. You do not believe the Great Spirit has sent me. I will leave Tukabatchee immediately, and will go to Detroit. When I arrive there, I will stamp on the ground, and will shake down every house in Tukabatchee."

Tecumseh stormed out of the Creek council, leaving behind a rift in the tribe. Some feared what would happen if they followed his advice; others worried what might become of them if they did not. Later, the Choctaws claimed that, as Tecumseh departed, a Cherokee warned him that if he ever tried to spread such a message in the Cherokee Nation he would personally kill him. If Ridge made that threat, however, he never spoke of it. But Tecumseh passed through the Cherokee land without stopping. His ideas, however, would spread.

Tecumseh had certainly made his mark on the Creeks. Some of them broke off from the tribe and adopted a new name, taken from Tecumseh's lesson. No matter how much the Creek chiefs pleaded for unity, the Red Sticks could not be swayed. When tremors from the New Madrid earthquake (the same quake that Ross had encountered on his trip west) shook the Creek Nation, many of them took it as a sign that Tecumseh had reached Detroit.

While Tecumseh was campaigning in Indian villages to the south, the Prophet had recruited so many followers at Prophet's Town that nearby settlers worried he was amassing an army. Friendly Indian chiefs told Harrison that the Prophet was inciting his people with talk of a coming war. It fit with other incidents that had occurred of late—stolen horses, a few minor skirmishes, an unexplained attack on a couple of whites. Harrison quickly recruited an army of nearly a thousand men to march to Prophet's Town.

On November 6, 1811, a delegation of Tenskwatawa's warriors met Harrison's army less than two miles from the village, where the Tippecanoe and Wabash rivers met. They asked Harrison why the army had moved so close to them, claiming they were peaceful Indians. The delegation promised the Prophet himself would meet with Harrison the next day, and asked that the soldiers not advance on the village before there was a chance to make a peace treaty. They even offered Harrison a comfortable spot to camp.

The Indians attacked the next morning, hours before daybreak.

The Prophet was no warrior, and he had no elaborate plan for battle. From the safety of his village he told his followers to attack, claiming the Great Spirit would not allow the white men's bullets to strike them. They believed him. Although Harrison's men were surprised by the attack, they quickly turned the battle in their favor. The Prophet urged his warriors to keep fighting, promising an easy victory would soon follow. It didn't. Harrison's men sacked Prophet's Town.

The surviving warriors could not hide their disdain for their false Prophet. In a single day he had been unmasked as a fraud and his folly had cost dozens of men their lives. His followers abandoned him. Harrison became a folk hero and used the battle in his campaign slogan a few years later when he ran for president of the United States.

After the battle of Tippecanoe, Harrison's men discovered that many of the guns and supplies the Indians had used were English, a finding that only fueled speculation of a coming war in which the Indians would align with the British. The United States hardly needed another excuse to move against the redcoats. Already, the British were sabotaging American trade. The Royal Navy had taken to blockading ports, firing on the occasional American ship, sometimes forcing United States sailors into their service. Finally, in 1812, these disputes added up to war.

Not all of the reasons for fighting were retaliatory. The United States wanted the British completely out of North America, and some members of Congress coveted the Canada territory. Additionally, many politicians feared the Indians would fall on the side of the British during territorial expansion. Some believed the British had been courting the Michigan, Indiana, and Ohio tribes as they inched closer to U.S. soil. Tecumseh would only confirm that fear. When he returned home and found Prophet's Town destroyed he was furious. His chance to build a great Indian confederation had been lost. Tecumseh had little choice but to do exactly what he had warned the Creeks he would. He set out for Detroit to join the British in the opening battle of the War of 1812. Americans' fears that the Indians would fight against them had been realized.

A month later, the Creeks officially divided into two factions and fell into civil war.

John Ross ignored the war for more than a year. If the attacks he suffered on his trip west had anything to do with hostilities sparked by Tecumseh and his brother, he did not realize it. The war concerned only those whites to the north, he believed. But Ross soon saw the escalation of forces firsthand. His grandfather's trading post sold a good percentage of its wares to soldiers marching into battle. Ross was opposed to supplying men on their way to fight Indians, but McDonald knew that refusing to do so would only bring trouble to the Cherokees. So far, the tribe had remained neutral.

In the summer of 1813, during a trading tour through the Alabama territory, Ross saw the beginnings of disaster. While visiting the Creeks he met Big Warrior, who told him of the turmoil in his tribe. The chief feared he would soon be overwhelmed by the insurgent Red Sticks. He likely spoke of Tecumseh's plan to unite the tribes against the white men and the destruction such a conflict would bring. Sitting among the Creek chiefs around the campfire at Tukabatchee, Ross first heard dire predictions of the end of the Five Civilized Tribes.

These warnings scared Ross. He may have worried about the Creeks but he was more concerned about what such a war might mean for the Cherokees. For his entire life he had been a passive observer of the events that shaped his tribe. Now, as a man sitting around a fire with the chiefs of the Creek Nation, he decided that he must do something for his people. And the best way to do that, he decided, was to help the Creeks. When he returned home, he asked Meigs to send reinforcements to the Creeks, and he even offered his services as ambassador to the tribe.

"The intelligence received from the Creek Nation at this present crisis is very serious," he wrote on July 30. "The hostile party is said to be numerous and if assistance is not given to Big Warrior and his party by the U.S. it is apprehensive that they will be conquered from the Superior force of the rebels."

Ross's note to Meigs was the first evidence of his political awakening. Perhaps it began as a concern for his family and business, but he realized the conflict the Creeks spoke of could have repercussions for all Cherokees. He could hardly have avoided hearing the talk among the tribesmen in his store, who watched nervously as the fighting grew more intense to the north and south. The Cherokees had stayed out of such conflicts for most of his adult life, but Big Warrior had told him they would not be able to remain neutral for long. Ross saw his offer as an opportunity to do something for his people, for his mother's people. He realized that he wanted to do more than run a trading post, that he needed to be involved in the tribe's business, to be part of something larger than himself.

Meigs would not hear of it, however. He declined to use Ross as a go-between with the Creeks, either because he thought the young man too inexperienced or because he wanted to spare him possible danger. Yet John Ross would soon have his chance. A month after Ross visited Big Warrior the Creeks suffered the most brutal massacre in Indian history. War was coming and there was no way to avoid it.

*   *   *

Shortly after the War of 1812 began a group of settlers and mixed-blood Creeks had taken refuge at Fort Mims near Mobile. Eager to stop the rebel Indians from joining the war, a group of white men from the fort, led by Daniel Beasley and Dixon Bailey, ambushed the Red Sticks at Burnt Corn, eighty miles north of Pensacola. The Red Sticks had bought weapons there from the Spaniards, and the men wanted to prevent them from using this cache. Beasley and Bailey launched a surprise attack that sent the Red Sticks fleeing into the swamp, but the rebel tribe regrouped. A year later they would get their revenge.

On August 30, 1813, a large band of Red Sticks led by William Weatherford, known as Chief Red Eagle, attacked Fort Mims. The settlers saw them coming and attempted to secure the fort, but one of the Creeks buried a tomahawk in Beasley's head just as he tried to shut the fort's gate. The settlers hid inside to avoid fighting, but the Red Sticks set the fort on fire to force them into the open. There, the Red Sticks proved viciously efficient at warfare. In a single day of fighting the renegade Creeks killed more than five hundred people and took half that number in scalps. They spared only the fort's slaves, whom they released. For a while, it would stand as the most brutal massacre in U.S. history. But even greater bloodshed was coming. The attack convinced the Americans that they could no longer ignore the feuding Creeks. The United States declared war on the tribe.

The fighting between whites and Indians rekindled old divisions among the Cherokees. Although The Ridge assured Meigs the Cherokees remained loyal to the United States, some members of the tribe had other ideas. The message of the fallen Prophet and Tecumseh had filtered into remote villages of the Cherokee Nation, and a group of superstitious Indians met at the village of Ustanali in the summer of 1813 to discuss how they should respond. There, in the mountains at the eastern edge of the Cherokee Nation, one tribal prophet predicted that a great hailstorm—like the one described by the Prophet—would destroy all but the faithful red men. He suggested they gather atop the highest peak of the mountains clouded by blue smoke in order to be closer to the Great Spirit.

After night fell on Ustanali a man named Charles spoke, and it seemed he took his entire message from the Prophet's own sermons. He claimed the buffalo and other game had disappeared because the Cherokees had taken to sleeping on feather beds and wearing white man's clothes. The books and domesticated cats that the Indians kept, Charles argued, were nothing more than tools of the white devil. As he spoke, another Indian beat a war drum beside the fire, adding to the drama of the moment.

"The Great Spirit is angry and has withdrawn his protection," Charles said. "The nation must return to the custom of their fathers. They must kill their cats, cut short their frocks, and dress as became Indians and warriors. They must discard all fashions of the whites."

As the beat continued, Charles roused the audience with a promise that, if they followed his instructions, their game would return and the settlers would vanish. Indians rose to dance around the fire, a ceremony that stopped only when Charles claimed anyone who disobeyed these commandments would be struck dead by the Great Spirit. The drum continued to beat.

One Cherokee not stirred by this talk was Ridge. He had quietly slipped into town to hear Charles speak and knew he must stop this nonsense. The Ridge feared these revelations would divide the Cherokees as it did the Creeks. After Charles finished, Ridge interrupted the dance. He moved to the front of the crowd and the Indians watched him with great interest. Here was a member of the council who, they assumed, would support the prophet's message. But he surprised them. The Ridge called Charles a fraud.

"My friends, the talk you have heard is not good," Ridge said. "It would lead us to war with the United States, and we should suffer. It is false; it is not the talk of the Great Spirit. I stand here and defy the threat that he who disbelieves shall die. Let death come upon me. I offer to test this scheme of imposters!"

There was a pause, as if the Indians were waiting to see if Ridge would be struck down. After a few seconds the warriors in the crowd charged Ridge, screaming in blind fury. He fought them off as quickly as they came at him—one man, two, then three. The Ridge held his ground, swing-ing wildly, knocking younger men to the ground as they attacked. Single-handedly, none of them were a match for the great hunter. But there were too many of them.

The men wrestled Ridge to the ground, pinning him in the dirt. He had not used his knife, not against his own people, but that did not stop them from pulling theirs. Ridge had misjudged the strength of the prophet's words, the fury of his followers. Among the mob, The Ridge recognized one of his friends, John Harris. And it looked as if Harris and these other Indians meant to kill him.

Before the enraged Cherokees could stab Ridge, Jesse Vann, the son of James Vann, and a few other levelheaded Indians rushed to his defense. They pulled enough men off Ridge that he was able to stand and fight back for a moment. But that only seemed to make the crowd angrier and Ridge knew he would soon be overwhelmed again.

Finally, one old man, a respected chief and staunch believer in the Great Spirit, calmed the mob long enough to allow Ridge to escape. As he retreated Charles rose to speak again, distracting the crowd from the only truth that had come out of the night: The Ridge had not been struck dead.

General William McIntosh, a half-white Creek and tribal leader, was visiting the Cherokees when Fort Mims was attacked. He had been sent to ask for help fighting the Red Sticks but the Cherokee were reluctant to intervene. After McIntosh's request was politely denied, Ridge escorted him home to Coweta, where they met with Big Warrior. The Creek chief warned Ridge, as he had Ross, that the Cherokees could not remain neutral forever.

"You must take one side or the other," Big Warrior said.

The Ridge reacted much as Ross had—he was inclined to help the Creeks. When he returned home in September Ridge took the floor dur-ing a council and made a passionate speech, arguing that helping the Creeks was not interference but self-preservation. The Ridge predicted that if they did nothing, the white armies would soon make no distinction between the

Red Sticks and other Indians. The actions of these renegade Creeks, he said, threatened the Cherokee tribe.

Despite his oratorical skill and logical message, the council for once remained unconvinced. The chiefs voted against any relief for the Creeks. Furious, Ridge vowed to make his own stand. He began to round up volunteers and, to his surprise, found many eager warriors. The council took notice. And after the Red Sticks killed a Cherokee woman near Etowah, Georgia, even the most ardent chiefs conceded that neutrality was no longer an option. The Cherokees' new principal chief, an old warrior named Pathkiller, gave his blessing to Ridge's recruiting efforts and directed him to support white troops in the Creek's war. It was a vote of confidence, and a shrewd bit of diplomacy. In a single gesture Pathkiller had endorsed a popular Cherokee leader and ingratiated the United States with the Cherokees. He had even earned a favor from Return J. Meigs, who had been asked to produce Cherokee fighters by the governors of Tennessee and Georgia.

The Cherokee intervention in the Creek War marked a new level of political strength for Ridge. Through sheer will he had stopped the prophets, swayed the tribal council, and built an alliance between the Cherokees and the United States government. To any informed observer, it seemed Ridge was on a path to become principal chief. For the time being, however, he made a proficient military recruiter. By October he had mustered some eight hundred Cherokee warriors to fight alongside the Tennessee militia, including a young trader named John Ross.

It was a turning point for Ross as well. In the course of a year he had gone from an apolitical businessman to an Indian warrior. Even if he did not exactly fit the part, and would not have been expected to join the fight, he wanted the Cherokee Nation's business to be his business. Moreover, it would give him the chance to prove himself a warrior, a true Cherokee.

As Ross, The Ridge, and the other Cherokees prepared to join the Tennessee army in Alabama, even the most superstitious Indians must have noticed that no hailstorm had come.

THREE

Horseshoe Bend

The bodies were scattered across the ruins of a burned Indian village, most of them reduced to little more than scorched meat and charred bones. John Ross saw a dead boy facedown in the dirt and an old woman slumped in the doorway of a small cabin, the remnants of her clothes tattered with bullet holes. Inside the house, there were at least a dozen more Indians, or what was left of them. They had been tortured, mutilated, and left to die in the fire. This was Ross's first glimpse of war, and it resembled nothing in the white man's history books. Those books never mentioned the joy some took in killing.

Before they'd set out the government Indian agent Return J. Meigs lectured them: do not kill women, do not kill children. Ross had to wonder if those rules did not apply to the white men who had done this. The dead were Red Sticks and, to be sure, he had signed up to fight them. But he had not expected this. This was not warfare, Ross thought. This was a slaughter.

Ross rode into the Creek village of Tallushatchee with Colonel Gideon Morgan's company in early November 1813, less than a month after he joined the Cherokee mounted forces. They had traveled from the fort at Hiwassee

Garrison into the Alabama territory, stopping at Turkeytown, the place of his birth. There, they learned the Red Sticks had gathered in a nearby village and set out on their own, without orders, to confront them. Meigs, who had traveled with them to Turkeytown, fawned over the Indians like a proud father but warned them to behave like white soldiers once they reached the battle.

"I flatter myself that, in the just and necessary war now commencing against the hostile Creeks your battalions will be considered as a respectable part of the army, according to your numbers," Meigs said. "The Generals Jackson, Cocke and White will consider you as entitled to their care and friendly attention, that you have provisions, ammunition and medical aid when necessary. In all of these you will have equal advantages with other troops. And of course it will be expected that you will be obedient to every order and regulation."

The Cherokees did largely as they were told but left nothing to chance. They knew some soldiers could not tell one tribe from another and would happily shoot any Indian on sight. For that reason, Morgan's men rode cautiously, wearing white feathers and deer tails as signs to the soldiers that they were friendly troops.

Many of the great Cherokee leaders rode with Colonel Morgan, including Charles Hicks, The Ridge, even Pathkiller (although the principal chief was too old to fight). Ross rode alongside his brother Lewis and John Golden Ross, their brother-in-law. Navigating the northern Alabama mountains was difficult for most white soldiers, but the terrain was so similar to the Cherokee country that the Indians handled it easily. When they reached the village, the Cherokees discovered they were too late by several days.

The Indians that the Cherokees found dead at Tallushatchee were victims of General John Coffee, the Tennessee militia, and decades of animosity. When the Creek War began it had taken little effort to round up settlers ready to fight the Indians. Some were patriotic and saw it as their duty; others wanted desperately to rid the countryside of the natives. A few simply considered it sport. Some settlers, it seemed, thought the Indians little better than wild animals.

Coffee stormed Tallushatchee with nearly one thousand men on November 3, 1813. Under orders from General Andrew Jackson they surrounded the village and quickly took dozens of Red Sticks prisoner. At first,
it appeared the casualties would be few. But then a number of the Indians—
one man counted nearly four dozen—retreated into a single log-and-mud
building. When Coffee's dragoons approached the door they were faced
with a woman sitting on the ground, blocking their path. She was stretching
a bow with her feet, her arms apparently too weak to set the weapon. When
she saw the men, the woman fired an arrow that hit and killed a lieutenant
named Moore. A young soldier named Davy Crockett—whose grandfather
had been slaughtered by Indians—later reported that this incident is what
sent the troops on their murderous rampage.

"His death so enraged us all, that she was fired upon, and had at least
twenty balls blown through her," Crockett wrote. "This was the first man
I ever saw killed with a bow and arrow. We now shot them like dogs; and
then set the house on fire, and burned it up with the forty-six warriors in
it. I recollect seeing a boy who was shot down near the house. His arm and
thigh was broken, and he was so near the burning house that the grease was
stewing out of him. In this situation he was still trying to crawl along; but
not a murmur escaped him, though he was only about twelve years old. So
sullen is the Indian, when his dander is up, that he had sooner die than make
a noise, or ask for quarters."

It was the first conflict between U.S. troops and the Red Sticks in the
Creek War, and it ended after a few hours with 186 casualties: 5 Tennesseans,
181 Indians. The next day, the famished troops had returned to the village
and ate the Red Sticks' food, including a stash of potatoes glazed with the oil
of burning flesh. The soldiers were too hungry to care.

Looking over the remnants of that battle, Ross could not help noticing
the disappointment in the eyes of some of his own people, upset that they
had missed the fight. Along with Morgan and Ridge he watched as some of
the Cherokees made sport of the find, scalping corpses even as the colonel
ordered them to stop. The rules of combat, Ross learned, did not apply to
the dead.

The Cherokees would not have long to wait for their first taste of war. Although the campaign against the Creek rebels included troops from five other states, the Tennessee militia, under which the Indians fought, did most of the fighting. That was largely because Jackson's forces were stationed in central Alabama, where most of the Red Sticks were situated. The first battle the Cherokees saw, however, was between Jackson and his rival Major General John Cocke. Cocke commanded the eastern Tennessee forces, but Jackson—who led the western Tennesseans—had overall authority. The two men had decidedly different ideas about how to proceed. Furthermore, Jackson believed Cocke was envious of his authority and withheld supplies to hinder his success. Whether that was true, Cocke did not easily bow to Jackson's will. The Cherokees soon found themselves caught in a struggle between two massive egos.

Shortly after Tallushatchee, Jackson received word that a village of friendly Creeks was under attack by the Red Sticks to the west at Talladega. The Creeks had sent a messenger to beg for the general's help, and Jackson collected more than a thousand men and rode out. He sent orders for Morgan's Cherokees to back up his troops, but Cocke intercepted the note and discarded it. He decided to take the Cherokees for his own use and set out for Talladega in a different direction, to share in the battle—and in the glory. His ambition would prolong the war by months.

Jackson's troops rode into Talladega on November 9 and quickly routed the surprised Red Sticks. The Creek village, a few huts huddled in a dusty field, offered little protection but the woods surrounding it gave Jackson all the cover he needed for a surprise attack. It was a decidedly one-sided fight: the Tennessee militia killed some three hundred Indians and lost just seventeen men. By then Jackson had learned of Cocke's subterfuge, but he chose to attack anyway. He was rewarded with an easy victory, but without the Cherokees for backup more than seven hundred Red Sticks escaped into the surrounding woods. Jackson's men did not give chase. In the forest the Red Sticks had the advantage. Without the Cherokee, who could have better fought the Red Sticks in their native environment, Jackson was forced to watch his decisive victory slip away.

Jackson's military prowess had an effect, however. The surviving Red Sticks were demoralized and humiliated by their defeat. When they regrouped to the southwest at a town called Hillabee, the rebel Creeks realized they could not win and decided to surrender. They sent a messenger to find Jackson, asking that he meet with them to negotiate a peace treaty. Jackson sent the envoy back to Hillabee with a promise that the fighting would stop, that he would sit down with them soon. But the Red Sticks never got that message. Cocke found them first.

The Red Sticks had made no effort to conceal their location, in part because they assumed Jackson would accept their request to suspend the fighting. But General Cocke learned of their position and quickly dispatched General James White and the Cherokees to Hillabee without bothering to consult Jackson. The Tennessee militia and Colonel Morgan's Cherokees set out immediately and cut a path of destruction through deserted Creek villages, stopping only long enough to burn a few huts and meeting sheds. Then, to conceal their approach, they rode through mountainous terrain on the far side of Lookout Mountain, finally reaching Hillabee before daybreak on November 18. In the gray dusk of dawn they surrounded the Red Sticks.

Fearing they would be left out again, the Cherokees stormed the village without waiting for the Tennessee militia. As Morgan's adjutant, Ross most likely did not fight but rather watched as his tribesmen killed sixty Red Sticks in just twenty minutes. They shot and stabbed their way through Hillabee in a blind fury, trampling food stocks, killing their animals. Morgan later wrote a boastful note to Meigs about the "cool and deliberate bravery" of his warriors. He did not realize the Red Sticks were not prepared, that they had been expecting a diplomatic party and not warriors.

It was never a fair fight. For the second time in two weeks Ross had the opportunity to survey the site of an Indian massacre. But this time his own people were to blame. He must have wondered if he was cut out for such work. Ross was no stranger to a gun. He had often used one for hunting. But he had never seen men shot before, never heard the sounds they made as they died. He said nothing but realized this violence settled nothing; killing begat only more killing.

The Ridge, John Walker, and Alex Saunders missed most of the battle. They had staked out the high ground to catch any escaping Red Sticks but few of them got that far. By the time the Tennessee militia joined in, the U.S. forces had taken 250 prisoners and used bayonets to slay the rest. The Ridge, Walker, and Saunders, for their part, killed three Indians and captured forty women. However, Ridge did not come away empty-handed. He collected several slaves for his own plantation, as well as a young Muscogee (Creek) girl. (Although slavery was not widespread in the Cherokee Nation, some wealthy Indians had appropriated escaped slaves from Carolina and Virginia plantations for years.)

When Jackson later learned that the slaves Ridge took belonged to a friendly Indian, he ordered them returned to their rightful owner. After stalling for several days, Ridge eventually complied, but he kept the girl and came to treat her as one of his own family. Jackson could not say much about that. He had adopted an orphaned Creek boy who survived the raid at Tallushatchee, a rare instance of the general showing mercy for any Indian.

The Red Sticks, of course, thought Jackson anything but compassionate. After the Hillabee raid, they believed Old Mad Jackson, as they called him, had betrayed them, had learned their position and sent his troops to kill them. Although Jackson was innocent the damage had been done. The Red Sticks would never consider surrender now. They were more determined than ever to kill the general and anyone who fought with him.

Not that Andrew Jackson was opposed to fighting. In fact, he rather enjoyed it. More than a decade earlier he had given up a promising, if uninspired, career as a politician to become a soldier. He had retired from Congress, returned to his plantation, and become a judge. Some suspected the move was part of a calculated plan to take a more active role in Tennessee's military. He campaigned to lead the state militia against Governor John Sevier's hand-picked successor, a battle he fought for so long that he very nearly found himself in a duel with the governor over it.

Fighting, quite simply, was what Jackson knew best. He'd been around it all his life—a prisoner of war as a teenager during the Revolution, he later watched settlers battle Indians for control of his adopted home state. Even as an adult he constantly found trouble. There were stories that he had once caned a man, ran a sword through another, and shot and killed a third in a duel. Throughout the Creek War, he nursed a gunshot wound from a brawl with two brothers in Nashville. The tall, lanky lawyer was too mean—or too stubborn—to let a simple wound, or much of anything else, stop him.

After the disaster at Hillabee, however, Jackson found himself momentarily out of the fray. Georgia troops engaged the Creeks at the end of November and Mississippi forces burned the tribe's Holy Ground in December while Jackson struggled with a mass desertion of his troops. In mid-December, the Old Volunteers of Tennessee claimed their tour of duty had expired. After stopping the men at gunpoint twice, Jackson finally had to let them go. In January, both the East and the West Tennessee forces followed. The war was getting away from him.

As 1814 began, Jackson was stuck at the nearly empty Fort Strother, out of men, and short on supplies, sleep, and patience. The gunshot wound bothered him, and he was irritated to be missing the war. In a letter to Major David Walker he sounded demoralized about both his losses and Congress's preoccupation with the war against the British instead of his campaign.

"It is as unnecessary as it would be painful to particularize the many causes which have suspended our operations, & brought disgrace, I am fearful, instead of honor upon the Tennessee name—it is enough to say, that I am left almost without an army, but with all my former determination to conquer the Creeks & realize the expectations & the wishes of the genl. government, even if they attend to other objects."

But Old Mad Jackson would not quit. As the new year dawned he began to recruit new troops.

John Ross returned to Chickamauga with his brother in late December. After Hillabee the Cherokees had spent a month in Creek territory with little to do. They grew restless and hungry as the military supply line had nearly broken down, significantly reducing their rations. Finally, on December 18, Morgan released them from their service. There was, at that point, no Tennessee militia to support. Before they disbanded, however, Morgan offered his troops a stirring speech meant to keep their spirits high. Standing on the banks of the Coosa River, he promised them that not fifty days would pass before their swords, lances, and knives drank the blood of their enemy. Most of the Indians, and even John Golden Ross, would return after a month of rest. The Ridge was inspired to continue recruiting Cherokees for the war.

Ross passed the winter catching up on work at the trading post and enjoying restful evenings with his family. In some ways, it was as if he'd never been gone; Chickamauga felt far removed from the war. The trading post was thriving and his family was healthy. Although he and Quatie lived with his grandfather, he visited his father and younger siblings regularly. Daniel Ross was still an important figure in his son's life but he never tried to impose his will on John. He would let him find his own way, even though he could tell his son was troubled by what he had seen.

Ross sometimes seemed weary; the war had made an impression on him that he could not explain to his family. He had always been more seasoned than his age, less emotional even than most Cherokees. Perhaps it was his wealth or his white blood, but he seemed to have attained the confident air of gentility. The insecurities of childhood behind him, he now dressed almost exclusively in the suits of the richest white men. But now other things weighed on him. The horrors of war had affected him deeply; he had learned that he had little stomach for violence. Yet at the same time he had never felt more like part of the tribe, a true Cherokee. He would return to fight when called, even if the brutality made his stomach turn.

Ross followed the war from home. News of troop movements drifted through the trading post on a weekly basis. By mid-January Tennessee had sent Jackson 850 new soldiers, enough to begin a new campaign. Aided by a few Cherokees who had remained with Colonel Morgan's company, Jackson attacked the Red Sticks at Emuckfau Creek. He recorded an easy victory there but two days later was lucky to escape at Enotochopco. The Red Sticks, fueled by their anger over Jackson's apparent double-cross at Hillabee, fought with renewed vengeance. They drove the Tennessee militia all the way back to Fort Strother. Jackson was forced to regroup once again.

It did not take long. By March the general had amassed an army of about five thousand men and began to devise a new plan. In anticipation of a spring campaign Morgan sent for his adjutant. He asked Ross to meet him at Fort Strother with as many Cherokees as he could round up. Ross collected a few dozen men, including his brother Lewis, and asked Meigs to relay the call to arms among the Cherokee towns, to summons all who wanted to distinguish themselves by "fighting and taking revenge for the blood of the innocent."

Ross left Chickamauga filled with patriotic bravado, and most likely unaware that Quatie was pregnant with his first son. He no doubt believed the things he'd seen had prepared him for further battles. But in the coming months the young trader would see horrors to make the war to this point seem not much worse than a game of ballplay. The next correspondence he sent to Return J. Meigs would be a lengthy casualty report.

The mood was tense at Fort Strother when Ross arrived in mid-March. Jackson had assembled an army that he swore would "crush the Creek Nation and . . . remove the danger of warfare by them for all time to come." But things were not going entirely the general's way. His longest-serving troops had become mutinous—they had barely survived the winter and didn't have enough to eat. Unable to placate his men, Jackson swore to make an example of the next man accused of mutiny. It was a threat he may have regretted.

When an eighteen-year-old boy was accused of disobedience to an officer, and then resisted arrest by drawing his gun, the court sentenced him to death. Normally, Jackson would have commuted the sentence or imposed a lesser charge, but he felt that if he went back on his word he would never be able to keep order. The general eventually ordered his men to kill the boy. The execution may have improved discipline but it eroded morale even more.

The Cherokees were in somewhat better spirits as their numbers swelled to around five hundred, some of whom had received promotions from

Morgan. The Ridge had been given the rank of major, and he was so pleased by the title he would use it for the rest of his life. The Cherokees were joined by a hundred or so friendly Creek Indians who believed Jackson would need all the help he could get against their violent brothers. These Indians complemented two thousand infantrymen, some seven hundred cavalry, and a hundred mounted riflemen from the Tennessee militia. Jackson finally had enough troops to end the war.

The army moved out on March 21, riding south through the northern Alabama valleys for thirty miles before stopping to set up a new base of command, which they named Fort Williams. With so many men at his disposal and a ready supply of lumber in the thick woods, it took little time to build a new garrison. Jackson was inching closer to the location where, it was rumored, the Red Sticks had fortified their position.

But delays plagued Jackson's operations for the better part of a week. The boat carrying supplies for the troops ran aground in the Coosa, and it would take two days for the equipment and rations to arrive downstream. With nothing else to occupy his troops' time, Jackson sent the Cherokees to scout the area. They passed the time burning deserted Creek villages. It seemed the Indians enjoyed the sport of burning Indian towns nearly as much as the white soldiers.

When their munitions and food finally reached the fort on the twenty-fourth, Jackson and his army began marching south, toward the last Red Stick village.

It took two days to cover the fifty miles between Fort Williams and the Red Stick town of Tohopeka, the troops cutting their way through dense forest as they went. The slow pace afforded the Indians time to converse with Jackson. Although many Cherokees had their own biases against whites, and even Jackson, a few were clearly awestruck by the general. As Morgan's adjutant, Ross had occasional dealings with Jackson but no close bond. The general seemed to hold the most respect for Indians who were warriors, like himself, and spoke the common language of the battlefield. For that reason, Jackson and Ridge came to know each other fairly well. Although Jackson had been upset that Ridge took the Creek slaves at Hillabee, they quickly put the incident behind them. On the road to battle Jackson gained a life-long admiration for the gallant Ridge.

The rest of the Indians simply amused the general. Another Cherokee chief, Shoe Boots, tried to impress Jackson by making the sound of a rooster, his calling card.

"Me crow like cock," Shoe Boots told Jackson, "but no chicken me."

Using mostly body language, Shoe Boots demonstrated to Jackson that he knew not to shoot an enemy in the back, but only the front. It's not clear whether Jackson actually agreed with these terms of engagement but he must have been amused by such antics, calling the Cherokees "friendly" in several letters home to his wife. It was a major concession by the general, who normally referred to Indians as "savages" and men like John Ross as "half-breeds."

Like most settlers on the frontier Jackson had grown up surrounded by people who both feared and hated Indians. He was raised on the belief that it was perfectly fine to evict the natives from their own land to make way for civilized people. Still, he knew that encroaching on Indian land carried a cost. When he came to Tennessee as a young man, he had seen the garrisons and understood why they had such high walls. In some ways the Creek War seemed the logical end to years of such tensions. He had to know this sort of conflict could arise with any tribe, even the Cherokee, but Jackson could be kind toward Indians, particularly if he thought they were his allies. But even then, he spoke to all Indians—even the oldest chiefs—as if they were children, unable to comprehend complex ideas.

If the Cherokees noticed this slight they said nothing of it.

On the night of March 26, Jackson and his men camped just six miles from the Red Sticks' fortification. The campground covered a dozen acres, and watches were set at the perimeter so no one could sneak up on the men. Many of the troops were anxious and stayed up late into the night, standing around fires and talking. The Cherokees kept mostly to themselves, but few could rest despite the hard march they'd made. It was difficult to sleep knowing the next day could be their last. The army moved out at 6:30 in the morning.

Jackson had drawn up an elaborate battle plan. He sent Coffee, Morgan, and the Cherokees to cross the Tallapoosa River downstream and come up behind the camp at Tohopeka, so as to prevent any Red Sticks from escaping. He told them the same thing he told his other forces: to be cool and collected, to follow orders with deliberation, and to "let every shot tell."

"Any officer or soldier who flies before the enemy without being compelled to do so by superior force and actual necessity shall suffer death," Jackson told his men.

If the Cherokees had actually heeded that command, the battle might have turned out differently.

The Red Sticks had named this land Cholocco Litabixee—"horse's flat foot"—but the white men called it Horseshoe Bend, and even Jackson had to admit the Indians had found a perfect place to make their last stand. The Tallapoosa dramatically looped around a hundred acres of high ground, creating a teardrop peninsula with a neck barely more than one thousand feet across. The village lay near the tip of the peninsula on a bluff, protected by steep banks and the deceptively wide river. The Red Sticks had built nearly three hundred simple log huts, laid out in no particular pattern. The ground was covered with stumps, remnants of the trees used to build their houses.

The high ground of the village gave way to lower, sloping land at the narrow neck, across which the Creeks had established a brilliant defense: a zigzag breastwork of logs, between five and eight feet high, which curved inward. The log wall was packed with rock-hard mud and its shape made it impossible to attack without becoming caught in the Red Sticks' cross fire.

Jackson recognized this dilemma when he emerged from the woods on a hill a few hundred yards from the wall. From that vantage he could see the entire valley, including the village beyond the wall. Hundreds of Red Stick warriors were gathered just behind it, and Jackson knew his men might take heavy losses if they simply marched down the hill. They were too far for rifle fire to do them any good, so he set in place his two cannons, one of which fired a three-pound ball about the size of an orange, while the other shot a six-pound ball roughly the size of a grapefruit. At 10:30 a.m., he gave the order and the militia commenced firing both cannons.

The noise rumbled through the otherwise quiet valley, but neither gun had any effect. The Red Stick defenses were holding. The wall would not come down.

The leaders of the Creek rebellion watched Jackson's bombardment with a measure of confidence. Their leader, Menawa, had prepared his warriors for this fight, and the prophet Monahee promised that the Great Spirit would protect them from the enemy's bullets, much as Tecumseh's brother had once told his followers. If Menawa did not entirely believe his prophet's claims, he at least had faith in his breastworks. The wall withstood two full hours of cannon fire.

Across the river from the Red Stick village the Cherokees were growing impatient. The echo of the cannon fire made them anxious to attack, even though they had been ordered to hold their ground. Coffee had been warned another band of Red Sticks might approach from their side of the Tallapoosa, and he was counting on the Cherokees to guard his flank and prevent more Creeks from joining the fight. But to the Cherokee warriors it sounded only as if they were missing out on the battle once again. With most of the Red Sticks distracted by Jackson at the neck of the peninsula, some of Morgan's men saw a chance to join the fight.

The Red Sticks had left a long line of canoes on the banks of the Tallapoosa, their only means of retreat. These boats, mostly hollowed-out logs, sat in the mud or were wedged behind large rocks that littered the river. A few Indians, including one warrior named the Whale, ignored Coffee's orders, dived into the water, and swam more than a hundred yards to the other side.

The Cherokees crossed the river undetected but were spotted and fired upon as soon as they reached the Red Stick canoes. The Whale took one shot but it did not stop him or the others. The Cherokees loaded the Whale into one canoe and brought another back across the water as their own troops provided a covering fire. When they landed, more Cherokees filled the two canoes and they crossed the river again, more quickly this time. Each of those Indians took another of the Red Sticks' canoes. That relay continued, under constant fire, until the Cherokees had them all, leaving the Red Sticks with no way to escape.

Then, while most of the Red Stick warriors guarded their fortification on the neck of the peninsula, the Cherokees—among them Morgan, Major Ridge, and John and Lewis Ross—loaded into the canoes and charged Tohopeka from the rear.

After two hours of shelling, Jackson conceded that his cannons could not take down the wall. Faced with no other alternative he told his men to charge the breastwork, an order his troops had been itching to hear all morning. But the task seemed easier than it was. The soldiers had to run down a hill with a drop-off so steep that it was hard to keep their balance, especially while carrying rifles. Once they reached the bottom it didn't get any simpler. The open land that led to the wall undulated in a series of uneven rises that left them stumbling as they came into range of the Red Sticks. They had to dodge arrows and gunfire coming from ports in the wall while clumsily trying to return fire. The scene was chaos. From the moment Jackson's men started down the hill, the quiet countryside erupted into a piercing chorus of war whoops and gunshots. In many ways it sounded like a game of the ballplay, but with heavy artillery and musket fire.

The Thirty-ninth Regiment reached the fortification first and shoved their rifles into the wall's ports, firing without any idea what, if anything, they were hitting. Pressed close to the wall, the militia fought in such close quarters to the Indians that some later claimed the Red Sticks' musket balls melted onto their bayonets. Jackson's men spent several minutes pressed against the wall with no way to advance. Finally, Major Lemuel P. Montgomery climbed to the top of the wall, stood atop it for a moment, and yelled out for his men to follow him. Before he could finish his call, a bullet struck him in the head and he fell dead, the first of many casualties that day.

The next man to scale the wall was a young ensign named Sam Houston, who repeated Montgomery's order and was promptly shot in the thigh by an arrow. But Houston ignored his wound and jumped over the wall. Soon others began to follow, and within a few minutes the fight quickly scattered all the way to Tohopeka.

The Red Sticks were surrounded. By the time Jackson's men breached the wall, the Cherokees were moving across the peninsula. Major Ridge ordered some of the men to set the village on fire in order to drive the Creeks toward Jackson's men. "The carnage," Jackson later wrote to his wife, "was dreadful." Bullets, arrows, swords, and spears sliced through the smoke and dozens of men fell dead every minute, some shot in the head, others gored. The ground was littered with trampled bodies, most of them Red Sticks who had not been protected by the Great Spirit, as their prophet had promised. Perhaps in atonement for this false assurance, Monahee was shot in the mouth. Menawa suffered seven wounds before falling on a pile of bodies.

Neither side had the edge on savagery. The Tennesseans killed an old Indian, apparently senile, who did not realize what was going on around him. Another soldier beat a young boy over the head and shot him, defending his actions by claiming the child would have grown into another Indian bent on revenge. According to Cherokee legend, one Red Stick nearly stabbed Jackson, but a chief named Junaluska swept in and saved him. Yet the Creeks could not remain on the offensive for long, as the Cherokees had forced them to defend two fronts at once.

The Cherokees moved through the Tohopeka in one large group, killing and burning as they corralled the Creek rebels between themselves and Jackson's men. Although the Red Sticks were largely preoccupied with the militia, they still outnumbered the Cherokees and most preferred to fight the smaller force. The Red Sticks were not completely helpless and took out several Cherokee warriors as they pushed toward the river in a desperate retreat. Morgan was wounded but kept on fighting. Ross stayed close to his colonel, avoiding injury. It is unclear how much fighting the young merchant did, but he would have had little choice but to fire on the Red Sticks. On that day, it was the only way to survive.

After little more than an hour Jackson had had enough. His men were winning, and he saw no point in prolonging the battle. He sent a soldier offering a cease-fire if the Red Sticks would surrender. But they refused to give up—they had not forgotten Jackson's apparent double cross at Hillabee. They shot Jackson's messenger and kept fighting but the battle was lost.

By late afternoon the remaining Red Sticks abandoned the fight and crept toward the river, using fallen timber and foliage to hide their movements. When they reached the water, however, the Indians found themselves stuck between Coffee's men, who were firing from the opposite bank, and the pursuing Cherokees. Some hid in brush along the riverbank while others dived into the Tallapoosa and swam for the other side.

Ridge jumped into the water to pursue the Red Sticks, and in just a few minutes he killed six injured Indians as they thrashed in the current. But as he attempted to plunge his sword into another the warrior turned on him. They struggled in the water, slipping off the rocks that jutted from the riverbed and nearly drowning each other. The younger man was injured but still as strong as the middle-aged Ridge, and neither could get the upper hand. Finally, unable to reach his knife, Ridge grabbed the Red Stick's own blade and plunged it into him. Even as he bled to death the man kept fighting until another Cherokee delivered the killing blow with a spear.

By nightfall it was over. Men would later say the battle was so violent the Tallapoosa ran red for days. Even though his men were exhausted, Jackson ordered a count of the dead. It fell to Ross to sort out the white and Cherokee casualties while soldiers tallied the dead Red Sticks. To keep from counting a body more than once, the militia men cut the noses off as they went, and the Cherokees followed behind to scalp some of the enemy dead. The blood would stain the ground at Horseshoe Bend for some time to come. In the end, the militia found 557 dead Creeks on the peninsula, and Coffee estimated that his men and the Cherokees killed another 300 trying to escape across the river. It was the single bloodiest day in Indian history.

Still, Jackson feared that even such a decisive battle would not end the war. Not all of the Red Sticks had been killed. In the night, the injured

Menawa woke up, crawled to the banks of the Tallapoosa, and found a canoe. He disappeared into the darkness.

John Ross reported to Return J. Meigs that eighteen Cherokees were killed in the fighting, including two men in Major Ridge's company. He noted that Morgan had been wounded only slightly, and that he, his brother, and his brother-in-law John Golden Ross had escaped injury. Besides the colonel, another thirty-five Cherokees suffered wounds he rated "severely" or "dangerously." By comparison, the Tennessee militia lost 26 men, while another 107 were wounded—the result of their frontal assault. By attacking from the rear the Cherokees had carried an element of surprise, which reduced their casualty rate. Or perhaps they were just better fighters. But Shoe Boots—the old chief who had entertained Jackson on the trail—was missing and the Cherokees feared he had been killed. They searched the battlefield for hours but could not find him. As some lamented the loss of their friend, they heard a noise like a rooster's cry in the distance.

The next day, the Cherokees set out with Jackson on the three-day trip back to Fort Williams. Despite the overwhelming victory at Horseshoe Bend, no one was sure if the war was over. Some Red Sticks had escaped, and there was a chance they would regroup and continue to fight. While many of Jackson's forces left for home when they reached the fort the general took a band of men on an expedition along the Coosa to round up the remaining Red Sticks. They found few of the defeated Indians. Most had simply disappeared.

In mid-April Bill Weatherford—Chief Red Eagle, the man who had started the war by attacking Fort Mims—walked into Jackson's camp and turned himself in. Jackson had put a price on Red Eagle's head and planned to kill him, but the Indian's bravery gave him a change of heart. Jackson valued honor, even among Indians. After a short meeting, Jackson let the chief go in the hope that Red Eagle might convince his brothers they should make peace.

John Ross had returned home to Chickamauga by then, free of any romantic notions of war he may once have had. If he regretted his decision to fight he told no one of it—Ross did not like to admit mistakes. But the fighting had taught him to keep a cool head in crisis and given him a measure of the stature he had longed for as a young man. He had risked his life for the tribe, and it gave him a newfound standing among the Cherokees. He had been respected before but now was considered an honorable man, if not exactly a warrior.

Ross was finished with soldiering, however, and resigned his commission less than two weeks after he'd watched Tohopeka destroyed. He would not fight again, and he never spoke of his own actions at Horseshoe Bend. Unlike many Indians, he did not feel the compulsion to brag about his exploits. Without a doubt, the battle had scarred him and he carried it with him the rest of his life. But he had learned valuable lessons about both war and Jackson.

After Junaluska saved him on the battlefield, Jackson had said, "As long as the sun shines and the grass grows, there shall be friendship between us." Ross, however, had reason to be skeptical. Months later, when Jackson negotiated a peace treaty with the Creeks, he took more than twenty million acres of their land and sent much of the tribe west. Some of that land had belonged to peaceful Creeks who had nothing to do with the war, but the general claimed it was the only way to ensure that both whites and Indians were safe, although in truth he believed the two races could not peacefully coexist, a common philosophy among whites of the time.

John Ross realized that if even just a few powerful white men shared Jackson's attitude, the Cherokees might one day face the same fate as that of the Creeks. Horseshoe Bend also taught the young trader another important lesson: no matter how brave or strong the Indians were, they would never be a match for the white man's army.

These truths would inform his decisions for the next five decades, when the fate of the Cherokee Nation rested solely with him.

FOUR

A Sharp Knife

Spring had come to Chickamauga by the time John Ross returned home in April of 1814. The drab landscape of winter had given way to dogwood blossoms and wildflowers, the rain had begun to replenish the rivers, and the days were growing longer and warmer. The Indians who lived near his grandfather's house were busy with the start of the planting season, while others fished on creek banks and children played in the fields. After his months on the burned and bloodstained battlefields of Alabama, the green hills of Tennessee and sloping profile of Lookout Mountain were a welcome sight to Ross.

The warm weather brought with it the promise of great business opportunity. The Meigs and Ross trading post stood at the gateway of the country's expansion, and everyone who followed the river west—settlers, U.S. troops, even some Indians—stocked up on supplies for the voyage. Ross hoped the tribe's recent alliance with the army would help his trade, and it certainly did not hurt his prospects to be in business with the son of a U.S. Indian agent. Return J. Meigs could steer lucrative government contracts their way. The trading post had done well while he was gone, and it would only pick up with the return of its more ambitious partner.

By the end of the summer Ross witnessed the birth of his first son, named James McDonald in honor of his great-grandfather. The baby forced him to acclimate himself to family life. He had spent little time with Quatie since their wedding, and this would prove to be one of the few periods of un-interrupted domestic life for them. He was pleased that Quatie raised young James as a Cherokee, just as his mother had done for him. Ross adapted to tradition easily—like his parents, never missing an opportunity to attend a green corn festival or local tribal meeting. Ross found himself accepted into Cherokee life more readily after his service in the war, but for the next year and a half he immersed himself in his business. He divided his time between Chickamauga and the trail, riding across Tennessee and Georgia to gather supplies for his shop.

Not even the death of his partner in 1815 slowed Ross. After Timothy Meigs passed away unexpectedly (he was only in his early thirties), Ross took on his brother Lewis as a partner. Lewis had worked for their grand-father and father for several years and proved to be Ross's equal in business, and perhaps even better with the books. The bond between them, formed in childhood, remained intact and their temperaments seemed a perfect fit; Lewis was content to stay home and mind the trading post while his older brother traveled.

The two worked in isolation much of the time. The trading post was sur-rounded by dense forest at the river's edge, a tangle of scrub brush and pine tree, the far bank more visible to them than the land just beyond their back door. There were only a few Indian homes in the miles around the shop, at the time little more than a shanty and a log hut where the ferryman hid from the brutal southern sun. Soon, more Cherokees would move into the area— they wisely built their villages near freshwater for drinking and bathing— and the trading post sat on one of the few spots where the river was easily accessible. The small town that grew up around the brothers' trading post would come to be known as Ross's Landing.

In the late summer of 1815 Ross rode south to Savannah and took pas-sage to Baltimore and New York on a luxurious ship, where he fit in perfectly with the white businessmen, even though ocean travel was new to him. He carried deerskins for trade and found a ready market in the modern northern cities. His travels in the North until then had been limited to a single trip to Baltimore, and the huge cities were a wonder to him. New York, in particular, was a staggering sight. Although New York was no longer the nation's capital, its port was growing, and the streets were lined with more buildings than Ross had ever seen before. In the past year, the city's population had grown to over a hundred thousand—more than five times as many people than in the entire Cherokee Nation—living on a single island. But no matter how much the city impressed him Ross was no longer tempted to move away from his home.

If he had ambitions beyond his trading post, Ross shared them with no one. He had realized he was no soldier and had so far shown little inclination toward politics. But his intellect and calm manners had made an impression on the tribe's leaders. While he was north, Ross received word that the principal chief Pathkiller had requested he join a Cherokee delegation to Washington City. Although Ross may not have relished the idea of cutting his business trip short, he could not ignore a request from the chief. He hurried home to get his assignment.

Pathkiller had waited more than a year for the United States to make good on several promises and he would be ignored no longer. The government had yet to repay the tribe for all the "marauding and plundering" of Cherokee property during the Creek War, done primarily by white troops under the guise of gathering supplies. And despite assurances from the War Department, there had been no militia brought in to protect the tribe's land from the growing number of squatters, hundreds of whom arrived each month. If anything, the Cherokees were treated worse than they had been before their alliance with the U.S. military.

The tribe also learned that the Creeks, in their peace treaty with Jackson, had given away several thousand acres of land the Cherokees believed to be theirs, a dispute that had lingered for years. Now this land had been declared open for settlement and white people paraded in quickly. In earlier times, the Indians would have chased away these squatters with force or intimidation. But Pathkiller, careful not to provoke the United States military, decided it was best to follow the agreements of their own treaties—and ask the government to do the same. Pathkiller had first appealed to Meigs, but his bosses in the War Department ignored all requests to respond. By the end of 1815 it had become apparent the Cherokees would have to go to the president for relief.

Ross had been selected to accompany five chiefs and Meigs to Washington, where they hoped to meet directly with President Madison. Someone had recognized the young man's particular skills and brought him to Pathkiller's attention. It could have been Gideon Morgan, Charles Hicks, or even Major Ridge, the men who had watched the way Ross handled his duties during the war. Whoever referred Ross, it was clear that influential Cherokees agreed he was an asset, for the mission he had been given was of grave importance to the tribe.

Pathkiller gave the delegation a long list of grievances to address and great latitude to solve them. He even suggested they might make greater progress if they bartered the last of their land in South Carolina, which the president had repeatedly asked to buy. Even though the tribe was determined to sell no more land, its South Carolina property held little value: far across the mountains, it was remote and unconnected to the rest of the nation. The principal chief left no question that, if it would help them solve their pressing problems, he would gladly give it up.

"The multiplied Intrusions on our lands by disorderly men from all the states of Territories of the United States by which our country is surrounded has become alarming to us," he said. "I wish you to make such representation of those intrusions as you may think proper to our Father the President. We do not doubt receiving such protections as by our treaties we are entitled; but as these intrusions still continue, and now nearly surround our whole Country; it is feared that they will so increase as to be very difficult to repress, if not impossible to be remedied."

If Ross wondered why Pathkiller had asked him to join a group of elders such as George Lowrey, John Walker, and Major Ridge on this mission, he got an idea soon enough. On every letter or document the Cherokees sent while in Washington, the chiefs signed their name with a simple X, for none of them could write or read the white man's language. But Ross could. That was his value to the tribe and, for years, it would serve him and his career well.

Washington was still recovering from the ravages of war when the Cherokees arrived in February 1816. The British had burned many of the city's public buildings in the summer of 1814 and more than a year later the city remained in disarray—the national Treasury and Department of State still operated out of private homes. The reconstruction did not slow the town's active social scene, and the delegates—a rare breed of guests in those days— soon found themselves invited to many lively parties, where they gazed admiringly at the wives of government officials dressed in the finest satins and silks. None of the Indians had ever seen such wealth, and they were amazed at the way these people lived, but the Cherokees were not intimidated. At one fete, Major Ridge serenaded the crowd with a Cherokee song so raunchy that Richard Taylor, a member of the council and the group's interpreter, refused to translate it.

"You don't want to know," Ridge joked. "It's just like a white man's song—all about love and whiskey."

Although Ross was not as gregarious or colorful as his colleagues, his refinement and classical education must have won over the Washington elite. The *National Intelligencer* newspaper was no doubt referring to the young trader when it described the visiting Cherokee delegates as "men of cultivation and understanding."

"Their appearance and deportment are such to entitle them to respect and attention," the *Intelligencer* reporter declared.

In part, the appearance of the chiefs was improved by the new clothes issued by the War Department. Ridge and many of the older Cherokees still dressed in skins and an ostentatious display of feathers and beads, and Meigs's bosses had given the Indians suits to make them more presentable to government officials. The Cherokees proudly wore these clothes everywhere while in the city. For weeks after their arrival the delegation did little more than mingle with the city's elite, winning over many scores of people, including Dolley Madison, the president's socially conscious wife. At one banquet, they learned that Jackson, now a national hero after the Battle of New Orleans, was in town. Worried he would be upset if he learned of their attempt to renegotiate the Creek treaty, the Cherokees said little of their mission publicly.

The delegation was finally granted an audience with the president on February 22. They met Madison at the Octagon House, an odd-shaped home that served as the president's residence and office while the fire-gutted Executive Mansion underwent renovations. The Cherokees must have been surprised by the sight of the diminutive Great Father, who stood barely five feet, four inches tall—shorter, even, than Ross. But they quickly recognized his air of authority. Although not as self-possessed as Jefferson, Madison was just as gracious a host. He greeted the Cherokee delegation warmly and thanked them for their service to the country. The president declared it a pleasure to receive friends, "especially my red brethren the Cherokees who have fought by the side of their white brethren and spilt their blood together."

If the Cherokees took the Great Father's hospitality as a sign that they would enjoy straightforward negotiations, they were wrong. Madison, one of the nation's founders, had not attained his position by being a pushover. For the entirety of the short meeting, the president did all the talking. He promised the Indians that any of their tribesmen permanently disabled in the war would receive the same pension benefits as white soldiers, and he assured them the government would pay for the damage done by troops to the Cherokee Nation—"as much as what is right."

Madison mentioned in passing that South Carolina would likely make the tribe a fine offer for its remaining land in that state, and then he graciously dismissed the delegates. He made no mention of the Creek treaty or its appropriation of Cherokee land and gave them no chance to bring it up. Like most chiefs, Ross noted, the president left the unpleasant tasks of governing to others.

It took more than a month to address the border dispute. War Department officials were eager to negotiate for the South Carolina land but dismissed the Indians' other issues out of hand. The Cherokees had immediately agreed to sell their South Carolina property, believing it might make the government more amenable to assisting them. Instead, acting secretary of war George Graham told Ross that Jackson believed the Creek treaty established a fair boundary. Ross promptly rescinded the offer to sell the South Carolina land. The Cherokees were surprised by his aggressive negotiating skills, something the language barrier and their temperament left them ill prepared to master. The trader knew how to bargain.

"We are also surprised to see that your commissioners were disposed to support the unfounded claims of the Creeks," Ross told Graham. "We can only observe, that we confide in the justice of the Government, and hope such justice as our nation are entitled to, will not be withheld from us, by the Government. We ask no more."

Graham would not bend, but when he was replaced by William H. Crawford—Madison's permanent choice for secretary of war—Ross renewed his efforts. He got an audience with the new secretary on March 12 and explained all that had happened since the war's end. The squatters had treated the tribe barbarically, stolen their land, and even killed a few Indians. The Cherokees did not exact revenge, he noted, out of friendship. In a very diplomatic way Ross told Crawford the Indians were acting far more civilized than the white men.

"It is foreign to the Cherokee people to feign friendship where it does not exist," Ross said. "You have told us that your Government is determined to do justice to our nation and will never use oppressive means to make us act contrary to our welfare and free will."

Ross proved to be a persuasive diplomat. For two weeks he talked Crawford into a stupor, and he won every point. His logic was hard to ignore, and he had an impressive understanding of the treaties between the government and the tribe. Clearly, Ross had studied these documents in preparation for the mission, and his knowledge of the history between the whites and Cherokees impressed his colleagues. Eventually it paid off.

After weeks of Ross's bargaining the secretary of war agreed to redraw the boundary of the Creek treaty, giving the Cherokees a fifty-mile swath of land in the Alabama territory. He also promised that General Jackson's troops would evict the illegal settlers. In exchange, the tribe sold its land in South Carolina for $5,000 and gave the United States the right to build roads through Cherokee land. Ross even allowed the government unlimited access to rivers and waterways throughout the Cherokee Nation, a concession he made only after the Cherokee chiefs gave their blessing. When Ross left the capital city in April, Crawford was no doubt glad to see him go.

While the other Cherokees lingered in Washington and took an excursion to Baltimore, John Ross returned home a hero. Through his negotiations the tribe had given up an isolated tract of land for a written deed to a much larger territory contiguous to the rest of the nation. No other Cherokee had ever displayed such savvy in dealing with white men, particularly in their own capital. It was as if the tribe's greatest disadvantage had been overcome.

Pathkiller would soon find many other ways to keep the talented Ross busy. The old chief was perceptive enough to recognize talent when he saw it, and the results of the trip provided enough proof that the young trader was useful to him and to the tribe. Ross, who enjoyed the prestige afforded him as a representative of the Cherokee Nation, would happily accept any assignment.

News of the amended treaty was not received well in Tennessee. It seemed federal bureaucrats had simply taken land from one tribe and given it to another—they were literally losing ground to the Indians—and that inspired some of the state's wealthiest and most powerful citizens to send formal protests to Washington. In Nashville, Crawford and Madison were criticized at public meetings. No one was more livid than Andrew Jackson. He had known about the Cherokees' claim to the land but dismissed it, arguing they had never really owned it to begin with. The general was mad: the Madison administration had made him look foolish, and this new treaty interfered with his ultimate goal, which was to remove all Indians from Tennessee.

An irate Jackson spent more than a month bullying government officials over the deal. He accused Return J. Meigs of helping the Cherokees swindle the United States, and warned James Monroe—the secretary of state with presidential ambitions—that the treaty could lead to problems for him on the frontier. Crawford, for one, had little use for Jackson's petulance. He noted that Congress had approved the treaty with little dissent, and ordered the general to get rid of the illegal settlers. Jackson refused.

The Tennessean was stubborn, relentless, and deadly efficient—it was for these reasons that some Indians called Jackson the "Sharp Knife." Jackson complained to Crawford that only "half-breeds" such as Charles Hicks and John Ross cared about the land, that "the real Indians, the natives of the forest are little concerned." Why else, he believed, would most Indians consider the land communal property? It was a foreign concept to most white men, one settlers often used for moral solace when taking Indian land. But he did not consider that the Cherokees were different from most tribes. They had been determined to hold on to their remaining land since Doublehead sold their hunting grounds.

From his home outside Nashville, Jackson sent one insistent missive after another throughout the summer. Finally, Crawford relented. Perhaps it was because he was considering a presidential bid, or maybe he just wanted Jackson to shut up, but Crawford suggested that if the general wanted to be rid of the Cherokees he should try to negotiate a new treaty. An idea was born.

Although Crawford repeatedly reminded Jackson that the president's position had not changed, he nevertheless appointed Jackson commissioner to the Cherokees, giving the general the legal right to negotiate. He even gave Jackson extra support by naming his friend General John Coffee commissioner to the Choctaws. Together, the two men devised a plan: Coffee would persuade the Choctaws to move west, while Jackson worked on the Cherokees and the Chickasaws.

That September, a group of Cherokee chiefs met with Jackson at the Chickasaw capital in the Mississippi territory. The general had no luck convincing the Chickasaws to move; they would not sell their land and at one point even produced a treaty signed by George Washington that guaranteed their rights. The Cherokees were just as stubborn. Jackson was not above a bit of trickery, however, maintaining the Indians were wasting their time trying to claim land in the Alabama territory. But he could not bluff either tribe. Instead, the general spent a week intimidating and bribing key chiefs until he got a treaty that granted 1.3 million acres to the United States. Under the terms of this treaty, the Chickasaws would get $10,000 annually for ten years, the Cherokees $8,000 for the same period.

Jackson thought he had won until some of the other Cherokees announced they were not authorized to make any land deals. The Indians apologetically told the general he would have to appeal to the council when the chiefs met in Turkeytown later that month. If Jackson wanted the land he had conquered in the Creek War he would have to face Pathkiller to get it.

At Turkeytown, most chiefs were outraged by Jackson's proposal; Charles Hicks and Pathkiller refused to consider it. Even without the tribe's toughest negotiators—Ridge did not attend and Ross was away on business—the Cherokees held firm. Rebuffed, the general remained in town for a week, meeting privately with individual chiefs. The Cherokees' governing council was not centralized and Jackson believed he could divide and conquer, much as he had done with the Chickasaws. After a while he resorted to bribery. When he left in October, Jackson claimed to have made a deal.

Later, Pathkiller and Hicks would swear that only a few minor chiefs had agreed to the treaty, but Jackson's proposal carried the principal chief's mark. Most likely, the old man had not realized what he was signing—it made little sense for him to give up land he'd fought so hard to regain, even if Jackson had promised him money. But the tribe made a serious mistake; Pathkiller let a year pass before complaining to Madison. By then it was too late. Jackson had moved on to a larger and more elaborate scheme to get even more Cherokee land.

During the Turkeytown council, Jackson introduced the chiefs to Cyrus Kingsbury, a missionary from New England who had spent much of the past year traveling in eastern Tennessee. He had been sent by the American Board of Commissioners for Foreign Missions to work with the Cherokees and was so successful that he wanted to open a permanent school. The general's endorsement of Kingsbury suggested his (and the country's) complicated, and sometimes contradictory, attitude toward Indians. Even though Jackson wanted every tribe removed from the Southeast, he was sincere when he urged the Cherokees to listen to Kingsbury and realize "the importance of educating their children." Some whites believed Indians would grow only more attached to their land if they were educated, yet others saw it as a way to make the frontier a safer place.

Kingsbury had no ulterior motives; he wanted only to help the Indians. On his seven-month tour of the Cherokee Nation, he told the foreign mission board, he had visited some of the most beautiful country he had ever seen but was more affected by the sight of the poor Indians, "so many people and large families of children entirely destitute of instruction, and living without hope and without God in the world." Kingsbury believed establishing a school in the natives' land was an opportunity to spread the gospel and help some underprivileged children.

He had planned an elaborate presentation for the chiefs, but the tribe's preoccupation with Jackson's treaty afforded Kingsbury little chance. He was not given the opportunity to speak for several days, and then he was not called upon until it was nearly midnight. He knew better than to bore his audience with a long lecture at that late hour, so Kingsbury boiled his message down to its simplest and, he hoped, most appealing terms.

"I told them we would take their children, teach them freely without money," he later wrote. "That we would feed as many as we could and furnish some clothes to those that are poor. That as we could teach more than we could feed, if the parents wanted to pay their board, we would teach all such freely."

The chiefs listened politely and promised Kingsbury an answer before he left. By 1816 most Cherokees had warmed to education. Daniel Ross had introduced the Cherokees to public education and since then some missionaries had opened a school at Spring Place. But the school was nowhere near as large as the one Kingsbury proposed, an entire campus of buildings that would take on hundreds of students, cultivate its own crops, and operate much like its own village.

Some Indians felt this sort of intrusion amounted to little more than giving land to white men, but others saw a chance to ensure their culture's survival. A school such as the one Kingsbury proposed would be proof the Cherokees were becoming more civilized. Some suspected it was a test, that Jackson's motivation was merely to gain evidence, by way of the tribe's presumptive refusal, that they were not interested in education. Other chiefs believed such a school would lead to great things. Perhaps the United States would treat the tribe as equals, some chiefs argued, if the Indians were more like them. After the council conferred, the chiefs gave the missionary his answer that night. He could establish his school once suitable land was found.

Later, Kingsbury could not recall which chief pulled him aside, but he remembered what he was told, even if he did not understand the double meaning of the message.

"They were glad to see me [the chief told him]; that they wished to have the school established and hoped it would be of great advantage to the nation," Kingsbury reported to the Board for Foreign Missions.

John Ross played an invaluable role in setting up the Brainerd Mission, which was named after an eighteenth-century missionary. His grandfather John McDonald sold Kingsbury a twenty-five-acre plantation little more than six miles east of Ross's Landing for just $500. The plantation included several buildings; all the mission board had to do was build a schoolhouse and boarding quarters for the students. Ross's trading post supplied the corn and other necessities. Over the years, Ross would do everything he could to ensure the mission's success, often extending credit to the missionaries, other times donating goods. His efforts were evident from the start. When Kingsbury sent for teachers and missionaries to run the school, he mailed them directions that led directly to Ross's trading post.

Major Ridge enrolled two of his children, Nancy and John, when the Brainerd Mission opened in March of 1817. He had boarded them at the missionary school at Spring Place for years but moved them because he was impressed by the men at Brainerd. The campus was growing quickly; the school had recently constructed a gristmill and a sawmill. When Ridge delivered his children the missionaries recorded in their logs the arrival of the "son and daughter of a chief" with "rich clothing, many ornaments & some knowledge of letters." Ridge's endorsement of the school would help it succeed—he would not entrust his oldest son to just anyone. John Ridge had always been a smart but frail child, affected from an early age with scrofula, a kind of tuberculosis that caused a swelling of the lymph nodes. At times, the boy could barely walk, but Ridge thought his son held great promise, if his health improved.

John Ridge would prove to be a bright, if sometimes difficult, student. During one class, some of the Indian students were having a hard time learning their spelling, so the teacher suggested they study fewer words at a time. Ridge, only fifteen, said "in a hasty and petulant manner" that he would not have shorter lessons. Such disrespect from one of the school's better students surprised the teachers. Shortly after his outburst, Ridge broke down in tears, "sorry he had given us so much trouble and pain."

Just two days after his son's tantrum Major Ridge made a surprise visit to the school. He was there to deliver the young Creek girl he had adopted during the war, but he'd also learned of his son's behavior and wanted to confer with the teachers. Tall with a broad chest, Ridge was an imposing figure. He surprised them with his knowledge of goings-on at the mission. The staff did not know how to respond, fearing they might anger the chief. But they found that although he lacked formal education Ridge was intelligent, sophisticated, and, on this day, apologetic.

"I heard that my children were so bad that you could not manage them, and had just to let them go wild," Major Ridge told the teachers. "I came to see if it was true. If they conduct so it will not be good to keep them at the school."

When the teachers assured Ridge that his children were well behaved his mood lightened. He would visit the school often over the years, always pleased by the progress of Cherokee students. As the tribe's dealings with the white men grew more complex, Ridge realized that his own lack of education limited his value to the tribe. He was gratified to see more Indians getting an education so that they might be of as much use to the tribe as John Ross had become. And he especially hoped his son John would have a bright future as a leader in the Cherokee Nation.

*   *   *

John Ross spent the spring of 1817 most concerned about corn. A poor year for the crop had left the area woefully short on supplies, and he could not fill the orders he had nor find any stockpile of it for less than $1.50 a bushel. The shortage forced him to reconsider the wisdom of his contract with the Indian Trade Department, a deal—no doubt secured by Meigs—that had proved lucrative. Now Ross was in the uncomfortable position of selling food that eventually found its way to the very settlers moving onto Indian land while some Cherokees went hungry.

Ross feared this arrangement could threaten his new relations with the tribe and, business aside, his first loyalty was to the Cherokees. Ultimately, he sought Meigs's advice. He wanted to maintain relations with the government, and he had his own livelihood to consider, but Ross was conflicted. Upon his return from Baltimore he had learned of the fraudulent treaty born of a trick by Jackson. Ross was so incensed that part of him wanted to cut all ties to the government that had allowed such subterfuge. Meigs convinced him to honor his Trade Department contracts.

Ross's conscience pulled him in two very different directions. He had followed closely in the footsteps of his father and grandfather, but unlike them he was part Cherokee. If there was any lingering question as to whether he more closely identified with his paternal ancestry or his Indian blood, the past three years had settled it. Although Meigs urged him to cultivate his business, he couldn't ignore the tribe's problems. He finally felt that he was one of them.

In May, Ross left his brother Lewis to mind the trading post while he attended the spring council at Amohe. The chiefs planned a formal protest against Jackson's duplicitous land treaty and Ross would help write whatever documents they decided to submit to the U.S. War Department. The controversial treaty, and the canniness by which Jackson attained it, had prompted the Cherokees to consider a change in their traditional hierarchy. There was talk of establishing a National Committee of thirteen men to conduct all Cherokee business, an arrangement that would prevent individual chiefs from signing any deal that affected the entire tribe. Pathkiller and Charles Hicks hoped such a committee, if recognized by the U.S. government, would thwart the efforts of unscrupulous Indian commissioners like Jackson and Coffee.

A day before the council started Ross rode through Spring Place, where he met Judge James Brown, his wife's brother and a prominent chief. There was little doubt Brown would be named a member of this National Committee and the two men discussed the politics of the restructuring as they rode the trail north. Ross thought the committee was a good idea and believed his brother-in-law was a wise choice for any such governing body. At one point, however, Brown joked that the tribe planned to put Ross "in purgatory" when they arrived. Ross stopped his horse, alarmed by the thought of offending the tribe, and asked Brown what he meant by that.

Had he, Ross asked, done something wrong?

Brown laughed and replied that Ross himself would almost certainly be appointed to the National Committee. Pathkiller held a high opinion of the younger trader, as did Hicks, who was now the second principal chief. Ross was not particularly happy about the information; he was now sure he was headed for trouble. As much as he wanted to be part of the tribe, he must have privately wondered if he was ready for such a commitment.

Major Ridge met them at Amohe. Ross had become acquainted with the great chief during the Creek War and admired him nearly as much as his grandfather. He knew that Ridge, as much as any other Cherokee, had encouraged the tribe to adapt to changing times and Ross had been heartened by his support of the Brainerd Mission. In 1817 Ridge was already one of the most influential men in the nation, and soon he would become one of the most important people in Ross's life. That day, Ridge escorted Ross into a private meeting with tribal elders, who told him that he would be appointed one of the thirteen National Committee members. It was not his blood or family ties that afforded him this acceptance to the Cherokee inner circle, nor the respect his grandfather had earned. It was Ross's mind and his education that appealed to the chiefs, traits that, ironically, he had developed in white schools.

Ross may have briefly worried about disappointing the tribe, not being able to do the job. But this was a greater opportunity than he had imagined. Not yet twenty-seven, and with only a few months' military service and a single diplomatic mission as experience, John Ross had suddenly become one of the most powerful men in the Cherokee Nation.

The new National Committee faced its first test a few weeks later. In June the Cherokees were due to collect their annual land payments at Return J. Meigs's new office in Calhoun, upriver from Hiwassee Garrison. Before they arrived they learned that an unexpected crowd awaited them there. Jackson, General David Meriwether, and Tennessee governor Joseph McMinn had gathered with several western Cherokee chiefs to address council. Realizing that nothing good could come of Jackson's surprise appearance, Pathkiller made him and his contingent wait a full week before the National Committee showed itself.

While the tribe fretted over a rebuttal to Jackson's treaty, the general had discovered a way to take even more land from the Cherokees. Earlier in the year, Congress had passed a law that required Indians living on Arkansas reservations to pay for that property with an equal amount of land in the east. In part, it was the fruition of a plan Jefferson had hatched when he made the Louisiana Purchase. Jefferson had sold Congress—and the southern states—on the idea of the huge land purchase in part with the idea that all the eastern Indian tribes could be relocated on that land; the president had known exactly what to say to get what he wanted.

More than a decade later the Congress—still controlled by the northern states—cared little about Jefferson's promise to the southerners and had done next to nothing to carry out those plans. The passage of the Arkansas law had been little more than an empty gesture to southerners. In fact, Jackson had not been given authority to enforce the law but he believed invoking it might force more Cherokees out of Tennessee. He had convinced the western chiefs to travel more than six hundred miles for this meeting, possibly by suggesting they could lose their homes if the eastern Cherokees did not give up any land. If that hadn't been enough reason for the trip, they were also told that their eastern brothers were withholding part of the tribe's annuities.

A large crowd had assembled at Calhoun by the time Jackson addressed the National Committee on June 28, 1817. The general noted unhappily that this new tribal governing body had been stacked with the very "half-breeds" he had complained about to Crawford a year earlier. Although the Cherokees clung to many old traditions, including a ceremonial fire that burned throughout their session, the tribe was changing. Some of these new chiefs wore suits and spoke fluent English. Jackson held his tongue, however, and tried to flatter the Indians, boasting of the tribe's advancements and brave service during the Creek War. He called them his "friends and brothers"— the first of several lies by Jackson, Ross noted.

When he finally got around to his reasons for this visit, Jackson made claims no one in Washington had ever suggested. He said Indians who wanted to secure property out west had to move now or the land would be given to white settlers—this after years of promises that white men would never inhabit the West. If the Indians chose to stay, he said they would fall under the control of the government.

"Those who remain and who have a wish to become citizens of the United States will be secured as such and proper reservations made, which will be theirs so long as they live on it," Jackson said.

He insisted the Cherokees had agreed to these terms years earlier, during their meeting with President Jefferson, and he even mentioned the Double-head treaty. The insinuation was that if the tribe did not give up its land in Tennessee, its brothers in Arkansas might lose their homes and the eastern Cherokees would be forced to share their remaining land. Brazenly, Jackson hinted that the president had ordered him to meet with the National Committee to discuss terms for removal.

"We are sorry to hear that some bad men have told you that we have come to take your land from you," he said. "To comply with this promise, made to the nation, we have been sent here by your father the President, and unless the chiefs and warriors of that part of the nation who have removed to Arkansas tell us in open council that they do not hold your father the president to his promise, we are bound in good faith to carry the exchange . . . into complete effect."

Jackson offered the Cherokees two unattractive options: they could live under the laws of the United States or move west. It was an ambitious power play and, by most accounts, a bluff. The general had no authority to make such demands, but he had the gall to call his proposal "justice for all." The members of the National Committee, shocked by the thinly veiled threat, promised they would deliver a response soon. The general graciously agreed to wait.

Jackson's message had the desired effect. The threat of falling under the control of white men was enough to persuade many Cherokees that they must immediately leave their homes, and several urged the National Committee to take whatever money Jackson offered. As the day progressed, the western chiefs joined the growing chorus, begging the committee to quickly strike a deal. Pathkiller and his council tried to calm the Cherokees, and even one of the tribe's most respected elders attempted to defuse the problem.

Nancy Ward, the mixed-blood niece of the legendary eighteenth-century chief Atakullakulla, was one of the few women allowed to speak at the council. Nearing eighty, she was still sought out by Cherokee chiefs for her sound advice and common sense. For all of her life she had promoted friendship between the whites and Indians, but she was no pushover. She assured her people the creator had given them this land and urged the chiefs not to sell any more land but to "keep it for our growing children." Her words had a minimal effect on the most anxious Cherokees.

John Ross had recognized Jackson's ploy for what it was and it infuriated him. During the general's speech, Ross was scarcely able to hide his disdain for Jackson's condescension and thinly veiled threats. Here was a man, in Ross's view, who had taken advantage of the uneducated Indians and orchestrated a fraudulent treaty that could cost the tribe several hundred thousand acres of land. That day, Ross formed an opinion of Andrew Jackson that he would hold the rest of his life. That day, Jackson became his enemy.

*   *   *

Ross's first task as a member of the National Committee was to draft a formal response to Jackson's request. As anxious as he must have been, Ross felt
an angry confidence stirring in him and his new authority freed him to act.
Since his days as a schoolboy in Kingston, he had wanted to stop the white
men who marched onto Cherokee land and claimed it for their own. Now
he was in a position to do something about it. Jackson's arrogance awakened
John Ross's political voice. And it was confident, blunt, and direct—all the
things young Ross had never been.

The next day Ross spoke for the entire committee when he read his
statement dismissing both of Jackson's options. He declared the tribe a "free
and distinct nation" and noted that "the national government has no policy
over us further than a friendly intercourse in trade." He continued, "Brothers, we wish to remain on our land, and hold it fast. We appeal to our father
the President of the United States to do us justice. We look to him for protection in this hour of distress."

With that pronouncement, Ross distilled the feelings of all Cherokees
into one clear, succinct message as if he knew their very thoughts. A legend was born, and from that day Ross's popularity would never wane. The
Cherokees at Calhoun had watched this young trader stand up to a powerful
United States general and refuse his demands. The tribe had called Jackson's
bluff, and Pathkiller dismissed the general without affording him the chance
to respond.

Jackson was unimpressed and set out to convince individual Cherokee
chiefs, one at a time, to relocate. He drew up a treaty and quickly collected
the signatures of the western chiefs. Before he left Calhoun he bribed nearly
two dozen eastern chiefs to sign as well. Later, when he delivered the document to the War Department, Jackson did not mention that it had not been
authorized by the Cherokee governing body or principal chief. He neglected
to tell Crawford the vast majority of chiefs—sixty-seven of them in all—
would not even entertain the idea. He did, however, promise that Governor
McMinn was prepared to assist those Cherokees who would move west.

Return J. Meigs realized the deception behind the treaty and refused to help enforce it—for once taking the tribe's side over that of his own government. That did nothing to slow McMinn, who spent the next six months cajoling, bribing, and threatening Indians to board riverboats bound for the Arkansas territory. He tempted stubborn Cherokees with whiskey or paid them out of an $80,000 appropriation secured from the U.S. government. He told congressional leaders the money was for "moving expenses." His tactics would become the model of forced removal.

The Indians who succumbed to McMinn, or accepted his bribes, were ostracized. One leading chief, Toochelah, was even removed from the council; Charles Hicks took over his job. Still there was little the National Committee could do to stop the governor, no matter how much the chiefs assured their people that Jackson had deceived them. By the end of the year McMinn had sent between three thousand and five thousand Cherokees west.

Ultimately, Jackson did more damage to his position than good by distilling the eastern Cherokees to their most resistant elements. McMinn deported only those Indians who were easily scared or already favored moving away from white settlers. The Cherokees who remained were more firmly and unanimously opposed to removal than ever before. Jackson had accidently created a stronger, more unified tribe, and incidentally provided them a common enemy. And John Ross would soon find a way to use Jackson's bluster and deceptions against him. But the general behaved as if he had done nothing underhanded. He even had the audacity to ask, later that year, if the tribe would supply troops to help him fight the Seminoles in Florida.

Over the next eighteen months there was a noticeable change in Cherokee diplomacy. Although the tribe's complaints about Jackson and McMinn went ignored by the War Department, U.S. officials recognized that the Indians had become more businesslike in their correspondence, more sophisticated in their legal arguments. Jackson attributed it to the "half-breeds" in general, but others had come to realize the problem was largely a single mixed-blood Cherokee, John Ross. The rising star of the Cherokee Nation—adored by Pathkiller, mentored by Charles Hicks and Major Ridge—was spending increasingly more time on tribal business and less at his trading post. To some, it appeared that Ross alone stood in the way of southern expansion. This was becoming a problem for the government. Finally, his interference prompted officials at the War Department to devise a plan to get Ross out of the way.

The offer was everything that Ross had wanted as a younger man. Thomas L. McKenney, the new superintendent of Indian trade, suggested the trader might be in line for a position at a government factory in the Arkansas territory, much like the one he had proposed building years earlier. The job would pay well, offer him a future on the frontier, and as a consequence take him off the National Committee. Perhaps Meigs had mentioned Ross's earlier ambitions. But McKenney did not know Ross's opinion of Arkansas, or how his priorities had changed.

Ross considered the offer seriously enough to ask Meigs for advice, but it's doubtful he entertained the idea for long, if at all. He tended to Cherokee business more than his own, even after the birth of his second son, Allen, gave him all the more reason to be distracted. Ross enjoyed his political work, felt that he was making a greater difference for his people than any businessman ever could. He was quickly amassing the respect he had seen paid to his grandfather over the years, and it flattered him. Mostly he had realized he was a Cherokee above all else.

The tribe likely never knew about the offer from McKenney, but soon Ross was rewarded for his decision to stay. In the fall of 1818 Ross was elected president of the National Committee. Four years earlier he had been a private citizen with almost no official ties to the tribe. Now he held a position of power second only to the principal chief and his second in command.

Ross proved to be a natural leader. Soon after the appointment, McMinn appeared at the council to offer the tribe $100,000 to move completely out of Tennessee. The governor had tired of laborious, piecemeal efforts to remove the tribe; he now wanted them gone all at once. When Ross declined the offer, McMinn doubled it, admitting he would have to pay in installments. Ross rejected that price, too, not even bothering to consult with the other chiefs—he could make decisions unilaterally. Ross even adjourned the meeting with the governor still standing before him, a clear message that

McMinn was not worth their time or respect. It was also a statement that Ross, operating with the confidence of Pathkiller, was firmly in charge.

Later, Ross sent a harsh warning to the governor, questioning his motives and demanding that he stop interfering with the Cherokees. In an attempt to embarrass him, Ross even sent an account of the tribe's meeting with McMinn to a North Carolina newspaper, most likely because he suspected the governor could stop a Tennessee paper from running the story. Ross offered McMinn's behavior as proof that the white men were out to swindle the Indians.

It was the first time Ross had used the press to fight government officials and campaign for public favor, but it would not be the last. Ross grew more comfortable, and cunning, every day. He was no warrior but he made a fine politician. He was smart and shrewd as the most successful businessmen, and his training and education served him well. Most of all, he knew the Cherokees did not have the military might to frighten the United States, but the white men had already shown they were afraid of his words. The Cherokees would use that to their advantage.

In early 1819 John Ross returned to Washington City as part of a delegation that included John Walker, Charles Hicks, and his former commander the Cherokee colonel Gideon Morgan. Pathkiller had sent them to sort out the confusion caused by Jackson and McMinn and gave Ross unlimited authority to solve those problems. The aging chief increasingly entrusted the tribe's day-to-day business to Hicks, but he preferred that Ross deal with the white men.

When the group left Knoxville on January 1, 1819, however, Ross was at a decided disadvantage. To promote his own agenda, McMinn had secretly bribed at least two of the Cherokees. Ross would not find out who these traitors were until it was too late.

John C. Calhoun was no fool. After meeting with the Cherokee delegation in early February, the new secretary of war realized that Jackson and McMinn had lied to him. They claimed the entire tribe was ready to move west—all it needed was a slight nudge. But John Ross and Charles Hicks told a much different story. And Calhoun found them significantly more reasonable, and civilized, than the Tennesseans.

Calhoun was from South Carolina, a state filled with the nation's most incessant troublemakers, and he quickly realized that his neighbors from Tennessee weren't much better. He had heard nothing of the manner in which Jackson—a native of South Carolina himself—had secured his treaties. He had not been told of the bribes, the tribe's refusal to negotiate, or the way in which McMinn had spent congressional appropriations. And when the Cherokees revealed that McMinn had even tried to sell the Brainerd Mission, Calhoun was dumbfounded.

As angry as he was, Calhoun would not simply give in to the Indians' demands. He harbored national political ambitions and could not risk losing the support of southern states. Ultimately, too, the plight of the Cherokees did not overly concern him. The best he could offer the chiefs was an honest assessment of their situation. He told the Cherokees they could not avoid further land cession, and he could not guarantee the tribe would be left alone if they dropped their protests and complied with Jackson's treaties. But Calhoun was not without a measure of pity, and he gave Ross and Hicks the friendliest advice he could. Unless they lived the same as the white settlers around them, he said, they would never have any peace.

"So long as you may retain more land, than what is necessary or convenient to yourselves, you will feel inclined to sell and the United States to purchase," Calhoun said. "The truth of what I say you know cannot be doubted, as your own experience, and that of all Indian nations, proves to be true. If on the contrary you retain a suitable quantity, no more cessions will be asked for or made, and they will be settled down permanently. You are now becoming like the white people; you can no longer live by hunting but must work for your subsistence. In your new condition far less land is necessary for you. Your great object ought to be to hold your land separate among yourselves, as your white neighbors; and to live and bring up your children in the same way they do, and gradually adopt their laws and manners. It is thus only that you can be prosperous and happy. Without this you will find you have to emigrate, or become extinct as a people."

Ross initially considered Calhoun much less diplomatic and accommodating than the Washington officials he had encountered on his previous visit. It seemed their past treaties held no value and the politicians were no longer willing to honor their commitments. But eventually Ross came to understand that Calhoun was right. Property that belonged to every Cherokee in fact belonged to no one, and was easy to take. The world had changed and the tribe must adapt. And since the Congress had passed a law that required the Cherokees to pay for the western land with land in the east, the delegation had no legal argument to make. Ross concluded their best chance to undermine Jackson's efforts would be to make a better deal with Calhoun. It was the sensible business decision.

The government estimated that one-third of the tribe had moved west: 15 percent prior to the recent treaty and another 10 to 15 percent as a result of McMinn's efforts. By that reckoning, the Cherokees owed the United States nearly a third of their remaining property: four million acres. Ross thought the numbers were slightly inflated but he could not argue, for he had no evidence to the contrary. When the details were sorted out the Cherokees gave the government nearly a million acres of land in North Carolina, including the Black Mountain range; 739,000 acres in Alabama; 536,000 acres in Georgia; and about 1.5 million acres of Tennessee land. That left the Cherokees with about eight million acres in northern Georgia, eastern Tennessee, and the western hills of North Carolina.

Calhoun never made any mention of moving the entire tribe west, even though McMinn and Jackson had requested he do so. The Cherokees, he decided, had given enough. In the end, Calhoun even chose to honor one treaty concession Jackson had never intended to fulfill. The secretary gave mixed-blood members of the tribe 640 acres each in Tennessee, land reservations that he hoped would help them to one day become United States citizens. McMinn would protest for months but Calhoun had come to believe the rumors that the Tennessee governor was a drunk and a fool. The Indians, Calhoun thought, acted more honorably.

The land reservations were not much of a concession. Calhoun was basically offering the Indians property they already owned. Ross's reservation was an island in the Tennessee River near Tellico that his late uncle William Shorey had left to him. Still, it became a sticking point in the negotiations. The Tennessee senator John Williams told Calhoun he would hold up the treaty in Congress if Ross was given any land; he wanted the trader gone, not given legal standing to remain in the state. Calhoun ignored the threat, and even included a stipulation—at Ross's suggestion—that part of the government's proceeds from the sale of Cherokee land would fund mission schools to educate Indian children. McMinn and Jackson were livid.

Although the land reservations were an important, and symbolic, concession, the poorer Indians never understood the deal. To some Cherokees, these reservations looked like bribes. Even though most Indians realized there was a difference between these reservations and the land Doublehead had been given years earlier, Ross would face his first political criticism for accepting title to land he already owned. But the land itself meant little to Ross; he wanted the precedent the reservations represented. Taking clear title to land supposedly inside the boundaries of the United States gave the tribe legal standing to remain there. As long as the Cherokees held those reservations, the United States could not force them to leave without breaking its own law. Pathkiller would applaud the decision, and mute criticism of the deal, by later claiming Hicks and Ross had saved the tribe. At that point, Indians could not imagine a nation breaking its own laws.

Despite the importance of the land reservations, even the Cherokees had to protest the bounty one member of the delegation was set to receive. In the negotiations, John Walker, a mixed-blood Cherokee who sometimes served as a spy for Tennessee politicians, managed to secure two 640-acre parcels, one for his home and ferry, another for a gristmill and sawmill. When he asked for a third reservation Ross finally spoke up.

Was this, Ross asked, a further bonus beyond the $500 bribe Walker took from McMinn?

Ross never said how or when he'd learned about McMinn's secret deal; perhaps it was a rumor, or a guess born out of growing suspicion about Walker's loyalties. He might even have remained quiet if Walker had not gotten so greedy. If he had any doubts about the validity of the rumor, Walker quickly put them to rest. The Cherokee became enraged, at first denying the charges and then lunging at Ross. Two other Indians had to hold him back. Walker was not given a third reservation and he abruptly stormed out of the meeting, convinced that Ross had soured the deal only to get a better one for himself.

The night before the delegation left Washington, Ross spent the evening working in his hotel room. Away from home for nearly three months, he had fallen behind in his own business dealings, especially since his brother Lewis had abandoned the trading post to accompany him to the capital. There were letters to write, arrangements to make, paperwork to finish. It was late, and he wrote quietly by the light of a single candle so as not to disturb Lewis and his brother-in-law James Brown, both of whom were asleep in the room.

A knock at the door and Judge John Martin, another Cherokee delegate, came in. Martin had just returned from the theater, saw the light on in Ross's room, and stopped to chat. He excitedly described the performance and explained the story behind it. The Cherokees had their own dances and dramas filled with symbolism and ritual, but their arts were much different from the elaborate productions staged by the whites. Ross was not nearly so enamored. He had been exposed to such things, if only in his father's books, from an early age. But the two men agreed Washington was an exciting city, full of many things they did not see in the Cherokee Nation.

As Ross and Martin talked, the door burst open and slammed against the wall. John Walker stood in the doorway, a knife in one hand, a brick in the other, casting a dark shadow on the ornate wallpaper.

Walker had murder in his eyes, a look Ross had learned to recognize at Horseshoe Bend. If the enraged Indian was surprised to find anyone else in the room it did not stop him or even slow him down. He glared at Ross for a moment, then spoke in a low, guttural Cherokee.

"I'm come to whip you," he said.

Before Ross could react, Walker threw the brick at him. With no time to get up, Ross tilted his chair backward to avoid being hit. The chair slipped out from under him, sending Ross reeling backward. He slammed his head into the wall just below the point where the brick struck it. The blow dazed him. Ross had no time to recover before Walker was on top of him.

Walker punched Ross and sliced at him wildly with the knife. The first slash got Ross in the left arm, a solid cut that drew blood. Pinned down, Ross could hardly fight back, but he swung his fists blindly. It was no use. The merchant diplomat was no match for the mad Indian. Walker stopped and raised his blade to stab Ross in the heart, but before he could John Martin was on him.

The two men struggled just long enough for Ross to jump up and draw his own knife, which he carried for decidedly more peaceful purposes. The noise of the struggle awoke Lewis and Brown, and they were quickly out of bed and standing in front of Ross. It took all three of them to hold down Walker. They told Ross to leave the room, said that they would calm Walker down.

Ross did as he was told, embarrassed by his retreat—it served as a reminder of his limitations as a Cherokee. He went across the hall to the room where Charles Hicks was sleeping. Inside, he noticed the blood pouring down his arm where Walker had cut him badly. When Hicks awoke, Ross told him what had happened. Ross worried that he had made a mistake, that he should not have confronted Walker in front of Calhoun. But Hicks assured him he had done nothing wrong. It was better that Calhoun saw proof that Jackson and McMinn were capable of such behavior.

Hicks spoke to him like an approving father, and it had a calming effect on Ross, restoring his confidence. But he would not get the chance to confront his attacker again. By the time Ross bandaged his wound and returned to his own room Walker was gone.

The delegation departed for Baltimore the next day. Once in the port city, the others set out for home by ship, but Ross decided to stay in Maryland. He claimed he had business in Baltimore, but he may have thought it wiser not to travel with Walker. Ross remained long enough to make a few trade deals but his true business was elsewhere.

In a very short period of time, Ross had gone from a bystander in the tribe to one of its leaders, and he was quickly growing into the role. The attack had done little to discourage him. For the great chiefs, such as Major Ridge, controversy and violence were a way of life. Ross resolved that a few cuts and bruises would not stop him from doing what he thought was right for his people. Yet in the future he could be more cautious.

For the time being, he felt heartened, having thwarted the campaign to remove Cherokees from their homes. But he was under no illusion that this new treaty would be the end of the tribe's troubles. The white men wanted them gone, and they would find a way to continue their efforts. The history he had read in books, and had learned from the other chiefs, taught him as much. And if Walker could be bought so easily, Ross knew other Cherokees might fall under Jackson's or McMinn's spell.

As he nursed his wounded arm on the long trip home Ross knew that the attack was only the beginning.

Part II

John Ross, undated

FIVE

A Traitor in All Nations

He stepped lightly through the woods, slow as a hunter, over brush and pine needles that padded the hard ground. This flat terrain, 250 miles from the hills of Chickamauga, was unfamiliar territory to him, the forest so thick with trees that little sunlight pierced the canopy of leaves overhead. In truth, he did not really know where he was; he knew only that a man had told him the house he sought lay beyond these woods. He accepted this because he had no other choice.

It was better that he go alone, John Ross had said before leaving his horse and the two men traveling with him. He needed to move quickly and quietly, avoid detection if possible. He did not anticipate a warm reception but he did not know what to expect. Now, creeping along in the muted afternoon light, he was nervous. He told himself the occasional crack of a twig, which sounded like gunshot to him, did not carry far in the forest. Ross was not much of a hunter. There were many things he did not know how to do—such was the curse of his mixed blood and mixed upbringing—but he supposed few Cherokees excelled at kidnapping.

He had been sent to find a little boy from the Osage tribe, a child who would become a slave if the people holding him had their way. The white men at Brainerd Mission had made it their business of late to rescue Indians in trouble, and many Osages had been taken captive in the past year. In the decade since the United States had banned further slave imports from Africa, demand had forced traders to become creative in securing new laborers, and they would stoop to almost anything. The missionaries recently had taken in a young girl named Lydia Carter and shortly after that had heard about this boy. Not yet five, he was stolen from his family in the west and traded east among whites and renegade Cherokees.

When the boy was spotted just beyond the boundaries of the Cherokee Nation, the missionaries and Return J. Meigs recruited Ross. He had agreed immediately. He could not turn down the missionaries who were doing so much for his people. Ross asked only that Meigs give him government authorization to claim the child. He left Brainerd on September 27, 1819. A week later he found the boy. Not a bad turnaround for an admittedly poor hunter.

When he stopped at the edge of the woods it was quiet enough to hear the running waters of a nearby river. The ramshackle house was there, just as the man said it would be, and the child was playing in front of it. The boy was thin and dirty and not wearing a stitch of clothing. He was alone. Ross looked to make sure no one else was around and crept out of the brush. A few steps more and he had the child in his arms. The boy did not protest. He had been passed around from one person to the next so often that he seemed to accept this as normal—the way of his life.

Ross could not abide the scene, a scruffy child, malnourished and left to graze in the yard like an animal. Even though he did not relish the idea of a fight, Ross felt he must confront the men who had done this. He called out to the people in the house, asked them to step outside. Soon a white man appeared on the porch and Ross could tell the man was afraid even before he said that he didn't want any trouble.

*   *   *

Ross had been told the man bragged to his neighbors that the boy was for sale, claimed the child was a mulatto, not an Indian. The white man denied ever having said that, but Ross said it did not matter. The boy was Indian and he had come to take him back to his people.

The man feigned concern, asked if Ross might leave the child a little longer, time enough to find him some clothes for the journey. It was a trick, Ross knew. He told the man he would not let the boy out of his sight for another moment. Sensing the resolve in Ross's voice, the man protested no more. Ross carried the boy into the woods and made his way back to his horse.

It seemed so easy. He had grown accustomed to exchanging hard words with politicians in the last three years, no longer had any fear of a negotiating table. But until then John Ross had not confronted men when the threat of violence lingered in the air. The rescue bolstered Ross's confidence, enough that during the weeklong ride back he was emboldened to free another Indian slave he heard about on the trail. When he reached the Brainerd Mission on October 10 the missionaries were so pleased they named the rescued boy John Osage Ross. The child had little to say but readily took to the school.

When the white men told the boy he would find a mother and father among them, he had said only, "Yes, and bread too!"

By the time of his twenty-ninth birthday, which fell during the rescue of the little Osage boy, John Ross was devoting almost all of his time to the tribe. Many days he did not even see Quatie or his boys—James, now five, and Allen, two. They were growing up quickly and took their father's time when they could get it. John Ross was also a less than regular presence at his trading post. Lewis, who had recently married, seemed content to manage the business while Ross tended to his many political commitments. He was at Brainerd Mission to greet the Great Father President Monroe, who had visited the previous summer. When the harvest came, Ross was away on patrol with the Lighthorse Guard, the tribal police force he was assigned to command, like Major Ridge before him. His undistinguished career as a soldier mattered little to the chiefs; they had come to believe Ross could do anything.

Despite the work that kept him from his family and offered little pay, Ross was in high spirits. There had been few problems with the United States government of late, and this period of calm allowed him some optimism. He told friends that he hoped "more liberal sentiments" toward Indians were beginning to prevail among whites. Perhaps prejudices of the past were fading with the old generation. Surely these changing attitudes, he believed, were due in part to the tribe's adoption of European traditions. President Monroe's compliments of the Brainerd Mission had flattered Ross, made him feel he had done something good for the Cherokees.

There were still troubles, to be sure. The work with the Lighthorse Guard took too much of his time, largely because General Andrew Jackson ignored squatters on Cherokee lands, leaving the tribe to deal with them. Jackson claimed he did not have the men to spare but Ross knew that this was a lie, that the general did not wish to help. But when Ross appealed to President Monroe, noting that by treaty the squatters were the responsibility of the government, he got no response.

So every time the Cherokees learned of a white family living on their land without permission, the unpleasant business of eviction fell to him. Ross would gather some men and investigate. If the claim was true, and they could not convince the family to leave by reading their treaties, the guardsmen would burn their home. Ross took no pleasure in this job. Even though the guard was justified in its actions, and even though many of these settlers had stolen livestock from Indians, the missions did not improve the tribe's image among whites, nor did they make Ross proud. He wanted to end the troubles between whites and Indians, not provoke them.

The incident that disturbed Ross the most occurred in the summer of 1820. A man named Atkinson had built a large farm on Indian land in Tennessee, and when James G. Williams—one of Meigs's subagents—told the man he was violating the law, Atkinson threatened him, ran him off. The Lighthorse Guard rode north to find Atkinson on June 17, bringing along another surrogate for Meigs to make sure there was no misunderstanding and to prove that the tribe was acting within its rights.

The house was deserted, as if it had been evacuated in a hurry. Ross hoped to avoid a confrontation and ordered his men to quickly burn the crops. These Cherokees were too young to remember the troubles of the previous century and followed their orders without any of the anger Ross had seen in his contemporaries during the war. While they worked, Atkinson and his family appeared on the other side of the river and crossed over to face the Cherokees.

Ross expected a violent scene, so he was unprepared for what came next. Atkinson stood quietly, watching his farm burn with tears in his eyes. Even though the man had been warned that he was living there illegally, Ross still felt guilty. He allowed Atkinson to gather his things, a few sheep and geese, and told him to leave. Unable to watch this sad old man any longer, Ross left the work to Elijah Hicks, son of the second principal chief. Hicks had recently begun courting Ross's younger sister Margaret, and Ross had a great deal of confidence in him. Still, Ross warned him not to hurt the man—that was not the way Cherokees behaved.

When Ross returned home he wrote to Jackson and insisted the general evict the remaining squatters. He claimed business obligations would not allow him the time to continue these expeditions. In truth, Ross just could not bear the work any longer.

Ross had plenty else to do. His trading post at Ross's Landing was one of the most successful in the region and his rickety ferry carried dozens of people across the Tennessee River every day. He had been charged, most likely at the request of Meigs, with establishing the first post office in the area and that only attracted more business and more people. An entire town was slowly growing at the edge of the forest surrounding Ross's Landing.

At the same time, Ross's own home was becoming ever more crowded. Ross had moved his father into his aging grandparents' two-story house that year. Then, in 1821, Quatie delivered the couple's first daughter. Jane was named for Ross's eldest sister, and she became her father's pet as he had longed for a little girl. Ross had a lot of mouths to feed, and he did so remarkably well given his prolonged absences. Some visiting missionaries said his cabin—with wide verandas stretching across the front and back—reminded them of the fine New England houses they'd left behind. The home was soon filled with Daniel Ross's large library of books, which John consulted often on the rare days he was not traveling. Ross lived a more cultured, more civilized, life than most whites in the area. A rich businessman with his own small group of slaves, Ross was hardly the savage Indian chief denounced by so many white settlers.

Of course, Ross was not doing the sort of work expected of a traditional Indian chief. By the early 1820s he was most concerned with reorganizing the Cherokee government into a system more closely modeled on the one whites had adapted from Great Britain. Although tribal council meetings still included some of the old ceremonies—priests dressed in elaborate, feathered costumes who called to order and dismissed meetings—the Cherokees were changing. Taking the advice Thomas Jefferson had offered nearly a dozen years earlier, Ross and other tribal leaders divided the nation into eight districts, giving each equal representation on the General Council, a bicameral governing body composed of the National Council and the National Committee. Ross likely culled the particulars of governing from his father's books, which he read at night. As president of the National Committee, the Cherokee version of a senate, Ross was paid $3.50 each day the council was in session. It amounted to about $50 a day in twenty-first-century dollars. Ross collected this money less than one month out of the year.

The Cherokees had grand plans for this new government. They talked of building a permanent Cherokee capital at New Town, a small village on flat pastureland about fifty miles south of Ross's Landing (and inside the territorial limits of Georgia). If the white men had an elegant seat for their government, some Indians argued, the Cherokees should as well. Ross seemed pleased by the idea, if for no other reason than it would be another tie to the land, another claim of ownership.

These grandiose plans, however, paled beside the work of an illiterate, mixed-blood Indian named George Guess. The son of a white man and a Cherokee woman who had been the sister of the famous war chief Oconostota, Guess—or Sequoyah, as the Cherokee called him—had grown up in the legendary lost tribal village of Chota, near Fort Loudon, Tennessee. He had not learned to read or write as a boy but this lack of education never occurred to him until later in life. Guess was working as a silversmith when one of his customers asked if he would sign a particularly fine piece of work. He couldn't do it. Later, Sequoyah went to Charles Hicks for help and the chief taught him to write his name in English. It was not easy for, like many Cherokees, he found the sounds and patterns of the white tongue as strange as the Cherokee dialect was to settlers.

Sequoyah studied the problem at length, treating the mysteries of language like a puzzle to be solved. He believed the Cherokees should have a written language the same as the whites and he tried to create one for years, patiently working through his failures and ignoring the ridicule of men who thought his efforts useless. By 1821 he had his breakthrough. Sequoyah distilled the unique sounds and inflections of the Cherokee tongue down to a set of eighty-six symbols that, when pronounced, were easily recognizable to anyone in the tribe. Many Cherokees who had struggled for years with English learned to read and write in Cherokee in a matter of days. Ross, who did not speak Cherokee fluently, would not bother to learn the tribe's written language, but he often used Sequoyah's breakthrough as proof of his tribe's cultural legitimacy.

When council met at New Town in October of 1822 it marked the beginning of the great Cherokee renaissance. Sequoyah's triumph was unveiled to hundreds of Indians. The council adopted Sequoyah's language to write official documents and ordered it taught to any interested Indians. Eventually, even the Bible would be translated into Cherokee for tribespeople to learn, and many did. The language unexpectedly converted many Indians to Christianity.

Some chiefs were so excited they suggested the tribe establish its own press and print a newspaper, a broadsheet written primarily in English, with much of it translated into Cherokee. No other Indians had such a luxury. Ross believed a newspaper would allow the council to quickly spread important messages throughout the nation. Even in 1822 Ross recognized the value of such an organizational tool.

In 1822 the new General Council voted unanimously never again to sell, trade, or give away another acre of land. It may have seemed an odd time to pass such a resolution. Jackson and McMinn had been quiet for years, and Meigs had just received approval from Washington to use military force to remove squatters on Cherokee land. But the council knew that meant little; Ross had recently intercepted a disturbing rumor that suggested this calm might soon end. Georgia officials had asked President Monroe to rid their state of all remaining Creeks, and Ross feared the politicians might soon turn their attention north.

He had good reason for such suspicions. He had heard from sympathetic friends in Milledgeville—the Georgia capital—that the state planned to send a delegation to New Town within months. Ross worked quickly to preempt any showdown. He sent a letter to John C. Calhoun that said no whites should bother looking for land in the Cherokee Nation. It would, he said, be a waste of money and time. Ross had grown so confident he barely bothered relating such troubles to Pathkiller. He knew what had to be done and was prepared to act on his own.

"If we had but one square mile left they would not be satisfied unless they could get it," Ross wrote on October 24, 1822. "But we hope that the United States will never forget her obligation to our nation of an older date than her promises to the State of Georgia."

Return J. Meigs had been around long enough to worry that Ross's ultimatum would only antagonize politicians in both Washington and Georgia. The old Indian agent knew the tribe would have little respite from a country eager to grow and feared the Cherokees would make themselves a target with such rhetoric. Despite his great affection for Ross, Meigs warned Charles Hicks to take a softer approach to diplomacy.

"It will not do to commit the government of your highest concerns into the hands of your young men," he said.

Hicks relayed those concerns to Ross but neither man was inclined to budge. Ross told Meigs he was reflecting the will of the entire tribe. It would be

Ross's governing formula for years—he would always be guided by the majority of Cherokees, even if most of them did not completely understand the way white men operated. In 1822, however, there was little dissension in the tribe: the eastern Cherokees were united in their decision to cede no more land.

Major Ridge spent the fall awaiting the arrival of his son John. Four years earlier, Ridge had sent the boy to Cornwall, a prestigious mission school in Connecticut, where he studied alongside the scions of the tribe's most influential chiefs, including James Vann's son John; Leonard Hicks, the son of Charles Hicks; and Ridge's nephew Buck Watie, who had taken the name Elias Boudinot. John Ridge had flourished as a scholar in Connecticut, but the harsh New England winters triggered a return of the boy's scrofula. He spent months bedridden.

His son's declining health worried Ridge enough that, a year earlier, he had made the nine-hundred-mile journey to visit John with thoughts of bringing him home. The old chief had dazzled northerners with his imposing presence, mannerisms, and fancy clothing. His white-topped boots and gold-trimmed jacket looked very much like a military uniform, which suited his name. Ridge was pleasant and charming, if a little wary of white men, but he soon grew disturbed by more than his son's illness.

John Ridge was under the care of John Northup's wife and during the boy's convalescence he had fallen in love with Sarah, the family's blonde fourteen-year-old daughter. Ridge approved of the romance only slightly less than the Northups did. It had little to do with prejudice. Major Ridge likely feared his son's infatuation threatened his future as a Cherokee politician. A white bride could prevent John Ridge from ever becoming chief; Cherokee women often married white men but few white women married Cherokee men. That was largely because few unattached women ever wandered into the tribe's country, but also because the Cherokees clung to a matriarchal society, where the mother's bloodline was most important. John Ross might have had less Cherokee blood than the young Ridge, but he had at least married a Cherokee woman. Ridge realized there was a great distinction.

After two weeks in the north, Major Ridge set out for home. He had been inclined to take John home then, but the boy was too weak to travel, or claimed as much because he did not want to leave Sarah. Since that visit the old chief had worried constantly about his son.

Mrs. Northup tried to discourage the romance for more than a year after that, but her daughter seemed as determined as the young Ridge. Finally, she told John to go home. If he could return in two years able to walk without crutches, she promised he would be allowed to propose to Sally, as the family called Sarah. In the meantime, the Northups sent their daughter to school at New Haven with hopes that she would meet more suitable callers. But Sally Northup was as smitten as Ridge, and no New England boy stood a chance of winning her affections.

John Ridge and his cousin Elias Boudinot sailed home in the fall of 1822. They landed in Charleston and made their way to the Cherokee Nation, where they were greeted with great fanfare. At homecoming parties for the two young men, John Ross seemed as proud as Major Ridge. Ross considered the boys worldly new voices that could be of great use to the nation some day. John Ridge particularly had grown into a serious young man, and his health seemed to improve each day. Ridge did not disappoint his father or Ross. He clearly had big plans for his future, but they were split between the Cherokee Nation and Connecticut.

Not long after Ridge and Boudinot's return, the Cherokees lost one of their greatest allies. On a cold night in January of 1823, Pathkiller visited the U.S. agent Return J. Meigs at Calhoun. The old chief was in poor health, and the sight of him concerned the agent. Meigs worried not only about Pathkiller but about what his passing might mean for the tribe. Pathkiller was the Cherokees' last link to the old days. In his time, he had been a moderate, diplomatic, and wise chief who seemed to know instinctively just how far he could push the whites. This younger generation knew no such boundaries. If the Cherokees lost Pathkiller, Meigs realized, it could jeopardize their future. More than that, Meigs worried about Pathkiller's health because he had a great admiration for the chief.

At eighty-two, Meigs was even older than the chief, but he insisted the sickly Pathkiller take his bed that night. The chief protested at first but finally relented. Meigs's kindness did not go unpunished. That night he slept on the floor and developed the first symptoms of pneumonia. It took hold of the old veteran quickly and Meigs passed away quietly just five days later, on January 28. John Ross was heartbroken.

The Cherokees realized just how great a loss they had suffered when President Monroe appointed former Tennessee governor Joseph McMinn as Meigs's replacement. From the tribe's perspective, there could hardly have been a worse choice. Although McMinn had grown up among the Cherokees in a family friendly to the tribe, he seemed to have forgotten his heritage. His recent history of bribing, coercing, and intimidating hundreds of Indians to move west seemed like an even greater sin in light of his past. The tribe could not forgive him for such transgressions, and the president should have known that. Monroe could not have insulted the Cherokees more had he appointed Andrew Jackson himself as the new ambassador.

At Pathkiller's insistence, Ross welcomed McMinn with a diplomatic letter. He appealed to the governor's sense of duty, reminding him of the role of an Indian agent. Ross wrote that he hoped the appointment would influence McMinn "to seek the true interest Welfare & happiness of the Cherokee People as a true friend & brother—so that equal justice may be extended to the red man as the white man."

McMinn had his own interests, his own ideas of justice. Within a month the new agent asked the tribe to cede a tract of land in Calhoun, where a tavern owner wanted to build a home. Ross had already given McMinn permission to plant a garden in the town but he refused to give the tavern owner any land. The new agent ignored Ross and invited the bartender to move in anyway. It was a sign of more conflict to come.

In 1802 the state of Georgia had given much of its western territory to the United States with the understanding that, in return, the federal government would rid the state of Indians. Jefferson had negotiated the compact while trying to win support for his Louisiana purchase; southerners had been wary about giving up any land, so the president was forced to make grand promises. The idea was that more land would be opened up inside Georgia's boundaries once the tribes were forced out. At the time Indian removal had seemed like a trivial concession, given the relatively small number of people in the state. For twenty years, the United States had made no effort to honor the compact.

In that time Georgia's population had doubled, growing from 162,000 in 1800 to more than 340,000 by 1820—and more people were moving in each day. These settlers coveted the state's fertile soil and temperate climate and did not want to share it with Indians. The state's recent effort to remove the Creeks was an attempt to force the federal government to finally make good on its promise. The Cherokees were aware of the deal but realized the agreement was vague and open-ended, promising only to secure title to Indian lands in Georgia when the government was "reasonably and peaceably able to do so." Ross realized the Creek offensive was only the beginning of a gradually turning tide.

In July of 1823 the Georgia Indian commissioners Duncan G. Campbell and David Meriwether showed up at Calhoun to request that McMinn arrange a meeting with the Cherokees. Ross was unsurprised by the visit but played ignorant, telling McMinn he had no idea what the men could want, and then apologized that the council's scheduled meeting had been delayed. He would make the commissioners wait for months.

It was a plausible, and truthful, excuse. Heavy spring rains had drowned most of the Cherokees' newly planted crops, wiping out acres of the tribe's corn supply. The Indians had learned that the agrarian lifestyle left much to chance and the weather. If it was not drought, it was a deluge causing them problems. A slight shift in meteorology could threaten the entire tribe with famine. Ross meant to delay the Georgians regardless, but in fact the food shortage was more than enough reason to delay a council. Major Ridge told Ross that if the council convened at the first of September there would not be enough food to feed the assembled chiefs.

The Cherokees had other problems by the time the chiefs met at New Town in October. John C. Calhoun had reneged on his earlier promise to send troops to remove illegal settlers. He claimed the Tennessee militia did not have the manpower after all, and the Cherokees would have to tend to the business themselves. Even though it violated the tribe's treaty, Calhoun refused to pay Cherokee soldiers to do the work, arguing that helping their own people was payment enough. For that reason, Ross was already in a foul temper, and in no mood to listen to more foolishness from the Georgians.

Campbell and Meriwether were surprised and disturbed by their first sight of New Town. Here on the north Georgia frontier, the Cherokees had built a modern city to rival most white outposts. Nearly a dozen log cabins ringed the town's center, connected by well-worn roads that circled the ceremonial field where Indians still enjoyed occasional ballplay. There was a community corncrib, although it was presently nearly empty, and a tavern had been built on the outskirts of town. The most impressive sight, however, was the Cherokees' government buildings.

When the tribe first selected the village for their new capital a few years earlier, they had built two simple open-air sheds to house council meetings. The sheds faced each other with ascending rows of benches and a log house at one end. By 1823 the sheds had been replaced by a two-story clapboard council house, the Indians' modest answer to the white men's capitol building. When the commissioners were invited inside on the morning of October 9, they were escorted to a small podium at the front of a rectangular room built of sturdy and squared hardwood logs, where they stood facing dozens of chiefs. At one end of the room a fire burned in a hearth, more a nod to tradition than a need for heat. It was an intimate, and intimidating, setting.

An interpreter translated as Campbell and Meriwether blathered on like untrained diplomats, bragging about the tribe's advancements, much as Jackson had done before delivering his unreasonable demands. The men claimed they were traveling under orders from President Monroe (which Ross did not believe) and mentioned Georgia's long-standing agreement with the United States. They explained that their population was growing much faster than that of the Cherokee Nation. The Georgians were cramped, they claimed, while the Cherokees had more land than they could tend. The disparity, they said, had been noticed by officials in Milledgeville.

"The difference is too great ever to have been intended by the Great Father of the Universe, who must have given the earth equally as the inheritance of his white and red children," Campbell said.

The arrogance of these men incensed Ross. These commissioners represented the people who had forced their way into Indian territory, set up towns, and stolen Cherokee property. And now they demanded the tribe move to make room for their growing numbers. It was not the implied threat that angered Ross as much as the way the commissioners spoke to the Cherokees: as if they were children, as if the Indians could not see through such a facile ruse, as if he were not smart—a sore spot for Ross. He had asked the more diplomatic Major Ridge to greet the commissioners, but by the time they finished speaking he had signaled to the chief that he would respond.

Ross did not speak with the eloquence of Ridge but he knew how to make a point. He curtly noted he made no claims to know the intentions of the Supreme Father—unlike the commissioners—but he understood Congress had passed laws guaranteeing the Cherokees the right to land that had been theirs hundreds of years before the first white man set foot in the country. The eastern Cherokees, he said, were not interested in moving west, a place where their brothers had suffered sickness and war. The Indians who remain here, he said, "love the soil which gave them birth." Ross could be subtle when he wished to be, and cutting when he didn't.

There was not much to say after that. Ross adjourned the meeting and escorted the men out of the building.

Campbell and Meriwether either did not understand or chose to ignore Ross's remarks. They remained in New Town for another week, appealing to chiefs in session and outside town. They sat with old Indians in the cabins in the town's center and around the ceremonial fires built at the edge of the woods on crisp fall nights. They offered trinkets, shared whiskey, and talked of the great friendship between the tribe and white men. To some chiefs, they argued the tribe had given up its right to the land when the Cherokees fought alongside the British during the Revolution, ignoring the fact that all their treaties had been signed after the war.

None of it did any good, and the commissioners quickly grew frustrated by the Cherokees' unprecedented unity. Government commissioners usually found it easy to divide and conquer tribes. There were always a few chiefs they could trick, cajole, or bribe. But the Cherokees proved different and the laws of their new General Council made it impossible to simply take the land one village at a time. Not only was an independent nation's capital inside the boundaries of Georgia troublesome, but the commissioners also believed the tribe's new government was a threat to the state's sovereignty. That opinion would soon spread.

The commissioners blamed Ross for their difficulties, especially when he delivered to them a formal answer from council on October 20. It was short and to the point: "Brothers, we cannot accede to your application for a cession." It was signed by Pathkiller, Elijah Hicks, Alexander McCoy, and Major Ridge, but the sentiment behind it was exactly what Campbell and Meriwether had heard from Ross himself. Despite this official rebuff the commissioners chose to remain in New Town a while longer. They had another plan.

The Creek ambassador General William McIntosh arrived in New Town on October 20 and the Cherokees greeted him with great fanfare. His presence was announced in the council house and a delegation ceremoniously escorted him to the White Bench, a seat which was reserved for the most respected dignitaries, and which Campbell and Meriwether had conspicuously not been offered the week before. McIntosh had been a close friend of the Cherokees for years. Like many of the Cherokees he was a mixed-blood Indian, albeit one with influential contacts among the white men. His cousin, in fact, was George M. Troup, the newly elected Georgia governor.

Because of his standing among the Cherokees, it did not seem odd that McIntosh requested a private meeting with the president of the National Committee later that day. But Ross was surprised by the message of the general, a man who, despite their political relationship, he barely knew. In one of the cabins recently built at New Town, McIntosh spoke to him candidly, as if they were old friends. He explained to Ross that it was useless to fight Georgia. It would only delay the inevitable—the white men would eventually get what they wanted. McIntosh suggested Ross should get the best deal possible for the tribe. And he, of course, offered to help. Speaking conspiratorially, the Creek ambassador promised it could be profitable for Ross to bend a little.

"I will make the United States commissioners give you two thousand dollars," McIntosh told him, "McCoy the same and Charles Hicks three thousand, and nobody shall know it."

McIntosh claimed that he had $12,000 available to pay anyone who helped secure a treaty with the National Committee. He did not identify the generous benefactors offering this money, or mention the $7,000 he stood to earn for brokering the deal. The ambassador merely said he had the authority to spend this money. As he talked, McIntosh seemed to think out loud, revising the allocation of the bribe; certainly McCoy, as secretary of the council, should get something, he said. The rest could be divided between Hicks, Ridge, and Ross. Surely, this small group could convince the senile Pathkiller to go along, and no one would ever have to know.

For a moment, Ross sat quietly and said nothing. To McIntosh, it may have seemed as if he were considering the offer but in truth he was stunned. This man, a friend to the tribe, trusted adviser to Major Ridge, was blatantly offering bribes to anyone who would sell Indian land. Ross knew that white men would stoop to such treachery but he was amazed to learn an Indian— and one trusted by Ross's own mentor, no less—would make such a proposal.

Ross recognized this scheme as the work of the commissioners. His first inclination was to simply walk out on McIntosh, but he quickly thought better of it. No one would believe him and the Creek might turn to someone more willing to make a deal. Then, he had an idea. Ross asked if he could have the offer in writing, to make it official. McIntosh promised that would not be a problem and left the cabin. The next day, the ambassador delivered a letter that included all the particulars of the offer. Ross immediately took it to the man he trusted most.

That afternoon, John Ross and Major Ridge met secretly in a cabin on the outskirts of New Town. Ross was excited—he had uncovered a bit of

subterfuge against the tribe and quietly enjoyed the idea of being a hero—
but Ridge was only disappointed. Ridge had been around too long to be surprised by anything, but he was saddened to learn the white men had gotten
to his old friend. However, he was proud of the way Ross had handled the
situation. It was a testament to his honesty, his commitment to the tribe. It
pleased him to know he had been right about Ross.

Ridge would not allow his friendship with McIntosh to color his judgment. His sense of morality was every bit as strong as Ross's. Without hesitation, he agreed they must take the letter to the council.

Ross had been smart to get the offer in writing, Ridge said, but he
pointed out that they had no proof the offer had come from the Georgians.
Ross felt foolish. He had assumed the money was supplied by Campbell
and Meriwether, but nothing in the letter verified it. Ridge told him not to
worry, that they would have their evidence before they went to the council.
He would pay a visit to his old friend and find out who was behind the plot.

Ridge proved that he, too, could be a master of deception. He went to
see McIntosh that evening with Alexander McCoy. It seemed that nothing was amiss, just old friends recounting their past adventures. They sat in
McIntosh's cabin for an hour without speaking of the offer, such was Ridge's
patience. If the Creek thought Ridge acted conspiratorially, he likely assumed his friend did not want to compromise himself. Ridge played the role
well. Without giving any indication that he had agreed to the deal, he gave
that impression by the things he did not say. When he finally did ask about
the deal, it appeared he was just being careful. Ridge said he needed to know
if the generous offer was sanctioned by the commissioners.

McIntosh fell into the trap. He assured Ridge that Campbell and Meriwether would personally honor the financial commitments he had made.
Soon, the mood in the room changed. Ridge's inquiry gave McIntosh the
idea that he had a deal, and that loosened his tongue. He began to brag about
the many treaties he had arranged and promised that everything would work
out to the Cherokees' satisfaction. McIntosh even offered to speak in favor
of the treaty at the council—to tell of all the wonderful deals he had brokered—if Ridge thought that would help.

"I'm certain," McIntosh said, "that if the Committee would fall in with his views, and say they despaired of being able to any longer to hold out against the United States, the old Pathkiller could readily be brought to yield."

Ridge and McCoy said their good-byes and stood to leave. But before he walked out of the cabin Ridge coolly thanked McIntosh for his help. He added that it would, in fact, be helpful if he attended the next session of the council.

On the morning of October 24, William McIntosh walked into the Cherokee council house and took his seat on the ceremonial White Bench. From there, he could look out over the crowd. He heard the low murmur of conversation as the chiefs speculated on the reason for this "special & important business," as the notice read. But as he watched the Indians make their way into the room McIntosh grew uneasy, and he wondered why he had not heard anything further about the treaty from Ridge or Ross. He was not sure what role he was supposed to play at this meeting. At one point, he noticed Pathkiller quietly sitting alone. When the old chief caught his gaze, he held it so long that McIntosh had to look away.

There was no ceremony this morning, no symbolic lighting of the council fire. One moment, Ross, Ridge, and other members of the committee simply appeared, walking in together. All of them took a seat except Ross, who walked to the podium carrying a handful of papers. He called the session to order and, without any explanation of the morning's business, began to speak.

"My friends, five years have elapsed since I have been called to preside over the National Committee, and your approbation of my conduct in the discharge of my official duties is manifested by the successive re-appointments which you have bestowed on me. The trust which you have reposed in me has been sacredly maintained and shall ever be preserved," Ross said.

"A traitor, in all nations, is looked upon in the darkest color, and is more despicable than the meanest reptile that crawls upon the earth—an honorable and honest character is more valuable than the filthy lucre of the whole world—therefore I would prefer to live as poor as the worm that inhabits the earth, rather than to gain the world's wealth and have my reputation as an honest man tarnished by the acceptation of a pecuniary bribery for self-aggrandizement.

"It has now become my painful duty to inform you that a gross contempt is offered to my character as well as that of the General Council. The letter which I hold in my hand will speak for itself, but fortunately the author of it has mistaken my character and sense of honor."

McIntosh froze. *They all knew*. It was why Ross and Ridge had not contacted him, why Pathkiller had stared him down. He had been tricked into attending the council, just as he had been tricked into revealing Campbell and Meriwether as the architects of this scheme. If he held out any hope that Ross and Ridge would allow him to remain anonymous, it evaporated when he saw Ross hand a single piece of paper to Alexander McCoy. It was McIntosh's letter to Ross.

McCoy unfolded the letter and read its contents, his voice overtaking the rising din. He ended his recitation on the most damning line in McIntosh's letter: "I will get you the amount before the treaty sign. And if you get any friend you want him to receive, they shall be received."

The Cherokees fell silent and stared at McIntosh, who squirmed on the White Bench but knew he could not escape. He watched as the principal chief stood to address the tribe. Pathkiller moved slowly, as if in great physical pain, and spoke haltingly, but there was outrage in his voice. He was astonished, Pathkiller said, and his grief ran deep. The chief told the Cherokees he had mistaken the Creek McIntosh as an honest man. It made him sad to think back on all the times he had confided in this man, whom he had considered a devoted brother.

"But all affection must expire before such a breach of trust," Pathkiller said. The council could do as it must, but "Treachery must not be overlooked."

Many tribes would have killed a man who attempted to betray them. A few generations earlier, the Cherokees might have done so as well. But by 1823 the tribe prided itself on its sophistication, its manners. McIntosh did not realize this, however, and feared he was about to die. He jumped up and, stammering over his words, tried to defend himself. He said he had no wish to force anything on the tribe. The course the Cherokees choose, he said, was entirely up to them. As McIntosh talked, he grew more confident, even managed to sound offended. He claimed that he had proposed nothing for himself, that he was only a medium for negotiation.

McIntosh stopped talking when he noticed Ridge in whispered consultation with Pathkiller and Ross. The three men spoke for a moment, and then Ridge stood to face his old friend. Because he was speaker of the council, McIntosh's punishment fell to him.

"You have stained yourself with eternal infamy and disgrace," Ridge said in a low Cherokee voice. "Never raise your voice again in the council of the Cherokee Nation. Now go, and quit the White Bench forever."

McIntosh did not protest or hesitate. He knew better than to argue with Ridge. He left the building immediately. Even though Ridge had allowed him to live, there was no guarantee the other Indians would show such benevolence. Outside, McIntosh climbed on his horse and, with a dozen witnesses watching him, galloped off. Campbell and Meriwether followed close behind.

McIntosh rode so long without stopping that his horse finally dropped dead from fatigue. He escaped New Town, but the Creek ambassador could not travel fast enough or far enough to save himself. Little more than a year later McIntosh was caught attempting to sell Creek land to the state of Georgia. His own tribe would prove much harsher than the Cherokees in their punishment. In April 1825, two hundred Creek warriors surrounded McIntosh's home on the Chattahoochee River. His wives and children were called outside before the Indians set the house afire. When McIntosh ran out of the burning building, he was shot by a dozen men and dragged into the yard, where one warrior plunged a long knife into his heart.

Despite McIntosh's pleas for protection, his cousin the governor had not come to his defense.

Three days after the Cherokees expelled McIntosh from their council John Ross sent a final note to Campbell and Meriwether. The tribe, he said, had peacefully and respectfully declined all requests from the United States to move west, and they certainly would not do so for Georgia. Ross said their negotiations were closed.

Campbell and Meriwether did not realize how badly they had erred. Their efforts to bribe John Ross had done something far worse than injure their credibility or squander Georgia's bargaining capabilities. They had given Ross the opportunity to prove he could not be bought. After the council of 1823, John Ross became the most politically powerful man in the Cherokee Nation. He had proved himself an incorruptible man, a hero—perhaps even a savior—to the Indians.

And a hero was exactly what the Cherokees needed, because Georgia would not give up easily.

SIX

One Generation Passeth

For the first two weeks of 1824, the weather in Washington City changed drastically almost every day. Unseasonably warm stretches in the high sixties were followed by bitter blasts of stinging wind off the Potomac and temperatures that plunged into the low twenties. Even to a group of hardy Indians the sudden shifts in the meteorology were miserable. John Ross felt that the city's inhospitable climate matched its temperamental politicians perfectly.

Ross, Major Ridge, and a large delegation of Cherokees had come to the city after months of waiting for letters that never arrived. Throughout the fall, they had sent countless dispatches to John C. Calhoun, asking the War Department to intervene against Georgia, illegal squatters, and McMinn. When it became obvious the secretary was ignoring the tribe, they set out on a trek through Virginia that was becoming an annual pilgrimage. Ross did not seem to mind. The Blue Ridge Mountains were beautiful; occasionally they saw a rare dusting of snow, and the game was plentiful. Throughout the journey, Ridge kept them entertained with outlandish stories.

The Cherokees planned to take their grievances directly to the president. They feared Georgia would continue to press for more land and wanted

Monroe to intervene on their behalf. In addition, they wanted the president to replace Joseph McMinn, who was actively campaigning to remove the tribe from Tennessee, hardly the job description of an Indian agent. And if possible they wanted troops sent in to rid their land of white squatters. It was a lot to ask, but Ross—with the memories of his past successes still fresh in his mind—was optimistic.

The capital seemed oddly quiet. In years past, the noise of various construction projects had filled the streets, echoing the country's zeal for expansion. Despite a growing population in the city, the building boom of the previous decade had slowed. The country's most aggressive expansion was occurring to the west; the south's growth had slowed by comparison, and Washington City, it seemed, had reached a plateau. Even Congress could not muster excitement for its own projects. The House of Representatives had recently tabled a motion to press forward with work on the long-standing plans for a towering monument to George Washington.

Following an economic crisis a few years earlier, the country was now embroiled in a debate over tariffs, which were meant to spur domestic productivity and lower dependence on imports. The country was divided geographically: the Midwest and West were pushing for higher tariffs, while the South opposed them. The House had passed one tariff plan a few years earlier but it had not been enacted. By early 1824 Speaker Henry Clay was working on an even more ambitious plan, and his work would drive a wedge into a country becoming large enough to have regional conflicts. The Missouri Compromise of 1820, which prohibited slavery in the former Louisiana territory, save for Missouri, had been only the beginning of discord that would consume the nation for decades.

The delegation checked into Tennison's Hotel, just a few blocks from the Executive Mansion. The grand lodge had become a favorite among visiting Indian dignitaries and it was not unusual to meet chiefs from any part of the country in its ornate lobby. The Iowa chiefs, in particular, were fond of the hotel's bar and the Choctaws often commandeered several rooms. It likely occurred to Ross that the hotel's thriving Indian business suggested the

Cherokees weren't the only tribe with diplomatic woes. Most of those Indians were in town to negotiate their own problems with settlers encroaching
on their land.

The Cherokee contingent occupied several rooms at Tennison's. Along
with the chief George Lowrey and Elijah Hicks, Ridge had brought his
daughter Sally, hopeful that some of his Washington friends could recommend a good finishing school for her. Perhaps he was angling for some bene-
factor to pay her tuition, as the government had done for his son. John Ridge
had ridden north with the group as well. He was on his way to Connecticut,
where he would finally gain permission to court Sarah Northup. Her parents would not be happy to see the young Ridge, but he had met their one
requirement—he could once again walk without crutches. Major Ridge had
to convince his son to remain in the capital long enough to gain some diplomatic experience.

The Cherokees got their meeting with President Monroe within a week,
but it did not turn out as they had hoped. Once they reached the Executive Mansion, the secretary of war informed them it was merely a social call;
Calhoun deftly steered the conversation away from business. Ross was frustrated but too mannerly to complain in front of the Great Father. He instead
delivered his usual message of friendship and limited the particulars of his
talk to an update on the tribe's recent political reorganization. Monroe listened politely but showed little interest in anything the Cherokees had on
their mind.

Within a few minutes they were interrupted by the arrival of John
Quincy Adams, Monroe's secretary of state. This son of the former president
displayed much more intellectual curiosity than Monroe, and he was most
impressed by the Indians. They were dressed in the fine suits of gentlemen
farmers and a few of them, like Ross, spoke impeccable English. Adams was
most interested in Ross's description of their advances in agriculture, and
he also listened quietly as John Ridge interpreted a speech by his father that
made several references to the Great Spirit—a sign of the chief's growing
interest in religion.

Ross left the mansion irritated; he had little interest in social calls and it was apparent neither the Indians nor the president wanted to take part in such folly. But the visit had not been a total loss. Ross did not realize it at the time, but the tribe in fact had gained an important and influential ally. John Quincy Adams later proclaimed the Cherokees "the most civilized of all the tribes of North American Indians."

For a week after that, Calhoun refused to discuss any of the tribe's problems. Ross finally appealed directly to Monroe in a letter, praising the president's "magnanimous and benevolent exertions" on behalf of the tribe and asking him to persuade the Congress to extinguish Georgia's claims to the land of his "red children." The president did not respond, but Ross soon heard from a livid Calhoun. Still he refused to address any of the Cherokees' concerns.

"The state of Georgia is now pressing for fulfillment of that clause, and the federal government is anxious to fulfill the agreement also," Calhoun said. "You must be sensible that it will be impossible for you, to remain, for any length of time, in your present situation, as a distinct society, or nation, within the limits of Georgia, or any other state."

Calhoun may have overstated Monroe's position because he was under pressure from Georgia's congressional delegation. But if he thought he could intimidate Ross with thinly veiled threats and frank language he was wrong. For several weeks, Calhoun found himself in a series of unwinnable arguments. When he questioned the existence and interpretation of past treaties, Ross produced clearly worded copies. Calhoun's contention that McMinn was an impartial agent was refuted with a half dozen written examples of the governor's blatant bias. Finally, Ross said the 1802 compact did not concern the Cherokees because the tribe was not a party to it.

"We beg leave to observe, and to remind you, that the Cherokees are not foreigners, but original inhabitants of America, and that they now inhabit and stand on soil of their own Territory, and that the limits of their Territory are defined by the Treaties which they have made with the Government of the United States," Ross wrote.

Eventually, Calhoun gave up. He realized Ross was technically right: Georgia had made a foolishly open-ended deal with an earlier administration at a time when relations with the Indian tribes were far less complicated. There were too many contradictory treaties now, too many agreements in writing, simply to evict the natives from their homes with no legal repercussions. Calhoun would admit none of this to Ross, but he told Georgia congressmen that the negotiations had reached a stalemate. He offered little hope of ever settling the matter.

The capital seemed like a very different place from what it had been on the Cherokees' previous visit. Weeks passed without an invitation to a single social function. Many nights they ate alone in the hotel dining room. The news from Congress did little to lift their spirits. Georgia had taken the report from Calhoun poorly, and one of the state's congressmen delivered a vitriolic speech against the Cherokees on the House floor. Playing to his constituents, he derisively referred to Native Americans as uncivilized beasts, heathens that lived on "roots, wild herbage and disgusting reptiles." His comments were reprinted in local newspapers.

A few nights later, the Cherokees spotted the congressman sitting across the room in Tennison's dining hall. George Lowrey, a rich and influential chief from Tellico, spoke up. In a loud voice he called out to the waiter, gestured to the sweet potatoes on his plate, and asked for more "roots." Some of the other diners picked up on the joke and laughed loudly as Lowrey made a great show of picking out a single potato from the waiter's serving tray. Within minutes, Lowrey called for "more roots" and went through the entire act a second time. Lowrey chewed loudly and happily as Ross and Ridge rolled with laughter.

"We Indians are very fond of roots," Lowrey declared loud enough for the entire room to hear. "These are the kinds of roots we live on!"

The diners roared in approval, save for the unhappy Georgian, who was eating the same meal.

The city warmed to the Cherokees soon after their display of good humor. It helped the Cherokee cause somewhat when John Quincy Adams began to invite the delegation to his regular Tuesday night dinners. There they met northern politicians, who had their own sectional differences with southerners and seemed sympathetic to the tribe's plight. Adams was charmed by the charismatic Ridge, whose name began to appear in the social columns, and the secretary of state believed Hicks and Ross were astute politicians, skilled as any member of Congress. Adams's support of the Cherokees opened other doors. Even Monroe's initial frosty reception seemed to thaw. The president hosted the delegation at several of his Wednesday night balls.

The Cherokees' growing popularity did not go unnoticed in Georgia. In March, the state's congressional delegation sent an acrimonious and insulting letter to the president, criticizing Calhoun's lack of progress with the Cherokees. They insisted Monroe honor the 1802 compact immediately and said the administration's failure to act constituted fraud. When news of these harsh accusations circulated through Washington Monroe was forced to respond.

On March 12, the president met with Calhoun and Adams to discuss his options. Monroe's eight years in office had been largely successful, and he had not accomplished such a rare feat by acting rashly. He did not like being bullied, however, and his closest advisers were divided on what he should do. Calhoun explained that Georgia was under great pressure to deliver more free land to its growing population, men and women who demanded homesteads and were uncomfortable living so close to Indians. He suggested the president not attack the state directly; it would look as if the administration was siding with Indians over citizens, potentially hurting their efforts on other fronts.

Adams conversely recommended Monroe expose the state's efforts to illegally take Indian land by force. The compact was not vague: it said the United States could obtain Indian land only through peaceful measures. The state's aggression was an ominous sign, Adams argued. Left unchecked, Georgia might stir up support among the other southern states. And then the country would have bigger problems.

Monroe deliberated for nearly three weeks. The question of Indian rights was growing more political, more controversial every year. Ultimately Monroe realized the country could not ignore its past treaties for the sake of political expediency. It would set a dangerous precedent. And the Cherokees had the law on their side. When Monroe made that point clear in his speech to Congress on March 30, 1824, he surprised the chamber by delivering what was to that point the strongest statement in support of Indian rights ever given by a United States president.

"I have no hesitation, however, to declare it as my opinion that the Indian title was not affected in the slightest circumstance by the compact with Georgia, and that there is no obligation on the United States to remove the Indians by force," Monroe said. "An attempt to remove them by force would, in my opinion, be unjust."

Monroe insisted that he remained an advocate for moving all Indian tribes west of the Mississippi, but not by force. The Cherokees' title to their land had been guaranteed in numerous treaties, he said, and the 1802 compact had no effect on those rights. Monroe quoted extensively from the compact to make his point, emphasizing a clause that stipulated the Indians would be moved "at the expense of the United States as long as the same can be done on reasonable terms." There was no time limit on the agreement, Monroe said, and the government had no compulsion to act immediately. The president said the United States honored its deals.

The Georgians were outraged: the president had done everything except call them villains. But they found some reason for optimism. Monroe conceded that Congress had the ultimate authority on treaty issues, and John Forsyth took the point literally. Within a few days, the Georgia congressman had his House committee draw up a resolution to immediately remove all Indians from the state. If the tribes would not leave peacefully, this resolution stated, the United States should use force to remove them. The resolution ignored the 1802 contract and the previous titles the Cherokees held to their land. Forsyth's nonsensical argument held that using an army to rid Georgia of the Cherokees would save the state the trouble of doing so later.

President Monroe's public support for the tribe took Ross by surprise. He had been distracted by new problems at home. White settlers had stolen the slaves of two Cherokee families and the General Council had sent word requesting Ross ask the government to intervene. The thievery highlighted the complicated pecking order of human rights in the early nineteenth century. Some Cherokees, including Ross, owned African and Caribbean slaves, and in theory this meant they held a higher standing in society than blacks. Still, some Indians were kidnapped into bondage, a result of the ban on importing new slaves. In this new world, one man's slave was another man's master. The tribe was as complicit as the white men in the peculiar institution—in fact, they had adopted the practice from the colonists—but Calhoun had no sympathy for their troubles. He referred Ross to Thomas L. McKenney, who was superintendent of a new government department that handled Indian affairs. McKenney offered no help either.

The increasingly complex web of bureaucracy created by Washington politicians frustrated Ross to no end. Every time he learned to navigate the halls of government the rules changed. Although Monroe had demanded that Congress honor its treaties, his own administration seemed unwilling to abide by them. While Ross spent weeks arguing with Calhoun and McKenney, Congressman Forsyth slandered the tribe daily to win support for his new resolution and representatives from several southern states quickly aligned themselves with him. Within two weeks his committee delivered its Indian removal proposal to the Congress. A single vote would force the Cherokees out of their homes.

Ross did not adhere to old traditions and saw no reason to remain quiet simply because previous generations had. The game, he realized, was changing—and changing quickly. Since the administration was unwilling to step in, Ross decided he must act. Perhaps it was his growing self-confidence, or maybe he was urged on by Adams, but Ross took it upon himself to confront Forsyth. On April 15, 1824, John Ross became the first Indian to deliver a petition to Congress.

This short but eloquent memorial was filled with echoes of America's own founding fathers. It was with "unfeigned regret and pain," Ross wrote, that the tribe discovered Georgia's "hostile disposition" toward them, but they would not allow anyone to steal tribal lands. The Cherokee Nation had voted never to cede another foot of its land and would never allow its people to be sent west. The claim made by Forsyth and Georgia governor George M. Troup that the tribe's resistance was the work of white men was mere "subterfuge."

Whether warranted or not, Ross drew a distinction in his argument between the "civilized" Cherokees and the other Indian tribes. The Cherokees, he noted, had turned their efforts to agriculture, manufacturing, the mechanical arts, and education. They had no desire to go to a land where food and water were scarce, where they would be forced to fight uncivilized tribes. The tribe had agreed never to fight again, unless it was at the side of the United States government, a subtle reminder of their efforts in the Creek War. The tribe simply wanted to "enjoy the blessings of civilization and Christianity, on the soil of their rightful inheritance." If the Cherokees were forced to leave their homeland it would undoubtedly lead to their extinction.

Ross had loaded his memorial with some persuasive and suggestive language. He slyly made the point that many Cherokees were Christians, giving them higher standing among the whites. And he equated removal with genocide. Ross asked the Congress for justice and the protection of Cherokees' rights, and he used the white men's own words against them.

"We expect it from them under that memorable declaration, 'that all men are created equal; that they are endowed by their Creator with certain unalienable rights; that among these are life, liberty, and the pursuit of happiness.'"

John Quincy Adams would later note in his diary that Ross had "sustained a written controversy against the Georgia delegation with great advantage." Even the Georgians grudgingly admitted Ross's remarks were eloquent but suggested it was proof the memorial was "not written, or dictated by an Indian." That criticism won them little ground. On the heels of the president's own defense of Indians, Ross stirred enough opposition among northern congressmen to kill Forsyth's resolution.

The success of Ross's memorial was due in part to his reasoned arguments. He wisely avoided strident tones that might further divide Congress. But Ross could not resist a defiant and patriotic response to the claims that he had not written the memorial. He told the newspapers the memorial "and every other letter was not only written, but dictated by an Indian."

He used even harsher language when he wrote to Joseph Gales and William Seaton, the editors of the *National Intelligencer,* a newspaper that was following the story. Ross told the editors if Georgia wanted to take their land and add to its fertility with Indian blood, the Cherokees would oblige them, "for we are resolved never to leave them but by a parting from them, and our lives together."

John Ross returned home that summer to find the Cherokees suffering through a prolonged drought. There had been little rain since early spring and the creek beds he played in as a boy had been reduced to dusty furrows of stone. The banks of the Tennessee River lay exposed to the blistering sun and the fields at New Town were withered brown. Even Lookout Mountain was parched, the trees along its ridge withered and dying.

Disease had set in, no doubt hurried along by a lack of sanitary drinking water. The rivers were stagnant and unmoving; the air was dead. The threat of smallpox hung over the tribe for weeks. In the remote villages of the North Carolina mountains some tribal elders passed the days with stories of the old times, when epidemics had nearly wiped out an entire generation. Many Cherokees were frightened and had taken to calling on conjurers to save them. The most superstitious Indians believed a horrible snake had brought on these troubles as punishment for abandoning ancient customs. It was as if there were two separate tribes called Cherokees: these old-timers, who clung to legend, and the modern tribe, represented by Ross, Ridge, and Hicks.

Ross could not help feeling a little guilty. He had spent months living in a modern hotel while the rest of the tribe suffered. He had seen how most Cherokees lived and knew it was less than ideal. A drought only made things worse; most Cherokees did not have wells but instead built their villages next to swift creeks and deep streams. When those streams dried up the loss of water could nearly kill a whole town of Indians. It was ironic, as conditions in the Cherokee Nation at that moment closely resembled the description of Indian life offered by the smug Georgia congressman. The lack of rain had killed most of the season's crops, and the Cherokees—thanks to their adoption of farming—were in fact living on a paltry diet of greens and roots.

There was little Ross could do, although he made efforts to buy some food for his people. With little political business to distract him, Ross had the rare opportunity to sleep in his own bed and pass a few weeks with his family. He was gone so often that he hardly recognized Jane, who was by then nearly three. His sons James, ten, and Allen, seven, would soon be off to school. He had little hand in raising the boys, which was not unusual for the tribe's chiefs. Under Cherokee custom, uncles were the dominant men in a child's life. Quatie understood this even better than John did, and seemed uncomplaining regarding his long absences. She came from a family of Cherokee politicians and had lived this lifestyle even longer than her husband.

Ross returned home just in time to say good-bye to his grandfather. John McDonald died in 1824 at the age of seventy-seven, in the house he had built nearly three decades earlier. McDonald's passing was mourned by the Cherokees. There would never be a white man so universally respected by the tribe.

He had lived long enough to see his grandson take on a prominent role in the tribe's business, and it made him proud. Ross had modeled his life on his grandfather's and although he said little about his passing—that was the Cherokee way—it hurt him deeply. He had tried hard to please his grandparents, adopting McDonald's business sense and his grandmother's devotion to the tribe. McDonald was one of his last, tenuous links to the world of white men.

McDonald left his eldest grandson his house, his business, and all his slaves, a sure sign of how he had felt about his grandson. The other Ross children could have resented this slight, but none of them said anything of it. There had been a dispute over the will of a relative when Ross was just a boy, and it had soured the family on talking about such matters. None of the other Ross children could have protested too much, however. John had lived with and cared for his grandparents since he was a teenager—ever since his mother died. John Ross had been the grandchild most devoted to John and Anne McDonald.

When his grandmother passed away a year later, Ross would be devastated. He would never forget the lessons she taught him, especially the idea that the tribe came before everything else. He would do his best to honor her words. John Ross credited Anne Shorey McDonald more than anyone else—even his mother—with raising him as a Cherokee.

Soon after the death of his grandfather Ross returned to his job at the trading post. It was still a profitable operation. Lewis had proved quite adept at balancing the books and had expanded their operations to several new outposts. It was lucky for Ross that his brother was so talented, for he himself had lost all interest in his own business. The tribe's future had completely consumed him.

Still, Ross found time to help his younger brother Andrew start a trading post near Turkeytown, in Alabama. Ross did not need the additional business but family attachment or guilt compelled him to help. Andrew, who had taken in his three youngest sisters when their father went to live with John and Quatie, was struggling to earn a living. The two had a strange relationship. Andrew idolized his older brother, and desperately wanted to be as respected, but he never seemed to fit in. And he did not have John and Lewis Ross's business acumen. His trading post never flourished, and John Ross would divest from Andrew's business after a few years, begging off because of his busy schedule. It was a slight Andrew would not forget.

More than with his family, Ross spent much of his time that summer with Charles Hicks. The second principal chief had become an important force in the tribe, as the man leading the Cherokees into their most progressive era. The two men not only held similar ideas for the future but had a shared heritage: Hicks was also the eldest son of a white trader and Cherokee mother and his children had been among the earliest students at the Spring Place missionary school. Many of those missionaries had noticed that Hicks doted on Ross like a son.

Most astute Cherokees also realized what was happening, even if Ross did not. With the blessing of Pathkiller, Hicks was completing Ross's training as a chief. He spent days recounting the tribe's oral history: legends and stories more complex and detailed than any Ross had ever heard from his grandmother. Hicks even turned over his own handwritten history of the tribe and in the coming years would add to those logs. Hicks understood that one generation passed and another took its place, and he was preparing Ross to take over the tribe as if it were a family business.

This new generation had found its voice of late. It seemed there was no shortage of bright, young Cherokees willing to become involved in tribal politics. John Ridge had returned from Connecticut with his new bride and, along with his cousin Elias Boudinot, took a great interest in Cherokee business. Along with men such as David Vann, the son of James Vann, they represented the tribe's future. It sometimes seemed the young Ridge saw himself in competition with Ross for the attention of both the tribe and his father. But even Major Ridge realized his son was still too young, and perhaps too immature, to lead the Cherokees. For the time being Ridge agreed with Hicks that John Ross represented the tribe's best chance for survival.

Ross returned to Washington City in 1825, this time to collect on unpaid debts owed to the Cherokees. Congress had sent half of the tribe's annuities to the western Cherokees and Ross was suspicious enough to wonder if it was an attempt to starve the Indians out of their homes. He was beginning to understand that true savagery came at the hands of smiling politicians, and he had little time for such games. Because of the lingering effects of the drought, the tribe was desperate for money to buy food. But for weeks Ross could get no one to meet with him. The entire city was distracted by the ongoing presidential election.

The 1824 vote had settled nothing. Four candidates had divided the nation enough that none of them had a majority of the votes. Andrew Jackson, who held one of Tennessee's seats in the Senate, had taken 41 percent of the states' electors against Secretary of State John Quincy Adams, who received about 30 percent. House Speaker Henry Clay and Treasury Secretary William Crawford of Georgia had each won more than 10 percent of the votes. The outcome of the election now rested with the House of Representatives where Clay, if he could not win outright, at least held considerable sway.

Because Jackson had not meddled with the Indians for a few years, Ross may have been most worried about a potential Crawford administration. But the Georgian had gotten the fewest votes and seemed least likely to prevail.

Ross watched the drama play out as he attempted to clear up the annuity problems. Calhoun, who had already been elected vice president, was not inclined to do any last favors for Ross. He even had the audacity to ask the Cherokees to cede the land currently held by Georgia squatters only to save him the trouble of removing them. Ross turned to the Indian Affairs superintendent Thomas McKenney for help, but it did little good. McKenney also ignored his request to appoint Silas Dinsmore the new Cherokee agent, in the wake of McMinn's recent death. Instead, McKenney gave the job to the former Indian commissioner Hugh Montgomery, who was hardly an improvement. Upon his appointment, the Cherokees invited Montgomery to move the agency to New Echota (the new name for the tribe's capital) but he refused, claiming the town was too full of drunk Indians who did not recognize the Sabbath.

At the same time, Major Ridge, his son John, and David Vann were also in the city acting as hired negotiators for the Creeks. The tribe was trying to nullify a fraudulent treaty negotiated by William McIntosh before he was killed and had asked Ridge to intervene because of his contacts in Washington. Although the Creek chiefs swore they never agreed to any treaty, Georgia legislators were using the document to drive the Indians out of the state. The situation had gotten so contentious the federal government had been forced to send in troops to stop the Georgia militia until the truth could be sorted out. Ridge met with Calhoun and McKenney and even called on Jackson at the Gadsby Hotel to solicit his help. Despite the general's underhanded tactics against the Cherokees, Ridge seemed to have a great affection for his fellow warrior.

"My heart is glad when I look upon you," Ridge told Old Hickory.

Ridge made a great show of comparing their white hair and recalling their days together on the warpath. But Ridge was naive if he thought the Tennessean would intervene against Georgia, whose support he needed to win the presidency. He ignored Ridge's request to investigate the Creeks' claims in regard to the fraudulent treaty.

It disturbed Ross to learn that Major Ridge was socializing with Jackson and working for the Creeks, but he said nothing of it. At least he had been discreet in his dealings, unlike his son and Vann. Their meddling in Indian affairs soon reached Pathkiller, who believed the two men had risked the tribe's goodwill on behalf of the Creeks. He promptly removed them from their newly appointed positions on the council. Major Ridge's involvement was quietly ignored.

As the presidential election moved to the House of Representatives, Ross could do little but watch the unfolding drama from Williamson's Hotel, an upscale rooming house popular with members of Congress. He composed a farewell note to President Monroe to express his "feelings of gratitude for the many blessings which they have enjoyed under the auspices of your parental administration." It was a sincere note for which Ross expected nothing in return. But it contained a hint of melancholy. He feared the next president would not be nearly as neutral, or fair, as Monroe had been—particularly if Crawford or Jackson won—but he could do nothing except monitor the proceedings at the Capitol. And then, a bit of luck.

On February 9, 1825, John Quincy Adams was elected the sixth president of the United States in the House of Representatives. It had come down to Adams and Jackson; Crawford never had a chance and Clay took himself out of contention after realizing he could not win even among his own colleagues. When Clay threw his support to Adams it sealed the deal. Jackson would sulk but quickly regrouped and began to plot his political comeback.

No one in Washington was more pleased by the outcome than Ross. The new president was not only sympathetic to the Indians but also understood the larger issues of sovereign rights. Best of all, the tribe needed no introduction to the new president—Ross and Charles Hicks had dined in Adams's home several times. Ross was so elated by Adams's election that he allowed himself to dream of establishing a state of Cherokee, a legal subdivision within the United States that would have the same rights, if not the same representation, as Georgia or Tennessee. He believed ultimately that this would be the only way the tribe could have permanent peace. The short, congratulatory note he penned to Adams from Williamson's Hotel hinted at such lofty notions, but Ross asked Adams only to dissolve the 1802 compact and dismiss Georgia's last claim to Cherokee land.

"The Cherokees if permitted to remain peaceably and quietly in the enjoyment of their rights, the day would arrive, when a distinction between their race and the American family, would be imperceptible," Ross wrote, adding that "for the sake of civilization and preservation of existence, we would willingly see the habits and customs of the aboriginal man extinguished, the sooner this takes place, the great stumbling block, prejudice, will be removed."

Ross realized his people were already beginning to live more like white settlers every day, and he knew the trend would only continue. Many of the old traditions of Cherokee culture were dying out, and he was more interested in preserving his people as a separate nation, with rights to their land and self-determination, than he was in ceremony or legend. But he was making vague promises. Ross understood that the future he predicted was decades away. He was only trying to buy time.

Following Adams's election the Cherokees moved forward with plans to convert New Town into a grand new capital. For several years, the council had met on that flat expanse of land between the Conasauga and Coosawattee rivers, referring to it in correspondence as "Newtown." But beyond the council house and a few private cabins there had been no further development. When Ross returned home that spring he appointed commissioners to finish the grand village. Eventually, more public buildings would circle a great square with an open field for ballplay and other gatherings. The land surrounding this town was divided into one hundred lots for individual families, a fairly new concept for the tribe. These year-round residents would own one-room cabins with fireplaces, corn sheds, and private gardens within a few yards of one another. And Ross made sure the plans included a print shop for a newspaper.

The council named the town New Echota in honor of one of the tribe's most important early villages. In the eighteenth century Chota had been the Cherokee capital as well as the home of legendary tribal leaders such as Atakullakulla, Oconostota, and Nancy Ward. Situated in the mountains along the Tennessee–North Carolina border near Tellico, Chota and the land around it had been lost in an early treaty. The decision to honor Cherokee history in the tribe's most modern city was a decidedly American tradition, echoing the place-names for New York and New Haven.

William Chamberlin, a teacher at the Brainerd Mission, rode south to visit the new capital shortly after construction on these additional buildings began. Amid the sounds of sawing and hammering echoing across the pastureland, Chamberlin found Major Ridge. The chief led him down the dirt streets on a tour that lasted more than an hour. He promised that even though the tribe had become modern, the Cherokees would not forget their customs, or missionary teachings—a chaplain would open each council with prayer. Chamberlin was touched by Ridge's newfound appreciation for Christianity and amused by his pride. Ridge bragged about the new buildings and compared New Echota to the great cities of the north.

"It's like Baltimore," Ridge boasted.

Just as this monument to a new Cherokee Nation was growing out of the earth, the tribe lost the most visible symbol of its past. On January 8, 1827, Pathkiller died at the age of seventy-seven. The principal chief had witnessed remarkable changes in his lifetime. He grew up during a period of war between the Indians and white men, fought in the American Revolutionary War, and watched his tribesmen murder squatters. Pathkiller had welcomed the coming of missionaries, who called him "the old king," and embraced their religion. And he had presided over the Cherokees as they adapted to peace, agriculture, and written laws.

Pathkiller had the wisdom to allow these changes to occur naturally, neither resisting nor pushing too hard. Ultimately, he realized that he was merely a transitional figure, that the future of the tribe lay in the hands of younger, more educated men. He had promoted John Ross to high office simply because he knew it had to be done. Perhaps symbolically the old chief became one of the first people buried in the cemetery at New Echota.

Charles Hicks would have little time to enjoy his promotion to principal chief. Two weeks after Pathkiller passed away Hicks died. At the fall council he had seemed fine, but heavy rains delayed his trip home. Forced to sleep in the damp woods, a bitter cold in the air, Hicks took ill. Throughout December he ignored the symptoms of a serious infection. He and Ross worked long hours to stop efforts by Hugh Montgomery, the new Indian agent, to build a canal through Cherokee land. But shortly after his sixty-ninth birthday the cold Hicks had caught developed into something more serious. He retired one winter evening complaining of dropsy, a swelling that covered his entire body. Hicks never got out of bed again and, on January 20, 1827, he died.

They took Hicks's body back to Spring Place for his funeral. He was dressed in white and laid in a simple walnut coffin. Six Indians carried him slowly to his grave. With Hicks's large family, John Ross, and hundreds of other Cherokees in attendance, Major Ridge—last of the great chiefs—delivered a touching eulogy for his friend. Ross watched sadly as his mentor delivered the final remarks on his political father. It's likely he had never felt so alone. Now he had no one to turn to for advice in dealing with the white men—Hicks was the only other Cherokee with such an extensive understanding of whites and their politics. If not for the death of these chiefs, Cherokee history might have turned out differently. Now Ross was on his own to make the hard diplomatic decisions for the tribe.

The state of Georgia saw great opportunity in the passing of the two Cherokee chiefs. In Milledgeville, the state's politicians told newspapers the two Indians most opposed to selling Cherokee land had died and "those who are left have their price," a statement that betrayed total optimism or a complete ignorance of the inner workings of the tribe. These politicians began to plot a new plan for taking the Cherokees' land. Tennessee had similar ideas and dispatched John Cocke and two other commissioners to negotiate for the remaining Indian land on the North Carolina border.

To these outsiders it appeared the tribe had no clear leader; there had been no time to appoint a second principal chief during Hicks's brief tenure. But neither state's high officials had a clear understanding of Cherokee politics. Until a new chief could be chosen, responsibility for the tribe fell to Ross as president of the National Committee and Ridge, speaker of the National Council. And those two were even more obstinate than their predecessors.

Ross took his new role seriously enough that in the spring of 1827 he sold his grandfather's cabin and moved his family closer to New Echota. It was not an easy decision. He had lived within sight of Lookout Mountain most of his life. But he had little choice. His increased responsibilities would require a great deal of his time and he could not spend his days on the fifty-mile trail between his home and the Cherokee capital.

Ross had a much smaller family to move by then. His boys James and Allen were away at a boarding school in Athens, Tennessee, and Ross's nineteen-year-old stepdaughter, Susan, had just married Ross's nephew William Shorey Coodey. Now, there were only Quatie; Ross's father, Daniel, and six-year-old Jane left to relocate. Ross at least ensured his grandfather's home would stay in the family. He sold the spacious cabin to Nicholas Dalton Scales, a Methodist missionary who had married Ross's niece Mary Coodey. Scales, who had been persistent in his efforts to convert Ross to Christianity, was even allowed to buy an interest in the trading post at Ross's Landing. The Ross brothers would no longer be around enough to manage it. Lewis and his growing family would soon follow John Ross to Head of Coosa, leaving Scales to run it.

John Ross built his new home on a bluff overlooking the Coosa River, just a few miles from Major Ridge's own sprawling mansion. It was a large house—two stories tall, seventy feet long, and twenty feet wide, covered in weatherboard like the fine homes he'd seen in the North. Inside, there was enough room for a large family as well as private quarters for his father, who was in poor health. It fell to Quatie to care for the aging Daniel Ross while her husband planted a garden and fruit trees on the property, then set up a ferry across the Coosa near its intersection with two other rivers.

Ross's new estate included 175 acres of land, making it one of the largest plantations in the Cherokee Nation. He maintained this property with the help of nearly two dozen slaves, most of whom he'd inherited from his grandfather. Perhaps owing to the influence of Scales, Ross allowed one cabin on his property to be used for Methodist church services on Sundays. He sometimes attended but usually only when Scales came down to deliver a sermon. Ross was a busy man and had never become fully comfortable with the tenets of Christianity.

Through the spring and early summer Ross and Ridge wore a trail between their homes. The General Council, most likely at Ross's urging, had scheduled a convention to adopt a Cherokee constitution, a document they hoped would solidify their standing as a legal nation. Ross had been named president of the convention but did little without Ridge's input. On occasion, Ross saw John Cocke, whom he remembered from the Creek War, at Ridge's house. Cocke was now one of several commissioners courting the Cherokee tribe on behalf of the government, and he tried for months to secure an invitation to a council. It never came. Ridge was not inclined to allow the men an audience at the constitutional convention, which was set for July 3, a date whose historical significance could not have been missed.

The document presented by Ross differed little from the United States constitution. And just as Congress was modeled on the British Parliament, the Cherokees based their new General Council on America's legislature. The seats of the National Committee and National Council were allocated evenly by districts to give greater representation. The constitution spelled out specific powers and duties for the tribe's judicial and executive branches, which differed slightly from their model. Previously, the principal chief had been selected by a few chiefs and served as long as he had the support of the others. Now, the General Council would elect a chief every four years. The Indians had basically adapted the U.S. Constitution to their own purposes, with one notable exception. The first article of the Cherokee constitution declared the tribe would safeguard its land against any encroachment by the federal government or surrounding states.

Despite this strong declaration of sovereignty, some traditionally minded Cherokees still protested. While the convention committee debated the new constitution in the stuffy council house, Indians dressed in traditional tribal garb delivered fiery speeches against it in New Echota's town square. It was a strange symbol of the Cherokee Nation's dichotomy in the 1820s—the old customs on display in the shadow of the tribe's most modern city.

One old chief named White Path declared that the tribe's new leadership had brought too much change and called for a return to the old ways. This drama frightened some of the missionaries present, including a man named Samuel Worcester. He planned to build a house on the outskirts of New Echota but worried that he had made a poor decision, that his family might be in danger. However, Ross assured him this opposition would soon pass.

"A noise which will end in noise only," Ross said dismissively.

On July 26, the convention adopted the new Cherokee constitution. White Path and his followers continued their protest, but there was no violence, only noise.

Nearly one thousand Cherokees returned to New Echota for the fall council. They camped on the public square and in the woods surrounding the town, some of them near the new house Worcester was building. Many of them had traveled to the capital to learn who would be the next principal chief. The constitution had set the four-year terms for chief to begin in 1828, a timing that was perhaps purposely tied to the U.S. presidential election cycle. This year, the council would appoint a chief to fill out the unexpired term of Pathkiller and Hicks. While members of the council waited inside cabins, dressed in their suits, the traditional Cherokees, wearing deerskins and leggings, waited on the edge of town by fires that sent smoke wafting into the crisp fall evening.

Ross did not concern himself with such politics, likely because he knew what was coming. For the moment, he was most distracted by work at the print shop that had been built within sight of the council house. In this small building the *Cherokee Phoenix* would soon begin publication. The first Native American newspaper would include content in both English and Cherokee, and Ridge's nephew Elias Boudinot had been chosen as editor. Ross had faith in Boudinot and was as proud of the *Phoenix* as anything the tribe had done. Perhaps because of his enthusiasm, he would supervise Boudinot much more than the young mixed-blood Indian wanted. At first the two agreed on nearly everything. Boudinot and Ross planned to include the full text of the Cherokee constitution in the first issue, which would not be printed until February 1828.

John Cocke and his fellow commissioners were in New Echota as well. Earlier in the summer they had distributed notices inviting Indians to the agency at Calhoun, where they promised to explain ideas to "promote their interest and happiness." In fact, Cocke was trying to buy 504,000 acres in Tennessee to build a canal, the one Ross and Charles Hicks had opposed a year earlier. Cocke believed that, following the death of Pathkiller and Hicks, the tribe was unorganized and could now be easily duped. But Ross and Ridge had little trouble seeing through his attempts and told Cocke he had to present his proposal to council, in Georgia.

After making the men wait in New Echota for more than a week, the council sent a letter signed by Ross and forty-four council members that noted the "Cherokee Nation has no more land to dispose of" and referred Cocke to the new constitution.

Nothing could distract the tribe from the business of selecting a new chief. Neither John Ross nor Major Ridge campaigned for the job, even though they had officially handled the duties of chief for many months. In past years Ridge would have been the likely choice. He was a senior member of the council and respected by all Indians, both the full-bloods and the mixed-blood Cherokees. If the nation had not changed so much in his lifetime, there is little doubt Ridge would have been elected. But he was the last of a breed. He represented the tribe's past and he knew it. Ross also wisely avoided any appearance that he wanted to lead. With little fanfare, the council chose William Hicks to finish his brother's term.

John Ross was appointed second principal chief for the year, and he accepted the position graciously, honored to take the place of Charles Hicks. He did not mind this supporting role, or if he did he would not show it publicly. When the newly appointed chiefs addressed the council, promising to improve education and stop anyone who tried to take tribal lands, Ross allowed Hicks to deliver the speech from notes he himself had written.

For the next year, Ross went about his business quietly, as if nothing had changed. It was an arrangement that seemed agreeable to the new principal chief. William Hicks's appointment had been a sympathy vote, a fact that everyone except the new chief seemed to understand.

There were no illusions about who was actually running the Cherokee Nation.

SEVEN

The Reins of Power

The summer of 1828 passed quietly. There were no new ploys from Georgians to steal Cherokee land, there were few problems with squatters, and even the harvest went well. With little to distract him John Ross spent more time in his own home than he had in a decade.

Although domestic life bored him—compared with the intrigue of politics, most things always would—this extended stay at Head of Coosa gave him the opportunity to oversee the planting, meddle in his wife's operation of the household, and tend to his own personal business. As each day passed without a new crisis, Ross grew more relaxed. By the end of the year Quatie would be pregnant again.

He had never known the luxury of passing entire months in the company of his family, and he enjoyed it, especially his afternoons with Jane. Ross shamelessly doted on his daughter. Now seven, Jane liked to sit on her father's lap in the house's fine parlor, snuggled up against the slight paunch of middle age forming around Ross's midsection. Throughout his life, Ross would be closer to his dark-haired daughter than to any of his sons—even

Allen, who worshipped him. Throughout the summer he kept delaying the painful prospect of sending Jane away to boarding school.

As second principal chief, Ross had little business to attend to—a woman caught selling whiskey to young boys, a request from the government to build a canal through the tribe's land in Alabama. William Hicks proved to be uninterested in the minutiae of governing, so Ross handled most of these matters himself, usually from Major Ridge's home. The old chief's mansion had undergone extensive renovations of late and was now one of the most handsome homes in the nation. Covered in plank siding that had been painted white, it resembled the New England mansions Ridge had admired on his trip to Connecticut years before.

Ross and Ridge had grown closer in the past year, perhaps in part because they both missed Charles Hicks and felt they had only each other for support. Most days, the two passed their time on the porch of Ridge's home, in the shade of great trees. There they watched the silent waters of the Coosa and talked about the old times, discussed tribal business, what might come next. Both knew the summer's calm would not last. Already, there were rumors of discontent brewing within the tribe.

They heard most of these stories from George Lavender, a young man from Knoxville who ran the trading post behind Ridge's house. The store had become an informal gathering place for Cherokees and Lavender learned new gossip each day. Lately, most of the Indians were talking about the treaty discussions the principal chief had had with some white men. That in itself was hardly news, as there were always whites coming around, trying to buy a few acres of tribal land. What disturbed many Cherokees was the suggestion that Hicks had not been adamant enough in his refusal. One man even claimed he heard Hicks wonder aloud how much he might get for his own property. It was not the proper response for any Cherokee, particularly the principal chief.

Both Ross and Ridge knew that these rumors, coupled with the new chief's questionable political skills, could doom his chances to win election for a full term. It did not matter if these stories were true, only that some people repeated them and others believed them. Hicks apparently did not realize the tenuous position he was in. Principal chief was no longer a lifetime appointment, despite Hicks's obvious sense of entitlement.

Ridge worried about who might rise up to lead if Hicks was not reelected. He knew his own opportunity had passed, and although it may have disappointed him he had made peace with such truths long ago. For years he had hoped his son John might one day be chief. But the time was not right. The boy was smart enough, but he was still young and immature, and it did not help that he had married outside the tribe. Also, there were still some powerful chiefs upset by the younger Ridge's lobbying for the Creeks in Washington.

John Ridge had spent much of the summer trying to rehabilitate his image. He was assisted by Elias Boudinot, who published long, eloquent letters in the *Phoenix* in an attempt to clear his cousin's name. Boudinot was fiercely devoted to John and proclaimed him an influential leader for a new era. Most Cherokees who read these declarations realized the editor's bias but had to admit the young Ridge was smart, like his father. Slowly, his past transgressions would be forgotten.

These days, however, there was no shortage of Cherokees who aspired to lead. For much of the summer, the names of these men filled an entire column of page three in the *Phoenix*. This list of candidates for General Council, a mix of traditional Indian names and those with a decidedly European tilt, reflected the changing demographics of the tribe: Deer in the Water, Crawling Snake, and Sleeping Rabbit were vying for seats against Richard Taylor, Archibald Campbell, and Walter Adams. Two names noticeably absent from the list were those of Ridge and Ross. Ridge seemed not to care about his own role in the new council; he was more concerned with what office Ross might hold.

Ridge had come to respect Ross for his diplomatic skills, his honesty, and his instincts. When White Path traveled the countryside stirring opposition to the constitution—spewing rhetoric of the old times much as Tecumseh once had done—Ridge had urged Ross to respond, to defend the council. But Ross refused. He told Ridge to be patient, that White Path's moment would pass. He had been right—the old man's movement died quickly—and Ridge was impressed by the younger man's wisdom. In some ways, it seemed his protégé had surpassed him in political savvy.

More than his political acumen, Ridge admired Ross's dedication to the Cherokees. He could have lived as a white man and never had to worry about removal. But Ross had chosen the Cherokees over the easy path and that, more than anything, endeared him to Ridge. Ross was like a son to him—in spirit, if not in blood.

As the summer wore on, Ridge used the *Phoenix* to subtly promote Ross as a candidate for principal chief without ever mentioning his name. In just a few short months the newspaper had become an important and influential voice in the Cherokee Nation. At Ross's direction, Boudinot published pages of articles explaining the new laws of the tribe, as well as news from around the country. It had also become a handy tool for delivering political messages.

Major Ridge rarely contributed anything to the paper but the rumors about Hicks and the tribe's first popular election concerned him enough to make him reconsider. In a letter dictated to his son, Ridge urged young Cherokees to become involved in the political process. He expressed support for Hicks and made it clear the threat of forced removal was the most important issue facing the tribe, an odd if telling juxtaposition. He noted that Congress had dedicated an obscene amount of money—$50,000 (almost $1 million in twenty-first-century dollars)—toward efforts to secure a Cherokee treaty.

"I know that you are decided friends of this our native country," Ridge said. "On the Oostanallee and Conuasaugee and towards the mountains we have never heard of the people's selling land; but only of their attachment to it. Only a portion of those living near the Tennessee River have been disposed to sell. But now the high water has subsided; now all is peace; now I believe that all the men in that section are true to their country. Our principal chief also I honor. I have never discovered him in the least thing out of the way, anything in the least degree suspicious. Now the time of our Coosewaytee election is at hand."

Ridge warned of the dangers that would come if the tribe hastily elected leaders who could be manipulated by white men. He mentioned his pity for the Cherokees who had moved to Arkansas only to find the land less fertile than they had been promised and nearly devoid of game. Ridge said the tribe must consider these factors when the elections came. "Let us hold fast to the country which we yet retain." He signed his letter, "Your friend, The Speaker."

It was a sly letter. On the surface, it seemed an endorsement of Hicks. But Ridge had also managed to subtly raise the question of the chief's dealings, enough to plant the seeds of doubt among the wiser members of the council. He had also characterized the candidate he felt would be best fit to lead the Cherokees into the future, a man who had the tribe's best interest at heart and who had proved he could not be bought. Ridge had perfectly described the man who had sat on his porch many a summer evening, watching the lazy Coosa drift by and listening to the crickets chirping in the fields.

If John Ross recognized the hidden message in his mentor's words he was politic enough to say nothing of it.

The Cherokees began arriving in New Echota during the second week of October 1828, camping under trees filled with yellow and brown leaves. They walked dirt streets lined with cabins, smokehouses, and corncribs, past dry goods stores, taverns, and the one-room office of the *Phoenix,* where Elias Boudinot posted news from New York and Havana along with a serial chronicling the adventures of seven Creek boys traveling the nation. Many of these Indians, who had never visited a true city, marveled at the new house built by the missionary and postmaster Samuel Worcester, a sprawling two-story home that rivaled Major Ridge's in size if not beauty. Hundreds of Cherokees had moved into or near the new city, slowly shifting even more of the tribe's population into Georgia. New Echota was not as large as a typical white city of day, but it was bigger than just about any Cherokee village before it. The new capital had grown into the tribe's most modern, and impressive, accomplishment.

Despite the outward signs of prosperity, some members of the tribe felt a growing sense of unease. In the nights before the council opened, concerned Cherokees sat around huge, crackling fires and discussed rumors of the Georgia legislature's plan to annex the tribe's land. Some claimed Indian commissioners would attend the council to negotiate a removal treaty. Many Cherokees feared their grand modern city would soon be taken by the white men.

On Monday, October 13, Hicks and Ross delivered an annual message—the Cherokee version of a State of the Union speech—that promised great things: the construction of a national academy, new plans to guard against voter fraud in future elections. Hicks outlined the tribe's plans for combating Georgia's land claims through the federal government. These ideas resembled Ross's past policies so much there is little doubt who actually wrote the address.

After Hicks finished, the newly elected National Committee met for the first time. There was no shortage of familiar names. Among the sixteen members were George Sanders, three Vanns, and even a Ross—Lewis, the second chief's brother. His election reflected John Ross's popularity and the committee's makeup. The council's upper chamber was the domain of the mixed-blood Cherokees, the younger, progressive men who were guiding the tribe. The next day, Lewis was elected president of the committee.

On Wednesday, the National Council was seated. The lower chamber was traditionally filled with members of the tribe's oldest families, and the election had not changed that. Most of the twenty-four members were full-blooded Cherokees from the original clans; even the former insurgent White Path had won a seat. But the council was missing one familiar name: Major Ridge. The longtime speaker's absence fueled speculation he would be a candidate for principal chief, and the gossip circulated in the tavern and around campfires for the next two nights. Going Snake was elected to succeed Ridge, and his first official duty was to meet with Lewis Ross to set a date for perhaps General Council's most important vote. They chose to elect a new chief on Friday, October 17.

William Hicks believed the election was merely a formality. When he was installed as chief in 1827, he thought it was his rightful place as heir to his brother. For years, Charles Hicks had been principal chief in everything except name, guiding the Cherokees with the blessing of the "old king,"

Pathkiller. William Hicks had always been jealous of his brother's prestige, the respect he commanded. He felt like the second son of a monarch, royalty in name only. In some ways, the thin, craggy, sometimes disagreeable Hicks had to remind Ross of his own brother Andrew: Hicks had the air of a man who felt he was owed something but never did much to earn it.

In the past year, William Hicks had shown only that he lacked his brother's vision and political skills. He had made few friends among the tribe and many had come to regret their decision to promote him. Hicks had been considered only a minor chief before his election, and he'd done little to change that assessment. The rumors of his cozy relationship with white politicians did little to improve his image. Any Indian who made friends with men who would take Cherokee land was considered weak or crooked, or both.

Hicks was oblivious of all this. He apparently never realized he had been appointed only as caretaker of his brother's legacy; he believed it was simply his turn. The truth was too stinging for him even to consider. William Hicks had been given a year to prove himself a worthy successor, and in that time he had done little to distinguish himself. The wiser Cherokees realized John Ross still handled most of the mundane, but important, business of the tribe. As a leader, Hicks seemed more concerned with his own stature than with the tribe's prosperity.

Even if Hicks did not recognize that his days as chief were numbered, many of his advisers did. Some of his closest friends had quietly urged him not to seek reelection. They made excuses: the trouble with Georgia would get worse and he did not need the headache; it would be better if he were not a target for the white men. They played on his vanity, promising to nominate him for second chief if he would accept it. But Hicks would not listen. He argued that, throughout history, chiefs died in office; they did not step down. But times had changed. In the past, chiefs never stood for reelection every four years.

On Friday morning, Hicks took a seat on the podium bench as Indians crowded into the room, blocking his view of the fire burning in the hearth. The audience, most of them members of the General Council, reflected the changing Cherokee Nation: some wore deerskins and moccasins, others sported fine suits and more closely resembled members of the white man's Congress. Their diversity was acknowledged by Richard Taylor of the National Committee, who had to stand and interpret the proceedings each day. Some of the men could not understand English, but then a few did not even speak Cherokee.

After Going Snake and Lewis Ross read the rules of the election, they called for nominations. The first man to stand submitted Hicks's name, as expected. But before that man could settle back into his seat another stood and said, simply, "John Ross." For a moment, no one said anything. If Hicks was surprised he did not show it. When it was clear no one else would be considered, the nominations were quickly closed.

Ross must have known he would be a candidate. He knew the council was unhappy with Hicks. Some members had no doubt spoken to him about the possibility of his nomination. If Ross coveted the role of principal chief, he kept such thoughts to himself. He would not campaign against a sitting chief; it was not his style. Yet he realized Hicks was not a strong chief and may even have thought he himself was the better choice. Ross also knew he had the support of most tribal leaders, not the least of whom was Ridge himself.

For the Cherokees, Ross was a logical choice. Time and again he had proved himself a smart diplomat, tirelessly devoted to the tribe and immune to bribery. He was everything that William Hicks wasn't. Additionally, Ross had held the trust of Pathkiller and Charles Hicks, the men who led the tribe into its renaissance. Hicks, in fact, groomed Ross for the position over his own brother and his own son. Ross had been anointed by the old generation and embraced by the new, and his experience made him more of a Cherokee than William Hicks's bloodline made him.

John Ross made an almost perfect candidate. He was a member of the tribe's prestigious Bird Clan, he had experience as chief, and he was rich enough so no one ever had to worry that he might be bought by the commissioners. He represented the tribe's greatest chance to survive in the white man's world. When the first vote was taken Ross received thirty-four votes; Hicks got six.

Hicks accepted the council's verdict gracefully but his resentment would build and in time his disgrace and anger would consume him. He had not expected to lose the election. In truth, the only real surprise in the council's vote had been that it was not unanimous.

In one short decade, the Cherokees had developed a written language, built a modern city, and adopted a constitution. Electing John Ross principal chief completed what was in many ways the tribe's greatest period of advancement. Before Ross, every chief had taken a lifetime to reach the position and all of them had been nearly full-blooded Cherokees. When Ross was sworn in on October 17, 1828, he was only thirty-eight and had served the tribe for barely more than a decade. He was the son of a white man who had nearly been killed by the Cherokees a generation earlier. Unlike every other chief, Ross had been educated in the white man's schools. He had trained to be a merchant, and his only military experience was a brief stint serving as secretary to Colonel Gideon Morgan fourteen years earlier. Most amazingly, Ross was only one-eighth Cherokee. And now he was the tribe's principal chief.

If Ross made any grand pronouncements or eloquent speeches that day they do not survive. Perhaps he allowed the message delivered by Hicks and himself to serve as an inaugural address. The *Cherokee Phoenix* made little of his election, almost certainly at Ross's direction. But the news soon reached Milledgeville, and it sent a strong message to the governor, who had once quipped that nineteen-twentieths of Cherokees were ignorant savages. These so-called savages had elected one of their most learned men to lead the tribe.

John Ross took over the tribe more completely than any chief before him. Soon after he was elected, the General Council—led by his brother Lewis—appointed Ross's confidant George Lowrey second chief and installed his brother Andrew as a justice on the Cherokee court. Major Ridge was named counselor to the chief. In one day, Ross took the reins of every branch of the Cherokee government and, with the council's help, surrounded himself with loyalists and family members. It was an incredible consolidation of power.

*   *   *

The 1828 presidential election was not nearly so civilized. For months, the
two campaigns had hurled accusations of adultery, prostitution, and even
murder at each other, highlighting the growing difference of political views
between the North and the South. It was the culmination of probably the
longest presidential campaign the country had ever seen. Andrew Jackson
had been a candidate for nearly four years, since the moment Congress chose
John Quincy Adams over him in the previous election.

Jackson had resigned his Senate seat in early 1825. He claimed it was
only proper he return to private life given the decision by Congress, but
most people thought he was just pouting. When he returned to Tennessee
Jackson immediately started to campaign again, while his supporters undermined the presidency of John Quincy Adams from his first day in office.

Old Hickory had friends in nearly every corner of Washington, including even Adams's own vice president, John C. Calhoun. Jackson's political
buddies branded Adams an elitist, and the president's high-minded speeches
did little to dissuade such notions. Like his father, he had a cold demeanor
and a sense of fairness that did not go unpunished. Adams often allowed
men in patronage jobs from the previous administration to remain in office. And that gave Jackson's cronies the luxury of undermining Adams from
powerful positions.

Adams had proposed a number of ambitious programs: a federal net-
work of roads and canals, a national marketplace, even a national university
to support the arts. He wanted to preserve public lands through conserva-
tion projects. These were ideas that would later be embraced by the country
but Adams had little support in Congress during his time. As a result, he
got almost nothing accomplished in four years. And Adams inflicted mortal
wounds on his political career with his position on the Indians.

Adams demanded that treaties with the Native Americans be honored
and declared that states could buy land only from tribes willing to sell. Although Adams ignored John Ross's request to intercede on the Georgia
compact—in fact, he kept the Cherokees at arm's length—he repudiated the

state's fraudulent treaty with the Creeks. That ruling alone would cost him the South, where few appreciated Indian rights. He could not have done himself greater harm had he personally endorsed Jackson.

Then the smear campaign began. Jackson's men spread innuendo and lies, claiming that while he was minister to Russia Adams gave one aristocrat a young American girl to serve as his sex slave. The president's supporters retaliated by calling Jackson a murderer, repeating stories of his duels and the underhanded way he had won them. Adams's campaign accused Jackson and his wife of adultery and bigamy, noting they married before Rachel Jackson was divorced from her first husband.

In the end, Adams did not have the stomach or the sleaze to keep up with Jackson. One month after John Ross was elected principal chief of the Cherokees Andrew Jackson won the 1828 presidential election by an overwhelming margin, taking more than 56 percent of the national vote. But the victory did not come without a price. Before Jackson could take office his wife died. The president-elect blamed the Adams campaign for causing her stress. He buried Rachel on Christmas Eve.

Jackson's election had repercussions for the Cherokees even before he took office. On the same December day Old Hickory won by a two-to-one margin in the electoral college, lawmakers in Georgia drafted a bill claiming all Cherokee land within the state's boundaries. This legislation required any white person living among the Indians to sign an oath of allegiance to Georgia or move. The Cherokees were given no option whatsoever; they had to leave the state by June 1, 1830, unless given permission to stay by the Georgia legislature. State lawmakers were so sure they would now have a friend in Washington that they passed the proposal into law barely two weeks after it was introduced.

A few days later the federal government renewed its own efforts to evict the Cherokees. On the same day Jackson buried his wife in Nashville, John Ross exchanged harsh words with Hugh Montgomery in Calhoun. The Indian agent claimed that a number of Cherokees "repeatedly told him" they wished to enroll and emigrate but feared repercussions from Ross and his "big men" in New Echota. He warned Ross the United States would protect these Indians if the need arose.

Ross accused Montgomery of lying and challenged him to produce these frightened Indians.

"I hope you are not disposed to give credit to every frivolous tale that may be told you by designing men, prejudicial to the nation," Ross said.

Ross returned to Washington that winter to seek help, but the trip was largely a waste of time. No one in the outgoing administration would help, and Congress adjourned in the spring, ignoring Ross's pleas that the Cherokees' mounting problems could decide "whether we shall continue as a people or be abandoned to destruction."

Ross was still in Washington on March 4 when Andrew Jackson took the oath of office. He could hardly have avoided the spectacle as the city filled with Tennesseans and other partisans, many of whom checked into Williamson's, the same hotel in which the Cherokees stayed, to be near the various balls and parties. Although Ross attended the ceremony and heard Jackson's conciliatory words, he was no doubt skeptical when the new president portrayed himself as a benevolent Great White Father to the poor red men.

"It will be my sincere and constant desire to observe toward the Indian tribes within our limits a just and liberal policy," Jackson said in his inaugural address, "and to give that humane and considerate attention to their rights and their wants which is consistent with the habits of our Government and the feelings of our people."

It is unlikely Jackson's supporters applauded such promises from their new president, but this did nothing to dampen the mood. The inaugural party at the Executive Mansion allegedly became so rowdy the new president had to escape through a window. Most likely, these revelers knew, as Ross did, that the rhetoric on that day was nothing more than pomp and circumstance. Most assumed Jackson was trying to appear more moderate to garner favor with northern politicians, who were expecting the worst from him.

Jackson's remarks also belied the complexities of his feelings toward Indians. He had grown up believing Indians to be evil and barbaric but he had no desire to wipe out entire tribes of people. The general admired some Indians, to be sure, as strong warriors and even worthy opponents, even though he did not believe they deserved the same rights as whites. He stated that giving the tribes land west of the Mississippi was "just and liberal." But Jackson was also a politician, and an astute one. He realized there was no way to avoid removal without sparking civil war.

Ross waited a polite two days to test Jackson's "just and liberal" policies. His brief note to the president included no congratulations, no feigned admiration, and no references to their past relationship. He simply asked Jackson to remove the combative Montgomery from office and give the Cherokees an agent who would serve as a better ambassador. He would have to wait in his hotel room more than a month before getting a response from the benevolent Great Father. And then the letter didn't even come from the president himself; Jackson had delegated the task of rebuffing Ross to John Eaton, the new secretary of war.

Eaton proved every bit as adept at quoting law and past treaties as Ross, and he was as stubborn as the new president. He claimed the Cherokees were to blame for their troubles with Georgia. The tribe had overstepped its bounds by establishing an independent government within the boundaries of the state, the new excuse for evicting the Indians. It was the Cherokee constitution, Eaton argued, that had compelled the state legislature to pass its new law, and there was nothing the federal government could, or would, do about it. Eaton promised to remove illegal squatters but informed Ross the president believed the most humane course of action would be for the new principal chief to lead his people west.

There, he said, "the soil shall be yours, while the trees grow or the streams run."

Ross would not give Eaton or Jackson the satisfaction of begging. He left Washington at the end of April, irritated that his first diplomatic trip as chief had been a failure. The prospect of returning home with this news held little appeal, so Ross sold his horse and traveled north by stagecoach. He planned to book passage south on a ship out of New York, but at Philadelphia he

decided to change course and go west to Pittsburgh, then sail south through
Ohio to Nashville. His meandering route was telling; Ross needed a break.
Washington and its politicians had drained him of all optimism, and the
tribe's position seemed more precarious than ever.

"What will be the result of the unnatural course which Georgia has
taken, or the ultimate fate of the Cherokee nation, I dare not attempt to
predict," Ross wrote to the missionary Jeremiah Everts during the trip. "But
candour compels me to remark that I sincerely believe the nation is prepared
passively, to meet the worst of consequences, than to surrender their homes,
their all and to emigrate."

In Ross's absence the pressure on the Cherokees had only increased. Georgia's deadline had been enough to drive off some Indians, many of whom set
out for the Arkansas territory that winter. Those who stayed could hardly
have been encouraged by a letter from Thomas McKenney, published in the
Phoenix, which claimed the federal government "looks to the fulfillment of
the compact with Georgia on the one hand, and the prosperity and happiness of the Cherokees on the other." For a letter that McKenney claimed was
not meant to be threatening or intimidating, it certainly carried a menacing
tone. Boudinot's decision to publish the note caused Ross to question the
young Cherokee's judgment. After that, the chief would begin take a more
active role in selecting the paper's content.

Under Boudinot, however, the *Phoenix* was becoming a diverse forum
for the tribe. That winter, not long after running McKenney's dispatch,
Boudinot included an anonymous letter from one Cherokee farmer that
seemed a rebuttal of the Indian Affairs superintendent's halfhearted assurances. The farmer suggested the tribe was destined to share the fate of the
Shawnees and Delawares, once powerful tribes that were now little more
than wandering nomads with no game to feed on, no land to call home.

"But in case we should emigrate as a nation, where are we to go?" the
man wrote. "Where is the country in the West that will be congenial to
Cherokee habits? *Alas! there is none.*"

Major Ridge had watched the mood of the Indians sour throughout the winter, and he grew more concerned with each passing week. Ridge had seen this before: when the Red Sticks divided the Creeks, when Tennessee had coerced thousands of Cherokees to abandon their homes. The only advantage the Indians had was their population; the sheer number of Cherokees in Georgia and Tennessee made it difficult for the whites to impose their will on the entire tribe. But even with such numbers the tribe could not survive another exodus.

As spring thawed the Cherokee country, Major Ridge set out on a speaking tour to urge his people to remain calm and resolute. At Turkeytown, just south of Willstown, he assured the Indians that Ross was doing all he could to hold their land. The old chief's power of oratory had not diminished with age; he often sounded like a preacher delivering a fiery sermon.

Ridge said while other tribes were rounded up as slaves and marched into the setting sun, the Cherokees had retained their homeland through reason and legal arguments. The tribe had been targeted not because it was weak, Ridge said, but because it was strong. The whites were scared as "we have unexpectedly become civilized, and because we have formed and organized a constituted government."

"It is too much for us now to be honest, and virtuous, and industrious," Ridge proclaimed facetiously, "because then are we capable to aspiring to the rank of Christians and Politicians, which renders our attachment to the soil more strong, and therefore more difficult to defraud us of the possession."

John Ridge traveled the Cherokee Nation with his father, transcribing his every word. The young Ridge sent these inspirational messages back to New Echota, where Boudinot published excerpts in the *Phoenix*. As powerful as they were, Ridge's words of assurance did little to soothe the Cherokees, even when his messages were reprinted alongside Jackson's claims of a just policy toward Indians.

When John Ross returned home later that spring he quickly joined Ridge's campaign. He was pleased to see the old man taking on this responsibility, but he also felt a measure of guilt that he had delayed his own return. Ridge realized the Cherokees, more than anything else, needed reassurance, and Ross learned from this oversight on his part. He would not reveal the melancholy that had come over him in Washington. For the first time in his life he exaggerated his efforts, offered reassurances that were—to say the least— overly optimistic. In the *Phoenix,* he reported on his business in Washington and suggested Congress would investigate the Georgia legislature's conduct. In reality, he knew it was nothing more than wishful thinking.

"If Georgia was to extend her laws over us it would be a violation of our treaties with the Genl. Govt. and of the laws of the United States," the chief said. "We don't believe [Georgians] will extend their laws over us. The Genl. govt. has too much respect for the Treaties to let them be violated."

In his efforts to calm the Cherokees, Ross also noted that the president's word was not the ultimate law of the land. Such remarks may have alarmed the more astute Indians because, to that point, Jackson had said nothing of efforts to remove the Indians. Ross had unwittingly revealed his true fears— that he did not trust any whites, especially the president. But it was a conclusion that had been building for some time. Over the years, he had watched the politicians in Washington play their dangerous and cynical games. None of their principles mattered so much as compromise, the making of deals. It was the aspect of politics that Ross hated most.

For the moment, Ross's political naïveté mattered little. The chief's feigned confidence convinced most Indians to delay their plans to flee. If any of those Cherokees had spoken directly to the chief they might have felt differently. They may have heard a small measure of desperation in his voice. Behind his bold promises, Ross was becoming very afraid that Congress would do nothing to protect his tribe.

For thirty years fortune hunters had searched the foothill streams of Georgia and North Carolina, encouraged by a Cherokee legend about a shiny yellow rock. An Indian boy allegedly found the stone somewhere in the mountains and his mother later sold it to a white man. She refused to say where the boy had found the trinket, no matter how much people pressed her. Men had been panning for gold, without luck, on the outskirts of the Cherokee country ever since.

In the summer of 1828, one of Frank Logan's slaves came upon a nugget of gold lying in a branch of the Chestatee River. No one knew if the slave had found it in Ward's Creek or Duke's Creek, but everyone who heard the story realized that if there was one piece there would be more.

The crowds began arriving within a week. Before the summer ended a small village of shanties, filled with aggressively territorial miners, thieves, and gamblers, had sprung up in the north Georgia hills less than fifty miles east of New Echota.

This new village was filled with the worst kind of settlers. The prospectors were ruthless and violent. Fights broke over small claims, swindlers found ways to make money off the suckers, and local Indians were robbed weekly. The town that grew out of this mining camp would come to be called Dahlonega, a corruption of a Cherokee word that translated loosely as "yellow money." The Cherokees had never seen such an invasion of their land, and there was nothing they could do about it.

At first, Ross did not even consider the financial implications of the country's first gold rush; the idea of mineral rights was a foreign concept to him. But Ross realized if gold fever reached Milledgeville then Georgia politicians would be more determined than ever to take the Cherokees' land. Within a year he was proved right. By 1830 the state's militia would occupy Dahlonega under the pretense of policing prospectors. But it seemed their primary goal was to prevent any Cherokees from taking gold off their own land.

Ross asked Hugh Montgomery, the Indian agent, to send in federal troops to protect the tribe's gold and its land. But after several months Montgomery apologetically reported that he could not get authorization from Eaton. He promised to keep trying, and Ross—perhaps naively—took him at his word. It was another of his failings picked up from Cherokee tradition. He was raised to believe men always told the truth.

*   *   *

At the same time Montgomery was commiserating with Ross about prospectors, he was also quietly signing up Cherokees to move west. President Jackson had ordered the Indian agent to discreetly entice as many families as possible to emigrate, leaving it up to Montgomery to decide whether such enticement included bribery. It was slow work, but between the distant threat of the Georgia legislature and the more immediate menace of gold prospectors it began to pay off. By the end of the year he had persuaded nearly five hundred families to leave their homes. As Ridge had feared, the Cherokees' numbers were slowly dwindling.

When the Georgia legislature passed its laws declaring authority over the Cherokees, President Jackson decided it was time to act. For years, Georgia politicians had stewed over Washington's dismissive attitude toward their efforts to secure Indian land. The population of Georgia had grown by another 160,000 since 1820, to more than half a million, making it one of the most populous states in the Union. Georgia needed land for these new residents.

The state also had a profit motive. Because it had been one of the original thirteen colonies, any land inside its borders that was declared public domain was owned by the state. In newer states, such as Alabama, public land by law reverted to the federal government. This was an important distinction, probably the sole reason other southern states did not pursue Indian land as aggressively as Georgia. The Cherokees stood in the way of Georgia politicians making a great deal of money from this additional land, and that put the tribe squarely in harm's way.

With a fellow southerner in office, these Georgians believed they had the freedom to pursue Indian land, even if it meant stepping outside the law. They were running out of patience with the Cherokees, and Jackson knew the situation could turn violent. The president could justify the actions of Montgomery by believing it saved the Indians to force them out of their homes.

Jackson would not explain this dilemma to the Cherokees. He had little interest in negotiating with the "half-breeds" he believed had caused much of these problems. He ignored letters from Ross all summer, then dispatched the Tennessee governor William Carroll to negotiate a removal treaty directly with the General Council, a blatant attempt to go around the chief. It was a ploy nearly identical to the one Jackson and Joseph McMinn had attempted a decade earlier: target mid-level chiefs and act as if removal was a foregone conclusion. But the Cherokees were no longer so easy to trick or manipulate.

Ross learned of Jackson's strategy and refused to allow Carroll an audience with the council. He told the governor it would be a waste of his time and sent him away with a message for Jackson: Ross was well aware of the president's "deep interest" in ridding Georgia of the Cherokees, but the issue had been settled. The tribe wished to remain on its land.

"No proposition could be made to change their disposition as to induce them ever to enter into a treaty on the subject," Ross wrote in his typically formal, if bureaucratic, English.

Carroll gave up easily. He reported to Jackson that subterfuge would not work, that the Cherokees were too well informed to be tricked into removal. He did not understand how anxious Ross had actually been.

The chief was so concerned by what Jackson might do next that in November he sent George Lowrey, William Hicks, and his brother Lewis to Washington to force a meeting with the president. Ross realized Jackson was avoiding him but hoped the president might receive a different delegation. He told his men to ask for federal assistance against Georgia as had been guaranteed to the tribe in several treaties. He did not expect Jackson to help but he wanted to know what sort of answer he would get.

Ross felt overwhelmed. In all his years as a member of committees he had always felt confident speaking for the tribe. But he no longer had Charles Hicks or Pathkiller to guide him. Now he worried about making a misstep, of doing something that might doom the tribe to removal. He could not bear the thought of being the Cherokee who failed his tribe. This was not a matter of vanity, not anymore; he did not want to fail his grandmother's people, his people.

These self-doubts were apparent at the fall council during his annual address, Ross's first as chief. At New Echota, Ross said everything he could to ease the worries of his tribe, speaking of their "sacred privilege" to meet on their own ground and outlining all the reasons the Cherokees should be allowed to remain on their land. For the most part, Ross sounded calm and confident, yet for the first time he allowed the Indians to hear a hint of worry.

"A crisis seems to be fast approaching when the final destiny of our nation must be sealed," he told the silent council house. "The preservation and the happiness of the Cherokee people are at stake."

Ross hoped the delegation would provide some clarity, if not answers. But before his men could reach Washington he learned of Jackson's plans from news reports. Ross realized he had sent Lowrey, Hicks, and Lewis on a fool's errand.

In his first annual message to Congress on December 8, 1829, President Jackson did his best to play the role of statesman. He gave a long dissertation on the state of foreign affairs with Great Britain, France, and Spain. He spoke of refunding excess money in the Treasury to the states after, of course, the United States paid its debts. But his benevolence quickly dissolved, allowing a hint of the old politician—and his simmering vindictiveness—to surface. Still bitter over his 1824 loss to Adams, Jackson proposed a constitutional amendment to stop future presidential elections from being decided in the House of Representatives.

Jackson saved his most duplicitous and calculated remarks for a major announcement on Indian policy. At first he sounded almost sympathetic, as if he were the ideological successor to John Quincy Adams or James Monroe. The president spoke of trying to introduce the natives to "the arts of civilization" but lamented the United States had most likely "thrust them farther into the wilderness" by constantly purchasing their lands. The southern tribes had made some progress, he conceded, but had used their advancements for nefarious purposes.

Without calling the Cherokees by name, Jackson said if Indians wished to live among the white men they must submit to the laws of Georgia and Alabama. No tribes, he declared, could be allowed to form their own independent government within an established state. Jackson knew he was saying exactly what the southern states expected; if he was trying to persuade anyone, it was only the members of Congress from the northern states.

"Would the people of Maine permit the Penobscot tribe to erect an independent government within their State? Would the people of New York permit each remnant of the six Nations within her borders to declare itself an independent people under the protection of the United States? Could the Indians establish a separate republic on each of their reservations in Ohio?"

It was a clever argument, reminding northern politicians the New England states had not always been so magnanimous when dealing with Indian tribes. On the surface, Jackson portrayed himself as a concerned father who wanted the best for his unruly children. These natives make a powerful appeal to "our sympathies," he said, but Jackson feared their cultures would disappear if they continued to live among white people. It was the closest he came to candor in his remarks.

"By persuasion and force they have been made to retire from river to river and from mountain to mountain, until some of the tribes have become extinct and others have left but remnants to preserve for a while their once terrible names," the president said.

Ironically, Jackson offered a fairly honest, and blunt, assessment of what had occurred on the frontier over the past several decades. But his solution was the same one that had been pushed since the days of Thomas Jefferson. The president suggested Congress set aside an "ample district" west of the Mississippi for any tribe that chose to relocate. There, these Indians could set up whatever form of government they chose. Only in the West, the president argued, would the Native Americans truly be safe. Of course, he claimed, they should not be forced to leave. Jackson said, "This emigration should be voluntary, for it would be as cruel as unjust to compel the aborigines to abandon the graves of their fathers and seek a home in a distant land."

Careful to avoid any new wave of sympathy for the Indians, Jackson made it clear the time had passed to debate the morality of taking Indian land. The president would not allow that discussion. He acknowledged this policy for what it was: political reality. "It is too late," he said, "to inquire whether it was just in the United States to include them and their territory within the bounds of new states." What's done, Jackson said, is done and the Congress would simply have to deal with the policy of its forefathers.

"That step can not be retraced," the president said.

In his eloquent remarks professing great concern for the Indian tribes Jackson made no mention of his recent orders to Governor Carroll or the Indian agent Hugh Montgomery. He also neglected to add that he himself had concocted many of the methods of "persuasion and force" that had been employed to rid the South of Indians over the years.

A month later Congress would be debating a comprehensive Indian removal bill.

EIGHT

A Dangerous Game

They rode fast, their horses pounding the hard winter ground like approaching thunder. There were thirty warriors in all, young men with paint on their faces that glistened like smeared blood against a dull sky. They were led by an old chief in buffalo headdress, their advance announced by a chorus of enraged screams that pierced the cold forest air like gunshot. They crossed the familiar hills and streams of their homeland without letting up, a specter of the frontier's past, a reminder that old times had not yet been forgotten.

As they approached the cabin the noise startled the family inside—it always did. The settlers first thought to hide but quickly realized it would do no good. They emerged when they saw the Indians dismount and use torches to set their home afire. Soon the sweet smell of burning wood overcame them. Outnumbered and frightened, these families never gave thought to fighting. They ran deep into the woods, not stopping to gather their belongings, their only thoughts of escape. If they looked back, and most did not, they saw only smoke and ruin. They ran until they could hear the awful screams no more.

Major Ridge felt like a young man again. He had not raided white homesteads in nearly forty years, yet here he was dressed as a warrior and storming the countryside. It was no longer the way of the tribe but he and Ross felt there was no choice. The settlers had begun to move in again. Despite his misgivings, Ridge was not above hamming it up a bit. The headdress was part of the show. The Georgia politicians called them savages, so Ridge would give them savages.

The Cherokees had had enough. They had petitioned Washington for more than a year, begged the secretary of war to rid their land of the new squatters. Every letter went unanswered. In December they had met with General John Coffee, the Indian commissioner, at Head of Coosa to sort out a border dispute with the Creeks. They sat on fine furniture in Ross's parlor and tried to discuss their problems. But when the Indians mentioned the illegal settlers Coffee told them they could not depend on the military. He suggested they solve their own problems.

Coffee had said this in front of nearly twenty members of the General Council, and not long after he left Ross gave the order. This was not political calculation on Ross's part, a gesture to pacify his council. The federal government simply had pushed Ross to his breaking point. Even a peaceful man has his limits.

Ross gave the mission to the man he trusted most, the only remaining Cherokee with any experience in this sort of work. At sixty, Ridge was still a frightening man. Ross told him to be humane, not to let things get out of hand, to kill no one. His men could not drink whiskey on the trail; they could not take scalps. But that did not mean they could not frighten the people who had willfully invaded their country, many of them fortune hunters, thieves, and drunks. Ridge assembled a group of younger men, including George Hicks, the former chief's son, none of whom had been alive during the frontier days. They set out on February 4, 1830.

For two days Ridge's band traveled the mountainous Georgia–Alabama border, burning homes and outbuildings, pausing only long enough to permit some of these evicted settlers to gather their possessions or round up cattle. No one dared oppose them or tried to stop the torching. Most seemed grateful they were allowed to live. The Cherokees had one great advantage on these raids: the settlers were too scared to protest because they believed Indians were capable of anything.

In two days, Ridge rid Cherokee land of sixteen families. It was a small percentage of the people who had taken tribal land but it was a start. The tribe had a legal right to conduct these raids, and Ross had even informed the Indian agent Hugh Montgomery of his plans. None of those finer points mattered to George Gilmer. Within a week of the attacks the Georgia governor condemned the Cherokee barbarism in newspapers as far away as Savannah. He noted with no small amount of satisfaction that these raids proved the Indians were savages. Gilmer did not report, however, that by that time Georgians had evened the score.

On the afternoon of February 5, Ridge's warriors burned the home of an alleged horse thief named Samuel Rowe. The man had built a cabin south of the Coosa near Vann's Settlement, and it was the last stop on the raid; they had gone as far as Ross had authorized them to travel. Major Ridge was tired after two days of riding and he set out for home as soon as the skeletal frame of the thief's cabin fell. He planned to get as far as David Vann's home or Saunders's old place before dark and return to Head of Coosa the next day. Some of the others chose to stay behind. They found a barrel of whiskey at the house and a few of them could not resist. The Indians had finished their work, so Ridge saw no harm in it. He even justified their small larceny, saying the man had probably stolen the whiskey anyway. When the others rode off four Cherokees—the Waggon, Daniel Mills, Rattling Gourd, and Chuwoyee—stayed behind to drink.

That's where the posse found them that night.

News of the Cherokee raids had spread quickly and it took less than a day for a few outraged Georgians to round up a gang of twenty men eager to retaliate. They arrived at David Vann's home shortly after Major Ridge passed through, but the councilman would not tell them where the chief had gone. They threatened Vann, but when they realized he was not involved, and would not help them, they left, though not before informing him they planned to burn Ridge's home as well as Ross's. The Cherokees, they said, would pay for this outburst.

That night, the posse found the four Cherokee stragglers from Ridge's band warming themselves by the ashes of Rowe's house. Still in their war paint, the Indians were groggy from drink; in fact, the Waggon was so drunk the others had tied him up so he would not hurt them, or himself. None of them were in any shape to defend themselves.

The Georgians beat Mills with the butts of their guns and stomped him while he lay on the ground. They tied up Chuwoyee and put him on a horse, but he could not ride with his hands and feet bound so they just beat him instead. The men then carried the Indian a mile down the road and dumped him on the ground, where he later died. The posse arrested the other three Cherokees and took them to the Carroll County jail.

The assault set off a minor war in the Cherokee country. For days, gunfire rained on northwest Georgia, the posse fighting every Indian they found. Charles Vann and John West were ambushed near Turnip Mountain and nearly killed before driving back their attackers. The short gunfight allowed Vann a good look at the men, and he recognized one of them as the Carroll County sheriff. As soon as the posse retreated, Vann sent several Cherokees off on different paths to get word to Ross: fighting had broken out and the chief was in danger.

When John Ross learned what had happened he sent a wagon to collect Chuwoyee's corpse and bury it, then demanded Montgomery arrest the men who killed him. The Indian's murder was proof, he said, that the government could no longer ignore the tribe's request for protection. Georgia lawmen had come onto Indian land where they had no jurisdiction, beaten a man to death, and planned to put other Cherokees on trial under the state's laws. Ross was livid. He wanted to use the episode to force federal action, but he warned his people not to retaliate or resort to vigilantism. That, he knew, might lead to a larger war, one the Cherokees could not win.

Andrew Jackson could not have asked for more. Within a month of his call for Indian removal, Congress began work on legislation that would rid the

East of Native Americans forever. The debate consumed Washington for months. The halls of the newly refurbished Capitol building echoed with long speeches full of venom and sectional rhetoric. Northern politicians who had rid their land of Indians generations earlier now found the process distasteful, or rather their churches did. Northern missionaries, who had worked for decades to convert the southern tribes to Christianity, pressured their representatives to oppose removal. To be sure, some of those politicians realized the Indian tribes were becoming more civilized, in the European sense of the word, and that made them more worthy of property rights. A few of these northerners may even have wanted to slow the growth of the southern states for fear that they would soon control the entire nation. Despite all this Jackson was happy. He had accomplished his immediate goal: his legislation calmed the land-hungry Georgia settlers.

In late February, the House Committee on Indian Affairs issued a report that declared the "advances" of southern tribes exaggerated and claimed "no respectable jurist" had ever stipulated the rights of Indians to hold their reserved lands. The committee concluded the tribes lost their rights to American land the moment the king of England claimed it. As proof, the report noted England had not needed the Indians to relinquish any deeds in court. The Cherokees were singled out as perhaps the most problematic tribe. Their efforts to establish a sovereign government, the committee concluded, could "produce the most serious mischiefs."

When the Indian removal legislation reached the Senate floor in April, northern politicians tried to delay a vote with filibusters. Theodore Frelinghuysen of New Jersey talked for three straight days on the plight of the Indians. Peleg Sprague of Maine reminded his colleagues the government had signed fifteen treaties with the Cherokees alone between 1785 and 1819, contracts that guaranteed their existence as a separate political community, undisturbed possession of their land, and the protection of the United States. He hinted that the president had violated the spirit of the law through coercion and subterfuge and demanded Jackson be taken at his word: removal should remain voluntary. On that point, Sprague would not compromise.

"Mr. President: I am aware that their white neighbors desire the absence of the Indians; and if they can find safety and subsistence beyond the Mississippi, I should rejoice exceedingly at their removal, because it would relieve the States of their presence," Sprague said. "But let it be by their own free choice, unawed by fear, unseduced by bribes. Let us not compel them, by withdrawing the protection, which we have pledged."

The debate in the House fell along geographical lines as well. Edward Everett of Massachusetts, an acquaintance of John Ross, predicted forced removal—"a soft word," as he called it—would turn into a militaristic herding of human beings, many too old and frail to be marched hundreds of miles across country. Everett said it made him sick to discuss such inhumane treatment of people "while reposing on these luxurious chairs, and protected by these massy walls, and this gorgeous canopy, from the power of the elements." White men, the old Cherokees would learn, could be prophets too.

Southern congressmen maintained the upper hand throughout the debate, dismissing the concerns of New England politicians as hypocritical grandstanding. They repeatedly pointed out that northern states had rid their land of Indians generations earlier and questioned the patriotism of men who would assail the humanity and character of the president and the Congress. In the Senate, Robert Adams of Mississippi said there was nothing "unbecoming the character of a great, just, and magnanimous nation" in the removal bill. If Congress was so intent on upholding the law, he suggested, it should start by executing the 1802 compact with Georgia.

"The bill under consideration proposes a mode by which this agreement may be performed; by which the Indian title to all the lands within the boundaries of that State may be extinguished, peaceably, and upon reasonable terms," Adams said. "Peaceably, because it is only to operate upon those Indians who are willing to remove. And upon reasonable terms, because they are to receive other lands in exchange for those which they give up; just compensation for improvements made by them; the expenses of their removal and settlement paid, and subsistence for one year furnished them."

As the argument raged on, copies of a book collecting two dozen essays in support of the Indians—and the Cherokees in particular—were distributed to members of Congress. The essays, published under the name "William Penn," had originally appeared in the *National Intelligencer* and were actually written by the missionary Jeremiah Evarts, a close friend of Ross. In his writing, Evarts stirred support for Indians among northern politicians and urged Christian benevolence toward the tribes. He criticized Jackson's hypocrisy gently while trying not to inflame the partisan nature of the conflict. Throughout the debate, Evarts maintained his anonymity as the author of the essays, although he lobbied for the cause even as the books were circulated. As William Penn he was vilified by southerners, especially a House member from Georgia named Wilson Lumpkin.

Lumpkin, who had written the original House committee report, claimed the man behind the Penn essays was part of a sect more savage, superstitious, and diabolical than the "authors of the pow-wow, scalping, slave and dog laws." For Lumpkin, there was no middle ground. In a speech that dragged on for hours Lumpkin said the missionaries who supported Indians were "intermeddlers" and "disturbers of the peace." The Cherokees had thrust their law onto the state by trying to arrest a Georgia man who sold whiskey to Indians. Lumpkin said the Indians had no right to punish the man, who was licensed by the state of Georgia to sell spirits. It did not matter that distributing whiskey on Cherokee land was against tribal law.

Lumpkin, a large man with a long face and hard, oversize features, was the model of a southern patrician. At forty-seven, he had collected a lifetime of biases against Indians. He was born in Virginia, but his family moved to Oglethorpe County, Georgia, when he was a boy. He claimed his family was subject to frequent "depredations from hostile and savage Indian neighbors," though he heard these tales from his family more often than he actually witnessed such acts. Like Jackson, he was a typical southerner, indoctrinated with prejudices against Indians from an early age.

"Amongst my earliest recollections are the walls of an old fort, which gave protection to the women and children from the tomahawk and scalping knife of the Indians," Lumpkin said.

Despite his biases, Lumpkin knew well that such descriptions no longer applied to all tribes. As a commissioner on Georgia's board of public works,

he had traveled the Cherokee country often and knew most of the tribe's leading men, including Ridge, Ross, and the Vanns. He considered Daniel Ross
"a shrewd and sensible man of good education," and his son John a "well-
educated man . . . who converses well, writes well and is a man of soft, easy
gentlemanly manners." He conceded the chief was a man of "good moral character," but there was more to it than manners. The Cherokees, he would later
admit, owned almost six million acres of the best land in Georgia, property he
had inspected closely as a commissioner. And Lumpkin, better than most of
his constituents, knew the state could make a fine profit off that land.

Lumpkin quickly became Georgia's voice in the Indian removal debate,
and most of his colleagues deferred to him. The only southerner who sided
with the Indians was to many their least likely defender. The Tennessean
David Crockett, whose family had been slaughtered by the Cherokees when
he was a boy, and who owed his election to Andrew Jackson's coattails, argued that Indian removal violated the Constitution's treaty clause. Crockett
said he wanted the Indians gone as much as anyone but, the famous frontiersman said, he had been elected to uphold the Constitution. Crockett had
broken from Jackson before but never in such public fashion.

On May 19, a few weeks after the Senate passed the removal bill by a vote
of 28 to 19, Crockett stood up in the House to make his final argument. A
tall man with a growing belly and dark hair a bit longer than was fashionable,
Crockett did not entirely fit the mold of a nineteenth-century politician.
He was folksy, more plainspoken than most, and that day he put on a show.
Gesturing wildly, shaking his hands as he made his points, Crockett said he
could not resolve himself to such "wicked" acts; he could not take land from
people who had held it for centuries. He acknowledged the silence of the
chamber, saying no congressman who lived within five hundred miles of him
would dare oppose Indian removal. There will be a reckoning for this stand,
he admitted. But he could not abet such a crime because he "had a settlement to make at the bar of his God."

Crockett understood the intricacies of the law but he preferred to
speak like common folk, putting his argument in its most basic terms: the
United States had made a deal to always protect the Indians, and even an old

country boy knew it was dishonorable to say one thing and then do another. Later, Crockett would write that he had rather be honestly and politically damned than hypocritically immortalized. By that time his prediction had come true. Crockett's speech cost him his seat in the House and did little to change the outcome. A week after his defense of the Indians the House voted 102–97 in favor of Indian removal.

Two days later, on May 28, 1830, Jackson hurriedly signed the Indian removal bill into law.

President Jackson abandoned Washington for the summer, returning to Tennessee for a vacation. He was tired and also eager to escape the politics at his beloved home, the Hermitage. In a short time, he had accomplished what he set out to do for his southern friends. The Indian removal legislation had passed more easily than he'd anticipated, but he would not rest on this victory for long. Soon after he arrived home, Jackson sent invitations to the Choctaws, Chickasaws, Creeks, and Cherokees to meet with him and discuss the business of removal. He wanted to broker all the necessary treaties and be done with this business as soon as possible.

The Indian Removal Act was technically a voluntary program, authorizing the government only to negotiate with tribes that wanted to relocate. But from the first Jackson treated it as a foregone conclusion. He understood the political reality. Now that there was an Indian removal law, the states would not rest until all the tribes had been forced out or killed. There was nothing he, or anyone else, could do about it.

In August, Jackson delivered that message to the Chickasaws in Franklin, Tennessee, just outside Nashville. The president told the Indians they must move west to avoid death or assimilation into white culture, but he prayed the "Great Spirit above would take care of, bless, and preserve them." Jackson's emotion so moved the Chickasaw chiefs—who understood removal was inevitable—that they immediately agreed to a treaty. But the deal was vague and promised to delay removal until suitable land elsewhere was found. Congress would not ratify the open-ended deal, and it took another two years to sign a new treaty.

It took that long to reach a deal with the Creeks, and longer still for the Seminoles. The Choctaws, who refused to meet in Tennessee, eventually welcomed a delegation onto their land and signed a treaty in September of 1830. Ultimately, some seven thousand Choctaws would agree to Jackson's terms to remain in their homes and become citizens of Mississippi, which would force them to abide by U.S. law. Another fourteen thousand would move west of the great river over the next few years.

Of all the Five Civilized Tribes chiefs, only John Ross refused to meet with Jackson. Against the advice of Jeremiah Evarts and some Cherokees, Ross ignored the president's invitation and spent the summer behind his writing desk at Head of Coosa. He was stubborn but justified his position as a reflection of his people's will. A few chiefs questioned him, but Ross could not be persuaded to take action—and no one dared argue with him. The principal chief at that moment was in mourning; a week before the Indian Removal Act had passed, on May 22, Daniel Ross had died.

Ross never said anything of the losses he suffered; outbursts of emotions were considered ill-mannered by Ross and most other Cherokees. But his father's death hurt him deeply. Daniel Ross had given his son every advantage in the world—education, money, a good home—and taught John to respect the Cherokees. His death not only was a great personal loss to Ross but also severed his last blood ties to the white race. Ross buried his father on the grounds of his estate at Head of Coosa. In the coming years, he would quietly pass many hours beside the grave.

Ross's refusal to respond to Jackson's invitation worried some of the more skittish Cherokees. A few of his advisers feared offending Jackson, but Ross realized nothing good could come of the meeting. Jackson did not want to help the Cherokees find a way to remain in their homes; he wanted only to negotiate a treaty. And Ross had no interest in that conversation.

For more than a decade Ross had tried to find solutions to the tribe's problems through politics. But when he tallied up his record he must have recognized the Cherokees lost more often than not when dealing with the Congress or any president. And Jackson was undoubtedly more unreasonable than any past occupant of the Executive Mansion. Ross, Lumpkin said, had "intellectual advantages," but he did not have to draw on any genius to realize that traveling to Nashville to meet the president was a waste of time.

"My earliest and warmest friends in Tennessee are generally his advocates —during the late war I held a rank in the Cherokee regiment and fought by his side," Ross wrote to Davy Crockett that summer. "But it is with deep regret, I saw, that his policy toward the aborigines, in my opinion, has been unrelenting and in effect ruinous."

Ross thanked Crockett for so eloquently arguing the Cherokee case and lamented it had done little to advance the tribe's cause. Yet it helped convince him to take a different course. Politicians, he had learned, would gladly ignore laws and treaties to placate voters. The courts, however, were bound by the law, and Ross knew the law was on his side. Soon, the chief began searching for an attorney who would take the tribe's case in a lawsuit against Georgia.

Ross first solicited Daniel Webster, the famous statesman who had defended the tribe in the past. When Webster politely declined Ross turned to William Wirt. It was a savvy choice. Wirt had served as U.S. attorney under presidents Monroe and Adams, gaining an intimate knowledge of federal policy. Wirt agreed to help but he couldn't work without a fee. Taking on such a politically unpopular case might cost him other business and take up a lot of time. Ross hired Wirt, even though he wasn't sure where he'd get the money. The tribe's finances had been effectively cut off by Jackson.

In the past, the federal government had always paid tribal annuities directly to Indian chiefs, giving the tribes a small amount of revenue. Jackson ordered the program restructured, insisting the money be paid to individual Indians. It was a clever ploy to shut down the tribes. When the annuities were divided among individual families, the money amounted to less than fifty cents a person. Most Cherokees wouldn't even travel to the agent's office to collect such a pitiful sum, and those who did were unlikely to turn it over to tribal leaders. Unless he could change that policy, Ross knew that eventually he, Ridge, and a few other wealthy Cherokees would have no choice but to pay the tribe's legal bills out of their own pockets.

By the summer of 1830 Georgia's pressure on the Cherokees had become relentless. The state found any excuse to arrest members of the tribe—they owed a debt, were prospecting in Dahlongea, had accused whites of stealing horses. Perhaps the state's most egregious act, however, was the arrest of George Tassel. Tassel, who had accompanied the Ross delegation to Washington in 1825, was accused of killing another Cherokee during a dispute at Talking Rock. The tribe arrested Tassel and scheduled a trial but before the case went to court a band of Georgia lawmen rode onto tribal land and took him away. In Hall County, Tassel was swiftly convicted of murder and sentenced to hang.

William Wirt believed Tassel's case provided the tribe a legal opening to sue. He instructed Ross to hire another attorney, William Underwood, to appeal the Tassel decision to the Georgia Superior Court and test the theory that Georgia had violated U.S. treaties by imposing state law on the tribe. It was a sound legal idea but Underwood never had a chance. The Georgia justices ignored his arguments of independent sovereignty and seemed enchanted by the solicitor general for Georgia's western circuit, who argued the Cherokees were "inferior, dependent, and in a state of pupilage to the whites." In deference to the political climate in Milledgeville, the justices upheld the conviction. Ross and Wirt were not surprised but they weren't finished.

In spite of the tribe's growing troubles, New Echota was festive as the time for the fall council approached. More families arrived each day to find the town busy with workers building an academy, library, and museum. By now the town was populated with hundreds of Cherokees in dozens of cabins. Any foreign traveler would have had a hard time distinguishing the village from an outpost of white settlers, except perhaps for the community sheds filled with corn, squash, and beans. Charity was one of the tribe's more civilized traits.

To watch these Indians go about their lives, it would have been difficult to see they were under any duress. Going Snake made a grand entrance in early October, sporting a frock coat and cockaded hat as he rode into town on a blooded mare. Parties in the town square lingered until the fires died, Cherokees drinking whiskey and smoking, telling tales of the old days that all of them realized had long since passed. No matter how late into the night these men traded stories, they did not shirk their reason for coming to New Echota. By day, hundreds sat outside the General Council building and listened to the proceedings inside.

On October 11, Ross rode into town to deliver his yearly message to the tribe. He had spent most of the summer sequestered at Head of Coosa, where there had been few distractions from his writing desk other than the birth of his new son—his second in a year—whom he named George Washington Ross. Cherokees had a long tradition of naming children after their favorite American president. With George and Silas Dinsmore Ross, born a year earlier, Ross once again had a full house. Jane helped her mother care for her brothers while Ross planned his next move. By the time of his annual address he was ready to reveal his plans for a lawsuit against Georgia.

Cherokee independence, he proclaimed that day, would be won in the U.S. Supreme Court. In as grand a manner as the bureaucratic chief could muster, he described the case in details that most Cherokees did not understand. But they recognized his confidence. If Ross believed they could win in court, the Indians believed him—he had never let them down before.

Ross's hopeful annual address fueled beliefs that the tribe's difficulty would soon pass. The council even forgave John Ridge for meddling in Creek affairs and elected him to the National Committee, where he was quickly appointed its president. For the moment, the Cherokees were optimistic. They did not foresee that this would be the last council meeting held in their grand and modern capital city.

John Lowrey watched these proceedings from the outskirts of New Echota, where he had been sent to propose a removal treaty. Jackson would not allow the tribe to ignore him any longer. But for two weeks the Cherokees had refused to hear Lowrey. The Cherokees considered uninvited guests rude and often ignored them. And Ross wanted to avoid upsetting the council with any talk of removal. Lowrey would not leave, however, and the chief finally relented.

The Cherokees heard Lowrey's message in the yard outside the council house, where Indians had dragged benches from inside the chambers.

Standing before this crowd on a bright fall day, John Ridge translated the written statement, which was unremarkable and tiresome—nothing they had not heard before. It would be better for them to vacate Georgia and settle in the West; President Jackson wanted only peace and happiness for the tribe.

The Cherokees were prepared to dismiss Lowrey until, at the end of his remarks, he revealed disturbing news: Georgia planned to survey Cherokee land, subdivide it, and distribute it among white settlers within the year. When that happens, Lowrey warned, the president would not protect the tribe.

"What then," Lowrey asked, "will become of you?"

Most Cherokees were too stunned by the news to say anything, but Major Ridge reacted violently. He jumped up and accused Lowrey of being an imposter, demanded to see his credentials. Ridge said he must be an agent of Georgia sent to trick the tribe. For a moment, the commissioner feared for his life. In truth, Ridge was enraged because he did not want to face the alternative: that the man was telling the truth. When the flustered Lowrey produced papers that proved he had been sent by the secretary of war Ridge sat down. But the meeting was over.

Ross refused to negotiate with Lowrey. The next day, he sent his own tiresome note, repeating the tribe's mantra that it would never again cede another foot of land. Ross argued that the government didn't honor past treaties, so there was no reason to believe new deals would be any different.

"The offer of new guaranties can be no inducement to treat," Ross wrote.

It was time.

John Ross awoke early on December 20, ordered a servant to saddle his horse, and set out from his house before the winter mist lifted off the Coosa. George Lavender met Ross outside his home and by sunrise the two men were on the trail south to face Georgia governor George Gilmer. With Ridge's trading post manager acting as traveling companion, aide, and bodyguard, Ross carried paperwork to Gilmer that he hoped might end this dangerous game.

For more than a month Ross had been overwhelmed. Jackson continued to send envoys after the council meeting, and the rumors of surveyors en route to New Echota threatened to panic the tribe. The Georgia militia had increased its patrols on tribal land, arresting more Cherokees every day. Hugh Montgomery told Ross the federal government would soon transfer protection of the Indians and their gold to those same militiamen.

Ross had been forced to delegate many of these growing problems. He depended on Ridge and the second principal chief, George Lowrey, to deal with local issues. When Jeremiah Evarts suggested there was some support in Washington City for the idea of repealing the Indian Removal Act, Ross was not optimistic but dispatched John Ridge and his nephew William Shorey Coodey to lobby for the idea. It all might have been too much if not for the good news from William Wirt.

Wirt had been busy. He'd asked a number of lawyers to examine the existing treaties and laws pertaining to the tribe and they had come to the conclusion that the Cherokees were "an independent, sovereign nation." That meant the Georgia legislature had violated the Constitution; the state could not supersede federal statutes by imposing its laws on an independent nation recognized by the United States. As a result, the U.S. Supreme Court had jurisdiction to intervene. Wirt filed a motion for injunction, using the Tassel case as its basis. Nothing could be done, however, until sixty days after Georgia's governor and attorney general were served notice. Wirt sent Ross detailed instructions on how to prepare the proper legal documents and told the chief to deliver them himself. Wirt filed his appeal in the Tassel case on December 12.

It took Ross a week to reach Milledgeville. He rode twenty-five miles a day through Georgia, he and Lavender dodging hostile state troops along the way. As they rode south, the rolling countryside gave way to flatland littered with settler cabins. Although Ross and Lavender were white enough to pass for Georgians, they avoided most people; they didn't need any more trouble.

When they reached the capital on December 26 Gilmer refused to see Ross. The state had learned of the court filing and the governor and attorney general were evading all attempts to serve them. The morning after Ross's arrival they left town. Meanwhile, the legislature had decided the court order violated states' rights and had no intention of obeying it. These lawmakers told the sheriff of Hall County to hang Tassel, which he did on December 24, while Ross was traveling. It was an arrogant defiance of federal law.

By January 1, 1831, Ross and Lavender had tracked Gilmer to Augusta. When the governor refused to meet with them once again, Ross served the papers on a local judge, the highest-ranking official in the city. He told the judge the state was in contempt of the Supreme Court, something a man of the law should understand. Ross waited to leave until he was certain Gilmer had received the papers, but he nearly stayed too long. The state militia had put out a warrant for his arrest. The governor swore that, for the outrage, Ross would end up in prison. Lavender had to smuggle Ross out of the city after dark.

Since 1789 the U.S. Supreme Court had held the authority to nullify any state action its justices thought violated federal law, treaties, or the Constitution. Chief Justice John Marshall had used that power for three decades to impose his own brand of federalism on the country, and it had shaped the court into a distinct and influential branch of the government. It was perhaps the most remarkable feat of Marshall's long tenure, which went back to the days of John Adams. And now, because of a simple case involving the state of Georgia and the Cherokee Indians, it looked as though all his work might unravel in a single year.

Marshall was both embarrassed and outraged by the way the state had ignored him, flouted his authority. Georgia had brazenly executed an Indian whose case had yet to be heard by the courts, and the southerners showed no remorse for this slight. In fact, as the Supreme Court's March session drew near, Georgia politicians roamed the halls of the Capitol enlisting the aid of other states' rights proponents to strip the high court of its judicial review over state governments. In Congress, it appeared there were plenty of men— mostly from the South—with that goal. Marshall sensed that he may have underestimated the politics of removal and feared he had walked into a trap.

While the Georgians rallied support to rein in the Supreme Court, John Ridge, William Coodey, and Richard Taylor fought to repeal the Indian Removal Act. Escorted by Davy Crockett, they stalked the Capitol's grand halls, pestering members of Congress to restore direct annuity payments to tribal chiefs and pass a new law to stop Jackson's removal efforts. Although the Indians found sympathizers it was clear the southerners outnumbered them. By March 6, the day after the Supreme Court convened, Ridge had abandoned his lobbying campaign and staged a desperate publicity stunt; a day of fasting and prayer outside the Capitol. Ridge had a greater flair for the dramatic than the bureaucratic Ross but got no better results.

Marshall postponed *Cherokee Nation v. the State of Georgia* for nearly a week after the court began its spring session. While the chief justice worried about how the case might damage his court's authority, Georgia had little to lose. If the justices struck down Georgia's Indian law, it would only fuel the efforts to limit their power, by furnishing proof that they had overreached. Although most justices recognized that the Georgia legislature had clearly overstepped its authority, they feared correcting the state could lead to all manner of turmoil. And in the end it still might not help the tribe. But Marshall was not a man to be bullied.

On March 11, 1831, William Wirt and his associate John Sergeant, an attorney for the American Board of Missionaries, began to lay out their case, drawing heavily on the Penn essays and Wirt's own opinions. Standing in the imposing courtroom, Wirt was warm and collegial and acted as if the entire case were a simple matter of common sense. He argued that the Cherokees' authority and right to their own land had been recognized in more than a dozen treaties ratified by Congress. As he spoke, he waved around his ornate snuffbox like a commoner in a tavern. When he tired, he turned the arguments over to Sergeant. No one from Georgia showed up to defend the state.

Wirt's arguments were largely for show; he and Sergeant were simply going through the official motions. While studying a way out of the mess, Marshall had read the case so many times he knew it nearly as well as Wirt. He had come up with a way to save the court and possibly help the Indians. On March 18, the Supreme Court ruled the Cherokees were not a foreign nation and therefore were ineligible to sue Georgia on original jurisdiction. Over the objections of a divided court, Marshall sidestepped the question of whether the state's law violated existing U.S. treaties. Historians would later characterize it as a "political sleight of hand" to save the court's powers.

Ross would be discouraged but Wirt assured him it was not a complete loss. In his order, Marshall had offered a hint of his true opinion, writing that "the Indians are acknowledged to have an unquestionable . . . right to the lands they occupy." Marshall declared the Cherokees a "domestic, dependent nation" under the protection of the United States. Although no one was sure exactly what that meant, Wirt was a good enough attorney to realize the chief justice had left the tribe several loopholes to exploit.

And soon enough Georgia would give the tribe another opportunity to do just that.

The president was in a talkative mood. On the day after Marshall's ruling, John Ridge went to the Executive Mansion for a farewell visit. His mission had been a bust and he hoped at least to get a sense of what Jackson might do next. He found the president for once eager to meet with the Cherokees. On that day, Jackson was friendly and hospitable, and—even though they had never met—treated the younger Ridge like an old friend.

"I am glad to see you, particularly at this time," the president said. "I knew, or I thought I knew, that your claims before the Supreme Court could not be supported. The court has sustained my views in regard to your nation. I blame you for suffering your lawyers to fleece you—they want your money, and will make you promises even after this, perhaps that they can make you safe. I have been a lawyer myself long enough to know how lawyers will talk to obtain their client's money."

The younger Ridge was surprised to find that he liked Jackson. Old Hickory seemed genuine and amiable, nothing like the devil he had been made out to be. His expansive mood was welcoming and reassuring. Perhaps, Ridge thought, Ross was wrong; this was a man who could be reasoned with. Taking advantage of the president's jocular mood Ridge spoke bluntly. He said, "As a statesman and a warrior, we do not believe you would blame the Cherokees for the efforts they had made to maintain their rights for liberty."

No, Jackson said, he didn't blame the tribe. In fact, he wanted the best for them, and he asked young Ridge to take that message back to the Cherokees. He wished no ill will on his friends. After all they had been through—fighting alongside one another—how could he be anything but their friend? It was as close as Jackson would come to revealing any hidden conflicts he harbored.

Jackson chatted with Ridge for more than half an hour. He mentioned treaties with the British, lamented the plight of the Catawba Indians in South Carolina, and reported that the Choctaw and Chickasaw exploring parties had just returned from the West after finding suitable land. Finally, Jackson excused himself and wished the Cherokees well. As he shook hands with Ridge, he made a casual remark that struck the young Cherokee as a not so veiled threat.

"You can live on your lands if you choose, but I cannot interfere with the laws of that state to protect you," Jackson said.

The president, Ridge later noted, smiled as he said this.

The Georgia Guard arrested the missionary Isaac Proctor on March 12 at the Carmel Mission near Table Rock, on the Alabama state line. They arrived in the early evening, surrounded the property, and sent a few men to round up all the whites inside. When he heard the knock on his door, Proctor did not resist. He had known they would come for him eventually.

The deadline had passed on Georgia's new law requiring any whites living among the Indian tribes to register with the state. Proctor had not complied because he would have had to swear an oath of allegiance to Georgia, and this was something that, on principle, he was not prepared to do, no matter what the consequences. And there were consequences. The legislation stated that anyone who failed to obey the law would be sentenced to four years in state prison. Proctor and Daniel Butrick, another missionary at Carmel, had sent a frantic letter to the American Mission board in January asking for advice and help, but the answer did not come in time. Butrick fled to North Carolina, out of Georgia's reach. Proctor chose to stay with his family.

The guardsmen held Proctor in a nearby house overnight and the next morning allowed him to tell his family good-bye before they set out. They rode into New Echota that evening and arrested Samuel Worcester, surprising many of his Cherokee neighbors. The next day, the blacksmith John Thompson was taken into custody near Hightower. The three men were jailed that night in Lawrenceville, where they were told they would soon stand trial. The guardsmen had no warrant for their arrests and believed they did not need one—after all, they were doing the work of the state.

Although many white men had failed to register under the new law, only Proctor, Worcester, and Thompson were arrested. Their unspoken crime—the reason they were singled out—was helping the Cherokees. The missionaries had been the tribe's greatest proponents, writing of Cherokee advancement in northern newspapers and championing their cause in Washington. The men also undermined Georgia's socially accepted reason for removal, that it was not safe for whites to settle near Indian tribes. The missionaries put the lie to that just by living in Cherokee country.

The men spent nearly two months in the Lawrenceville jail before convincing a judge to release them. The missionaries argued that, as local postmasters, they were federal agents not subject to state law. The judge had to agree. Governor Gilmer was so incensed he appealed to Jackson, who fired the men two weeks later. The governor had them immediately rearrested.

The Georgia Guard terrorized the Cherokees throughout the summer. Although the troops treated the captive missionaries civilly—allowing Worcester nightly visits to his home, where his wife had just delivered their third daughter—they mercilessly taunted and harassed the Indians. On occasion, the troops became violent. Guardsmen killed twenty Creeks in a minor border dispute and later shot two Cherokee boys who had wandered too close to the gold mines. One afternoon, guardsmen discovered an Indian baptism under way and ordered all the Cherokees out of the water. They then rode into the stream on horseback, mocking the ceremony and laughing as they made a great show of "baptizing" their animals.

Elias Boudinot editorialized in the pages of the *Cherokee Phoenix* against this and other sacrileges, pointing out the inherent racism behind the state's actions. He did not know how close to the truth he was. That summer, Governor Gilmer sent agents into the Cherokee country to investigate John Ross's blood ties to the tribe. The governor wanted to bolster his argument that the tribe's resistance was caused by a bunch of half-breeds, that the savages themselves did not care about the land. Hugh Montgomery supplied the men with some genealogical information but, since it did not help their arguments, the Georgia politicians quietly discarded the information.

John Ross, who did not know of the efforts to investigate his lineage, urged the Indians not to fight the guardsmen or attempt any act of vengeance for the litany of injustices. He believed the state was trying to provoke the Cherokees or at least intimidate them into emigrating without a treaty. In any case, it seemed to be working. The Georgia Guard set up a headquarters on Cherokee land at Hightower, just east of New Echota, and no one dared to say anything about it. Most Indians simply left the town. Hightower became another piece of tribal land ceded to the white men.

At first, Ross tried to communicate with the tribe exclusively through the newspaper, publishing letters that urged them to go about their business and ignore the troops. But he soon realized that was not enough. That spring he set out on a three-week speaking tour of the Cherokee Nation, visiting every village in Georgia and Alabama. He even stopped once to talk near his old home, in a town that would one day be called Rossville.

It was the most extensive traveling in his own nation Ross had done since becoming chief, and it left him conflicted. While many Indians lived in glorious towns similar to New Echota, others huddled in muddy camps on the sides of mountains that never saw sunlight. Although the tribe enjoyed better conditions than many Indians, a lot of Ross's people were suffering. It reminded him why he was fighting. These people did not aspire to riches and fine homes. They wanted only to live on the land of their forefathers and not face the constant fear that white men would take it from them. It was, to Ross, shameful what the whites had done to his people.

Ross did his best to reassure these Cherokees that they would be safe. He passed hours with local chiefs, met young families and old men—all of whom were thrilled to have the principal chief come into their homes. And although he was not a gifted orator, like Major Ridge, Ross could occasionally be inspiring, even elegant.

"The busy tattlers and intriguers who are ever ready to prey upon our vitals by false insinuations, will, no doubt, endeavor to persuade you to believe that there is no hope left for you on this side of the Mississippi: nay, the coarse voice is even now beginning to be heard rustling from the 'forked tongue' o'er the plains, hills and mountains throughout the land, therefore beware and suffer not yourselves to be deluded by them. You have for the time past met oppression and injustice with fortitude and forbearance and I trust you will persevere in his prudent course; as it will not fail in due time to lead you to a safe deliverance from all the troubles you are experiencing under the cruel and unjust measures pursued by the state of Georgia and the President toward us."

To the few cynical Indians he met in his travels, this proselytizing might have come off as little more than a campaign speech. But Ross was trying to project confidence and promise safety at a time when his tribe most needed to hear it. For years, he had been a politician. Now he was beginning to fulfill the traditional role of an Indian chief. He was their father, their protector, and their savior, even if he didn't quite believe it himself.

In August, Colonel Nelson of the Georgia Guard ordered Elias Boudinot to visit him at his camp in Hightower or face jail time. The troops were upset by the *Phoenix*'s relentless editorializing against the state and wanted to take it out on someone. Nelson threatened to beat Boudinot for what he claimed were libelous articles but said he would go easy on the editor if he told them which missionaries had written the offending pieces. When Boudinot said he had written every one of the articles, Nelson scoffed. No Cherokee, he said, was smart enough to write like that. However, Boudinot was at least smart enough not to point out he had a much finer New England education than any of his captors. Guardsmen harassed the defiant Boudinot for hours, but eventually they let him go.

By the middle of September all but two of the arrested missionaries had accepted pardons in exchange for signing oaths of allegiance to Georgia. Once released, all of them left the state. Only Elizur Butler and Worcester refused the deal. Both men opposed the offer on principle, but Worcester had another reason to be bitter. While he sat in jail his infant daughter died, and he was not there to comfort his wife. There was no way Worcester would sign the oath. Such personal hardships mattered little to Georgia officials, however. On September 16, a judge sentenced Worcester and Butler to four years of hard labor at the state prison in Milledgeville.

John Ross offered the missionaries' wives money so they could visit their husbands, but in truth he had little to spare. The trouble with Georgia had hurt business, and these days he spent more money than he took in. Ross had to borrow $500 just to pay part of the tribe's legal bill, and he still needed to send Wirt another hundred dollars. But he felt responsible for the plight of Worcester and Butler. They had become embroiled in politics that did not concern them, casualties of a legal war. In a letter to Wirt, Ross noted that at least the missionaries, as U.S. citizens, could appeal to the Supreme Court. The thought lingered.

As the time of the fall council approached, Ross was interrupted almost every day by worried chiefs. Georgia's new Indian law prohibited tribes from meeting inside the state's boundary, and anyone who violated that order could be imprisoned. Many Cherokees feared that the Georgia Guard, camped at Hightower, was simply waiting for the General Council to convene in order to arrest everyone. Ross told every Indian who showed up at Head of Coosa the same thing: the meeting was mandated by the constitution and not even he could break tribal law. His bureaucratic responses did little to instill confidence.

Ross had already considered the scenarios and saw no reason to cancel the meeting. If the tribe altered its plans, it would almost be admitting that the Cherokees were subject to state law. And if guardsmen did arrest him and the other chiefs, Ross knew such a scene could win them a great deal of sympathy in Congress. It was dangerous but Ross was desperate. After weeks of receiving anxious visitors, however, Ross had little choice but to consult his executive council.

The meeting was not particularly useful. With more than twenty chiefs gathered at his home one afternoon, Ross made his feelings clear, although he did not mention the possibility of council members being arrested. Because no one wished to cross the chief there was little dissension. The only caution they took was to print notices for the meeting in Cherokee, a language no one in the Georgia Guard could read. The General Council decided to meet at New Echota, as planned, on October 10.

Ross thought the matter was settled until Major Ridge, Ridge's son John, and Elias Boudinot visited him a few days later. The men marched into the chief's house and told him he had to reconsider his action and either call off the meeting or move it beyond the reach of the Georgia Guard. These demands did not sit well with Ross. He had become accustomed to giving orders, not taking them. It seemed to him the two younger men were using Major Ridge to gang up on him, and he was suspicious of their motives. Irritated, Ross told them the issue had been decided. The executive council had agreed to meet at New Echota and there was nothing he could do.

John Ridge said such a meeting was impossible.

"Why do you think so?" Ross asked.

"Because," Boudinot spoke up, "I have taken much pains to ascertain the sentiments of the members of the General Council; and I have discovered that some of them, rather than attend at New Echota, will resign. Such an event will be most embarrassing to the public interest. An omission to assemble will break up the representation which, at this moment, is rendered peculiarly important."

The Ridges agreed. A council at New Echota would be sparsely attended and almost certainly would be disrupted by Georgia Guardsmen. There could be horrible consequences if thousands of Cherokees saw their leaders dragged away as prisoners. Before the council members could be freed, the remaining members of the tribe would flee, perhaps even be evicted from their land. And then all they had fought for would be lost.

Ross was skeptical. He had heard none of these rumors and had little sympathy for men who lived in fear. He argued that it would insult Cherokees to move the meeting, that it would insinuate they could not be discreet. Ross had never appeared so aggressive. He may have been overreacting to questions about his judgment. Whatever the reason, Ross soon worked himself into a rant.

"Suppose the members should be arrested," he said. "What then? Can they not give bail and return? And when driven from the place of a constitutional meeting, they will have the strong plea for a change that it was by force and not to be avoided."

After a minute Ross calmed down. He had not convinced the Ridges or Boudinot and may not even have convinced himself. He realized it was risky; Ross knew everything could play out exactly as Boudinot predicted. And such a spectacle might scare many Indians into leaving on their own, diminishing their numbers even more. Reluctantly, Ross gave in.

"As mine is but a single opinion, and I am now only one against three, I will do this, gentlemen," the chief said. "I will ask the members here. We will meet at my house as private persons and then discuss the expediency of assembling at New Echota or elsewhere."

On Wednesday, October 5, the forty members of the General Council quietly gathered at Head of Coosa to discuss new plans. The newspaper editor had correctly reported the mood of the council: many chiefs feared a meeting at New Echota could be a trap but were unsure what to do about it.

Privately, Ross suspected even deeper subterfuge at work. He worried that violating the new constitution would serve only as an excuse for more change. The document he had worked so tirelessly to perfect would be worthless if the Cherokees abandoned it at the first sign of distress. This would suggest the tribe's government had broken up, or had never been a serious body to begin with. Such a perception could hurt the tribe's legal arguments, he realized.

In his opening remarks to the informal council Ross stressed that they were assembled only for a friendly discussion, that the tribe was making progress in its efforts to hold its land.

"The continuance of a peaceable, firm and prudent course on our part cannot fail to crown our efforts," he said. "Therefore let harmony and union be our motto, and I earnestly beseech you to beware of innovation and disorganization."

In customary fashion, the Cherokee leaders debated as separate bodies. The National Council moved to Ross's yard, while the upper body remained in the house. Led by John Ridge, the National Committee quickly and unanimously voted to move the council, while the full-blooded Cherokees who held the majority in the National Council chose to stay in New Echota. But when the two bodies convened, and speeches were made, the resolve of the old-timers withered. Ross and Lowrey, who voted to meet in the Cherokee capital, were in a slim minority.

The chief took this defeat gracefully and offered to meet whenever and wherever the members of council chose. After some debate they picked Chattooga, in Alabama, on the western outskirts of the Cherokee Nation. Its only advantage seemed to be that it was far from the jurisdiction of the Georgia Guard.

The Cherokees were right to worry. In Milledgeville, the incoming Governor Wilson Lumpkin appealed to Jackson for help with the tribe. He told the president that "a crisis has arrived in our political affairs, in the Cherokee portion of Georgia, which cannot remain in its present attitude." Lumpkin said many Georgians feared their "domestics" might take note of how the Indians ignored the white man's law and get unsavory ideas. By raising the prospect of a slave rebellion Lumpkin was informing Jackson that he, even more than the previous governor, was intent on forcing the Cherokees out of Georgia for good.

Ross was in a foul mood. For more than a month nothing had gone well, and this fact spoiled the optimism he had built up on his speaking tour. It began with the disastrous fall council. At Chattooga, the council was forced to meet in dilapidated shacks, crammed onto coarse benches in front of rude pulpits. There hardly could have been a worse setting to debate the tribe's situation. They suffered through the elements in a barren field while their great modern city sat deserted. The Cherokees were regressing, and they were nearly broke. In his annual address Ross had been reduced to asking his tribe for money to keep the government running. Georgia had done this to them.

Since then, state and federal agents had roamed the nation at will, enlisting Indians to emigrate. These men used bribes and intimidation, but Ross told William Wirt that so far only "a few worthless white men" had succumbed. He bragged, somewhat unconvincingly, that his people would not follow such a course. Perhaps Jackson could send agents to enroll Georgians, he joked. Maybe they'd move west themselves and solve his problems.

By November 30 despair consumed Ross. He spent the morning at Head of Coosa with his brother Andrew preparing the paperwork for another delegation to Washington City. Andrew had been visiting his brother more often of late. Ross knew Andrew was in debt and suspected he wanted a loan but he could not turn his back on his brother. He allowed Andrew to help him as much as he was able, gave him what little money he could spare.

On this day, he had asked Andrew to help him gather supplies for the Washington delegation. The council felt it necessary to lobby Congress for relief. Ross knew it was pointless but he humored the council and appointed John Ridge, John Martin, and his nephew Coodey to make the trip. Although Andrew may have wanted to go, Ross did not trust him with such important business. His brother's commitment to the tribe was casual at best, and he had proved less than stellar at managing his own business affairs; he certainly could not be expected to debate government officials. Ross had little hope for success and feared that even if the tribe could reach an accord it would not be the end of their problems.

"It would be extreme folly to believe the Cherokees could again be duped into confidence of the good faith of the U.S. and take new shelter under the protection by settling on land to be assigned to them beyond the Mississippi," he had written to Wirt days earlier.

That afternoon Ross and his brother rode to Major Ridge's trading post to secure supplies for the delegation. When they were done, they paid their respects to the old chief, sitting in the parlor of his fine mansion, talking about nothing in particular. Ross had become cautious around his old mentor. The business with moving the council had left Ross defensive. For the first time he feared Major Ridge did not approve of his actions. They avoided unpleasant subjects until their conversation was interrupted by a rude man who called himself Harris, a North Carolinian who claimed to be looking for his stolen horse, and said that the thief had used Ross's ferry.

Ross tried to ignore the man but it seemed Harris turned up everywhere he went for the rest of the day—along the trail, at the ferry, and, finally, on the road to Coodey's house. It could not be a coincidence. The man acted too suspicious.

Earlier in the day Ross had volunteered a local Cherokee named Oonehutty to help Harris find the horse thief, and by the time the Ross brothers next saw them it appeared they had their man. Harris claimed that a Mr. Looney had stolen his horse. That piqued Ross's curiosity and he began to ask questions. Looney seemed nervous; Harris was evasive. Finally, the men dropped back on the trail.

Andrew spotted him first. Harris had gotten off his horse and crouched beside a tree, his rifle pointed directly at John Ross. As Andrew yelled for his brother to watch out, Harris cocked the gun and spoke.

"Ross I have been for a long time wanting to kill you, and I'll be damned if I don't now do it."

The shot reported as Ross turned his horse and rode off into the woods. He looked back and saw Andrew coming up behind him just as he heard the second shot. They turned off the trail, hoping to lose the men, and circled back to Head of Coosa late that night.

The next day Ross learned that Oonehutty had saved his life. The Cherokee had wrestled the gun away from Harris after he fired the second shot. Oonehutty was slightly injured in the brawl but Harris got away.

Ross said little of the shooting that day as he escorted his delegation to Gainesville. Boudinot would pester the chief for two months before he wrote an account of the incident for the *Phoenix*. When he did, Ross was overly nonchalant, although privately the attack must have worried him a great deal.

He did not know the man, had never seen him before, and did not believe this Harris had been trying to settle a personal grudge. Most likely, Ross knew, someone had sent him, probably Georgia politicians or perhaps even Old Mad Jackson. But it was a third alternative that worried him most. Harris could have been hired by someone in the tribe, an Indian who believed Ross had become an obstacle. That concerned Ross more than any danger to his own life.

He no longer knew who to trust.

Part III

The Trail of Tears by Elizabeth James, 1939.
Illustration courtesy of the Oklahoma Historical Society Research Division.

NINE

Turning Point

On January 26, 1832, the learned men and women of New York City braved a storm of ice and snow to hear the sad plight of the Cherokee Nation. They gathered at Clinton Hall, a grand new building at Nassau and Beekman streets that was becoming a base of the city's intellectual set, home of the Mercantile Library and, soon, the University of the City of New York. One local newspaper noted that, given the weather, the program was "more fully attended than we had any reason to expect." The draw that evening was two Indians, Elias Boudinot and John Ridge, who were on a speaking tour to raise awareness—and money—for their tribe. These well-spoken young Cherokees told an amazing story, and the people of New York were enchanted.

Although Boudinot spoke first and explained their mission, it was Ridge who made the stronger impression. He told a sad tale of broken deals and bribery, trickery and abuse suffered by his people, the arrest of the missionaries, and the ongoing efforts by Georgia to steal their land—things that seemed quite foreign to the progressive men and women in the audience.

"You asked us to throw off the hunter and warrior state: we did so. You asked us to form a republican government: we did so—adopting your own as a model. You asked us to cultivate the earth, and learn the mechanic arts: we did so. You asked us to learn to read: we did so. You asked us to cast away our idols and worship your God: we did so."

The New Yorkers were so touched by the tribe's tales of woe that Ridge and Boudinot were convinced to remain in the city long enough to give their presentation a second time. The *Commercial Advertiser* suggested Ridge did not know the power of his speech to "stir men's blood." By the time he finished speaking that first night, one reporter said, there was neither one unmoved heart nor a single eye that did not glisten with tears of pity. There were still some people who recognized injustice when they heard it. Ridge and Boudinot left the city with $800 in donations and more than six thousand names on a petition to Congress.

The speaking tour had been a spontaneous idea, born of frustration. Ridge had originally set out for Washington on a diplomatic mission. But the trip had been a waste of time. Secretary of War Lewis Cass refused to let him talk with the president, said Jackson would not intervene. The only way the tribe could save itself further embarrassment was to move far away from Georgia. Jackson wouldn't even give Ridge an audience this time and left the dirty work to an underling.

"Your people," Cass told him, "are not in a condition to resist."

As cold as his words were, Cass was not without a measure of sympathy. He explained that an ongoing dispute with Georgia could result only in "incalculable injury" to the tribe.

Ridge was defiant, going so far as to publicly call the president "a chicken snake." But he had a growing fear Cass was right, and that prospect made Ridge sick. He had spoken with some western Cherokee chiefs visiting the city and they told him all the tribe's land beyond the Mississippi amounted to barely enough for half the Indians still residing in the East. Ridge did not know enough not to believe them. He feared thousands of Cherokees might end up homeless.

Ridge was quickly learning the duplicitous nature of Washington politics, much as Ross already had discovered. Ridge was shocked to hear that the president had denounced South Carolina nullification weeks earlier while standing in Brown's Indian Queen boardinghouse, the very hotel where the delegation was lodged. The idea of Jackson condemning one state for flaunting federal law while aiding Georgia's effort to do the same was, Ridge said, "nefarious hypocrisy."

When Boudinot stopped in the city on his way to a gathering of newspaper editors in Philadelphia, he and Ridge devised the plan for a speaking tour. They would visit all the large cities in the East and "awaken American citizens" to the crisis facing the Cherokees. Both had spent years in northern states and understood New Englanders well. Such a tour might allow them to raise money for their legal bills and the tribe's subsistence. Ridge realized he could do no worse in New England than he had done in Washington and rode out of town with his cousin.

In Philadelphia Ridge met with Thomas L. McKenney, the former head of the department of Indian Affairs in Washington. McKenney had broken with Jackson over his Indian policy and planned to write a major history of the North American tribes. The old bureaucrat offered to "bury the hatchet" and publish pro-Cherokee letters in various northern newspapers. In return, he asked only for a sketch of Sequoyah's life to include in his book. Ridge was impressed. When he finally wrote to John Ross, on January 13, informing him of the plan to raise money, he declared without realizing the irony that McKenney was "apparently as strong a friend as we have."

After two presentations at Clinton Hall in January Ridge and Boudinot were suddenly in high demand. In February, their audience at New Haven filled "every slip, aisle, nook and corner, both floor and gallery" in the Center Church. There, they repeated their story, emphasizing how Washington, Adams, and Jefferson had promised to leave their land alone, only to have this new generation of politicians threaten to take it away.

The *New Haven Religious Intelligencer* wrote a sympathetic article about the Cherokees, describing Ridge as "rather tall and slender . . . with a profusion of black hair, a shade less swarthy and with less prominence of the cheek bones than our western Indians." In a soft voice, Ridge told the assembly he was unashamed of his race, but sorry to tell of the evils of the white men in Washington. The Connecticut audience drafted a memorial to Congress on the spot. Ridge did not mention he had taken his bride from the state, recalling the less than approving reaction his wedding to Sarah had received. Even folks up north had limits.

By early March they had raised $2,700 for the tribe, even though Boudinot took ill and had to cancel plans to speak at Salem and Newburyport, Massachusetts. He and Ridge took refuge with the American Board of Missionaries in Boston and eventually delivered another presentation at the Old South Church. They might have continued on, but one afternoon a man came into the mission office and asked if Ridge and Boudinot had prepared for bad news out of Washington.

"No," Ridge said, "we are not prepared."

Braced for yet another setback, the two Cherokees were confused when the man broke into a wide smile. The Supreme Court, he said, had ruled in favor of the missionaries in Georgia. Ridge and Boudinot were so excited they hastily packed and set out in the snow for the capital.

The U.S. Supreme Court heard the first of three days of oral arguments in *Worcester v. Georgia* on February 20, 1832. William Wirt had worked throughout the winter on his case, relying heavily on his associate John Sergeant. A rising star in Washington, Sergeant had just been named Henry Clay's running mate in the upcoming presidential race. There could hardly have been a better legal team.

Worcester was a defense of United States citizens who had been detained under Georgia's Indian laws, and there was no question the Supreme Court had jurisdiction this time. Wirt hoped a focus on U.S. citizens would provide enough political cover for John Marshall to issue an opinion on whether Georgia's law, which had been used to imprison the missionaries, violated federal policy, specifically, the tribe's treaties. A verdict in favor of the missionaries would be, by extension, a victory for the Cherokees.

Wirt was ill and absent from the courtroom for much of the trial and Sergeant handled most of the arguments. He wisely contested the case on the grounds of federalism, Marshall's first concern. Georgia had passed laws that conflicted with federal statutes, Sergeant said, and violated treaties ratified by the United States Congress. When he mentioned the Cherokees, he referred to them by Marshall's own definition of the tribe, a "domestic, dependent nation." Sergeant was playing to his audience.

Georgia had once again not bothered to put up a defense. Wilson Lumpkin, the state's new governor—who, as a congressman, had written much of the removal bill—believed there was no need to send his lawyers to Washington. The state had won its last case without representation and believed Marshall would be no braver this time. But Lumpkin overestimated his own power. Georgia's flagrant disdain for the Supreme Court infuriated Marshall and emboldened the chief justice to assert his own authority. He would not let states' rights undermine his court.

It took little more than a week for Marshall to issue his opinion, and when he did it was a powerful statement in defense of Indian rights. On March 3, the Supreme Court ruled that Georgia's arrest of the missionaries was unconstitutional, as were its attempts to govern the Cherokee Nation. Marshall could have taken the safe route and ruled only on the arrest of Worcester and Butler, but he chose to flex the court's muscles and remind Congress of its power as the law of the land. The chief justice wrote that the state had no right to extend its laws over Indian nations, which had "always been considered as distinct, independent political communities, retaining their original natural rights, as the undisputed possessors of the soil."

The Cherokee Nation, he noted, had been recognized in more than a dozen treaties with the United States. The treaties of Holston and Hopewell guaranteed the tribe the right to self-government. The discovery and settlement of Indian land by Europeans in no way suggested conquest, as southern politicians had claimed. Georgia had violated not only federal law but the political rights of the Indians. The Cherokees were a nation, Marshall said, recognized by the government and—until recently—the state of Georgia.

The federal laws took precedence, the court declared, and the United States had the authority to protect the Indian tribes.

"Protection," Marshall wrote, "does not imply the destruction of the protected."

The Supreme Court decision went far beyond what John Ross had hoped. The court had upheld the Cherokees' legal and political rights, and its decision could not have come at a better time. Ross had nearly lost hope that winter. When he heard about the ruling he wrote a brief note to Martin and Coodey in Washington recounting the mood in the Cherokee country.

"Our adversaries are generally down in the mouth—there are great rejoicings throughout the nation on the decision of the Supreme Court upon the Cherokee case. Traitors and internal enemies are seeking places where to hide their heads."

Ross's celebration was premature, however. When the court's ruling reached Milledgeville, Lumpkin was defiant and signaled that he had no intention of obeying John Marshall. He announced publicly that he would hang Worcester and Butler before he would let them go.

John Ridge returned to Washington in April. The Supreme Court decision had revived his flagging spirits and, like Ross, he felt the tribe was well on its way toward independence. But when he checked into Brown's Indian Queen Hotel he learned little had changed. Despite the court ruling, Lewis Cass continued to push for a removal treaty. Sympathetic congressmen said there was little they could do. They advised the Cherokees to get the best deal they could and move on. Jackson had made it clear that the court held no sway over him. Newspapers reported that when the president heard about the ruling, he said, "John Marshall has made his decision. Now let him enforce it if he can." It was a bit of journalistic embellishment that played to the president's renegade nature. In fact, Jackson had said something far more chilling. He had declared the decision "stillborn."

John Ridge soon learned the same thing: everyone he spoke to said that Georgia would not give in and that the federal government would not give up. Frustrated, Ridge one day marched into Lewis Cass's office to demand the government stop its efforts to move his tribe. But Cass told Ridge that he was out of touch. Cass claimed many Cherokees were despondent and ready to emigrate. The source of this intelligence was John Walker Jr., the son of Ross's onetime attacker. Walker had tried to make his own deal, promising that the Cherokees in Tennessee and North Carolina would sign a treaty. Cass informed Ridge that the president preferred to deal with the entire tribe but threatened to negotiate with the renegades if he must.

Ridge could hardly believe what he was hearing. He argued that the Senate would never ratify such a deal, that the government was bound by the Supreme Court decision. Had Marshall not ruled the tribe had been guaranteed a right to its land? Cass told him that he was quibbling, and assured him the Cherokees would not "regain their rights." Ridge demanded to see the president.

That meeting went no better. Jackson was cordial but cold. In their short encounter, Ridge was direct. He asked if the Supreme Court ruling would be enforced and Jackson told him it would not. No matter what Marshall's ruling implied, Jackson said, the tribe had no hope of keeping its land. Georgia intended to take it and he refused to stand in the way. It was over.

The president suggested Ridge himself must lead his tribe through this difficult time, a transparent attempt to stoke the young man's ambition and undermine Ross. Jackson told Ridge to go home and persuade the Cherokees, for their own good, that the fight was finished. It was a request he never would have made to Ross. But then, the president thought the young Ridge more susceptible to threats, easier to persuade than the chief.

"Advise them that their only hope of relief is in abandoning their country and removing to the west," Jackson said.

Ridge made no promises. Although Jackson frightened him, Ridge maintained his composure—he would not allow the president to see that fear—and reiterated the tribe's tired position. He later told his cousin Stand Watie that to save the tribe "it will, I fear, be first necessary to cut down this Snake's head and throw it down in the dust." It was a hollow threat. Even the younger Ridge knew his people were no match for the United States and its military.

Ridge said nothing about this realization, but Jackson saw it in his eyes. The president later told his friend John Coffee that Ridge now realized "it is better for them to treat and move."

Jackson was right. It seemed every day brought another setback, and Ridge fell deeper into despair. Congress would not intervene, Georgia would not release the missionaries, and Jackson would not rest until the tribe had left the South. Ridge had looked in the president's eyes too—and he knew there was nothing he could do to change Jackson's mind. Ridge was not nearly as stubborn as Ross; he recognized the political reality. Even the missionary David Greene had sent him a letter recommending Ridge give up his fight.

"It makes me weep to think of it, but if your friends in Congress think all further efforts in your behalf will be useless . . . you must make the best terms you can and go."

It would be the most difficult decision of his life. Ridge knew once he started down the path to removal, there would be no turning back. He had no desire to give up but, after weeks of analyzing the situation, Ridge ultimately concluded there was no other way. If the Supreme Court could not stop the president, no one could. Ridge could imagine how the situation might unfold: Georgia would continue its aggression until violence erupted. And then the Cherokees would be killed, for his people could not hold off the white men's army. John Ridge was beginning to think like a leader, albeit one with a message no Cherokee wanted to hear. But Ridge was certain he knew what would come, and he could not let that happen. He began to lay the groundwork for surrender.

As April passed, Ridge began to hint he was open to negotiating, while still denying it publicly. On the street in Washington, where spring had finally thawed the city, Martin and Coodey ran into General Daniel Newnan, a congressman from Georgia. They told him—he later claimed—the delegation had "consented to recommend to their people to make a treaty with the government." When Newnan gave an account of his conversation to a Washington newspaper, Ridge was forced to deny it. "There is not the least ground for any such suggestion," he told the *National Intelligencer* in a letter that was, curiously, signed with his Cherokee name: Skah-Tle-Loh-Skee. He may have felt the need to bolster his Cherokee credentials.

A week later Ridge and the others met with Cass to hear the specifics of the treaty offered by the government. The secretary promised the Cherokees fertile ground, near the tribe's western band, and the authority to establish their own government. The United States would pay the tribe's bills for a year and then pay an annuity for its land in Georgia, Tennessee, and North Carolina. The government would even compensate the Cherokees for the buildings at New Echota. It was, Cass assured them, a generous offer. Ridge was polite but declined to take the treaty to the tribe. He feared that if he even broached the subject he would be killed on the spot.

In mid-May Ridge, Martin, and Coodey left Washington. Ridge had made his decision but knew he could not present such an opinion to John Ross or the General Council. The chief was headstrong and, emboldened by his court victory, would never consider a retreat. But, Ridge knew, Ross had not seen the look in Jackson's eyes, had not heard the determination in his voice. Somewhere along the trail leading to his home, high in the mountains of Virginia, Ridge decided he must go to his father. He would listen without prejudice. He would know what they should do.

John Ridge had realized that if he could not convince his father he was right he would never be able to convince anyone.

The surveyors arrived in April. More than five hundred men marched through Cherokee towns and villages, planting stakes as they divided the land into lots of two hundred acres—forty acres in the gold country. They camped where they wanted, trampling through gardens and town squares. It was meant to be an intimidating sight and it was. The state of Georgia was subdividing the Cherokee Nation.

The state planned to distribute the land through a lottery system. There was no schedule for this land giveaway; settlers were told it might take place in the fall, or perhaps even the next year. In truth, Wilson Lumpkin had not thought that far ahead. He ordered the survey teams into the Cherokee country before he was actually ready simply because he wanted to send a message: he would not only ignore the Supreme Court ruling but openly defy it.

Stand Watie, who was acting editor of the *Phoenix* during his brother Elias's absence, tried to reassure his worried tribesmen by pointing out they had the law on their side. He noted that each of the five hundred and more men trespassing through the nation risked fines of $1,000 and a year in prison for illegally setting boundaries on land that was not their own. The president of the United States even had the authority to use military force to stop them, he slyly noted.

"It is surprising to see men of good and liberal feelings, & who would no doubt feel highly indignant were they charged with dishonest conduct towards an individual in his private capacity, deliberately invading the rights of thousands of their defenseless fellow beings, in open violation of the law," Watie wrote.

He even took to quoting the Bible in the paper: "Remove not the old land mark; and enter not the field of the fatherless; for their redeemer is mighty; He shall plead their cause with thee."

In May, Elias Boudinot directed his brother to reprint a Washington newspaper article that claimed the delegation had tried to sell the tribe's land. The *Phoenix* also ran the article that included Ridge's denial, but without any reassuring editorial comment attached to it, which was otherwise a common practice. To make matters worse, Watie reported that "a proposition of a treaty will be sent on to the Principal Chief in a few days from the War Department."

It's unclear whether Boudinot meant to brace the tribe for bad news or was testing the waters to see how such an idea would be received. Ridge may have revealed his recent change of heart to his cousin, one of the few men he trusted. If Boudinot was simply hoping to see what reaction the story got, he did not have to wait long to find out. When the new issue of the *Phoenix* was distributed, the Cherokee chiefs were enraged.

Solely on the basis of one newspaper article, the General Council branded Ridge, Martin, and Coodey traitors and insisted they be put on trial. It did not matter that these men were relatives and close associates of

Ross—the council demanded justice. Men were sent out to find the delegates, with orders to bring them to New Echota as soon as they crossed into Cherokee country. The charges were so upsetting that the council did not stop to think about the implications of setting in motion the possible execution of both Major Ridge's son and the chief's nephew. This was treason.

John Ross did not contradict the council's demands because he knew it would only make matters worse. He was also too sophisticated to be flustered by a single newspaper article. Ross suspected that Newnan was referring to John Walker—Ridge had informed Ross of the renegade Cherokee's dealings in a letter. But the chief was livid that Boudinot had chosen to publish the inflammatory article in the first place. For four years Ross had worked closely with the editor, never exerting complete editorial control but sometimes suggesting which stories should be included, and which should not. When Boudinot had demanded more pay as editor, and the council refused, Ross had paid him out of his own pocket. *Is this how loyalty is repaid?* Boudinot knew better than to print such sensational stories, Ross thought, especially without consulting him.

Ross feared that Boudinot had put the delegation in danger or, worse, had his own agenda. He had felt the first kick of rebellion in Boudinot when the editor stood with the Ridges in favor of changing the location of the council, but now he had crossed the line. In a statement printed in the *Phoenix,* Ross publicly chastised Boudinot. He assured the tribe there were no treaty negotiations and claimed the report from Newnan was "well calculated to mislead the public mind." He said it was wrong to cast prejudicial light on members of the delegation until they were able to vindicate themselves. His measured argument did little to calm the excited council. But the men were not arrested when they returned home.

By early June Ross began to fear there was some truth to Newnan's claims. He had interviewed Ridge, Martin, and Coodey separately upon their return, and each told him the same story: they had made no progress, the government was determined to get a treaty, and their friends in Congress could not help. None of them admitted how far they had strayed from their original mission, and they all discounted Newnan's account. Ross was confused by the story and the tepid reaction to the Supreme Court decision. He did not understand it all but soon would.

A week later, Elisha Chester arrived at Head of Coosa with a message from the president. Jackson wanted a removal treaty and was prepared to send negotiators to New Echota that summer. Ross insisted there had been some mistake. The tribe won its case in the Supreme Court, he told new Indian Affairs commissioner, and had legal standing from the highest authority to remain in their homes. He said that not only would he not discuss a treaty, he demanded the president obey the law and protect the Cherokees from the state of Georgia.

Chester seemed genuinely surprised by the chief's response. He politely explained that he had come, in part, on the advice of the tribe's friends in Congress. Ross eventually recognized the confusion in Chester's reaction: he was a man who had expected an entirely different response. And Ross had to wonder why.

It was not an easy conversation for John Ridge. He sat in the darkened parlor of his father's sprawling house, recounting all that he had learned on his trip. He was much more forthright than he had been with Ross but still he found it difficult to reveal his true feelings. For decades, his father had been one of the great defenders of the Cherokee land—he'd fought, even killed, those who tried to take it. No one, not even Ross, felt the same attachment to the Cherokee country that Major Ridge did. And now his son was about to recommend they abandon it. He did not know how to begin.

Ridge underestimated his father. Major Ridge understood even before his son spoke; he had read the trouble on his boy's haggard face when he'd arrived. In some ways, the old man must have felt he was looking in a mirror. He had not been elated by the Supreme Court decision. While Ross had felt vindicated, Major Ridge knew the ruling was little more than the hollow words of white politicians. How many promises had the tribe heard over the years, and how many had been broken? Ridge was not so taken by the courts of the white men and their sense of justice.

Major Ridge judged the condition of his people by their suffering, and he knew the situation to be far worse than anyone else dared admit. While white men divided up their land for sale, the Cherokees were reduced to attending fireside parties to celebrate a court decision most of them did not even understand. John Ridge had worried that his conclusions would disappoint his father, even shame him. But Major Ridge was in some ways proud that his son had reached a difficult conclusion and was brave enough to share it with him. He had long hoped John would become a great leader of the tribe, and at last Ridge believed that the time was drawing near.

For weeks after their conversation the old chief traveled the nation talking to enrolling agents, and he learned nothing to contradict all that his son had told him. But Major Ridge did not need to see a great deal of proof. If there was one thing the old man loved more than the Cherokee land, it was the Cherokee people. And he too had come to believe—as his son did—the only way to save the tribe was to give up its land. Although the Ridges would deny it for a long time, the son convinced the father to support removal that day in his house beside the Coosa.

Some Cherokees began moving west that spring. They told enrolling agents their chiefs had filled them with false hopes, and they no longer believed the tribe could protect them. The rumors of a coming treaty prompted some Indians to make deals with the commissioners. Despite their denials, many men began to whisper that Boudinot and the Ridges had been bribed, that it was only a matter of time before the white men persuaded the rest of the council to go along.

John Ross was so disturbed by the signs of Cherokee resignation that he set out on another speaking tour and announced July 19 would be a day of fasting and prayer. Rather than comfort the tribe, it only fueled speculation that something was amiss. To many, Ross seemed unsure of himself.

It was not only the common Cherokees who worried; members of the council were unsettled too. They demanded a report from the Washington delegation, unconvinced by Ross's assurances that there had been no negotiations. On Tuesday, July 3, Ross gathered the chiefs at Head of Coosa to plan a special council. John Ridge pushed for them to meet at New Echota, contradicting his earlier position. Ross overruled him and would not allow a vote. He also had changed his mind. Now he feared New Echota held too many distractions, and the Georgia Guard would undermine his ability to maintain control of his increasingly fractured tribe.

The Cherokees would not return to the remote village at Chattooga; it was too distant and uninviting. They decided instead to meet in Tennessee, home to the tribe's great capitals of the past. For their new council grounds, they chose a narrow valley just across the state line, a flat expanse of field at the base of a forested ridge that stood some two hundred feet high.

Bordered by the mountain and a dense forest, it was a quiet, beautiful piece of land, comfortable and defensible. No one could sneak up on the tribe at Red Clay, as they called their new village. Ross sent workers to build a meeting shed for the council at the foot of the mountain, near a spring that provided an endless supply of cool drinking water. In many ways, a few Cherokees noted, it would have made a better capital for the tribe than New Echota. And they might have avoided a lot of trouble.

A generation earlier, Ridge, Martin, and Coodey might have been killed on the spot. When the council met at Red Clay in late July the delegation delivered a brutally honest assessment of the tribe's predicament. They relayed the threats of Jackson and the advice of missionaries and friendly members of Congress. Ridge was smart enough to stop just short of recommending the tribe emigrate, but his opinion came through clearly. Most of the old chiefs were too shocked to say anything. Through Ross's influence, however, the council did not put the men on trial.

Although he tried to protect the Ridges, Ross could not abide their dissension. He had never had to deal with such flagrant mutiny from his inner circle. And now it had all happened so fast. He decided to post on a tree near the shed a copy of the Newnan report, which suggested these men were renegades, talking out of turn, and that their efforts had undermined the efforts to hold Cherokee land.

It was a turning point for Ross. In all his years, he had been unwaveringly honest and open about his dealings. But now he feared a stark assessment of the tribe's position might lead to a rash decision that could not be undone. And he would not allow that, not while there was still a chance they might keep their tribal land. Nor would he allow Boudinot to publish an account of the delegation's report in the *Phoenix*. But Boudinot, still upset by Ross's public reprimand earlier, would not be complicit in any censorship. He quit.

Boudinot made a great show of relinquishing his position. He had his resignation letter read to the council and two hundred other Cherokees at Red Clay on August 1. He urged the tribe to reconsider its staunch opposition to a treaty before it was too late, reiterating his cousin's message in stronger terms, and confirming all the rumors circulating through the Cherokee Nation. He became the first member of the Ridge family to publicly oppose Ross.

"I do conscientiously believe it to be the duty of every citizen to reflect upon the dangers with which we are surrounded," Boudinot wrote, "to view the darkness which seems to live before our people—our prospects, and the evils with which we are threatened; to talk over all these matters, and, if possible, come to some definite and satisfactory conclusion, while there is time, as to what ought to be done in the last alternative. I could not consent to be the conductor of the paper without having the right and privilege of discussing these important matters."

Boudinot's resignation put Ross in the unfamiliar position of defending himself before the council. The next day, he argued the editor's decision to print views so divergent from that of tribal leaders—and therefore the tribe—could lead only to confusion and problems. Ross reminded the chiefs their rights had been affirmed by the Supreme Court, and said that the federal government would eventually live up to its obligation. The truth, Ross said, would continue to be printed in the *Phoenix,* but he would not allow it to become an outlet for propaganda.

"The toleration of diversified views to the columns . . . would not fail to create fermentation and confusion among our citizens," said the chief, "and in the end prove injurious to the welfare of the nation. The love of our country and people demands unity of sentiment and action for the good of all."

It was not an entirely convincing argument. The wiser Cherokees could sense a tinge of desperation in Ross.

Ross appointed his brother-in-law Elijah Hicks to replace Boudinot, a move that allowed him to keep the *Phoenix* completely under his control. And he wasted little time making use of his familial ties, asking Hicks not to print Elisha Chester's remarks at Red Clay that summer.

The commissioner had observed the Cherokees at work for more than a week while awaiting a turn to speak, and he came away with some interesting and accurate conclusions. Chester would later report to Lewis Cass that it appeared some of the mixed-blood and educated Cherokees had softened their views on emigration, although none would publicly admit this. But the full-blooded Cherokees remained adamantly opposed to removal, and Chester believed Ross was pandering to those Indians to remain in power.

Ross ignored Chester as long as he could, but the council finally insisted on hearing his message. Chester, however, did not put his insights to good use. In his opening remarks he could not have upset the council more had he tried. He noted the president "has recently been informed of a change of heart . . . on the subject of removal." From there, the meeting turned to disaster. He outlined an offer identical to the one proposed to Ridge and even subtly threatened the tribe.

"Shut your eyes, I entreat you, to bad counsels, if any should be offered you," Chester said. "Whatever may be told you, it is impossible you can remain here. . . . And if you persist in the effort the time of regret will come, I am afraid, after the most injury to yourself."

The Cherokees did not respond well to threats. They immediately dismissed Chester, sending him back to Washington with a letter to Cass stating their opposition on removal and requesting federal troops to protect them from Georgia's continued harassment. The chiefs did not realize how preposterous their demands must have seemed to the agent. They were in no position to make ultimatums. They could not even meet in their own capital.

If any members of the council had begun to have doubts they would not dare voice them for fear of being in the minority. The pressure to continue fighting for their land was so unanimous that even the Ridges signed the document. Major Ridge realized change came slowly to the Cherokee Nation, and in order to maintain any credibility for the coming debate he could not openly rebel. John Ridge likely signed because his father told him to, or he feared what might happen if he did not.

It was difficult for Major Ridge to remain silent as he watched John Ross make what he considered a series of mistakes. Ridge had always believed Ross had the tribe's best interests at heart, but he was beginning to question Ross's motives. The chief appeared more stridently opposed to a treaty then even the full-blooded Cherokees, and that made little sense to Ridge. An educated man should realize how precarious the tribe's situation had become. He feared Ross had become accustomed to power. For proof, there was the business of the election.

The Cherokee constitution mandated elections every four years, and the Indians were scheduled to cast ballots for a new council that summer. But some members of the General Council suggested they postpone the election for fear of interference from Georgia, and for the sake of not changing leadership during troubled times. A few suspected it was simply a ruse to allow the current chiefs to hold their seats. The Ridges believed Ross had orchestrated the postponement to avoid an election that might pit him against John Ridge. The Cherokees did ultimately decide to wait. John Ross would continue as principal chief indefinitely.

Heavy rains kept Ross sequestered at Head of Coosa through September and into the first week of October, delaying the start of the fall council. The Cherokees returned to Red Clay on October 8, deciding the new camp would serve as their temporary capital until the trouble with Georgia passed. Elisha Chester attended the meeting again, this time with Indian agent Hugh Montgomery. Both men avoided the Ridges for fear of causing them more problems. They had little else to do, however. Most of the Cherokees kept to themselves, huddled under lean-to sheds, stoking fires, and waiting for the rain to pass. Fat clouds and a thick mist hovered over the hillside, weather that matched the tribe's mood. No one cared to hear anything from the commissioner; nor did Ross, who finally arrived on October 10.

Ross had come prepared to combat the Ridges' whisper campaign for a treaty and used his anger to elevate his rhetoric beyond its usual bureaucratic pitch. In the middle of his usually laborious annual address, Ross offered a fiery repudiation of removal and the land beyond the Mississippi. It was a stark warning to anyone who thought life would be better on the plains.

"Here then is a country, in extent, agreeable to the report of the surveyor, six hundred miles long and two hundred miles wide, bordering on the States of Missouri and the Territory of Arkansas spreading over an extensive prairie badly watered and only skirted on the margin of water courses and poor ridges with the corpses of wood," he said.

There, Ross continued, the Cherokees would mingle with civilized and uncivilized tribes alike and eventually be governed by white rulers. All of the tribe's current benefits, all its existing treaties, would be extinguished. For any Indian who casually wondered if life would be better in the West, Ross painted a frightening portrait.

As Montgomery listened to these horror stories, he wondered if Ross actually had the support of the tribe, or only the illusion of it. He knew the Ridges no longer agreed with Ross and suspected others felt the same way. The Indian agent, who did not realize the speech was out of character for Ross, came to believe the chief might be a demagogue. He later told his bosses in Washington that Ross ruled the tribe as a tyrant who did not allow dissension. It was an unfair assessment but clearly the chief had made mistakes. He could have used the Ridges to debate the merits of removal, to prepare the tribe for unhappy possibilities. At that point, though, Ross was unwilling to accept the possibility. He did not plan to lose.

While Ross delivered his sermon Montgomery ducked out of the council shed and told his interpreter to mingle with the Cherokees. Try to discern, he said, how the Indians really felt. For several days the man lingered at the edge of council fires and strolled between sleeping huts, eavesdropping on conversations and engaging what few Indians would talk to him.

The interpreter offered Montgomery an impression of a tribe in turmoil. A growing number of the mixed-bloods and white men in Indian families were indeed willing to consider removal. They had tired of the unending tension with the state of Georgia and the federal government.

A few believed Ross hopelessly naive or blind to the truth, but they would never admit such feelings publicly. They still respected their chief. The vast majority of the Cherokees, however—the full-blooded Indians who controlled the tribe—were completely opposed to moving west. And, the interpreter said, those Indians still believed that John Ross could do no wrong.

In the final days of the council, John Ridge decided he could wait no longer. He suggested that a new delegation travel to Washington and learn more about the proposed treaty. It would do no harm, he argued, and the tribe might learn useful information from such talks. As a peace offering, Ridge even suggested Ross accompany the men to ensure the tribe's interests were protected. At first, his suggestion seemed to do nothing except solidify the growing opinion that he favored emigration. Yet, tellingly, the proposal did not provoke a violent reaction.

The Cherokees voted against Ridge's proposal but ultimately decided to send another delegation to the capital. The group was stacked with anti-treaty Cherokees and Ross was asked to accompany them. Ridge considered it a minor victory. Ross was not stupid; Ridge believed once the chief talked to Lewis Cass and Jackson he would come to the conclusion that the tribe must make a deal. If not, it would prove Ross was ignoring reality.

Montgomery was also encouraged. The reconnaissance of his interpreter had convinced him it was futile to deal with the tribe's factions. Ross was the key. Only Ross, Montgomery knew, could persuade the tribe to abandon Georgia. If Cass could convince the Cherokee chief he had no hope of winning, it could change the entire situation. On October 31, 1832, Montgomery sent a letter of advice to the secretary of war.

"If . . . the present delegation, and particularly John Ross, can be brought over, I apprehend but little difficulty with the balance of the half breeds," Montgomery suggested, "and then the great mass of the Indians will follow, as a matter of course."

TEN

The Schemes of Traitors

John Ross had been in Washington nearly a month when he learned that John Walker was on his way to negotiate a Cherokee removal treaty with President Jackson. The news came from John Ridge, in a long letter that made no mention of the growing animosity between them. Ridge reported that Walker had tried to recruit several Indians to his cause, including Elias Boudinot. But Ridge claimed the renegade Cherokee found no support from within the tribe.

"General Jackson did urge to have Delegation composed of those who had lost all hope of the reestablishment of our nation to face you at Washington in order as he tho't to drive a bargain, I can have now no doubt," Ridge wrote. "But the aforesaid Gentlemen are too high-minded, patriotic, & honorable to acknowledge Jack Walker as a leader there is also no doubt."

Ross thought it was a suspicious note. Ridge praised his abilities as a statesman and promised he had kept his own feelings on removal private, so as not to extinguish the "high hopes" of others in the tribe. He urged the chief to consult the best minds in Washington and to remember that the "well being of the whole people" was his responsibility. If the tribe could not continue as a nation in Georgia, he added, "I hope we shall attempt to establish it somewhere else!"

It seemed to be a peace offering but, in fact, it may have been a warning. Ridge knew Ross would get no better reception in Washington than he had. He believed the chief would soon realize their situation was hopeless and let go of his stubborn optimism, and Ridge wanted to help him reach that conclusion. It was the unspoken message of the letter. Ridge was giving Ross one more chance to come around.

Although he would not admit it, perhaps not even to himself, Ross could hardly disagree with Ridge's assessment of the mood in the capital. For weeks, he and Lewis Cass had argued back and forth, each man repeating himself to the point of monotony—the same tired debate that had dragged on for years. Ross was too stubborn to give in but, unconsciously, he was coming to accept reality. Most days, he refused to make the ten-minute walk down Pennsylvania Avenue from Brown's Hotel to Capitol Hill. He knew that it was pointless, that Congress would not help him.

For more than three years the Cherokees had been arguing only with themselves. In that time, the federal government had not changed its position in the slightest. Perhaps Ross kept trying because he believed it was his job to promote the agenda of his tribe's majority. Or maybe he could not grasp the concept of a government not keeping its word. Ross also had grown more obstinate over the years. Had he listened to the Ridges, debated them openly in the council, he might have nudged the Cherokees toward a voluntary removal. A generation earlier, nearly half the tribe had been ready to move. Now most full-blooded Cherokees would hear nothing of the idea. The Ridges believed Ross pandered to that constituency, but the truth might have been the opposite. Ross, who refused to bow down to the white man's rule, might have hardened the tribe against any thought of moving west.

Eventually Ross managed to get two meetings with Jackson. He would never give a full account of their talks but others who were there said words were exchanged that need not have been spoken. Jackson seemed interested only in the Cherokees' land in Georgia and Tennessee. When Ross asked why he did not demand the tribe's land in Alabama and North Carolina the president was vague. Jackson seemed not to care at all about Alabama and said the mountains of North Carolina held little value to white men. In fact, neither state had pressed him for removal nearly as hard as had Georgia and Tennessee.

The two men argued for half an hour, two warriors locked in a battle of words. Each deftly countered the other's arguments, neither willing to concede a point. Ross tried to use Jackson's own law against him—removal was a voluntary program, he noted, and the Cherokees would not volunteer to leave. Jackson, in turn, attempted to speak the language of Ross's business: money.

The president offered $2.5 million to the Cherokees if they would leave the South. When Ross didn't answer, Jackson thought he saw an opening. He upped the ante: $3 million, that is, if the tribe would move without government assistance.

Ross would not consider the offer and tried to turn the argument once again. "If you have so much money at your disposal," he said, "buy off the Georgia settlers and end this dispute."

Jackson quickly grew frustrated, weary of debating Ross. The chief could not be intimidated, like Ridge, could not be bluffed, could not be bought. It was a stalemate. Jackson knew the only sure way to win was to use military force. But he did not want the political complications that might arise from breaking his own law. Finally, the president used his last weapon: candor.

Jackson offered Ross an astute assessment of frontier politics. He explained that Georgia would not give up, that its militia would continue to arrest Cherokees until they forced a war in which the Indians would be hopelessly outmatched. Congress would not intervene and threaten the shaky union on behalf of an Indian tribe. Eventually, the president said, the Cherokees would be killed, and those who survived would fall under the state's laws.

It's hopeless, Jackson said.

Ross listened to the president's speech without any show of emotion, without any reaction. He could not help but hear the truth in Jackson's voice. These were not idle threats, he knew. But Ross would not admit this to Jackson, or perhaps even to himself. Even though he knew everything could come to pass just as the president predicted, he told himself he could not give up. Not yet.

Ross left Jackson's office that day with much on his mind. He could not deliver Jackson's message to his people. Vanity may have guided him; he did not want to admit he had failed. He may even have worried about being cast out as chief. Ross knew that if he were no longer chief, the Cherokees would turn to someone who might lead them into an unwinnable war, or they would simply give up and retreat to the West. Neither option was palatable to John Ross.

By the time Ross returned home in April of 1833 the tribe was on the verge of civil war. A small but increasingly vocal number of Indians had begun to side with the Ridges and talk openly of removal. The Cherokees called these malcontents the Treaty Party, while the loyalists distinguished themselves as the National Party. The division brought a new level of discord to the Cherokees.

The violence started in early April, when two Indians nearly killed each other in a field not far from Major Ridge's home. During a ballplay match, one Cherokee called John Fields a traitor and said he should be killed. After the game, the Indian who insulted Fields was attacked on a nearby road and beaten unconscious. His friends retaliated, jumping Fields and one of his associates at Lavender's store. Fields was stabbed but not hurt badly, while the other man was beaten with a ballplay stick. One of Ridge's slaves was injured when he tried to break up the brawl. The incident convinced Major Ridge that the rhetoric must be toned down before the Cherokees did more harm to themselves than Georgia or the United States could do.

Controlling these Indians would prove impossible. There were factions within the factions, each with a different leader and agenda, and alliances seemed to change daily. Even the former chief William Hicks struggled to regain control of the tribe. Hicks, who had gotten old and absentminded, still stewed over his election loss to John Ross. He felt he deserved to be principal chief. Hicks had initially joined the White Path rebellion, and later visited Governor Lumpkin to draw up a removal treaty. He may have thought he was saving the tribe, or he may have just been making a grab for power. The government's Indian agents had recognized Hicks's discontent and courted him, put grandiose ideas in his head.

At the same time, John Walker continued to pester Hugh Montgomery for money to lead a delegation to Washington so he could negotiate a treaty. Walker had dreams of becoming principal chief when the tribe relocated, and he had some influential allies, including Ross's own brother Andrew. The chief's youngest brother had fallen even deeper into debt and the idea of moving away and starting over may have appealed to him. The tribe had treated him no better than William Hicks, in his opinion. His judgeship had not lasted, and he felt his brother did not respect him. He had no great love for the tribe, unlike his brothers John and Lewis, and was intrigued by the idea of the bonus he might earn by brokering a deal for the tribe's removal. Andrew showed he had more savvy for rebellion than for business.

The National Party remained optimistic by clinging to rumors. John Vann claimed the United States would soon buy out Georgia's interest in Cherokee land, and others said members of Congress had urged them to continue their fight. There was no supporting evidence for these stories, but anyone who discounted them was branded a traitor. Walker told Montgomery much of this false hope had been spread by John Ross's own advisers.

Even if Ross had nothing to do with those rumors he had begun occasionally to mislead the tribe in order to maintain order. When the council met in May the chief was uncharacteristically vague. He conceded that the president would not intervene against Georgia, but he said Jackson's stand against nullification in South Carolina offered the tribe some hope. The president had declared the Constitution and U.S. law had jurisdiction over any individual state. That, Ross weakly claimed, was proof the administration would ultimately intervene to enforce their treaties. To bolster his argument he claimed that Elbert Herring, the U.S. commissioner for Indian

Affairs, was sending troops from Charleston to evict squatters from the "assailed parts of your country."

Some later said Ross seemed embarrassed while making his remarks, as if he had done something wrong. In truth, the chief knew he was being less than forthcoming. He claimed unnamed government officials had offered him $80,000 to make a treaty but told them nothing of Jackson's assessment of the situation. Ross justified this selective reporting as necessary for the good of the tribe. He worried that if the council realized he had accomplished nothing, this fact could strengthen support for this new Treaty Party. His closing remarks did little to boost anyone's spirits, however. He was too honest to promise a good outcome. He could not lie outright.

"Should it become necessary, I will in a subsequent communication, express my views in regard to our public affairs in more general terms," he concluded.

The Cherokees listened to their chief on the muddy floor of the open-air council shed at Red Clay, a setting that did little to reassure them. At New Echota, they had the luxury of ignoring bad weather from the comfort of their modern council house. Now, they were again at the mercy of the elements, and constantly reminded of the fact. This was not the civilized future they had once imagined.

No matter what Ross did, it seemed something or someone conspired against him. A few days after the chief's address, John Ridge told the council it was time to chart a new course. He was careful not to explicitly endorse removal but Ridge did his best to undermine Ross's credibility. Ridge had learned that Herring's promise of protection extended only to Cherokees in Tennessee and North Carolina and not Georgia. If he had hoped to portray Ross as a power-hungry liar, willing to tell the Cherokees anything to stay in office, his plan backfired. When Ridge revealed that he had written to Lewis Cass for clarification, many chiefs were offended he had gone over Ross's head. It made him seem too ambitious, as if he, not Ross, was hungry for power.

Ridge was not Ross's only problem; nearly his entire executive council had turned against him. The wiser Cherokees realized they were running out of options and the chances of holding their land became slimmer every day. Ross's refusal to admit this worried many of the tribe's most learned men. Some had come to believe he was dangerously misguided and feared his dedication to a lost cause could lead the Cherokees to ruin. These men secretly prepared a letter to the General Council, laying out these concerns and urging the members to reconsider their opposition to a treaty. Before this position paper was delivered to the council, however, William Shorey Coodey, Ross's nephew, gave a copy to the surprised chief.

The letter was a thinly veiled endorsement of removal signed by many of the most influential men in the nation—Major Ridge, Charles Vann, Elias Boudinot, John Walker Jr., William Hicks, and Coodey. For once, it seemed all the various factions had united. John Ridge had not signed the document, realizing perhaps he already had overstepped his bounds. The document was a stark assessment of the Cherokees' predicament and warned the council its present course would "not result in the restoration of those rights" that had been taken from the tribe.

"It must be obvious to you, that the affairs of this nation have been brought to a crisis never before known or anticipated by its citizens generally," the letter read. "And believing, as they do, that the preservation and perpetuation of the Cherokees, as a nation, should be the first and greatest object . . . they trust that those upon whom the confidence of the people have [sic] been bestowed, will prove themselves worthy of their nation, and capable of conducting its affairs as the exigencies of circumstances may require for the general welfare."

Ross was shocked. His closest advisers said the same thing Jackson had; it was as if they had been in the same room. They had his attention and, he realized, the upper hand. If all his advisers turned against him, the General Council—and the entire tribe—might lose faith in him, in their fight. In some ways the chief felt they were all traitors, but he knew better than to force their hand. He would handle the situation diplomatically. Ross begged the men not to publicize the letter until he'd had a chance to discuss it with them. Coodey convinced the others to agree.

The executive council crammed into a small cabin and argued with the chief for two days, their absence the source of many rumors around Red

Clay. Somehow, they managed to keep the subject of their discussions secret. It was hardly a fair debate, as the Ridges led the arguments against Ross. Ross had only George Lowrey, his assistant chief, on his side. Coodey and Ridge could not be persuaded to destroy the letter, but Ross finally convinced them to delay its release. If he had not made any progress with the federal government by the fall, Ross would present the letter to the General Council and lead the debate over its content. Neither side was entirely happy, but both walked away with reason for hope. The Treaty Party had finally forced a concession from Ross, and the chief had bought himself five months.

Ross had agreed to the deal partly out of political expediency, but he must have understood that the possibility of holding the tribe's land grew dimmer each day. His closest advisers had come to the same logical conclusion as had the president. And, much as he resisted the idea, he knew it was a fair assessment. Yet he also recognized that the General Council and his tribesmen were not ready to hear such a possibility stated outright. So when the council reconvened he offered several resolutions, one of which marked a strategic shift in his views.

Mixed with mundane position statements—one approving the Washington delegation's conduct, another declaring the secretary of war evasive and unresponsive to the tribe's questions—Ross included a resolution that raised the possibility of the Cherokees abandoning their homeland. The document objected to moving west of the Mississippi but added the caveat "without a more settled policy on the part of the General Government."

The resolution said if the president would intervene and stop the illegal actions of Georgia, the tribe would send a delegation to meet with Congress. If Congress ruled Georgia had the right of control over tribal land, the delegation "will come to immediate terms satisfactory to the Government." It was more of a concession than most Cherokees understood. By now Ross knew the Congress would not support his position. He was quietly preparing his people for the possibility of removal, even while he desperately searched for a way to avoid it.

Ross also slipped in a glimpse of his latest solution. The resolution said the tribe would not relocate on U.S. land if it came to that, but instead move far enough west to be beyond the reach of the white men. They considered Texas and Oregon territories as possibilities, and Ross even had thoughts of moving the Cherokees to Mexico. The council approved Ross's plan on a silent vote. No one particularly wanted to put his name on the document.

John Ridge believed the anonymous vote was a trick by Ross to appease the Treaty Party without leaving any proof he had contradicted his public statements. After the resolution passed, Ridge demanded it be made a matter of record and published for all Cherokees to read. The council agreed. But a few moments later, while Ridge was distracted by the sight of his father speaking in a nearby grove, Judge Taylor took the resolutions from the dais, jumped on his horse, and rode off with John Ross. The incident would go unreported in the *Phoenix,* and most Cherokees would never learn exactly what the General Council had reluctantly agreed to.

Major Ridge's speech at Red Clay that day marked the close of the spring council. The old man seldom spoke in public anymore, but his words still carried considerable weight. He took a spot under a large tree within sight of the council shed, but out of earshot, and talked to the dozens of Indians who had gathered around him. For several minutes, Ridge went on about the tribe's troubled history with the white men. He said their current problems reminded him of the Red Sticks, how outside forces had divided the Creeks and led the tribe to ruin. He urged his people to bury their party animosity and do no harm to one another. Even as he preached unity, Ridge tried to nudge his people toward a more receptive opinion of emigration.

"In case we should conclude to seek a new home," Ridge said, "let us go in the character of true friends and brothers."

The Indian Affairs commissioner Benjamin Currey, who witnessed Ridge's speech, later told Lewis Cass that one disillusioned Cherokee approached him at Red Clay and offered a plan to speed along a treaty. They met in the darkness on the edge of the forest, far from the council fire. This unnamed Indian suggested he deliver Jackson's message directly to the Cherokees so they would see that Ross had not accurately explained their predicament. This man, who perhaps was John Ridge or Elias Boudinot, advised the government to blame Ross for the tribe's problems and to stop negotiating with him. If the United States government refused to recognize him it might eventually diminish his considerable influence over the tribe.

In the summer of 1833 the winners of Georgia's land lottery began arriving to claim their land. Every day, Indians were evicted from their homes as new settlers showed up to take them. One man even moved into Ross's grandfather's house. Many of the educated, mixed-blood Cherokees fought their evictions with lawsuits, but most did not understand the white men's legal system. When the new owners appeared, many scared Cherokee families simply packed up and left. The fleeing Indians kept enrolling agents busy for months. By the fall nearly twelve hundred Indians had signed up with Hugh Montgomery—so many that the agent hired workers to build a new receiving station for these émigrés.

At the same time, Alabama officials arrested a Cherokee accused of killing another Indian on tribal land. It was a case nearly identical to that of George Tassel. Although Alabama courts eventually ruled the deputies had overstepped their bounds, Cherokees who had believed they were safe in Alabama began making plans to leave the state. Slowly, but steadily, the Cherokee Nation was losing its population.

During that dangerous summer, the rivalry between Ross and John Ridge became even more pronounced. Elijah Hicks, acting as the chief's surrogate, led a concerted attack in the pages of the *Phoenix*. He criticized Ridge for his unauthorized communications with Lewis Cass, Benjamin Currey, and Governor Lumpkin—"the very man who is at this moment robbing our children of their inheritance." Hicks and Ross believed that if the younger Ridge's machinations were more widely known it might turn the Cherokees against the Treaty Party. Ross had enemies coming from two directions—he had to fight not only Georgia and the federal government but some of his own people—and they forced him to rely even more heavily on propaganda.

Whether Ross considered John Ridge a political rival is unclear, but he obviously feared the young man's efforts to influence opinion on the subject of removal. Hicks called Ridge's efforts a "dark spot on our national virtue" that, after much mature and careful consideration, had to be exposed. Ross was careful not to attach his name to this criticism but the Ridges knew Hicks would not publish such inflammatory statements without the chief's blessing.

Ridge was working against Ross even more fervently than anyone realized. He spent the summer recruiting Indians to the Treaty Party and at the same time was corresponding with the president, sending his letters through the Tennessee general R. G. Dunlap. He suggested Jackson fund an exploratory party of Cherokees to survey western lands so they could see for themselves that the land beyond the Mississippi was well suited to their needs. He also asked the president to delay his effort to enroll Cherokees, as it diluted the number of Treaty Party members.

Dunlap offered an astute assessment of the tribe. He believed both Ross and John Ridge were acting in good faith. Both, he told the president, had altruistic motives and similar goals, but they had very different ideas about how best to achieve these. The president wasn't interested, however. He refused to stop Montgomery's enrolling efforts. The Indian agent appeared to be making great gains. Every Indian who left on his or her own was one less they would have to force out.

Ross remained sequestered at Head of Coosa until the fall, when he appeared by the council fire at Red Clay on October 15. His silence through the summer, while many Cherokees fled, had raised some concerns the chief would soon give up his fight. Treaty Party Indians arrived at the council grounds sure that Ross was prepared to lead the debate on removal. He had made no progress over the summer, so they expected him to admit defeat. Instead, Ross was defiant and stubborn as ever, and he turned to propaganda.

Standing in the council shed Ross delivered an annual address that sounded like a preacher's sermon. Usually devoid of emotion, on this day the chief's voice strained as he spat venomous denouncements of the Cherokees who had betrayed the tribe. He downplayed the success of Jackson's enrolling agents, suggested those who left had been coerced or bribed with whiskey. He claimed many of those Indians had no true claim to citizenship in the nation and had given in to frivolous self-interest. Ross's outbursts surprised many of the Indians; they had never seen him so angry, so desperate. He said the tribe must resist the oppression of the federal government and called for unity—on his terms.

"On all important questions, when a difference of opinion arise [*sic*] in regard to their rights and interest, the sentiments of the majority should prevail, and whatever measure is adopted by that majority for the public good, should be the duty of the minority to yield, and unite in support of the measure, this is the rule of order, sanctioned by patriotism and virtue; whilst a contrary course would lead to faction, confusion and injury."

The subtext of his message was clear: anyone who resisted him was a traitor to the Cherokee Nation. But Ross was not finished. He downplayed the tribe's many setbacks and overstated the importance of what little good news he had to report. The chief used an Alabama court ruling against state deputies who had arrested Cherokees as proof of the tribe's progress.

To John Ridge, it appeared Ross had turned into a ruthless dictator. Ridge had known the chief would not listen to reason and now it appeared he would squash any opinions contrary to him. It seemed Ross had become everything Ridge accused him of being. And now the chief was using a meaningless court ruling to renege on his promise to debate emigration.

Ross felt he was providing the tribe the very kind of leadership it needed at the time. Normally a gentle, soft-spoken man, he made it clear he was no pushover. Any weakness, he knew, would be exploited. The chief refused to concede that all hope was lost, perhaps suspecting the tribe held more power than it realized. After all, the removal law had been passed three years earlier, yet the Cherokees had stood their ground and not been forced out. But he had to know that the Georgians, and the president, were making progress toward that goal.

The General Council remained committed to the chief and asked him to return to Washington to negotiate with Jackson, to find some way out of the situation. His delegation was stacked with members of the National Party, a clear signal the council was not ready to consider removal. The council even gave Ross power of attorney, despite the objection of John Ridge. The chief had argued that the president would not meet with him unless it appeared he had the power to broker a treaty. Ridge believed it gave one man too much power and, in truth, he no longer trusted Ross with such authority. The Cherokees, however, were still willing to give Ross anything he wanted.

The men set out at night, using the darkness to slip away from the Cherokee country undetected. They did not tell the Ridges, or anyone else, about their plans for fear that they would be killed. They were on the trail of John Ross, who had left for Washington days earlier. Their plan was simple: they meant to stop the chief's mission, take over his delegation, and negotiate a removal treaty. And if Ross got in their way they would stop him.

These men operated outside the Treaty Party, without the Ridges' knowledge, and had less than noble motives. They meant to overthrow the council, sell the Cherokees' land, make a tidy profit, and escape west before anyone knew what had happened. Among these men were two members of Ross's own family.

William Hicks and Hugh Montgomery were behind the scheme. Growing more feebleminded every day, Hicks had become obsessed with the power he had lost to Ross. He believed he could regain his position atop the tribe once it was settled in the West, an idea the Indian agent may have planted. But then Montgomery was receptive to any idea that led to removal.

In December, the deposed chief had called a small band of Cherokees to the Indian agent's office on the Hiwassee. There, they plotted their coup. The group sent word to Jackson that they were ready to negotiate and assured the president they would lead the tribe once it was relocated beyond the Arkansas territory. This shadow government—a "kitchen cabinet," as the *Cherokee Phoenix* would later call it—unsurprisingly elected Hicks as its principal chief.

The bumbling cabal made a series of mistakes in its first day, however. Many of the Indians had already signed up with enrolling agents, and a few even left the country immediately after their meeting. They thought this would show their commitment to emigrating but it only removed them from the rolls of the tribe they claimed to represent. Most important, Hicks did not accompany the delegation. Instead, he sent two of Ross's own relatives; Thomas Jefferson Pack, a distant cousin; and Andrew, the chief's brother. Andrew was no more adept at politics than business but he felt much the same way Hicks did: unappreciated and passed over. His brother had never given him any attention, any important role to play in the tribe. He had been ignored long enough. This break from his brother was freeing for Andrew but his plans were doomed from the start. The *Phoenix* would describe Andrew's betrayal in Shakespearean terms, while others would say he did it only because he was deep in debt and hoped to profit from the treaty. In the end, neither excuse would save Andrew Ross.

Despite their unofficial status, the group had some reason for optimism. Andrew and T. J. Pack rode out of the Cherokee country with John West in early January, carrying an invitation from President Jackson. It seemed the president was ready to meet with any Indians inclined to willingly leave Georgia.

The president was not opposed to simply going around Ross; divide and conquer was, to him, an acceptable diplomatic strategy. But Andrew Ross was so completely inept—"destitute of the science of governments," as the *Phoenix* later reported—that Jackson found himself wishing he had tried harder with the chief. He quickly realized these Indians had no standing, legal or political. Dealing with them would be a waste of his time, Jackson realized. They understood so little about treaties it was if they did not speak the same language. Not even Congress would approve a treaty signed by such inconsequential men.

Jackson listened to the "kitchen cabinet" delegation for only a few minutes before dismissing them. He finally told Andrew Ross that if he wished to negotiate a treaty, his delegation would have to come back with some chiefs of great standing in the tribe—men such as Major Ridge, he suggested. Andrew Ross apparently did not recognize the slight and did as he was told. He set out for home the next day.

The meeting was not a complete waste of time for Jackson. Hicks's delegation had unwittingly achieved a minor victory, although not exactly the one they had planned. When Ross found out his own brother was negotiating with the president his resolve crumbled. It was not the familial betrayal that did him in—nothing surprised him anymore, not after Major Ridge's change of heart—but rather the sense that he was losing control. Ross realized that if renegade Indians such as William Hicks and Andrew represented yet another tribal faction, the Cherokee Nation could soon dissolve into civil war.

Jackson's willingness to meet with Andrew proved that the white men would deal with any Cherokees ready to do business. And Ross knew that the president had a singular interest in negotiating. At his own meeting with Jackson, the president had said that nothing—*nothing*—short of removal would satisfy the government. Ross finally understood those were the truest words the president had ever spoken to him. And if inept men such as William Hicks and Andrew Ross negotiated for the Cherokees, the chief knew the tribe could end up homeless. Ross decided he had to alter his course, and quickly.

In a series of letters to the president, Ross went far beyond the mandate of the General Council. He proposed vacating Georgia if the Cherokees could continue to live in Alabama and along the Tennessee–North Carolina border. He asked if the tribe could cede a portion of its territory to Georgia and become United States citizens, a deal Jackson himself had once suggested. Ross was becoming desperate. The president refused every offer.

Finally, Ross told Jackson if the Cherokees were forced to move they would relocate beyond the boundaries of the United States, a last-resort solution he had been pondering for nearly a year. But the president said he would not allow that to happen. The country, Jackson said, was bound by treaty to keep the Indians within the limits of the United States. It was the only agreement Andrew Jackson was prepared to honor.

The white men fawned over Major Ridge. When he arrived in the capital that May, Ridge was treated like royalty, invited to parties nearly every night. He attended these fetes good-naturedly and spoke to the Washington elite through an interpreter—Ridge had long since given up trying to speak English in public. Still, the old warrior charmed nearly everyone he came in contact with, including Senator George Gilmer, the former Georgia governor.

Gilmer acted as if he had met a celebrity and later gushed over the old chief's dignity and nobility, calling him the "finest specimen" of American Indian.

On this visit, Ridge was asked to sit for his portrait, a painting that would find its way into McKenney's comprehensive Indian book. It is the image of a man every bit as regal and imposing as his Washington hosts described him. In it, he is depicted as a large man wearing the fine suit of a gentleman farmer, and his white shock of hair stands in stark contrast to his ruddy complexion. But it is the expression on his face that dominates the image. Ridge is frowning, his brow furrowed as if deep in thought. It is a testament to the artist's eye, for at that moment Major Ridge was deeply troubled.

He had been forced to slip away from his home like a fugitive. When Ridge agreed to accompany Andrew Ross to Washington, rumors that he planned to sell Indian land spread through the nation within a day. The reaction had been even worse than Ridge had feared. A small band of Cherokees assembled to ambush the old chief, but he eluded them by taking a long, wandering route out of the Indian country. He meandered over hills and through trees and scrub he had known all of his life. Even though he was willing to give up the Cherokee country, he still loved it, knew every inch of it. And it was hard to follow the trail of an old hunter.

Once he reached Washington, however, Ridge refused to support either of the Ross brothers. Each of their proposals gave him reason for concern. He believed Andrew Ross wanted only the commission he'd earn from brokering a treaty and was willing to concede anything with the promise of nothing in return. The fate of the tribe meant little to him, and this indiference was a sin the old chief could not abide. But Ridge was also disturbed to learn of the various solutions suggested by John Ross, particularly the idea of Cherokees becoming U.S. citizens. He feared such a plan would relegate the Indians to the lowest class, where they would be marginalized until the entire tribe was wiped out. Separate, the Indians maintained a level of respect. As citizens, Ridge feared they would barely enjoy better status than slaves.

After several weeks the distraught Ridge left the city with Elias Boudinot. He refused to help Andrew Ross, whom he considered a con man. But he was most disappointed with John Ross. Without the General Council's endorsement of a removal treaty, Ridge said, the chief had no more power to make a treaty than his brother. It seemed to him that Ross had become as duplicitous as John Ridge claimed. It disappointed him, seeing his apprentice so desperate. Gone was the self-assured young politician Ridge had championed years earlier. It seemed that Ross was no longer an honest man, was little better than Hicks or Walker. Ross appeared obsessed with winning without considering the cost to his people. Ridge left Washington dejected, in a dark mood. The old chief had wasted several weeks in the city with nothing to show for his efforts except a new portrait, which was hung in the offices of the Indian commissioner Elbert Herring.

Andrew Ross eventually negotiated a removal deal. In June, he signed a treaty that gave the Cherokees just $25,000 annually for twenty-four years and a small amount of money for various other projects. It was a pitiful deal, far less than the government had offered John Ross, but it included $1,000 for Andrew. Ridge, Boudinot, and even John Walker Jr. had refused to sign it and members of Congress refused to ratify it, just as the president had predicted they would.

John Ross remained in Washington another month, waiting for a package sent by Elijah Hicks. At the chief's request, the *Phoenix* editor had collected a petition signed by thirteen thousand Cherokees opposed to removal, and Ross hoped the sheer number of signatures would give Jackson pause. The president only laughed. He called the petition a forgery.

"The whole nation don't exceed ten thousand," Jackson said.

"You are under a great mistake, sir," Ross said. "There are even many more than thirteen thousand in the nation."

"Sir," Jackson said, mocking Ross's own feigned politeness, "I will bet what you please that the population does not exceed ten thousand."

"No doubt your Excellency believes so," Ross countered, "but the population far exceeds the number stated; and I can assure you if you think otherwise, the agent whose business it is to report these matters truly has done you great injustice."

Jackson did not care, and Ross realized nothing more he said could move the president. It was another turning point for Ross. He had long believed in the rule of law, cherished the notions of democracy. He had not given up when the Indian removal law passed because it had included the word "voluntary." For several years, he had searched for legal standing to fight the Cherokee cause. He now knew that none of it mattered, that nothing he did would convince the white men to leave his people alone. He had been naive, and he had led his people astray. John Ross knew that, barring a miracle, he would have to return to Red Clay and broach the subject of removal with his people. But Ross would not admit this to the president.

The Georgians were getting scared. A group of settlers sent Governor Lumpkin a note in May of 1834 claiming the Cherokees were planning to massacre whites "when the corn is fully grown." They claimed this story had been told to them by a young Indian girl whose grandfather was a chief in the tribe. She said her grandfather had gotten orders to organize the Indians in groups of twenty or thirty to attack settlers. These men claimed Ross had given the order. It looked as if the tribe, pushed to the point of desperation, had decided to fight back.

For all Lumpkin's bluster and disdain for the Cherokees he gave the report little thought. Even if he had not known Ross was in Washington, he realized such attacks were out of character for the Cherokees. He told the men these stories were nothing but rumors spread by settlers trying to spark a war.

"But that anything like a plan of general hostility has been arranged and agreed upon by the remnants of Cherokees, I am very far from crediting," Lumpkin wrote. "I know that ten days ago the two delegations at Washington were seriously engaged upon the subject of negotiating a final treaty with the Federal Government. And I know that intelligent men among the Cherokees rely upon negotiation, and have too much light to countenance the idea of hostilities. I attribute all the desperate acts which have been or may be committed by the Cherokees to the wicked and selfish influence of certain citizens of Georgia who are, and have long been, engaged in the diabolical work of endeavoring to produce a state of anarchy and civil war in the Cherokee section of our state."

It was a telling letter. Even Lumpkin had grown tired of the ever-increasing demands of settlers, and he revealed more respect for the Cherokees than he ever had shown. But that made little difference; Lumpkin knew that, politically, he could not oppose the will of the people. That month, he told Senator John Forsyth it might become necessary for the state to remove the Cherokees by year's end, "peaceably if we can, forcibly if we must."

Before that could happen violence would erupt in the Cherokee Nation. But Lumpkin and the settlers had little to worry about. Rather than slaughtering Georgians, the Indians were far more intent on killing one another.

Many Cherokees had begun to blame their troubles on the efforts of the Ridges, Walker, and William Hicks to secure treaties. The whites would not want their land so desperately, these Indians believed, had it not been offered to them. The way Cherokees interpreted the news of Ross's failure to get a deal worked to his advantage; many Indians believed these factions had sabotaged his efforts. Ross did little to dissuade this way of thinking. It was a serviceable excuse.

Upon his return to Head of Coosa, John Ross learned just how deeply the resentment against the Treaty Party ran. A group of Cherokees was plotting to kill his brother and cousin for signing their failed treaty. Ross did not encourage these men but did little to stop them either. His brother had betrayed him, so he could hardly blame the Cherokees for the way they felt.

Ross may have worried he, too, was a target. Quatie told him some men had been lurking around their home for weeks, scaring the children. In fact, they were only prospective buyers. The man who won Ross's land in the Georgia land lottery was looking to sell. Ross would file a suit to stop the sale, like many other wealthy Indians, but it didn't keep the settlers away. Everyone knew the Cherokees had no standing in Georgia courts.

In August 1834, less than a month after he returned home, Ross called a special session of the council. He hoped to calm his irate tribe but he only made matters worse. Ross outlined the various proposals made in Washington in an attempt to gauge the tribe's reaction. But the crowd at Red Clay nearly turned into a lynch mob. Tom Foreman, the Cherokee sheriff, interrupted the council to demand Major Ridge be held accountable for his trip to Washington. For all of the chief's talk of loving the land, Foreman claimed, Ridge was a hypocrite: he was interested only in the kickback he would get for brokering the deal. Foreman called the Ridges a gang of traitors.

Someone in the crowd shouted, "Let's kill them!"

Before anyone could make a move toward the old chief, John Ridge stood up and shouted, begging them to listen to what he had to say. Major Ridge, he said, had defended his country with "distinguished zeal and ability" for years. He loved his land and his people but now saw that both were in danger and only one could be saved. The younger Ridge asked, "Is a man to be denounced for his opinions? If a man saw a cloud charged with rain, thunder and storm . . . and urged his people to take care . . . is that man to be hated or respected?"

Major Ridge would not allow his son to defend him for long. The old warrior stood to face the crowd, seemingly unaffected by their threats. He had seen angry mobs before, and they did not frighten him. Although the younger Ridge was well spoken and passionate, nothing he said matched the simple power of his father's presence. This was the man who had killed Doublehead and stood up to Tecumseh, had spilled the blood of both white men and Indians who threatened his people. Major Ridge stood and told the Cherokees it did not matter if they liked him; he was not so vain to wish for honor this late in his life.

"It may be that Foreman has better expectations and that he should in slandering men establish his fame among you," Ridge said in Cherokee. "But I have no expectation that he will enjoy it long, for we have no government. It is entirely suppressed. Where are your laws? The seats of your judges are overturned. When I look upon you all, I hear you laugh at me. When harsh words are uttered by men who know better . . . I feel on your account oppressed by sorrow. I mourn over your calamity."

Ridge's words paralyzed the crowd so completely no one made a move when Foreman again called for them to be shot. The Cherokees' respect for the old chief was greater than their rage, and they feared he spoke the truth.

The council would not dismiss the sins of the Ridges so easily. Elijah Hicks quickly assembled a petition signed by more than one hundred Cherokees that called for both Ridges and David Vann to be removed from the executive council. Their crime was "maintaining opinions and a policy to exterminate the existence of the Cherokee community on the land of [their] fathers." The petition ordered the men to attend the fall council ready to answer these charges.

While the council argued about its next step, Major Ridge and his son slipped away through the forest, eluding Foreman and a posse of armed men waiting to kill them. John Ross later claimed he helped the Ridges escape. It was a further sign of the conflict Ross felt. No doubt he had guided Elijah Hicks to make his motion against the Ridges. Even though Ross no longer wanted his mentor to hold official standing in the tribe, neither did he want any harm to befall Ridge.

John Walker Jr. was not so lucky. Shortly after the council Walker was riding toward Hiwassee when he was shot out of his horse's saddle and left to die on the trail. He had been one of the first men to publicly oppose Ross, had attempted to secure his own treaty, and had been in Washington with Ridge and Andrew Ross. Even though he too declined to sign Andrew's treaty, his crimes against the Cherokees were serious enough. First blood had been drawn.

The threat of violence lingered throughout the summer of 1834, whispered plots repeated around campfires. Some Indians claimed the Ridges had hired Seewakee to assassinate John Ross, and others swore Thomas Woodward would kill the Ridges at the chief's behest. Andrew Ross and T. J. Pack went into hiding to avoid the dozens of men who demanded they be executed. The men who shot Walker were arrested by Tennessee authorities but later released when the state conceded it did not have jurisdiction in the case. No one would ever be prosecuted for the murder. By September Ross would hear reports that Benjamin Currey, Jackson's own enrolling agent, had threatened to see the Cherokee chief killed—even if he had to do it himself.

On Wednesday, September 10, Major Ridge visited John Ross at Head of Coosa. They sat in the chief's ornate parlor and tried to get to the truth of these rumors. The chief received his old mentor graciously and for a while they tried to talk as they once did. It was a sad occasion; sitting together as they had on so many afternoons the men realized how far apart they had grown. Each assured the other that these assassination plots were without merit, and that they had no ill feelings toward each other. But that was not entirely true. Although it is doubtful either Ross or Ridge sought to have the other killed, their differences were now irreconcilable. Ridge believed Ross was leading the Cherokees down a path toward destruction; Ross thought his oldest and closest adviser had become soft, allowed himself to be influenced by his son. As much as they tried, neither could see the other's point. But they agreed on one thing: all this talk of murder must stop. Cherokees did not kill Cherokees. Those days had passed.

Ross tried to make peace with John Ridge a few days later. In a letter, he assured the younger Ridge he had no part in Woodward's alleged plot, had not even heard of it until Major Ridge told him. "It is high time," Ross said, "that all such mischievous tales should be silenced.

"With the utmost sincerity and truth, I do assure you, that whatever may be the character of those reports they are false," Ross wrote. "At no time have I ever directly or indirectly expressed, insinuated nor even entertained any such feeling toward yourself or any other person."

Ross appealed to Ridge's growing leadership role among the tribe and suggested they work together to restore unity among the Cherokees. To prove he meant what he said, Ross called Woodward to his home a few days later and asked if he was plotting against the Ridges. Ross later told Ridge the man denied having ill designs toward anyone. Ross assured Ridge that Woodward's story had checked out when the chief questioned other Indians.

The tentative peace would be short-lived. In October the rift in the tribe widened even more as Currey attempted to persuade the council to adopt the treaty negotiated by Andrew Ross. The chief's brother had been in hiding for months, and the council refused to discuss the matter. Currey left

Red Clay dejected and frustrated and later told his bosses the Cherokee Nation was in chaos, the council a "fallen government."

Ross tried to make good on his promise to John Ridge but he only made matters worse. He refused the council's demands to put the Ridges and Vann on trial to face impeachment charges. Ross may have believed he was doing them a favor, perhaps even saving their lives. But John Ridge didn't see it that way. He felt a trial would have given him the chance to clear his name, and perhaps even sway some of those council members most adamantly opposed to emigration. Ridge suspected Ross canceled the trial to avoid that risk, not as any act of kindness.

The council reluctantly went along with Ross but refused to drop the charges against the Ridges and Vann. John Ridge considered it an insult to have to live with the unanswered charges against him and left Red Clay immediately. It would be the last General Council he attended.

A month later, John Ridge called his own council near his home at Running Waters. Fewer than a hundred Cherokees attended, but those who did were among the most influential men in the nation: Elias Boudinot, Alexander McCoy, John West. Over three days, the men drafted a memorial to the U.S. Congress that set forth the "right of their people to the soil on which they live, and their sense of wrong done them" but also recognized that they could have no peace in their current homes. For that reason, they had "turned their eyes to the country west of the Mississippi."

The group elected a Washington delegation to follow John Ross, who had been ordered back to the U.S. capital by the General Council. This group, led by John Ridge, was ordered to join Ross, meet with Jackson, and force negotiations for a removal treaty. But to accomplish this, Ridge knew they first had to escape the Cherokee country with their lives.

By establishing its own governing council, the Treaty Party had in essence seceded from the Cherokee Nation. In the eyes of most Indians they now were undoubtedly guilty of treason.

ELEVEN

1835

It was a moonless night in April. The trail was dark and John Ross rode alone, the silence broken only by the sound of his horse clopping on hard-packed red earth. He had been traveling for nearly a month and had never felt so tired, so weary. The trip to Washington had been a disaster. He'd been tricked, made to look a fool. Now Ross wanted only to be home. The problems of his tribe, he feared, had become insurmountable, but for the moment he could not think about a solution. First, he needed rest.

Ross did not need light to guide him—he knew every rock and tree along the trail. And even though the threat of violence lingered, he was not wary of riding alone through these woods, his woods. He was certain no men would be hiding in the tall stands of pines he passed and, in truth, he was too tired to care. He knew there was nothing he could do about it anyway.

By ten o'clock he was close enough to see the silhouette of his home in the distance. There, at Head of Coosa, a family he barely knew lived in anticipation of his infrequent visits. His daughter Jane was gone, enrolled in a North Carolina school, and he missed her terribly. At the same time Allen, the son who worked hardest to remain close to his father, had returned home and was planning to marry young Jennie Fields, a local girl from a good family. Even the smallest of his children were now taking lessons, although it would be a few years before Silas and George were old enough to go away to boarding schools. Quatie kept him informed of these developments as best she could and rarely spoke to him about his business, or if she did he did not find it of enough consequence to repeat. He knew she worried, and he did not make matters worse by telling her how hopeless it had become. Ross barely wrote to her when he was away.

If he had written to Quatie, what would he have told her—that John Ridge and Elias Boudinot, who he'd come to despise, had outmaneuvered him? They had surprised him in Washington and he feared they would entice Jackson to negotiate a treaty. In a panic, he had attempted to make a deal for the Cherokees' land. He suggested the tribe would accept $20 million to move west of the Mississippi, knowing he did not have the authority to make such an offer. But then these were desperate times, and he had become a very desperate man.

Ross had allowed the negotiations to go all the way to the Senate, believing even his supporters in the government would balk at such an outrageous sum and put an end to any talk of a treaty. Instead, they voted to give the Cherokees $5 million. Ross had made a mistake. He argued such a deal had no legal standing, but this did little good since he himself had suggested it.

Now there was even talk that he was no longer the chief. The Cherokee Nation had ignored its constitution and not held an election since 1830. Ross had not faced a vote of the people in seven years; he served at the pleasure of General Council chiefs who had extended his term along with their own. He remained in power because he did exactly what the people wanted, and now he had gone to Washington and betrayed their faith. But he felt he'd had no choice, and secretly he wondered if the Ridges were right, that all was lost. Ross had no idea how to explain such intricacies of diplomacy to his people. They would not understand. The Cherokees only knew what was right, that the land had belonged to them before the white men had ever come.

As Ross rode through the gate of his property he saw a man in the shadows —one of his servants, he assumed. The man followed him to the front of the house, where Ross climbed off his horse. The chief didn't recognize the man who took the reins, but then he had little to do with the operation of his home anymore. Without making eye contact or waiting for a reply, the chief ordered the man to put up his horse, feed him, give him some water. Ross walked up the steps and into the house and found it was no longer his.

Inside the home he had built for his wife and children Ross found the family of a man named Stephen Carter settled down for the night. Carter was unpleasant, even rude, although he could hardly have been expected to act otherwise at such an hour. He told Ross that Georgia agents had given him possession of the home only a few days before, and he had the paperwork to prove it. Quatie and the children had been turned out; Carter did not know where they had gone.

Ross stood there quietly, bone-tired, confused, and helpless, unsure of what to do next. He had no place to go, no idea where he might find his family. Finally, Carter recognized Ross's distress, took pity on the chief, and offered him a room for the night.

It was the final blow. Carter had made the gesture out of kindness, but Ross took it as an insult. The chief was humiliated. He was nearly as white as this man, and probably richer, yet he was treated like a poor servant, someone to be pitied. He did not want to accept the offer, could not bear the idea of sleeping as a guest in his own home. But, in truth, he was simply too tired to set out in search of his family. Quatie, he knew, would have found a safe place.

Yes, Ross said humbly, he would like to stay for the night.

Ross awoke early the next morning and walked the grounds of his home for the last time. He noticed his corn crop was untouched and saw his cattle and sheep grazing in the distance. He stood beneath one of his majestic oak trees and spotted the peacocks, once Quatie's pride and joy, roosting on an outstretched branch. Finally, he visited the graves of his father and one of his own children, who had died as an infant. They would never be forced to leave their home. John Ross lingered until he could stand it no longer. He quickly gave an order for his horse, paid for his room and board, and set off to find his family and a new place to call home.

* * *

John Ridge returned home in much better spirits than Ross. He carried with him gifts for Sarah and his children—clothes, shoes, trinkets—as well as newspapers to distribute at the next council. Ridge expected Ross to lie about what had happened in Washington and was prepared to expose the chief with published reports of the delegation's dealings. It would, he thought, force the Cherokees to see they had been deceived and be enough to make them reconsider a treaty. Ridge believed he'd beaten Ross, perhaps even saved the tribe.

When the president concluded he would get nowhere with Ross, he had asked the retired Reverand J. F. Schermerhorn to negotiate with John Ridge and Boudinot. This move not only tricked Ross into bartering but allowed Schermerhorn to reach a deal with the Treaty Party, one the president was prepared to honor if Ridge persuaded the majority of the tribe to support it. Ridge told his father that Jackson's offer of $4.5 million for Cherokee land was "liberal," one that every Cherokee would embrace as soon as he explained the deal.

"The poor Indian," he told Major Ridge, "enjoys the same rights as the rich—there is no distinction."

Jackson had appealed to Ridge's ego, offering to fund a Cherokee scouting party to the Arkansas territory and promising military protection for his home at Running Waters. While Ross's home had been sold at auction, Georgia protected the property of the pro-treaty Cherokees. Governor Lumpkin had blocked efforts to sell Elias Boudinot's home and the legislature passed a law protecting Major Ridge's ferry and home. The young Ridge became so enamored of the man he'd once called a snake that he named his new son after Jackson.

Ridge's elation soon turned to paranoia. He spotted Indians lurking on the outskirts of his property, some wearing disguises, others wrapped in blankets to hide their identity. These men, he suspected, were waiting to kill him—and he was right. Word of the Treaty Party's efforts in Washington to sell tribal land had gotten back to the nation. Ross's most ardent supporters believed Ridge had interfered with the chief's efforts to save their homes. Ridge and Boudinot had feared this would happen but justified their actions as patriotic. They believed they were acting in the best interest of Cherokees who had been deceived by Ross. They only had to hope the rest of the tribe realized that before they were assassinated.

Benjamin Currey sent troops to guard Running Waters and threatened to hold Ross responsible for the death of any Treaty Party member. Currey's main purpose, however, was to make sure Ridge went forward with plans to host a council. The purpose of this meeting was allegedly to vote on who would receive the tribe's future annuity payments, but Ridge also hoped to present the treaty and win enough converts to get the deal ratified.

Even though he timed the council to coincide with a green corn festival, only a few dozen Cherokees showed up, nowhere near enough to claim a majority support for the treaty. Currey believed Ross had sabotaged the meeting, sending out couriers to warn people not to attend. Ridge adjourned the meeting after two days, blaming the poor attendance on the planting season and heavy rains. In truth, he had little support among the vast majority of the tribe.

The General Council officially rejected the president's offer for a treaty a week later at Red Clay. The Cherokees seemed largely united but signs of the growing rift had become obvious. Most members of the council urged the assembled Indians to "hold on—be united, and all will be well shortly," but that did not stop one chief, who actually voted in favor of the treaty. Crawling Snake, the speaker of the council, pointedly asked that the tribe "stick to Ross." Yet never before had any official acknowledged there might be another option.

While the chiefs met, Ross was largely preoccupied with his new house. He had found his family staying with friends and moved them to Tennessee, beyond the jurisdiction of the Georgia Guard. He bought some land from a white farmer at Flint Springs and built a modest cabin just a few miles from Red Clay. This new home was closer in size and style to his grandfather's place in Rossville than to his sprawling mansion at Head of Coosa. The cabin, just a one-room shack with a stone fireplace and modest porch, more closely resembled the home of an average Cherokee than a rich chief. It may have been a sign that he did not expect to be there long.

On May 19 Ross finally appeared at Red Clay, where he offered a brief report on his trip to Washington. He was careful not to incite violence against his opponents in the tribe, but Ross encouraged "decisive and unequivocal disapprobation" of those people who had tried to negotiate a treaty on behalf of the Cherokees. He did not mention the Ridges by name but he did not have to do so. The council acknowledged the Treaty Party's efforts by passing a resolution to condemn Currey for his attempt to hold a competing council at Running Waters.

The mood of the tribe worried John Ridge enough that he wrote Governor Lumpkin to ask for military protection. He called Ross's supporters "banded outlaws" and suggested the governor organize a group of men to hunt down these vigilantes. He feared his assassins would not lurk in the woods much longer.

"You must break up this incubus or nightmare which sets so heavily upon the breasts of the ignorant Indians," Ridge wrote. "Depend upon it that it requires but this measure to dissipate the mists which now blind the eyes of some of our people. John Ross is unhorsed at Washington and you must unhorse him here."

John Ridge had long considered himself—and all that he did—"loyal opposition" to the Cherokee leadership. If he had once held political aspirations, however, he knew his chances had passed. Ridge believed he was doing the right thing and was willing to take considerable risks to achieve these goals, but he must have realized that relaying information about other Cherokees to the state of Georgia would be considered treasonous by many Cherokees. He felt he had no other choice, however. Ridge had committed to doing anything it took to get the Cherokees out of Georgia.

Ridge's plea worked. Within two weeks Governor Lumpkin ordered Colonel William Bishop to quietly and covertly protect John Ridge, his family, and his associates. He told the colonel to stop the Cherokees from meeting in Georgia and, if he had the opportunity, "arrest John Ross."

"Trust nothing to men who continue to excite the Indians to resist the operation of the laws of the State over them, or who encourage their appealing to other authority than that of Georgia for protection," Lumpkin wrote in his orders.

After years of pressure, the Cherokees were at their breaking point. Even though many of them had already emigrated, and a growing number turned to the Treaty Party, most remained dead set against removal. But they had been weakened, and Jackson realized it. The president suspected that a growing number of Cherokees wanted to put this trouble behind them; all they needed was another nudge. He would provide it.

Jackson's newest Indian commissioner, Schermerhorn, arrived in the Cherokee country later that spring. The parson's negotiations with Ridge and Boudinot had been so successful Jackson thought the rest of the tribe should hear from this man of the cloth. Schermerhorn accepted the assignment eagerly and suggested he might bribe some chiefs to speed the process along. Jackson assured him that this would not be necessary.

Soon after he set up his office at the Indian agency in Calhoun, Schermerhorn learned John Ross was at his brother's house a short distance away. He sent an introductory letter to Lewis Ross that stated he would like to meet the "leading men of the nation," particularly the chief. Although John and Lewis Ross were too savvy to be taken in by the flattery, they rode over to the agency out of curiosity. Any intelligence about the opposition could only help.

The pleasantries did not last long. Ross knew the commissioner was planning to host a meeting at Running Waters on July 20. The stated purpose was to discuss whether individual Cherokees or the chief would receive the tribe's annuities, but Ross would not fall for that trick; he realized Schermerhorn was there to promote a treaty. Ross offered to gather the entire tribe at Red Clay but the commissioner balked, claiming the site had already been chosen. He wanted the session held at Ridge's home specifically to exclude the majority of the tribe. The two men argued for a week.

Ross first considered advising Cherokees to stay away from the meeting but worried Schermerhorn might, through coercion or bribery, persuade the Indians who did attend to sign his treaty. Ross ultimately decided a strong showing was the best course. He quickly dispatched messengers to request the presence of all Cherokees at Running Waters on July 20, ensuring there would be a majority opposed to removal. They were told to bring their own food and meet near John Ridge's home the day before. Ross's word alone drew more than twenty-five hundred Cherokees.

In a pouring rain they came from as far away as a hundred miles—old men, women and children, members of the General Council. They gathered on July 19 in a clearing just two miles from Ridge's property, where they huddled under blankets and makeshift shelters. As the storm carried on into the evening they ate parched corn, leaving their horses to feed on wet grass and drink from a stream that threatened to overflow onto the campground. Ross did not even have a blanket and suffered throughout the night, too polite to take blankets that could be used by others. On the edge of the forest Ross spotted members of the Georgia Guard, armed with rifles, who had been called in to make sure no one harmed Currey, Schermerhorn, or the Ridges. This is what his tribe had come to, Ross thought: summoned by white men and left to rot in a cool summer storm.

The rain had not stopped the next morning when the crowd gathered at Running Waters, but Benjamin Currey—Jackon's enrolling agent and Schermerhorn's partner—took his time to appear. He did not want to start without Schermerhorn, who was still in Rome (the new name given to Head of Coosa), and asked if Ross minded opening the assembly with a prayer. Ross demanded Currey speak now. He would not allow his people to remain in the open, "overwhelmed by the rain" at the general's whim. Currey acquiesced.

It began like a church service, with the Cherokee preacher John Huss offering a prayer, followed by a hymn. The spiritual was drowned out by members of the Georgia Guard, who played drums and fifes in time with the music. Currey stood before the crowd and explained that he wanted to see a vote of the assembled Cherokees on how the tribe would like its annuities for past treaties distributed. But there were greater issues at stake. He said Ross had deluded them, that no matter what they did "it will not save your country."

Ross realized he had been goaded into assembling the tribe so the Treaty Party and Indian commissioners could confront him. He had been lured into a debate and could not afford to appear weak. When he rose to respond, Ross claimed he had no quarrels with those who had an honest difference of opinion. He said that he was not a party man, harbored no hostility toward the Ridges, and wanted only to "promote the best interests of my people."

Ross intuitively knew exactly what he needed to say to calm the Cherokees, and his political skill both impressed and unnerved Currey and the Ridges. He had claimed the high road and, without uttering a disparaging word, put Schermerhorn and the Treaty Party on the defensive.

John Ridge followed the chief and was forced to agree with Ross's call for unity. He defended his efforts to negotiate a treaty as his "honest convictions." But when he criticized Ross for failing to offer the tribe a reasonable plan to end their troubles, he convinced no one of his altruistic motives. The Cherokees had no interest in such talk and grew restless. Ross told Currey he had to take the vote now, before his people left to seek shelter from the rain.

It took nearly two days. The Indians stood in the incessant downpour, lined up before the stage, to have their votes tallied one by one. Despite Currey's attempts to persuade them—asking some, "Don't you want the money?"—it soon became clear the Cherokees overwhelmingly favored giving the annuities directly to the tribe's treasurer. When Schermerhorn arrived he tried to stop the voting so he could speak but Ross would not allow it. They had come for a vote, the chief said, and they would have one. Some of the pro-treaty Indians tried to distract their fellow Cherokees— starting a game of ballplay, sending women through the crowd with bottles of whiskey—but the Cherokees resisted every temptation, and Ross kept them in line and voting.

At the end of the first day the Cherokees returned to the field where they had passed their first night at Running Waters. Ridge offered Ross a bed in his own house and said he and his father would stay with the tribe. Sarah, Ridge told Ross, would treat him well. It may have been simple courtesy, or perhaps he was extending an olive branch to the chief, one last attempt to mend the growing divide. Ross declined, saying he saw no reason he should fare better than his people. If it was meant as a slight, neither man acknowledged it.

Late in the second day of voting, Schermerhorn demanded he be allowed to speak and, once again, Ross denied the request. He told the commissioner he could speak after the voting but could not guarantee the crowd would stay to hear him. The struggle between the two did not go unnoticed by the crowd, and the chief clearly had the upper hand, the Indians on his side.

"Aye," one Cherokee called out, "he may speak, but we needn't listen." Others, most likely planted members of the Treaty Party, voiced support to hear the man out, arguing "we are the weaker and must do as we are bid." Ross did not give the preacher his audience until all the ballots were in. Still, most of the Cherokees stayed to listen.

Schermerhorn talked for three and a half hours. He used the podium as a pulpit, delivering a fiery sermon meant to frighten the Indians into submission. By the time he finished the Cherokees had a new name for the man with the strange name. They called him "Devil's Horn."

Schermerhorn claimed to be their friend, that it was his dream to be useful to the Indians. He rambled on about his friendship with Jackson and warned the Cherokees not to be excited by the prejudices that had been spread against him. They should follow the example of the northern tribes, who chose to "emigrate and live" instead of remaining in their homes and rotting.

"Take this money," he cried, "for, if you do not, the bordering states will forthwith turn the screw upon you tighter and tighter, till you are ground to powder. And look not for mercy—for the measures of the present ruler of America will not change with his successor, whom I know as I do know myself. Do you complain of wrongs? Remove and you can retaliate, and if the white man here oppresses you, there you can oppress him."

Schermerhorn did nothing to change the Cherokees' opinion. Only 114 Indians voted to disburse annuity payments to individual members of the tribe. The rest—2,225 Cherokees—demanded that the money be sent to the tribe's treasurer. Major Ridge tried to offer an amendment that the money could not be used for legal fees but the Indians would not listen even to him.

Schermerhorn left Running Waters embarrassed and less than hopeful he could get a treaty out of the stubborn Cherokees. It was a blow to his massive ego. He had thought he could sway the Indians with a frightening sermon and a few threats. But he now realized nothing he said could move the Cherokees. No matter what he or the Treaty Party proposed, the majority of the tribe looked expectantly to Ross before reacting. In their darkest moment, it seemed John Ross had become more than a politician to these Indians, more than a chief. He was their prophet.

Schermerhorn later told Jackson and Cass that Ross's sway over the tribe was complete, that these natives "do only what they were bidden." His opinion of Ross strangely mirrored the Cherokees' own name for the preacher. Schermerhorn called the chief "the Devil in Hell."

John Ross had just sat down for breakfast on July 31 when he heard the horses outside his cabin. On the road, the Ridges and a band of nearly twenty men were approaching his gate and the chief stepped outside to greet them. He could afford to be magnanimous, for it appeared he had won. Ross invited them to dine with him and ordered a servant to feed their horses.

Although he acted as if their visit was nothing out of the ordinary, Ross was caught off guard. He had ignored a request by Schermerhorn to meet with the Treaty Party at the agency headquarters two days earlier. Ross begged off, sending a letter to the Ridges stating he would gladly meet with them but such talks should include only Cherokees. He was relieved to find Schermerhorn was not among the men in his front yard.

The Ridges must have been surprised by the chief's modest accommodations, a cabin very nearly swallowed up by the rolling hills that surrounded it, so small many of the men were forced to sit outside with the horses. But they said nothing of the chief's change in his fortunes. John Ridge told the chief he had brought a letter for him. They had planned to send it by courier but their trip home passed so close to Ross's home they had decided to deliver it personally.

The men spent the morning chatting pleasantly, avoiding their recent troubles. There had been few private conversations between them in months and Ross wondered if there was not something more to this unexpected visit. But the Ridges were worried as well. The threats against them had increased and, although Ross denied it, they feared he was behind these plots. None of those things came up. On that morning, there was no maneuvering, no posturing, and no calculation. They were simply men who all wanted the best for their people but had different ideas of how to achieve that goal.

As they stood to leave, John Ridge handed Ross the letter and asked for an official meeting of the National and Treaty parties. He planned a green corn festival for August 24 and hoped that any council could be held well before or after that date. Ross said he'd consult with the people but did not want to take them away from their crops at an inconvenient time. The letter Ridge delivered simply said that he agreed the Cherokees should meet to confer on the "affairs of our much afflicted nation." The note only highlighted how strained their relationship had become.

"We have no feelings of a private or personal character which can interpose or prevent the restoration of brotherly confidence and harmony among ourselves," Ridge had written.

There was, however, little harmony for the rest of the summer. The Georgia Guard arrested James J. Trott and Elijah Hicks, Ross's brother-in-law, for compiling a list of losses the Cherokees had suffered because of the state's interference. Just before Ridge's dance, four pro-treaty Indians were killed. A man named Hammer was beaten to death and a Cherokee named Crow was murdered at a dance after begging people in attendance to join the Ridges. A few days later, two Ridge supporters named Murphy and Duck were stabbed to death. And a fight nearly broke out when a group of Cherokees found John Martin tipsy from drink and nearly asleep.

"Ho! Martin! Rouse up, old fellow," one of them called. "A treaty we mean to have and a treaty we will have, and there's but one way."

"What's that about treating?" Martin asked, rubbing the sleep from his eyes. "I've had enough treating to last me awhile."

"I tell you," one of the Cherokees said, "we must have a treaty and we will—John Ross won't make one and we must look to John Ridge."

Martin took the bait. He stood up and shouted, "John Ross forever!"

When his tormenters responded with cries of "John Ridge forever," the old man raised his fists. The Cherokees ignored the challenge but continued to tease him.

"The only way to settle the nation will be to settle John Ross."

"John Ross forever!" Martin interrupted.

"If John C. Martin would be a service to the nation he would do up John Ross," one of the Indians suggested. "Aye—what if we are going to kill John Ross and make a treaty?"

"Kill John Ross?" Martin asked. "Kill John C. Martin first—what do you want to kill John Ross for?"

The Cherokees called Ross an enemy to his country and argued all enemies should be killed. Martin replied there was an enemy to the Indians much worse than Ross—John Ridge.

"Then you're not for killing John Ross?"

"Kill John Ross? Kill fifty John Ridges before I'd see John Ross killed," Martin said.

The Indians later reported Martin's threat to U.S. troops, who promptly arrested the old man. It took Lewis Ross a week to get him released. Martin argued that he'd been drunk, that the other Indians had started it, and that he had not meant to threaten John Ridge. But he made this confession only after spending a week in jail.

The harassment of Martin notwithstanding, John Ridge feared Ross was behind most of the attacks. The majority of the men beaten or killed were members of the Treaty Party. At the same time, however, some Cherokees had come to believe the chief had given up his fight. Several Indians stopped by his cabin at Flint Springs in the weeks after the Ridges' visit. They wandered out of the woods as if they were casually passing through and interrupted Ross at his writing desk. All of these men asked the same thing: had he joined the Treaty Party?

"No," Ross told one of these Indians. "Why do you ask?"

"Because the Ridges say you have," the Cherokee reported. "They tell us—'Why attempt longer to resist, when even your own chief gives way to us?'"

Ross might have dismissed such talk as idle rumor but he had come to realize that, in spite of all the proclamations of unity and friendship, the Ridges were coordinating a new campaign against him. In mid-August, the Georgia Guard burst into the home of Elijah Hicks and confiscated the printing press for the *Cherokee Phoenix*. The soldiers, accompanied by Stand Watie, Boudinot's brother, took all the typefaces, books, and papers.

The timing was more than coincidental. That very day Ross had sent several Indians with a wagon to New Echota to move the printing press to Red Clay. But guardsmen beat Ross's men to Hicks's home and the press, effectively shutting down the chief's best way of communicating with his own people. Without asking, Ross knew Boudinot had tipped off the Georgia Guard.

In late August 1835 John Ross was distracted by the arrival of a visitor with a strong interest in Cherokee history. John Howard Payne, the New York actor and playwright who had penned the song "Home, Sweet Home," showed up unexpectedly at Flint Springs one summer afternoon with letters of introduction from several members of Georgia society. He had gained interest in the tribe almost by accident. After spending much of his adult life in Europe, Payne—who dabbled in several arts—had returned to the United States with plans to start a literary magazine.

Payne wandered into Georgia while on a tour to gather materials and subscribers and met a doctor named Tennille who told him about Cherokee history. Tennille mentioned that Charles Hicks, a former chief, had written extensively on the tribe, and had left the material with Ross when he died.

Tennille, the brother of Georgia's secretary of state, believed Ross had maintained those writings and perhaps even added to them. The idea of such a rich, unmined history intrigued Payne.

Payne found Ross living in a "log hut of but one single room, and scarcely proof against the wind and rain" that was, he later wrote, one of the "humblest dwellings in his nation." Ross was gracious, unaffected, and—Payne was surprised to discover—very nearly white. He was not the picture of a great Indian chief; he was short and quiet, with a craggy face, and showed the first signs of gray in his hair. Ross had kept Hicks's history of the tribe but sadly reported that he had not continued the notes. Ross offered Payne complete access to Hicks's work but would not allow him to take it. The papers were sacred to Ross, for they were a window into his tribe's past and the only thing he possessed that had belonged to the old chief. Ross invited Payne to stay at Flint Springs, regretting that he could not offer finer accommodations.

Payne had planned only a short visit but decided it was worth the time to make a copy of the Cherokee history. For several days, he sat at Ross's dining table transcribing the legends of Cherokee customs and beliefs, the history of the tribe's dealings with the white men—a saga apparently racing toward its climax. Payne was mesmerized by the story, thought it might make a good book. At the end of the fourth day Ross asked him to stay until the fall council. He suggested Payne could better understand the tribe by observing a council and meeting the tribe's greatest chiefs.

Ross was a generous man, but he had ulterior motives for this hospitality. He realized Payne had the ability to tell the Cherokees' story to a larger audience than had yet heard it and saw a chance to win support through public opinion. Through September, the chief spent an increasing amount of time with Payne, relating the stories of broken treaties, tricks, and bribery, of his encounters with Jackson and the conduct of Georgia's politicians—all from his perspective of course. By October Payne had become an unabashed Ross supporter. In his eye, the chief could do no wrong. He would soon learn not everyone shared his view.

*   *   *

John Howard Payne would never forget the sight of the Cherokees' solemn march to the council. The Indians emerged from the forest as if they were a part of it, dressed in tunics and sashes, long robes, and turbans or hats, carrying their belongings on blankets bundled and slung over their shoulders. The long, silent parade reminded the writer of the "old scripture pictures of patriarchal procession." Their path took them by Ross's home, and the chief came out to greet them. As they approached, the Cherokees formed two lines, each filing past Ross and taking his hand for a brief moment. It was, for Payne, a sad show of respect from an afflicted people.

Despite that bit of ceremony, Payne found the tribe divided when he reached Red Clay. Although the majority of the Indians still backed Ross, the Ridges had won some converts. The Cherokees segregated themselves around separate council fires across the wide field to avoid arguments and violence. Some of this tension, Payne believed, stemmed from the presence of the white men who had come to speak and monitor the progress of treaty talks. Currey and Bishop were there, but Payne was most surprised to learn that Schermerhorn, the man whom the Cherokees called the Devil's Horn and who was a former schoolmate of his, was in attendance as well.

The writer met these men one evening in a cabin near the council grounds. They were loud, bombastic, and Schermerhorn—Payne noted—cursed quite a bit for a pastor. The men showed him the anti-Ross documents they had drawn up, told of the progress made by the Ridges, and bragged that they would "have a treaty in a week." Schermerhorn apparently had recovered from the embarrassment he'd suffered at the hands of Ross a few months earlier.

"John Ross is unruly now, but he will soon be tame enough," he said.

Bishop asked Payne for his assessment of the situation. The writer said the Cherokees should be allowed to keep their land as the tribe had been there first and been recognized as the rightful owners by treaty and the Supreme Court. It was purely Ross's opinion, and Bishop dismissed this as the sort of silly romantic notions he expected from a northerner.

"It is not that I am from the north that I think as I do," Payne said, "but because I am jealous of our national honor and prize the faith of treaties."

"You would feel differently if you had the same interest we have," Bishop said.

"I should hope I would forget my interest where it went against my principles."

Bishop only laughed at Payne's proclamation and neither mentioned the tribe for the rest of the evening. After Payne finally excused himself, he did not talk with the men again. He believed that Schermerhorn underestimated Ross. And when Payne next saw him, at the close of council, he considered chiding the preacher for his unfounded confidence, but thought better of it.

John Ross delivered a masterful annual message on October 12. He renewed hope among the tribe while bracing them for disappointment; he undermined the Ridges while inching ever closer to their views. Standing beneath the council shed on a cool morning he spoke loudly, forcefully, in a speech that came as close to a sermon as he could manage. Schermerhorn had to watch in envy as the bureaucratic chief once again beat him at his own game.

In recounting his trip to Washington the previous winter, Ross claimed he might have reached an agreement with the federal government if not for the interference of "unauthorized individuals." He called for unity in the face of illegal arrests of Indians by Georgia officials, and said he had come to realize the white men had no desire to see their difficulties "speedily, harmoniously, and honorably terminated." Ross blamed Jackson for putting pressure on the tribe that was "calculated to produce dissentions and divisions among the people, which can but result in evil and ruinous consequences."

Although Ross must have understood it would be useless, he proposed sending one final delegation to Washington and suggested this group be empowered to negotiate a treaty if it came to that. It was an important but subtle point. Ross was telling the tribe he would try to save their land, but anyone paying attention could see that he feared the end would come soon.

"And, should it please the Providence of God to extricate us from the difficulties which surround us, and once more to permit us to enjoy prosperity and happiness, let all participate in those blessings," Ross concluded. "But, on the other hand, should it be His will that our nation shall be doomed to inextricable adversity and extinction, then, as one people, let us be united, and calmly disappear with colors flying, and leave a character on the page of history that will never dishonor the name of the Cherokee nation."

For the next two weeks Ross repeatedly prevented Schermerhorn from addressing the council. He told the agent that the tribe would gladly receive any new proposal from Jackson but had no interest in hearing an offer for removal. Every time the preacher asked for consideration, Ross found creative new ways to stop him. He questioned Schermerhorn's authority to negotiate; he told him the time to introduce new business had passed. The old man was furious.

During the council, Ross called the Ridges into a private meeting with his top supporters and ordered the two sides to make peace. The chief said they had to work together to plot the tribe's course. It seemed to be an admission that time had run out. He asked the men to jointly write the orders for the new delegation. It took two days to reach an accord. Ridge found Ross's wording too ambiguous and Ross's men thought the Ridges were willing to concede too much. After three days, Ridge walked away satisfied that Ross had conceded there would be a treaty, even if the orders were vague. After more wrangling, the delegation was stacked three to one with members of the National Party. The Ridges did not argue, believing they had finally won.

On the last evening of the council nearly two thousand Cherokees gathered to approve the delegation's orders. The document was practically guaranteed to pass because it included a formal refusal of Jackson's $5 million offer. Ridge believed the refusal was a ruse to distract the Indians from another clause, one that said only treaties made by Ross's delegation would be binding. Ross was preparing his people for the likelihood of removal, but Ridge considered it trickery.

"The question was, Are you willing to take five millions of dollars for your country? No, no, was the cry of the people," Ridge later wrote. "Some few of the better informed were placed in different positions to lead the way, and the Indians, without knowing the difference between 5,000 and five millions, said No! They did not understand. Then the question was put, Are you willing to give full power to these twenty men to do your business? The answer was, Yes. They were dismissed, and they scattered that very night. There was no deliberation."

For all his disdain, Ridge was complicit in a different type of subterfuge. Long after most Cherokees were gone Schermerhorn finally spoke at Red Clay. He announced that a meeting would be held at New Echota on December 21 for the Cherokees to negotiate a treaty "on their own land," an irony that escaped the commissioner. The most chilling thing he said, however, was that any Cherokee who did not attend would be counted as voting in support of whatever deal was made.

Schermerhorn felt his own trickery was sanctioned by the highest power. He later told Secretary of War Lewis Cass that "the Lord is able to overrule all things for good."

On Saturday evening, November 7, John Ross helped Payne transcribe the last of Hicks's Cherokee history. The writer planned to leave the next day and ride south to see Stone Mountain—the giant rock outcropping near Atlanta—before heading north. Payne had spent so much time visiting he had not finished his copying. Ross was happy for the distraction. Earlier in the day the man who sold him his Flint Springs land showed up and demanded the property back. The man offered no explanation and Ross could not reason with him—he just kept telling Ross to get off the land. A scuffle broke out between the man and some of the chief's servants, who eventually drove the man off and built a crude fence to mark the property line. Payne suggested the man was part of a larger plot to harass the Indians. Ross could not disagree.

Just after eleven p.m., as they worked by candlelight, copying the notes of a 1794 meeting between Cherokee chiefs and George Washington, Ross and Payne heard a sound like rolling thunder—galloping horses, barking dogs, yelling men. Within seconds they heard boots clacking on the porch, and a man yelled out to the chief.

"Ross! Ross!"

Before the chief could get up a man kicked in the door and two dozen soldiers stormed into the cabin with their pistols drawn and knives unsheathed. One stuck the barrel of his pistol against Payne's chest while another pointed his gun at the Cherokee. Ross recognized the men as members of the Georgia Guard, but he did not think it prudent to point out they were beyond their jurisdiction. Before the chief could speak one of the men did.

"You are to consider yourself a prisoner, sir," said the guard with his pistol aimed at Payne.

"Well, gentlemen, I shall not resist," Ross said calmly. "But what have I done? Why am I a prisoner? By whose order am I taken?"

"You'll know soon enough," the man said. "Give up your papers and prepare to go with us."

The men grabbed the papers Ross and Payne had been copying, rifling through them as if they were looking for something but didn't know exactly what. Ross was unflustered by the intrusion; he had seen so much trouble that this harassment did not bother him. If these men meant to kill him, Ross knew he would already be dead. But Payne had never had such an experience and was visibly upset. He protested when the men gathered up the documents.

"These, sir, are my papers," Payne said. "I don't suppose you want them."

One of the soldiers pistol-whipped Payne in the mouth for speaking up.

"Hold your damned tongue."

As Payne fell to his knees the soldiers turned their attention to the cabin. They tore through drawers and cabinets carelessly, taking the house apart. One demanded all the letters the chief had written recently, while another man packed up the history papers. After a minute Absalom Bishop— brother of the Georgia Guard's colonel—ordered Ross and Payne to get their horses. They were leaving. As soon as they got on the trail thunder sounded and the skies opened up.

They rode in the rain for miles, soon crossing into Georgia. Ross and Payne were surrounded by guards—twelve in front of them, twelve behind. The soldiers seemed unaffected by the downpour, laughing, singing, and telling obscene stories as if they were drunk. Ross remained quiet, trying to think of a way out of the situation. Payne pulled up alongside Bishop, hoping to reason with the officer. To his disbelief, he found the man humming "Home, Sweet Home." When Payne pointed out that he'd written that song, Bishop was not impressed.

Sometime after midnight they stopped at a tavern to eat and get out of the rain. Inside, there were drunks singing and the guardsmen joined in. The prisoners were free to wander around the bar, and Payne quickly spotted a songbook open to the sheet music for his song. He showed it to Ross, who smiled at the private joke. The tavern belonged to Wilson Young, the man who had hit Payne back at Ross's cabin, and the writer tried to strike up a conversation with him. Young was more impressed by Payne's song than Bishop had been and the two men were soon talking about French literature. Bishop broke up their conversation after a few minutes. He said they'd lingered long enough and marched Ross and Payne back out into the rain. The posse set out again and rode through the night, reaching Spring Place the next morning.

They were locked in a small, windowless log hut with a fireplace and a few bunks that were little more than rough-hewn boards littered with straw. A Cherokee, the son of Going Snake, was chained to a table. He said he'd been arrested for failing to give his name for a census but that the charges were a lie. Ross and Payne were exhausted and tried to sleep amid the racket outside. The writer was horrified to hear the guards bragging about their exploits, making fun of children who screamed for their mothers. Payne could not take it and after a few hours called the quartermaster to ask if he could send a letter to Currey. The guards would not allow it.

Two days passed before they learned of the charges against them. Young visited them on Tuesday, bringing books for Payne and a change of clothes for Ross. Despite his violent outburst earlier, he seemed friendly toward the men. He told Payne he would like to subscribe to his magazine and asked to borrow his confiscated pistols. It was clear he was just another Georgian following orders. He knew nothing of the Georgia Guard's plans but had heard why Ross and Payne were arrested, and he revealed it after half an hour of conversation. Payne had been detained, Young said, because he was a suspected abolitionist. Ross was accused of interfering with a government census of the Cherokees. Payne laughed at the charge but Ross was outraged.

"Who has accused me of such nonsense?"

"Currey," Young told him.

"Are you an officer of the United States?" Ross asked.

"No."

"Then how did you come to obey the orders of Major Currey?"

"In Georgia," Young said, "it's not law, it's all power."

The days got hard to count. Ross and Payne were not allowed to leave the hut, which had grown rank from being packed with a rotating number of prisoners. The guards harassed them, forced them off their bunks, and made them sit on the floor. Ross said little but assured Payne they would get out eventually. They collected what information they could by listening to the guards outside. One of the chief's brothers had come to Spring Place, demanding to see Ross, but was turned away. A few days later one of Ross's sons—most likely Allen—was allowed to see his father on the condition they discuss only family matters. When Ross attempted to speak to the boy in his clumsy Cherokee, the guards broke up the meeting and made the boy leave.

Young returned a few days later, carrying news of the Georgia Supreme Court elections and a paper that included remarks from Governor Lumpkin. The outgoing governor's farewell address included a venomous passage against Ross, and Young asked Payne to read it aloud. When Payne refused Ross spoke up.

"Read it," Ross said.

Payne was tortured by the lines he read, but they seemed not to affect the chief in the slightest. Ross craved information, knowing that any insight about the people who held him could give him an edge. Ross had already learned much from eavesdropping on the guardsmen. He knew that, despite their outward confidence, the Georgians still weren't sure Washington authorities would back their efforts. Ross seized on that bit of uncertainty.

When he heard that Bishop was leaving for Milledgeville on November 13 he asked to send Lumpkin a letter.

Bishop explained that Lumpkin's term had expired, and Ross did not know the new governor, William Schley. He decided instead to send his note to George Gilmer, the former governor and congressman. He told Gilmer he was supposed to leave on a diplomatic mission to Washington by the month's end. If he did not go there would be no chance of securing a treaty with the Cherokees. It was a bluff, but it was the best he could do.

"This delegation has been vested with the fullest powers to settle these unhappy difficulties upon such basis as will secure the present peace and future prosperity of the nation," Ross wrote.

Bishop suspected a trick. He realized the letter was ambiguous and demanded the chief add a postscript clearly stating he was ready to negotiate a treaty. Ross had no choice but to pen the addendum, but he was far too clever to play into the soldier's hands. He wrote, "Permit me to add that I hope you will be fully persuaded of my earnest & sincere desire that the delegation may be successful in settling this."

The next day, Young visited for the last time. He was riding to Milledgeville with Bishop and said he would make sure Ross's letter was delivered. He apologized for hitting Payne—saying, "I've hated it ever since"—and asked again to borrow his pistols. Payne offered to sell them to the man but Young could not afford them. Payne said he was sorry he could not give them away but joked that he wasn't keeping the guns because he planned to escape or feared for his life.

"I suppose our lives are safe enough," Payne said.

"Maybe not," Young said as he walked out of the hut.

John Ridge was furious. He'd been away from home nearly a week before he learned of Ross's arrest. No matter how he felt about the chief personally, Ridge knew this was a grave mistake. These reckless Georgians had made Ross a martyr, and may have sabotaged any chance of a peaceful removal. The Cherokees already considered their chief a saint; now he had gone to jail fighting for their freedom. If some Indians had begun to doubt Ross, that was over now. And if, God forbid, some overzealous guard killed him, Ridge knew it would start a war. He had to do something. On November 14, Ridge got on his horse and rode as quickly as he could for Spring Place.

The Georgia Guard had set up its prison camp near James Vann's house, just twenty miles south of Red Clay. Ridge had no trouble getting in—most of the men recognized him and a few had even guarded his house over the summer. But Colonel Bishop was not inclined to listen to his ranting. It took nearly an hour of warnings about war and political backlash before Bishop finally relented and sent two guards to fetch Ross.

When the men led Ross into the room he was dirty and pale, emaciated from the meager rations he'd been given. But the jail time had not taken his dignity. Even as a prisoner Ross retained the quiet confidence of a president. When Bishop offered the first official explanation for his arrest—he was suspected of working with Henry Clay and John C. Calhoun to lead a slave rebellion—Ross just laughed. These were serious charges, Bishop explained, punishable by death. Abolitionists were not treated kindly in Georgia, he noted, before walking out of the room.

There was no need of formalities between the two Cherokees, for both understood what was at stake. Their talk was brief, open, and frank. Ridge knew the charges were ridiculous and conceded that Schermerhorn had most likely orchestrated Ross's imprisonment. He agreed with Ross that the real purpose of the charade was to prevent the chief from going to Washington; nothing else explained the timing. Both of them knew where this path led. Ridge promised he wouldn't leave without Ross, and he did not have to explain why. No matter what their differences, both knew the tribe's future depended upon Ross's release.

Payne was nearly in a panic by the time Ross returned to the cell. When he asked what was happening he was amazed by the chief's demeanor. Ross had just been told he would likely be executed by the state of Georgia, yet he seemed amused.

"It's all out now," he said. "We are both abolitionists and here for a capital offense. We are the agents of some great men, Mr. Clay, Mr. Calhoun, Judge White, Mr. Poindexter, and the Lord knows who; and we have plotted in concert with them to raise an insurrection among the negroes, who are to join the Indians against the whites."

Ross's ability to joke signaled a confidence he would get out of this, not only because—in this instance—he trusted Ridge, but because he knew that no one of any import had trumped up such fantastic charges. If Jackson had wanted him arrested, he would have at least found more plausible coconspirators —Ross had tried for years to enlist Clay and Calhoun to his cause with no success. If something happened to him, it would undermine the president's and the state's efforts to remove the Cherokees. He knew this, and eventually these Georgians would figure it out. And if they didn't, Ross knew Ridge would explain it to them.

Ross met with Bishop and Ridge again that evening and for several hours the next day, Monday, November 16. Ross said little to Payne about the dealings, except to whisper that he'd gotten Hicks's history papers back. That night, Payne was allowed to join the group for a dinner. No business was discussed, but at the end of the evening Bishop told one of his guards that "Mr. Ross is discharged."

Ross visited Payne later that night on the pretext of collecting his things. He quietly assured the writer he would be free soon but the Georgia Guard believed he was responsible for some unflattering stories that had appeared in state newspapers.

"You have never published anything about Bishop or the Guard in Lumpkin County, have you?"

"Not a syllable, either in Lumpkin County or any other county in Georgia or elsewhere."

"You may as well explain that when you see Col. Bishop," Ross said.

Ross set out with Ridge that night, eager to get back to Tennessee before Bishop changed his mind. They rode through the late hours, finally reaching Ross's worried family at Flint Springs early that morning. There was little for the two men to discuss; they had both done what they had to in order to avert disaster. It changed little between them.

The next morning, after Ross had gotten some sleep and a good breakfast, he wrote to a friend of his father's, James Donohoo. He asked the man to help Payne get out of the South unharmed. Though he worried about Payne's safety, he knew the writer was just a bystander—the guardsmen had been after him, Ross. Three days later the writer was indeed released; the charges against him were dropped. Payne had told the Georgia Guard the truth, that he had not written anything about them. But that would soon change. He would not forget how he and Ross had been treated.

Ross spent the final weeks of November preparing for his trip. The delegation had fallen apart in his absence. Elias Boudinot refused to go because he doubted Ross would ever agree to a treaty, something Ridge had alluded to on their ride to Flint Springs. But when Ross asked for a reason, the former editor simply said, "I cannot go to Washington." He suggested sending Stand Watie in his place but Ross had another replacement in mind.

Two days before the group was scheduled to leave, Ross asked John Ridge if his father might go with them. Major Ridge was the most respected full-blooded chief the Cherokees had, both among the tribe and in Washington circles, and Ross wanted his counsel once again. If there was a compromise to be had, Ross knew the old man could find it. But Ridge declined without giving a reason, and Ross was forced to take George Chambers instead.

Ross nearly lost the services of the younger Ridge as well. No sooner had the delegation began its journey than Ridge received a copy of a Knoxville newspaper, the *Register,* in which John Howard Payne had written a scathing account of his arrest by the Georgia Guard. In the article, he called the militia "banditti" willing to break federal law to oppress the Cherokees. He told of the false charges against Ross, claiming the ruse was an attempt to force a treaty on the tribe. Currey publicly called Payne a liar, but the ensuing scandal forced Bishop to resign his post and eventually led the Georgia legislature to disband the state guard.

John Ridge believed Ross had put Payne up to writing the article. Before they traveled forty miles Ridge declared that he would not go on. The chief, he claimed, was "diametrically opposed to me and my friends, who will never consent to be citizens of the States, or receive money to buy land in foreign parts." Ridge would not even speak to the chief. Instead he sent a note warning Ross not to forget the best interests of his people, neglecting the fact that he and the chief had very different ideas of what his people's best interests actually were.

"I trust that, whatever you do, if you can effect a treaty, that the rights of the poor Indians, who are nearly naked and homeless, will not be disregarded."

Ross pleaded with Ridge to reconsider. He assured Ridge he had not told Payne what to write or settled on "any fixed course." He promised that he wanted only what was best for the "whole Cherokee people" and urged him to continue for the sake of tribal unity. Ridge stayed with the group but feared that Boudinot had been right about Ross, that Ross had no interest in negotiating. If Ridge knew the true reason his cousin had remained in Georgia he said nothing of it.

Ross considered the matter settled and rode with the delegation as far as North Carolina, where he stopped to visit his daughter, who was attending school at Salem. Jane was among the best students at the Moravian institution, which was one of the oldest, most prestigious girls' schools in the country. She had grown into a strong woman with her father's loyalty to the tribe, and would become one of Ross's closest confidantes. When Ridge and the others set out into the Virginia countryside, Ross told them he would meet them in Washington City a month later. By the time he caught up with the others, however, the entire game had changed.

New Echota was cold and quiet, a frontier ghost town. Two years of Cherokee exile had left the public square overgrown, the dirt roads hidden beneath fallen leaves, and the once grand government buildings empty and neglected. Only a few wary Indians still lived in the former capital, families who awaited their eventual eviction by Georgia troops. When Schermerhorn arrived in mid-December for his own council, some of those Cherokees were recruited to clean up the dirty and musty buildings to accommodate him.

The tribal elders began arriving on December 19, some making their first trip to the old capital in years. Most of them were members of the Treaty Party, but there were a few opposed to removal who simply felt they should be there. The vast majority of Cherokees thought it treasonous simply to attend, and others feared they would be arrested by Georgia troops. Few were enticed by the commissioner's promise of free blankets for all. Schermerhorn had expected as much—that's why he had announced any absent Cherokee would be counted as voting in favor of whatever action was taken. The Indians who chose to attend would straggle in over a few days; fewer than one hundred would ultimately show up.

Ross's disgraced brother Andrew appeared publicly for the first time in more than a year. Andrew Ross had remained hidden since his failed attempt at a treaty but felt safe enough to show up at New Echota while Schermerhorn's guards were present. Most of the other Indians ignored him. Andrew's attendance made Schermerhorn happy, if for nothing else than symbolism. Even the chief's own brother was against him.

Major Ridge was among the earliest to arrive, although it is unclear if he declined Ross's invitation to attend Schermerhorn's negotiations. He stayed with Elias Boudinot, one of the last Cherokees living in New Echota. For several days the small band of Indians enjoyed a social atmosphere they had missed for the past few years. They huddled around fires, smoking pipes and eating connahani, the Cherokee version of grits. Most avoided the unpleasant talk of what would come next, preferring to revel in their past glory on the site of their greatest achievement. It was something of a reunion. It was also, they realized, the end of an era.

On December 22, the Cherokees gathered in the council house to organize themselves, electing John Gunter the presiding officer and reinstating Alexander McCoy as secretary, a position he lost in part because of his pro-treaty views. The next day, the preacher spoke for several hours about the wonderful treaty they would make, promising to throw out the deal rejected at the General Council. He spoke to the Cherokees as if they were simple children, and even the Cherokees who supported Schermerhorn, such as Boudinot, cared little for the man. Members of the Treaty Party did nothing to quash the rumors that he was a clumsy, drunken womanizer, and certainly not a holy man. But few doubted his gift for oratory. By the time he finished speaking the Cherokees were so tired they did nothing else for the remainder of the day.

Major Currey made his appearance on December 24 to read a draft of the proposed treaty. An Indian translated his words into Cherokee. Despite Schermerhorn's assurances, the treaty was nearly the same as the one already refused by the tribe: the Cherokees would be given $5 million for all of their land east of the Mississippi. Currey promised the government's help moving the tribe and funds to pay for the Indians' necessities for a year afterward. Additional consideration would be paid to any Cherokee given a land grant in the 1817 and 1819 treaties. Currey promised that the United States would never take the Cherokees' new land or incorporate it into the country's own holdings—without the tribe's permission, of course. He even suggested the Cherokees would be given a seat in Congress at some undetermined point.

Finally, the bottom line: the tribe had two years to leave Alabama, Tennessee, and Georgia.

While Currey spoke, an ember escaped the council house hearth. The fire had been stoked into a rage to ward off the bitter December cold; Schermerhorn's blankets were not keeping the tribe warm enough. The errant ember floated upward until it settled in a rafter and, ultimately, caught the roof on fire. The Cherokees ran from the building while a few men fanned at the ceiling with the free blankets and stood on the benches to tamp out the fire. Eventually the Indians were called back inside and Currey resumed his talk. The few anti-treaty Cherokees in attendance believed the blaze a perfect symbol for these "unlawful proceedings."

The council house fell silent when Currey finished. This was the deal and the Cherokees knew they would get no better. Few said anything or offered a hint of how they felt. In truth, the Indians were torn. The entire Cherokee conflict now came down to their decision and it pained even the most pro-treaty Indians to cast their vote. It was Major Ridge who first rose to speak.

In his later years, the old chief had become increasingly reluctant to speak in public. It was only his distress that compelled him to intervene in what he knew should rightfully be the decision of younger Indians. He did not want to give up his homeland any more than Ross, but he had become convinced they had no choice. It did not matter that the tribe had the justice, morality, and the support of sixteen thousand Cherokees on their side. Ridge knew there was no way to win a game in which their opponents had the luxury of changing the rules. So the old man walked to the dais and gave his support to something he had once killed others for doing.

Speaking in his native tongue, Ridge urged the Cherokees to sell their land to white men.

I am one of the native sons of these wild woods. I have hunted the deer and turkey here, more than fifty years. I have fought your battles, have defended your truth and honesty, and fair trading. I have always been the friend of honest white men. The Georgians have shown a grasping spirit lately; they have extended their laws, to which we are unaccustomed, which harass our braves and make their children suffer and cry; but I can do them justice in my heart. They think the Great Father, the President, is bound by the compact of 1802 to purchase this country for them, and they justify their conduct by the end in view. They are willing to buy these lands on which to build houses and clear fields.

I know the Indians have an older title than theirs. We obtained the land from the living God above. They got their title from the British. Yet they are strong and we are weak. We are few, and they are many.

We cannot remain here in safety and comfort. I know we love the graves of our fathers . . . We can never forget these homes, I know, but an unbending, iron necessity tells us we must leave them. I would willingly die to preserve them, but any forcible effort to keep them will cost us our lands, our lives and the lives of our children. There is but one path to safety, one road to future existence as a Nation. That path is open before you. Make a treaty of cession. Give up these lands and go over beyond the great Father of Waters.

When Ridge finished speaking he looked out on the Cherokees and saw tears raining from their eyes. For years, Ross had offered them hope, promised them salvation. But now their oldest, most respected chief told them the unhappy truth, and they knew he was right. There was no hope, and if there was salvation to be had it lay in the land of the setting sun. It was finished. When the old man stepped down from the podium, tribal elders stood to greet him. One by one, each took Ridge's hands and embraced him. They told him they would follow him west.

The Cherokees hosted a feast on Christmas Day, during which they drank and tried to avoid discussing the choice that had already been made. The pastor Schermerhorn was not opposed to working on the holy day, suggesting the Indians select a committee of twenty Cherokees to negotiate the particulars of the treaty with himself and Currey. It was a clever ruse. The commissioner knew a treaty signed by fewer than a hundred Cherokees might be dismissed by the United States Senate as unrepresentative of the tribe. A unanimous committee of twenty chiefs, selected by an undetermined number of Cherokees, would look infinitely more official. The elected group included Ridge, Gunter, and Boudinot, who had given his own self-serving speech denouncing Ross and praising himself for the difficult decision he had made to stand up to the chief.

"We can die, but the great Cherokee Nation will be saved," Boudinot had said. "Oh what is a man worth who will not dare to die for his people?"

The man appointed to the committee that most pleased Schermerhorn was the last one chosen: Andrew Ross, the chief's brother. Even the Cherokees realized having the signature of a Ross on the treaty would lend it some weight in Congress. The men in Washington likely would not realize Andrew was an outcast from his own tribe, his own family.

The committee met for hours on Monday, and that evening they announced they had reached an accord with the Indian commissioner. Little had changed from the document Currey had read to the council four days earlier, but the group voted in favor of the treaty with little discussion. The elated Schermerhorn asked that a delegation travel to Washington with him to present the agreement to President Jackson and the Senate. It was not a simple request. Nearly fifty Cherokees volunteered to go, and no one wanted to whittle down the list for fear of angering one faction or another. Schermerhorn smartly declined the invitation to choose the Indians who would travel with him. The question was temporarily left unsettled.

The committee gathered for one final time on Tuesday evening, December 29, 1835, at Elias Boudinot's house. The location ensured only a small group would witness the final reading and signing of the treaty. With a fire staving off the cold, the document was read by candlelight in a room crowded with two dozen men. When the reading was finished there was a pause, as if no one wanted to be the first to put his name on the treaty. Despite their good intentions, all of them had lingering misgivings that, by making a deal with the so-called Devil's Horn, they were betraying their own tribe. Finally, Gunter signed and was followed by Schermerhorn. When the commissioner finished he handed the quill to Major Ridge.

Still illiterate at the age of seventy, Ridge waited while someone wrote his name high on the document, just beneath the commissioner's name. All he had to do was make his mark and the Treaty of New Echota—as the Cherokees later came to call it—would become official. His endorsement was all Schermerhorn needed for proof of the treaty's legitimacy, to win ratification in the Senate. Even though he realized that signing the document was an act of hypocrisy—had he not killed Doublehead for far less serious crimes?—Ridge knew he had been beaten. The only way to save his tribe was to reverse a course he had set for himself and the Cherokees decades earlier. He bent over the table and scrawled a simple mark on the document. When he finished, Ridge quietly acknowledged he had decided his tribe's fate, as well as his own.

"I have signed my death warrant."

TWELVE

Where They Cried

There were rules for visiting the president. John Ross could not discuss treaties or settlements, was not allowed to present any petitions or evidence to further his cause. Lewis Cass warned him that Andrew Jackson had no interest in personally handling such minutiae. This was simply, for lack of a better term, a courtesy visit.

When Jackson invited Ross into his Executive Mansion office at eleven in the morning on January 7, 1836, the president was more than courteous; he was affable and expansive. The two men chatted for half an hour, and it was Jackson who first brought up the treaty. The president said he had "hoped the propositions sent out would have been acceptable to the Cherokee people." It had always been his intention to protect the tribe, he said, but he regretted that was not possible so long as they lived among the whites. It seemed he was commiserating with Ross, but the chief suspected Jackson was merely employing a new tactic. Ross repeated the same mantra about the tribe never ceding another foot of land. He was disgusted by Washington bureaucrats, but sometimes he found himself droning on exactly like one. The president let Ross's remarks pass.

It soon became apparent Jackson was far less strident than he had been in the past. He even suggested he would entertain "alterations" to his treaty, something Cass had refused to consider. The president offered no specifics but said he was interested in Ross's ideas and asked that he submit them to the secretary of war. He promised that Cass would respond in kind. Jackson had no intention of debating Ross personally but he appeared this day ready to deal.

Ross was not given to bouts of optimism but the president's attitude gave him a measure of hope. Schermerhorn claimed Jackson would not even receive him, but after less than a week in Washington he had secured the president's blessing to negotiate. Ross thought it was because Jackson would soon leave office. By the end of the year a new president would be elected and he no longer would be burdened by the demands of temperamental Georgia politicians. Ross also thought Jackson looked noticeably older, more tired than he had been at their last meeting. The chief understood all too well how the demands of executive office aged a man.

Ross left the mansion somewhat encouraged. He had planned to wait out Jackson's term and appeal to his successor, but now he believed it might be better to bargain with an outgoing president with no concern for politics. Perhaps Jackson was being honest. If that was so, Ross thought he might win some concession from Washington, perhaps even be able to retain some of the Cherokees' land. For a moment he forgot his own rule: never trust a white politician.

In a week both Ross and Jackson would learn what had happened at New Echota, and that would change everything.

Reverend James J. Trott called it "the late Christmas trick." Trott's letter, which provided a detailed account of the New Echota meeting, reached Ross at Mrs. Arguelle's boardinghouse in mid-January. At first Ross did not grasp the significance of the news. He mentioned it to Cass only in passing, pointing out that his delegation was the only body authorized to negotiate with the government. He assured the secretary if such a convention were held it was certainly against the will of most Cherokees. He gave the story little credibility; after all, he had not been told of a meeting.

It never occurred to Ross that a treaty signed by a few dozen Indians, many of whom already had enrolled to emigrate, would be taken seriously, much less accepted, by Jackson or the Congress. By the time he realized the opposite it was too late. Schermerhorn and the leaders of the Treaty Party were on their way to Washington.

Major Ridge would not face Ross. When he reached the city in early February with Schermerhorn, Ridge sent the chief a copy of the treaty along with a formal note that attempted to explain his reasons for signing it. They were, by Ross's measure, pitiful excuses: Ridge claimed that the Cherokees feared Jackson would not meet with the delegation, that some people in the government had convinced them there was no other alternative to removal. It was a letter of defeat, nothing Ross had not heard before. Finally, Ridge asked the chief to approve the treaty, offering to make any alterations or modifications he felt necessary.

Ross was furious. It was the same basic deal rejected by the council, nothing more. He would not even respond to Ridge. The letter did not sound like the same man who had groomed him for Cherokee leadership, who had preached the tribe's sacred connection to its homeland. Ridge's note was most likely a letter of the committee, he knew, probably written at Schermerhorn's direction. In the entire note, Ross could find only three words he believed actually came from his old mentor, one sad message he distilled from several paragraphs of rambling: it was necessary.

Ross tried to pass off the treaty as just another complication, yet another fire to douse. But he was afraid. He felt his control of the tribe slipping away. This was the moment he had dreaded for years, the time when a large contingent of Cherokees chiefs would overrule him and accept removal. He could foresee any number of unpleasant scenarios unfolding—a civil war within the tribe, a military slaughter of Indians unwilling to move, genocide—but he could not allow himself to panic. There was not time.

The assistant principal chief George Lowrey knew of the treaty weeks before Ross and anticipated what the chief would need to combat the Ridges. Although the tribe was battling a new outbreak of smallpox, Lowrey circulated a petition against the treaty signed by nearly fourteen thousand Cherokees and sent it to Washington. It reached the city about the same time as Schermerhorn's delegation. The document made it clear how the majority of Cherokees felt about the treaty.

When Ross received the petition he forwarded it to Lewis Cass with a cover letter signed by John Ridge and Stand Watie, who had accompanied him to Washington. But by the time it was delivered the two men had abandoned Ross. They had begun to act strange days earlier, avoided the chief at the hotel. Within a day of Schermerhorn's arrival, Ridge and Watie moved out of Mrs. Arguelle's and into the hotel where Major Ridge was lodged. There, they signed the treaty of New Echota. Ross called it John Ridge's "fourth entire revolution in politics within as many months: varying as often as the moon, without the excuse of lunacy for his changes."

The arrival of Schermerhorn and his treaty changed the climate in Washington. Despite the president's recent promise, all of Ross's efforts to negotiate were rebuffed. At one point, Herring told Ross "you are laboring under extreme misapprehension in believing that you have been recognized by the Department as the duly constituted representatives of the Cherokee Nation." As far as Washington was concerned, the government had reached an accord with the Cherokees.

Jackson quickly embraced the new treaty and pushed to have it ratified by Congress, even though he had to know it was a shameful ruse. A cursory examination suggested the treaty was at best illegal, and more than likely fraudulent. Schermerhorn claimed that the agreement had been approved by the tribe's General Council and that more than five hundred Cherokees were present at its adoption, but neither claim was true. Even government agents charged with promoting a treaty criticized Schermerhorn's tactics. Major William M. Davis, an enrolling agent, said the preacher's methods had been a "series of blunders first to last." The treaty would not hold up under scrutiny in court but Jackson would make sure it never got that far.

The deception was apparent on Capitol Hill, however, and debate over the treaty consumed Congress for nearly two months. The tribe's friends fought to have the treaty voided. Former president John Quincy Adams, who had been elected to the House in 1830, called it "an eternal disgrace upon the country"; Senator Henry Clay, a potential presidential candidate, introduced legislation that would automatically force rejection of the treaty; Davy Crockett denounced the whole business as shameful. Daniel Webster, Henry Alexander Wise, and Theodore Frelinghuysen all expressed disapproval publicly. President Jackson ignored all charges that the treaty was a fraud. For all his many critics, he knew he had twice as many supporters in Congress.

On March 8 Ross delivered a lengthy memorial to the Senate. He had studied the treaty and outlined legal problems with it, the subterfuge employed by Jackson's agents to win it. He urged senators to "dare not unite with, and sanction the acts of a small faction, to which, they well know the Cherokee people would never yield their assent."

Although Ross's allies believed he had made a strong case—and gathered around to congratulate him in the ornate halls of the Capitol—it did not affect the outcome. After several weeks of debate the Senate approved the treaty 31 to 15, one vote beyond the two-thirds majority needed to ratify it. Ross turned his attention to the House, believing the treaty would be unenforceable if the $5 million it provided to the tribe was not paid out. But this was useless. The House approved the payment and Jackson signed the treaty into law on May 23, 1836.

While the other Cherokees returned home, Ross stayed in Washington and continued his fight for another month. He addressed Congress in June, detailing Schermerhorn's underhanded tactics, and asked Congress to investigate. He outlined his arguments one final time in a "Letter from John Ross" published in *Niles' Weekly Register*. Finally, he realized it was useless.

It had all happened so fast. In less than five months a small band of rogue Cherokees negotiated a treaty, carried it to Washington, and saw it adopted as law—and the president of the United States was complicit in the scheme. A few dozen Indians and the unbending will of Georgia politicians had decided the fate of a nation. The Cherokees had two years to give up their homes, leave the land of their forefathers, and march into unknown western territory.

*   *   *

Ross returned home to find the Ridges trying to prepare the Cherokees for removal and undermine his efforts to build opposition to the treaty. They found a ready audience in their own followers but could make no headway with the full-blood clans. Most Cherokees were simply confused; if more had understood what had happened the Ridges likely would have been killed.

The chief had been appointed chairman of a committee to appraise Cherokee property prior to removal. The treaty required the federal government to reimburse any Indian who had been granted private land in previous treaties, as well as those who had property confiscated by Georgia. To any poor Indian who took notice, it appeared the wealthy Cherokees were dividing up the treaty money before it was even distributed. John Ridge and Elias Boudinot sat on the committee and claimed Ross was appointed its chairman out of respect. But Ross suspected they wanted it to appear he had endorsed the treaty, and so he refused to serve. The chief's supporters followed his lead, leaving the valuation of Cherokee property entirely in Ridge's control.

Wilson Lumpkin would be lured out of retirement to help the committee, and later he reported to Washington that most Cherokees stubbornly refused to give up their land. He said the Indians were "enveloped in a gross darkness, who know nothing, except it comes from Ross." Lumpkin had spent so many years trying to deal with the tribe that his warning could not be dismissed as idle rhetoric. He told Indian Affairs officials that he had seen no signs the tribe was preparing to move.

"They intend to die here," Lumpkin wrote.

The Ridges called a September 12 meeting at New Echota to explain the treaty and sway Cherokees to their way of thinking. But Ross countered with his own council at Red Clay, forcing the Ridges to cancel. They refused Ross's summons to appear at his meeting.

The Red Clay council resulted in nothing except a new petition protesting the treaty of New Echota and another Washington assignment for Ross. Before he journeyed north, however, the council asked him to lead a delegation to consult with the chiefs of the tribe's western band. The western chiefs had maintained good relations with the government, and council members hoped they would intervene. It was wishful thinking, but there were no other options.

It took three weeks to reach the western Cherokees, a trip slowed somewhat by a lame horse that forced Stephen Foreman to give up the journey. The Cherokee land lay just beyond the boundary of Arkansas; the territory had been established as a state earlier in the year. For some of Ross's men it was their first look at this mysterious country they had heard so much about. They were surprised to see that, beyond the plains, the land returned to a form more like their own homes. The wooded, rolling hills and shallow, rocky streams were surprisingly similar to the terrain of northern Georgia. It was not home, but not nearly as bad as it had been made out to be. Ross wasn't interested in the land, however. It was not the home of his people and, as far as he was concerned, it never would be.

Ross spent three weeks in the West. In that time he conferred with the chiefs, visited relatives who had already migrated, and tried to avoid arrest. Indian agents in Tennessee had learned of his mission and asked the western superintendent, William Armstrong, to jail the chief if he tried to "incite" opposition to the treaty. Armstrong did not want to meddle in politics and avoided Ross by conveniently retreating to nearby Fort Gibson. But his surrogates warned the western chief John Jolly to meet with Ross in private to avoid any possible legal trouble.

The western Cherokees had their own reasons to oppose removal. They did not relish sharing their land and feared that consolidating the two bands would severely dilute their political power and deny them separate annuities. A contentious reunion could lead to violence or even civil war. Ross hoped those factors might scare Congress into reconsidering. Jolly understood all of this without Ross having to explain it, and in early December he appointed a delegation to accompany the eastern chiefs to Washington.

Bad weather forced the Indians to travel so far south they eventually wandered back into Tennessee. The western Cherokees were delighted by the chance to visit their former homes and asked for a short detour. Ross agreed, but the group was intercepted by a messenger carrying a letter from Lewis Ross, warning his brother that he was walking into a trap. Jackson had ordered General John E. Wool to watch the Ross cabin. There were soldiers stationed around Flint Springs.

"I do think there is nothing more certain than you will be arrested if you remain a day at home," Lewis wrote.

Ross avoided the soldiers by splitting off from the group and traveling alone to Knoxville. The delegation met him there a few days later and the group rode through North Carolina to Salem so the chief could visit his daughter, Jane. He rested at the school for days in the company of his daughter and the missionaries. Before resuming their journey, the party sold their horses at Salem and took a new stagecoach to Washington. It was easier riding but Ross did not like the lack of control and felt they were wasting time. They did not arrive in Washington until February 9, 1837, just a few weeks before President Jackson would leave office.

The capital was busy with the upcoming transfer of power and the Cherokees avoided Jackson so they could deal directly with his successor, Martin Van Buren. Ross hoped the new president, who had been elected in November and would take office in March, might change attitudes in Washington. But no one was interested in reviewing the treaty, and the western Cherokees proved to be of little help. They grew tired of the city quickly and departed, having settled nothing. Upon their return to the Arkansas territory, they would begin to plot ways to retain their power after the removal, which even they now recognized was inevitable.

Ross found Van Buren no more receptive to his suggestions than Jackson had been. In fact, Ross correctly suspected that the new president was doing little more than following his predecessor's policies. Van Buren had no time to meet with Ross but offered to reinstate the tribe's annuity payments. It was a hollow gesture.

Congress did offer Ross some hope. One committee promised to investigate the chief's claims against Schermerhorn, but it quickly became apparent the men were primarily interested in evidence that might embarrass the preacher. Before Ross checked out of Mrs. Arguelle's boardinghouse he met with Joel Poinsett, the new secretary of war, who was evasive and not much more help than Cass. When Poinsett was asked directly, What will the government do if the Cherokees refuse to abandon their homes next year? the secretary had no answer.

The trip, as unsuccessful as it was, convinced Ross of only one thing: he would not yet give up. As long as the Cherokees remained on their land, he believed there was a chance to have the treaty voided. He suspected the farce at New Echota had been a trick to make him accept removal and he would not fall into the trap by conceding.

John Ross returned to Tennessee after another visit to Salem, where Jane expressed concern about her father's health. She noticed he was distant and preoccupied, unable to rest, and she hated to see him travel in such a state. Ross had been away from home for months, and upon his return he found that many Cherokees had set out for the West on their own and others were preparing to follow them. He convinced as many as he could to stay—the fewer Indians in the tribe, the easier they would be to move. He also had to quash rumors he had joined the Treaty Party.

In Ross's absence, one of his overseers had submitted claims for the chief's property at Flint Springs and Head of Coosa to Ridge's appraisal committee. The panel concluded Ross was owed $23,665.75 for the two properties and his land reservations, a sum that made him one of the richest men in the Cherokee Nation. Boudinot suggested that because a claim had been submitted for Ross's property, he now approved of the treaty. Ross was livid. It did little good to point out that John Ridge had granted himself nearly as much money, and even more to his father.

Ross left no questions about his position when he finally addressed the General Council at Red Clay on August 3, 1837. Standing in the rustic council shed, a translator turning his English to Cherokee, the chief recounted his trip to the western land, the government's attempts to arrest him, and his meetings with the new secretary of war. These stories, similar to ones he'd told for years, could not have meant much to most Cherokees. But they understood all too well when Ross claimed that the land reserved for their tribe was "worthless to the Cherokees, as it can never be settled for want of wood, water and tillable soil—it being situated in a bleak region and represented almost entirely by prairie country and covered with stones."

Even if he neglected the fact that the western Cherokees were more than happy with their home, the chief convincingly argued that moving to such land would lead to their destruction. Ross could be hyperbolic when it suited his purposes. He said the Cherokees should not abandon their homes because it would give the impression they accepted the treaty as valid. If they must remove, he said, they should be allowed to find some other, more suitable land.

It was a subtle sleight of hand. Ross had condemned the removal and then suggested obliquely that the Indians might indeed soon have to leave their homes. Most Indians never noticed the conflicting message.

A few days later the Indian agent John Mason Jr. arrived at Red Clay with a message from the president. Mason was greeted amicably and given use of a warm cabin with dry pine needles on its floor. Ross even took time to entertain Mason and an Englishman named George Featherstonhaugh at his cabin. The men noted that, along with vegetables from the summer harvest, Ross was reduced to serving an unidentified meat for dinner. Ross did not eat with the men. It was Cherokee custom not to eat with guests, but it may have left the Englishman wondering if there was enough food to go around.

Featherstonhaugh was impressed by the Cherokee country and later boasted of the "copious limestone spring," the "beautiful trees," and the picturesque setting of Red Clay. He could understand why the white men wanted it so badly. Mason, meanwhile, spent much of the weekend watching the Indians through the spaces between the logs of his cabin. A series of campfires burned on the perimeter of Red Clay, and Indians huddled around them in the light rain. Occasionally, a few Cherokees would wander down to the spring for a drink. These people did not look intimidating or dangerous, Mason realized, and he took no joy in his mission. But he had orders to carry out. He emerged from the cabin only once that weekend, to meet with General Nathaniel Smith, the man expected to supervise the Cherokee removal.

On Monday, the horns of Indian messengers called the men of the Cherokee Nation to the council shed; the women and children were told to remain by the fires. Mason was given an interpreter, the same as Ross had had. The president, he said, was "guided by justice" and wanted only safety and happiness for the Cherokee people. That could come only through removal, when they were far away from their current lands. Mason informed them their move would begin in the spring. By the end of the next summer they would be settled in the West.

"There, Cherokees, in our new country, you will be far beyond the limits or jurisdiction of any state or territory," Mason said. "The country will be yours; yours exclusively."

The tribe listened politely but ignored his message. Still, Mason came away sympathetic to Ross and the Cherokees. When he returned to Washington, he made no one happy by reporting that Ross could not change the opinion of the tribe on removal if he tried. He described the chief as a peaceful man and said his opposition to removal was sincere, "not a mere political game played by Ross for the maintenance of his ascendancy in the tribe."

After Mason's speech, the council members voted to send Ross and another delegation to Washington to try once again to settle these difficulties. It was as if the Cherokees did not understand what they had been told, either by Mason or by Ross. They never stopped to consider that their delegations had not been successful since the days of President Adams. Ross spent more time away from his people than with them, and it never made any significant difference in their plight. They did not realize they had lost, or that they would never see Red Clay again.

Shortly after John Ross and his delegation set out for Washington, John Ridge left the Cherokee country for the last time. For the past year Ridge had divided his time between growing crops to feed Indians along the trail west and serving on the committee charged with sorting out the details of removal. He limited the time he spent around anyone associated with the chief or General Council. His cousin Elias Boudinot constantly argued they should leave the country, fearing they would be killed. But Ridge stoically went about his business, all the while keeping a watchful eye on the woods surrounding his farm.

Ridge could not have been happy about his predicament. He felt it was his duty to prepare the tribe for removal, but he had been abandoned by the Georgia officials who'd promised him safety. Since the treaty was signed, the state had allowed white settlers to do anything they liked on Indian land, and that included building a trading post on Major Ridge's land. The Ridges complained to government officials but got little relief. When they hosted a meeting to review plans for the removal few Cherokees attended, but Lumpkin and a few other state and federal officials showed up. The men offered no protection from the settlers. Lumpkin had even called for more troops to come in, not to help the Ridges but to control the restless Indians.

Major Ridge had been gone for months. He accepted government transportation to the new country earlier that year, fearing his poor health would not allow him to survive the long trip on his own. On March 3, 1837, he left Ross's Landing on a flatboat carrying nearly five hundred Cherokees to their new homes. His wife, his daughter, and one of John's children had traveled with him.

The first few days were terrible. Major Ridge was exposed to the elements on the deck of the flatboat and his condition worsened. Finally, he was transferred to the steamer *Knoxville* and given private quarters. But when that boat ran aground at Decatur the group had to trek across land until they reached deep water, where the *Newark* carried them the rest of the way across Tennessee and into Arkansas. Soon after Ridge departed it was rumored he had died on the route, but that was just a story from the trail. Despite a bad cough Ridge made it to the boundary of the western Cherokees.

Major Ridge settled in an area called Honey Creek, near the border where Arkansas and Missouri met. The land there closely resembled his property at Head of Coosa, but that was not the primary reason for Ridge's choice. The tract he chose was nearly fifty miles north of the Cherokee settlement, far from the land his people would soon call home. He no longer cared to live among his own tribe. Major Ridge had become an exile in exile.

John Ridge and his family followed six months later, traveling with Elias Boudinot and his new bride; Boudinot's first wife had recently died. They rode alone, preferring to avoid both the military and other Cherokees. Along the route they stopped to have their horses reshod at Nashville and, while there, borrowed horses to visit the Hermitage. Ridge was still enamored of Jackson, and he told the old man that he'd named his son after him. Jackson seemed grateful.

Ridge and Boudinot reached Honey Creek at the end of November. Although Boudinot would eventually mingle with the other Cherokees, Ridge decided to follow his father's example, avoid politics, and distance himself from the tribe. He built a fine house near his father's and together they opened a trading post. To his friends, Ridge claimed that his new home was beautiful and peaceful, and that he was finally content. He would remain there for more than a year and miss all the trouble the treaty he signed eventually brought upon his people.

John Ross wasted another eight months in Washington. For much of that time he was distracted by various federal agents who asked him to help them negotiate with the Seminoles. The military was tied up in its second war with the Florida tribe, a conflict sparked by a removal treaty signed against the wishes of most Seminoles. Their chief Osceola had been captured under questionable circumstances. Poinsett asked Ross to vouch for the government's fairness and integrity. To Ross, it seemed these men had little shame, much less any sense of irony.

Ross resisted Poinsett's overtures for months, but when the secretary of war suggested his help would be looked upon favorably, and perhaps benefit his own tribe, Ross had little choice. He justified his diplomacy as an effort to save Indian lives—he knew the Seminoles could not win against the United States. He dispatched Cherokee messengers to deliver his promise that the government would act honorably if the Seminoles would send an envoy to negotiate.

When the Seminoles followed Ross's advice, their delegation was arrested and thrown into prison. Ross was outraged but could do nothing other than send a short note of apology. He had been betrayed once again. But Ross could not dwell on it. He had larger problems.

Back home, Cherokees were starving and confused. They were harassed by military officers for not enrolling to emigrate, and they found this perplexing. Most Indians thought the issue was still under negotiation. When Ross heard about these troubles from his brother Lewis, he asked Mason and the Congress to intervene. But no one on Capitol Hill would listen to him.

Lewis Ross, still his brother's conscience and closest adviser, finally told him what no other person was willing to say. Lewis wrote to Ross that he was "tired to death" and that, if he could not win in Washington, perhaps it was time to tell the tribe they had failed and had to move. Ross heard about the trouble at home only through letters but Lewis was living it. Alone in a Washington hotel room, Ross was stung by Lewis's message. He believed his brother and understood he had been deluding himself. He'd been blind. Even his brother knew their time had run out.

One month before the removal deadline Ross offered to sign a removal treaty. It was a signal of defeat. Anyone who knew the chief would have recognized this decision as proof that his political future meant nothing to him. Agreeing to sign a treaty, no matter what the content, would likely lead to his expulsion from office. But John Ross knew there might not be any other way to save his grandmother's people, his people.

Ross promised Poinsett the Cherokees would leave peacefully—and on their own—but they would need another two years to prepare. In return, they would emigrate without government aid or funding. The secretary was not inclined to bargain but, after a few weeks, allowed that an extension might be granted. Poinsett had very clear motives. If he was able to secure Ross's signature on the treaty, it would remove any doubt of the treaty's legitimacy, and that might be worth another two years of complaints from Georgia.

However, Poinsett would not put his offer in writing and the Senate flatly refused the suggestion. Wilson Lumpkin, who had recently been elected to the Senate, complained that the government should stop listening to "this man Ross." Lumpkin declared Ross should be sent to New England or "Hayti" and Elias Boudinot—"a man of education, refinement and a high moral sense of propriety"—could lead the tribe out of their troubles. Most senators ignored Lumpkin but it did not matter. By that time the May deadline had passed. It was done.

Not another moon would pass before the Cherokees started moving west.

General Winfield Scott delivered that message to a few dozen Indians at New Echota on May 10, 1838, just two weeks before the removal was scheduled to begin. The imposing general had arrived in Georgia to take command of the troops already stationed throughout the South, and he was not pleased by the chaos he found. The Cherokees had done nothing to ready themselves for the move and Scott blamed Ross for this. While the chief was away in Washington, the Indians still held hope that their fate was not settled and ignored the buildup of troops and enrolling agents who urged them to sign up for the move. Most Cherokees went about their business as if there were no shadow over their land; many were actively planting gardens for the summer crop.

Scott told friends that Ross had done a disservice to his people. The Cherokees foolishly clung to hope that Ross would save them yet. Scott tried his best to convince them otherwise.

The few Cherokees who listened to Scott that day heard him explain there would be no escape; his troops would gather up the Indians and send them on their journey. The general said he hoped to do this kindly, with every bit of mercy, but warned he would use force if necessary. He urged them not to resist, for it would mean nothing less than the destruction of their tribe.

"Will you, then by resistance compel us to resort to arms . . . or will you by flight seek to hide yourself in mountains and forests and thus oblige us to hunt you down?" Scott asked.

The Indians looked as if they did not understand and had no intention of obeying. Scott worried a conflict similar to the Seminole War could erupt any day. By his own estimate four-fifths of the Cherokees were opposed to the move and he feared brute force would be the only way to take them. That was something he did not want to do. He ordered his remarks printed on broadbills and circulated throughout the nation to nudge the Indians, and the initial reaction was good: nearly one hundred Cherokees traveled to the Indian agency office at Calhoun to enroll. But soon the slow trickle of Cherokees stopped.

In late May Scott drew up plans to gather the Cherokees in a few locations and hold them until it was time to start sending groups west; he did not want to round up Indians while trying to direct the move. He sent orders to the troops scattered throughout Georgia, Alabama, Tennessee, and North Carolina on how to go about this task. Soldiers were told to swarm Cherokee houses without warning, giving the Indians no time to put up a fight or even pack their belongings. Families would be taken at once and brought into one of several camps. The men must be polite and not use profanity. Scott underscored his final order: his soldiers were not allowed to fire on any Cherokee who ran. That, he feared, was a sure way to start another war.

Over the final week of May and into early June the scene played out hundreds of times. Soldiers surrounded a house while one officer knocked on the door—or kicked it in—and ordered every Indian out. The Cherokees had no time to take anything except what they grabbed on the way out the door. Only the reactions differed. Few Indians resisted; most accepted their fate passively. One old Cherokee woman filled her apron with corn and insisted on feeding her chickens before she was led away. Others begged for time to pack their most valued possessions. Soldiers surprised one Indian returning from a hunt, a buck slung over his shoulders.

Scott had to stop Georgians from interfering on several occasions. Early in the roundup, a group of citizens arrested sixteen Cherokees near New Echota and asked permission to publicly beat them with whips. They were frenzied, spewing hateful, racist language. The general refused and sent them home. It seemed the settlers were behaving more savagely than any Indian.

Most of the soldiers gave little regard to allowing families to remain together. Some Indians returned to find their wives gone; children who were outside playing got left behind. In a few instances, scared Indian children ran from the soldiers and disappeared into the woods. Their mothers were not allowed to go after them. Those who ran were simply left behind or collected by another family. One old man called to his children and grandchildren to kneel in prayer with him. As the family fell to the ground and prayed aloud in their sharp, guttural native tongue, their voices tinged with anguish, some of the young soldiers wondered why they had to cause these poor, peaceful people such pain.

Not all the soldiers felt any such sympathy. Most of Scott's men followed orders and showed a measure of compassion, even ambivalence, but inevitably others took great advantage of the situation. Some drove the Indians with bayonets, barked at them as if they were herding swine. They showed little sympathy, forcing men, women, and children to march toward the camps for days with little rest. One Cherokee, enraged to see a soldier poking his children with a gun, hit the man with a rock. The entire procession stopped while the soldiers beat him with a whip.

A few of Scott's men chained the Cherokees like criminals, and others molested the women. As some Indians were led away from their cabins, they looked back to see white looters ransacking their homes, taking all they could carry. The soldiers could not stop them and in some instances even joined in. The Indians were not allowed to take weapons. Soldiers confiscated all guns and knives, making vague promises to return them when the tribe reached its destination.

On occasion, the soldiers became violent. They shot a confused deaf-mute who turned right on the trail when he was told to go left. They gave one Cherokee a hundred lashes with a whip when he struck a soldier who had shoved his wife. But the worst incident, the one that would become an infamous symbol of the removal, occurred near the mountains the Indians called "the place of the blue smoke." One morning, Scott's troops surrounded the cabin of an old Cherokee named Tsali. Inside, the soldiers found five Indians: the old man, his wife, his brother, and two sons. They ordered the family out at gunpoint.

The soldiers marched Tsali's family down a trail headed for Rattlesnake Springs, one of several outposts where Cherokees were being held. As they

walked one soldier, irritated by how slowly the Indians were moving, prod-
ded Tsali's wife with his bayonet and told her to "hurry it up." Tsali could
not abide the thought of the man hurting his wife. He lunged at the soldier,
wrestled his gun away, and stabbed him with his own bayonet. At the same
time, Tsali's brother attacked and killed another soldier. The stunned troops
had no time to react and watched as the five Cherokees dropped their belongings and disappeared into the forest.

It was exactly the sort of thing General Scott had wanted to avoid. He
feared the incident might inspire other Cherokees to fight their captors and
spread insurrection through the entire tribe. But soon he devised a plan to
turn Tsali's rebellion into a lesson that would prevent any more trouble for
his men. He would make an example out of him.

Tsali's family had taken refuge with Utsala, a Cherokee chief harboring
nearly two hundred Indians high in the fog-draped mountains, terrain where
Scott's men would not venture. Some of the North Carolina Cherokees, who
lost their land in the 1819 treaty, had chosen to remain in their homes and become citizens of the state. There was some debate over whether they would be
allowed to stay once the removal began, despite their land reservations.

The general sent Utsala a message through William H. Thomas, a man
trusted by the tribe. According to tribal legend, Scott promised he would
allow Utsala's Indians to remain in the mountains if Tsali, his brother, and
his sons turned themselves in. It was not an overly generous offer as most
whites considered the area, which they would come to call the Great Smoky
Mountains, too rugged and unmanageable to settle. No one would notice a
few hundred more Indians living in those hills, Scott reasoned.

Utsala recognized the good deal for his people, but it was not the Cherokee way to force their own to surrender. For a day no one spoke of the offer.
But Tsali realized that he could save his wife and many other members of the
tribe, so he sent Thomas back with a message promising to meet Scott's men
on the trail where the attack occurred. Utsala's warriors escorted the four
Cherokees while Tsali's wife remained with the North Carolina Indians.

Scott's men were, as ordered, brutal. They lined up Tsali, his brother,
and the eldest son on a firing line. Then, to demonstrate just how powerless

the Cherokees were, the soldiers forced Utsala's warriors to shoot Tsali, his brother, and the older boy. The troops allowed Tsali's younger son to escape so he would go back and tell the other Indians what had happened. It was a strong warning and would have the desired effect: no other Cherokees would dare attack Scott's men.

Later, some would say Tsali's attack on the soldiers was premeditated, part of an organized resistance to removal. Contradictory evidence and stories would linger for years. Ultimately, Tsali succeeded in showing the world how savage, how unforgiving the United States government was. His story would become legend among the Cherokees. Tsali's fate, though, was only the beginning of the tribe's most tragic year.

In less than a month the military rounded up more than sixteen thousand Cherokees. The Indians were jailed in small camps across the nation or corralled at one of three larger forts: Gunter's Landing, near the Tennessee–Alabama border; Rattlesnake Springs, close to the Indian agent's office at Calhoun; and Ross's Landing, within sight of the chief's former trading post. These stockades were like fortresses, two hundred feet wide and five hundred feet long with walls between eight and sixteen feet high. There was only a single gate. Inside each of these camps a few small cabins ringed a great dirt field. The Indians had no privacy and no sanitary facilities, and there was no shelter for most, who were forced to sleep on the bare ground.

The Cherokees had been taken in the clothing they wore at the time and many had little more than rags to cover them. They were exposed to the hot, unforgiving sun by day and left to chill at night. The missionary Daniel Butrick noted many Indians passed the time standing, penned like horses, or lying in the dirt like pigs. For food, they ate berries and roots; there were no vegetables, no milk. They ate musty cornmeal, rank bacon, and salted pork fat—if they were lucky.

The drought led to rationing; the creeks were soon too dirty to provide drinking water. It took little time for healthy Indians to fall prey to malnutrition and dysentery. One man who visited the camps declared them a death sentence for any child under the age of one or any adult over the

age of sixty. Hundreds of Cherokees succumbed in the first few weeks—
so many that the Indians soon began to suspect the doctors were poison-
ing them and refused medicine. The missionaries who lingered around the
camps to monitor the treatment of the Indians cried while watching these
weak Cherokees, standing in the intermittent spring rain, hold shivering
babies by a fire to keep them warm. Every day, the missionaries helped
carry the dead to shallow graves.

When alcohol was smuggled into the stockades, some Cherokee men
chose to drink and escape their troubles rather than witness all that was happening around them. Some of them grew belligerent and fought with soldiers or other Indians. Men were beaten, killed. This continued as long as
there was whiskey, which was a long time.

The soldiers provided little help and some even used their position to
swindle the Cherokees out of what few possessions they had left. A Bap-
tist missionary named Evan Jones said he watched the troops conspire with
looters to take anything the Indians brought into the camps. They promised
food and clothing, things that never came. When Indians died, the soldiers
took what few possessions they'd had. General Wool noted, with some sympathy, that ninety-nine out of a hundred Indians would arrive in the West
penniless. Jones urged the soldiers to stop the pillaging but he was ignored.

"The poor captive, in a state of distressing agitation, his weeping wife almost frantic with terror, surrounded by a group of crying, terrified children,
without a friend to speak a consoling word, is in a poor condition to make a
good disposition of his property, and in most cases stripped of the whole, at
one blow," Jones wrote. "Many of the Cherokees, who were a few days ago in
comfortable circumstances, are now victims of abject poverty."

Butrick watched six soldiers surround two young Cherokee women hiding in the shade of a tree, trying to force them to drink. Other military officers, he knew, had ignored women going into labor, in some cases leaving
them on the trail during the march to the stockades. The missionary was
later told that a few soldiers forced one married Indian woman, whose husband had not been caught, to drink whiskey until she was delirious. Then
they raped her. After that her entire family shunned her, leaving her to suffer

in isolation. The missionary must have wondered what Jackson had meant when he spoke of a kind and charitable policy toward the Indians.

The first group departed in early June. More than a thousand Cherokees and their guards boarded a flotilla of hundred-foot flatboats for the trip west, a difficult voyage along rivers that in some places, because of the drought, were too low to pass. Save for the breeze off the water it was scarcely more comfortable than it had been in the camps; Indians were crammed onto the rickety boats like cattle, some forced to lie down on the decks. These boats were overloaded with people and timber and a few quickly sank. When a few of the boats ran aground, the Indians were ordered ashore and forced to walk. Many of them did not even have shoes for a march that stretched over four months. There was not nearly enough food to feed them all and the weak soon began to die. Later, some would say those were the fortunate ones.

Two more parties of nearly a thousand Cherokees each left shortly after the first, only a few days apart. Somewhere along the route the third group heard that further parties had been delayed, most likely because of the poor conditions. Some Indians took the delay as a sign John Ross had returned to save them. Hundreds escaped the boats and disappeared into the woods, where they would make their way east, back to their homes. Some of those Cherokees were recaptured and put back in the camps; others fled into the mountains and joined Utsala. In the midst of the confusion, a Cherokee woman went into labor on deck. A soldier drew his knife and killed her, sparing himself the trouble of delivering the baby.

The Indians who remained with the third detachment suffered for their obedience. The boats ran short on water and food, and the summer heat was relentless. As many as five Cherokees died every day. Only a few hundred of the first group would cross the Mississippi, and even fewer would live to be greeted by their western brothers. One party left Ross's landing with some eight hundred Cherokees. By the time the group reached Paducah, Kentucky, there were only 489.

Scott called off the removal for the remainder of the summer. He realized few Cherokees could survive the trek in the hot months. Keeping the

Indians caged in stockades was barely a better alternative, one that became increasingly difficult when the majority of his troops were called away to serve as reinforcement in the escalating Seminole War. But there was nothing else to do with them. The Cherokees would have to wait. Some did; others simply died.

The sight was heartbreaking. John Ross reached Camp Aquohee, the stockade at Rattlesnake Springs, in mid-July. Although many of his people were nearly too weak to move, thousands still rose to greet him, to shake his hand, or simply touch him. Their chief had returned and they hoped he brought good news. But Ross was in little better shape than his incarcerated tribe. He had been traveling for most of the past two years and the trip from Washington had worn him out.

When he stopped in Salem to visit Jane, Ross had received a letter from Lewis detailing all that had happened. It sapped whatever strength he had left. Ross was so distraught he could barely manage a response to a note from John Howard Payne. He wrote to his friend that the unhappy condition of the Cherokees "makes it difficult for me to write you anything in detail. This I must defer until I shall have reached the encampment of my Nation."

Jane accompanied her father home. She had left her school, realizing her father needed her, and she would never go back. Jane was horrified by all that she saw—the camps, the suffering, the death—but Ross had been expecting it. He stayed with his people for hours after his return, listening to their sad stories and saying anything he could to comfort them. But he could not deliver any good news. He no longer had any.

That day, many Cherokees told Ross, if it was time, they were ready to fight. It broke his heart—many of them could not have lifted a gun if he ordered them to do so. They were defeated, but not beaten, and it tortured him to see the Cherokees suffer. But Ross had no answer for them. He simply said he would talk with them shortly, after he met with General Scott.

Ross had sent word to Poinsett asking to be put in charge of the removal, for the sake of his people's health. By the time he met with Scott the general had received his orders: Ross would lead the removal. The decision initially angered Scott but he soon saw the benefits. He was shorthanded and the situation was beyond his control. People were dying every day because of the government's ill-conceived plan, and Scott was not heartless enough to be unaffected by it. He knew the Indians would respond better to their chief. Ross could keep the peace more easily, and that was Scott's primary concern. The decision likely saved hundreds of lives.

Poinsett's order carried only one condition: Ross had to evacuate all Cherokees by September 1, and Scott would remain on hand to make sure he followed that order. The chief got busy immediately. He negotiated to allow his brother Lewis to sell supplies to the government and together they began to cobble together all the things his people needed to make the journey: food, water, blankets. Free of the bureaucracy that plagued the general's operation and more committed than any white men to the well-being of the Cherokees, the Ross brothers soon secured hundreds of thousands of dollars' worth of merchandise. The costs were so enormous the government at first refused to pay.

Later, some would accuse Ross of profiting from the misery of his people. But Ross did not care what anyone said. The only way to get supplies for the journey was to pay for them, and he did not have the money to buy everything. He was trying to save the lives of as many Cherokees as he could as quickly and as best he knew how.

Andrew Jackson, ailing and infirm at the Hermitage, was outraged when he learned of Ross's appointment. Acting as if he were still the president, Jackson demanded that Nathaniel Smith be put in charge of removal and that Ross be arrested immediately.

"What madness and folly to have anything to do with Ross, when the agent was proceeding well with removal, on principles of economy that would have saved at least 100 percent from what the contract with Ross will cost," Jackson wrote. "Why is it that the scamp Ross is not banished from the notice of the administration?"

Scott ignored Old Hickory. It was Poinsett and Van Buren's problem now.

Ross was concerned that Indians who were hiding in the forest might be found and herded like cattle or even killed. Soon after he took over Ross sent messengers into the woods to convince the remaining Cherokees to come out and prepare for removal. While he awaited their return he spent a few days with his family, the first time he'd seen them since the previous fall. His wife was growing frail, and the sight of her shocked Ross. He would keep Quatie close by him as he worked. Jane, now seventeen, took over most of the duties of running the household.

On July 21, Ross called the General Council members into session at Camp Aquohee to tell them their fight was over. He would not waste their time with a long recitation of what he'd done in Washington, Ross told them; suffice to say he had failed. The best they could do, he said, would be to make the journey to their new homes safely.

"When the strong arm of power is raised against the weak and defenseless, the force of argument must fail," Ross said. "Our Nation have been besieged by a powerful Army and you have been captured in peace from your various domestic pursuits. And your wives and children placed in forts under military guard for the purpose of being immediately transported to the West of the Mississippi—and a portion of them have actually been sent off."

Ross told the Cherokees he was proud of their conduct. They had "wisely and with Christian firmness" maintained peaceful relations with the white men throughout a long period of hateful opposition. They had avoided the fate of the Creeks and the Seminoles. In the face of adversity, the Cherokees had shown their moral superiority, and Ross predicted history would judge them well. But now, he said, it was time to go. He would lead them into and out of the wilderness.

When he finished, it was clear the Cherokee Nation would follow John Ross anywhere, even if they did not want to go. Grown men cried, but not nearly so much as they would later.

The summer passed slowly in the camps. More Cherokees died every day. The missionaries watched food supplies dwindle until mothers became too weak to nurse their babies. The heat took some, dysentery many others. In

their cages the Indians regressed, afraid of all white people, even the missionaries trying to help them. Some learned the doctors sent to help them were
not trained for the work; a few were not even medical doctors but dentists.
They remained opposed to taking medicine, clung to their whiskey. Ross visited the camps often, even set up his office at the Rattlesnake Springs camp in
Calhoun. But he could do nothing to save his people. Many Cherokees had
received a death sentence the minute Scott's troops took them into custody.

Despite Ross's best efforts he would not have the entire tribe moving by
September 1. Although the Cherokees suffered as long as they were in their
camps, he knew their fate might be worse on the long trail that summer. No
significant rain had come by September and the earth was parched. He tried
to wait for the fall, but every day the window for moving closed further.
Urged on by Scott, Ross had to make his final preparations.

He organized the remaining Indians into thirteen parties of nearly one
thousand Cherokees each and assigned each group a doctor, an interpreter,
and a leader. The drought left the rivers shallow, cutting off the most attrac-
tive route, so they would have to travel overland. The weakest among them
would be loaded onto wagons, and some had horses, but the majority had to
walk. Ross set out a path that took the detachments northwest out of Ross's
Landing to Nashville, where Lewis would meet them with additional food,
blankets, and as many boots and socks as he could find. There would not be
enough for everyone.

The route would take them from Nashville into Kentucky, where they
would march through Hopkinsville. The Cherokees would cross the Ohio
River just east of Paducah and Fort Massac, and the trail then led them
through the wilderness of southern Illinois. They would traverse the Mississippi just north of New Madrid. From there, the parties would split up
to avoid the Ozark Mountains, some traveling south into Arkansas, others
taking the northern route, planned by the military, that led them across the
plains of Missouri. The shortest route was more than seven hundred miles;
the northern route more than eight hundred. Ross hoped these large parties
could avoid the harshest winter weather by making the journey in less than
three months. In reality, it took an average of five.

The first group set out on Tuesday, August 28, led by Hair Conrad. He took more than seven hundred Cherokees with him on a journey that eventually lasted 143 days. Nearly a hundred Indians would die on the trail, and nine babies were born. Ross led the group in prayer before they set out, then a bugle sounded and the wagons began rolling. Ross's nephew William Shorey Coodey assisted the travelers departing that day. He would never forget the sight of his people turning to the west and marching out of the Cherokee country forever.

"At length the word was given to move on. I glanced along the line and the form of Going Snake, an aged and respected chief whose head eighty winters had whitened, mounted on his favorite poney passed before me and lead the way in advance, followed by a number of young men on horse back.

"At this very moment a low sound of distant thunder fell on my ear. In almost an exact western direction a dark spiral cloud was rising above the horizon and sent forth a murmur I almost fancied a voice of divine indignation for the wrongs of my poor and unhappy countrymen, driven by brutal power from all they loved and cherished in the land of their fathers, to gratify the cravings of avarice. The sun was unclouded—no rain fell—the thunder rolled away and seemed hushed in the distance."

Four days later the second group moved out under the command of Ross's brother-in-law Elijah Hicks. The following Monday, September 3, Jesse Bushyhead led the third group. For the rest of the month, detachments left on an average of one every four days, although on September 20 two groups left. John Benge took one group, Situwakee led another, and Ross entrusted James Brown with the ninth party. Ross had personally selected all of these men for the same reason: he trusted them. Some were full-blood Cherokees while others were mixed-blood members of the tribe. None of them knew what lay ahead. By the end of the month only two detachments remained in the old country.

The trouble began immediately. The drought ended abruptly at the beginning of the month and the ensuing deluge swamped the dry land. Dusty trails were suddenly muddy, impassable. Wagons could not make it through the Sequatchie Valley, and one farmer refused to allow the Indians to cross a road on his land. The first detachments did not travel a hundred miles before they were stopped and forced to wait for days. Some Cherokees deserted their parties and tried to make their way back home. For the ones who remained only misery followed. What food they carried had to be rationed; it was soon apparent there wasn't enough. Hicks sent a letter to Ross to inform him the group's wagon master had died, and that old chief White Path—who had led the failed Cherokee rebellion a decade earlier—would not survive the trip. He may have drunk some tainted water. Hicks lost several Indians each day.

"Necowee has given himself up to the bane of death," Hicks reported in one letter, "and I have all together lost his services."

Ross had no choice but to keep sending his people out; the military insisted they leave, and every day they waited put them on the trail deeper into winter. Before October ended the twelfth detachment set out from Ross's Landing, leaving only one more to depart. No one realized it at the time, but the Cherokees were marching into what would be remembered as one of the harshest winters of the nineteenth century.

The worst of it would not come until after they had left Tennessee. The Indians were resupplied by Lewis Ross in Nashville and again in Hopkinsville, where kind Kentucky settlers took up a collection to feed the Cherokees passing through. Some pastors opened their churches for a lucky few Indians to spend a warm night, but there was never enough room for everyone. By daybreak they were walking again at a slow, humble pace. Many days they barely managed five miles, only a fifth of the distance healthy people could have walked. Most of the Cherokees were too weak to walk from sunrise to sunset, but they had no choice, lest they be left behind. Some fell dead from exhaustion and famine. The lucky ones were buried.

A few Indians rode in covered wagons while the rest walked alongside at a slow pace, hunched by the burdens they carried—mothers with their children, men toting what few possessions or supplies they still had. They had to contend with not only the elements but also unscrupulous men along the trail. Every day, the Indians were greeted by settlers who wanted to take advantage of them. Many people considered the Indians rich because of the money they had received for their land. The price of a dozen apples, normally six cents, would rise to fifty cents the farther west they traveled.

Babies were born on the trail, and babies died on the trail. The young were the first to go, and then the old, their deaths sped along when the wagons broke down, as they inevitably did, and the Cherokees were forced to walk. The cold grew worse with each passing week. Many days they walked for hours into a headwind that chilled their bones and screamed in their ears, battering their faces with dust off the plains and filled their eyes with dirt, bringing more tears.

The removal had turned out to be little more than a human cattle drive. The Cherokees had been broken in the camps during the summer and sent on their death march. It was, in many ways, even worse than the stories the shamans had told of their removal decades earlier. Those predictions had described the barren nature of the western lands; they never included any depiction of the horrors the Cherokees would endure just getting there. If their fate had been left to the United States military, it might have been even worse. But that was little comfort for the thousands on the trail.

The air of death followed the Cherokees as they continued west, and the sight of them alone was enough to frighten some of the whites who met them along the trail. The kindest ones offered help, or at least asked about their journey. One man later described the heartbreak of watching one of the parties stop for the evening.

"The forward part of the train we found just pitching their tents for the night, and notwithstanding some thirty of forty waggons were already stationed, we found the road literally filled with the procession for about three miles in length. The sick and feeble were carried in waggons—about as comfortable for traveling as a New England ox cart with a covering over it—a great many ride on horseback and multitudes go on foot—even aged females, apparently nearly ready to drop into the grave, traveling with heavy burdens attached to the back—on the sometimes frozen ground, and sometimes muddy streets, with no covering for the feet except what nature had given them . . . We learned from the inhabitants on the road where the

Indians passed, that they had buried fourteen of fifteen at every stopping place, and they make a journey of ten miles per day only on average."

Not everyone the Cherokees encountered was sympathetic. Some people stole from the Indians, knowing they were too weak to fight. In Illinois, a group of men claimed they found a dead Cherokee and demanded money for burying him. Other families refused to let the Cherokees rest on their land. One detachment had to set up its camp in three different locations before being left in peace. They cooked in shared pots and passed sickness back and forth. Whooping cough took many of them. Pneumonia got the ones who didn't die from malnutrition first. Sometimes as many as two dozen people passed away in a single night.

Every day the march stopped several times while weak Cherokees buried the dead on the very spots where they fell. While some handled that grim task, the strongest among them hunted for turkey and deer to feed the travelers. One missionary who watched the sad caravan pass later remarked that he had seen the "look of death" in the eyes of the sick lying in those slow wagons. Children lost their parents, parents lost their children.

Thomas Clark Jr., an old friend of Ross's who left in one of the final parties, tried to warn the chief of the worsening conditions. On December 17 he sent Ross a note from Nashville that said, "The agents for supplying have been under the impression for some weeks that it would be impossible for the last detachments to pass thro' Missouri this winter for two reasons—the severity of the winter and secondly the scarcity of supplies." But it was too late. By then even Ross had set out.

A month later, Clark was sure he would die before reaching his new home. The cold, sickness, and endless walking had taken their toll on him. He had grown tired of watching Indians die every day, of burying mothers next to their children in unmarked graves at the edge of desolate fields. He had crossed the Ohio, which was filled with ice, and faced the prospect of more ice in the Mississippi. It would take some of the groups more than two days to cross the frozen river, relaying back and forth in rickety boats.

Clark sent Ross a final note from Jonesboro, Illinois, the words of a broken man: "I have waited until I am almost thread bare in patience and yet am undetermined what will be best for you. I never felt as anxious to see any person in my life as I do now to see you."

Eventually Clark made it, but more than a quarter of his party didn't. They walked into a terrible winter storm, facing winds the Cherokees had never been exposed to in the deep valleys of Tennessee and Georgia. The biting cold stung their skin, gave them frostbite, and froze the tears to their faces. Some Indians called on their old religion to get them through. At many a camp shamans chanted into the night.

"Long time we travel on way to new land," one old Cherokee later recalled. "People feel bad when they leave Old Nation. Womens cry and made sad wails. Children cry and many men cry, and all look sad like when friends die, but they say nothing and just put heads down and keep on go towards West. Many days pass and people die very much."

No one would ever know exactly how many Cherokees died in 1838 and the first months of 1839—at least four thousand, a full quarter of the eastern tribe, although some suggested the number was twice that. It was difficult to know for sure, because no one thought to tally the dead as they were buried. At the time, no one thought of anything other than survival.

In later years the Cherokees would come to call their tribe's long march of death "the trail where they cried." No one made the journey without losing at least one member of his or her family. That included John Ross.

It was December 4 before the last Cherokee party left. Ross had held back more than two hundred of the oldest and sickest Cherokees to travel with him. Because of the heavy fall rains the rivers had risen enough to allow them to sail west, the most forgiving route. But it took Ross weeks to finish his business at the Indian agency and pack up his belonging, carefully storing the Cherokee papers of Charles Hicks, and his own letters, in heavy trunks.

In the midst of this sorrow, Jane Ross chose to marry. In the town the white men called Cleveland, near Rattlesnake Springs, she wed Return J. Meigs IV, the son of Timothy Meigs, her father's former business partner. Ross gave his blessing and, in the bargain, gained another hand to help with the final details of removal. Jane helped her mother pack and kept a watchful eye on Silas and George. Ross's older boys were not a part of the removal. Allen would make the journey later; James remained up north. As Ross and Quatie gathered up their children to leave the cabin at Flint Springs, settlers lingered in the yard, ready to buy the chief's cattle and take possession of his home. They would not leave him alone, even in his final moments.

John Ross left the Cherokee country from the place where he had first made his mark: Ross's Landing. As he loaded his family and dozens of sickly Indians onto their boat, he looked out in amazement at what was already happening to his home. In the old days, the trading post had been surrounded by woods with a few errant Cherokee shacks visible in the distance. Now, as the last of his people prepared to leave, federal soldiers were clearing the land with saws and axes, outlining streets for Chattanooga, the great town that would soon grow up in the shadow of Lookout Mountain.

The steamboat *Victoria* carried them into the harsh western winter. John Ross watched much of the land pass from the ship's deck, and it reminded him of his first voyage west, but the wind bit into his skin and soon forced him inside. Sleet and snowstorms kept the boat cold and damp, and many of those not already sick became infected on the voyage. A soldier would later recall that Ross's wife gave her only blanket to a sick child on the boat. For her charity, Quatie was forced to shiver on the deck throughout a sleet storm. Within a day she had developed pneumonia.

Ross and Jane tended to Quatie as best they could, too stubborn or strong to let the cold affect them. She said little and seemed to accept her fate stoically. Every day she grew weaker and Ross was frustrated to be, once again, so helpless. He and Quatie had had an odd relationship, but Ross loved her. He often felt guilty for leaving his poor wife to run his home and raise his children while he had roamed the country on behalf of the Cherokees. And what had it gotten him? He had failed—failed his people, failed her. Ross thought about these things as he did his best to keep his wife warm, counting the days as the gray countryside drifted by.

Shortly after the steamboat reached Arkansas Quatie Ross passed away. In later years, John Ross lamented his martyred wife's fate in a few letters, saying more about her suffering than he ever said of her life. Ross did not complain about the injustice or take an unusual amount of pity on himself—if he did, he told no one. The chief surely realized he had suffered no more or less than the rest of his people on the trail. The exile of the Cherokees had been more horrible than he had feared it would be in his darkest nightmares. By then, however, it was over.

John Ross buried his wife in the cold, winter ground of Little Rock—as hundreds of Cherokee men had done for their wives before him—and then set out on a monthlong walk. A new home and an uncertain future awaited him where the trail ended.

THIRTEEN

Retribution

A cold wind greeted the Cherokees at the end of the trail. Winter lingered in the West and there was no escape from the biting chill that swept across the Great Plains. It stalked shallow valleys, rustled barren trees, and left the ground frozen. The land here was gray and bleak and lifeless, a desolate expanse that stretched to the horizon. It was the worst time of year for the Cherokees to arrive; there would be no relief from the weather for weeks, and it was the first thing most Indians noticed about their new home. In the East the spring would already have begun to thaw the earth. At first, it seemed their journey had not ended. The only difference between their first month in the new country and their time on the trail was they no longer had to walk.

Their first impression of the new country was not good. In some ways, this land beyond Arkansas was remarkably similar to their home—the rocky streams and thick forests of the Ozark foothills resembled Georgia and Tennessee, and the Illinois River shared much in common with the Hiwassee. But few Cherokees noticed these things. It simply was not their home.

After all they had been through, their pessimism was understandable. These gray and brown hills provided little shelter from the harsh wind, and the flat land seemed endless. Many would notice that the trees here were shorter. They feared there was little chance of finding game, imagined the ground less fertile for their crops. All of their hope, it seemed, had died on the trail.

Their plight did not end with the spring thaw. They were hungry and sick, and the Cherokees who met them—the Old Settlers, they called them—treated them cautiously, as if their misery might be catching. The eastern Cherokees felt like outcasts, abandoned and unwelcome. Some of those who survived the trail passed away shortly after arriving. The trail would continue to claim victims for months. All this new country offered those poor souls was a cold, hard burial ground.

John Ross reached the settlement in March of 1839, just another homeless widower. Not only had he lost Quatie but he soon learned that his youngest sister, Margaret, was "in a very dangerous condition" as a result of the journey. Ross could find no more words of comfort for his brother-in-law Elijah Hicks than he could his own children. He rarely showed his true feelings or spoke of personal troubles. Perhaps it was the politician in him, or maybe there was simply too much to be done to give in to emotions. As it had been for years, his tribe came first.

Instead of camping with the rest of the tribe, Ross moved in with his sister Jane and her husband, Joseph Coodey, who had settled in the West a decade earlier. He accepted their hospitality graciously, set up a small office in their home, and left the care of George and Silas to his daughter and sister. He secured a large, flat tract of land at Park Hill and hired men to build him a small cabin. Within a week he was overwhelmed by the simple task of feeding his people.

In the coming months, the Cherokees would find the land in this new country quite different: harder to till, less fertile. Given the scarcity of food it was a considerable problem. The government had not lived up to its promise to provide rations and many Cherokees were starving. The Indians who traveled west by boat had been given fifteen days of rations when they landed and were assured more would be distributed from a store that would soon be set up in Indian territory. Two weeks later there was still little food or clothing for those Cherokees who had marched across Missouri, and much of the beef distributed at the camp had gone bad. After months in the government camps and weeks of traveling, most Cherokees were so malnourished they could barely move. When they complained, troops in the area told the Cherokees to pick up food at a depot on the Arkansas border, more than fifty miles away.

Ross asked General Matthew Arbuckle, stationed in the new Indian territory, to intervene. The Indians refused to eat the rancid meat and begged for salt pork or bacon, but government contractors wanted to charge exorbitant prices for such luxuries. These things, Ross noted, were supposed to be supplied as part of the contract between the tribe and the federal government. Ross thought Arbuckle a reasonable man who might step in on his behalf, with more authority than an exiled Indian chief could summon.

"The health and existence of the whole Cherokee people who have recently been removed to this distant country demands a speedy remedy for the inconveniences and evils complained of, and unless a change of the quantity and kind of rations as well as of the mode of issuing the same be made ... the Cherokees must inevitably suffer."

Arbuckle was sympathetic and spoke to the contractors but could do little more than send the complaints to Washington.

John Jolly, principal chief of the western Cherokees, died just before the last of the exiled Indians reached the new land. His passing further complicated the politics of combining the tribe's two branches. The migrating Cherokees had decided by a vote of the General Council to retain their own constitution and government after the move. But they had ignored their biggest obstacle: the western Cherokees already had a government.

The western tribe was controlled by a small group of chiefs. There was a legislative body, a council of sorts, but one with far less district representation than the eastern model. Such disparities had meant nothing in the past—the two branches of the tribe did not need similar governing structures to coexist hundreds of miles apart. They split the land annuities from Washington based on population, one-third to the western Cherokees and the rest to the eastern tribe. There had always been minor disputes but never any real trouble; the vast distance between the two bands afforded little interaction.

Ross had believed he could find a solution with Jolly, a reasonable chief with whom he was on good terms. But the old chief's passing changed the political landscape. Less than two months after Ross arrived the western Cherokees elected John Brown to serve the remainder of Jolly's term and then appointed John Rogers and John Looney as assistant chiefs. And they would not submit to the incoming majority. These new chiefs, eastern Cherokees who had moved west more than ten years earlier, had no intention of giving up their new power.

Even in defeat and exile Ross felt his work was not done. Privately, he hoped to negotiate a new purchase price for the eastern lands, something he could do only as chief. The old country was gone, divided up among white settlers—he conceded that and knew they could not go back. But he thought Washington might be more generous now that the Cherokees had emigrated. John Brown threatened these plans. In the past, the western Cherokees had often argued for a greater share of the tribe's annuities, and Ross did not imagine that anything had changed.

Ross asked the western chiefs for a joint council to discuss their reunion. He was diplomatic, gracious, and respectful but Ross still had the air of a man accustomed to getting his way. After dealing with the polished politicians of Washington for years, he may have underestimated his western brothers. Initially, they ignored his request, said such business could wait until the fall. But Brown ultimately agreed. He saw an opportunity to set the tone for the coming debate.

More than six thousand Cherokees gathered at the Takatoka campground near the Illinois River on June 3, 1839. The western council grounds were crude even by the standards of the temporary capital at Red Clay. The tribe's leaders met under a simple roof held up by a few posts, leaving council members completely exposed to the elements. Many of the Indians in attendance were eastern Cherokees who had camped close to the nearby river. But they were given no special consideration. John Ross would not be given the opportunity to speak for a week; the opening address, reserved for the chief, was delivered by Brown. Ross did not object but his patience would not last long. Brown's welcome sounded very much like a veiled threat.

"We joyfully welcome you to our country. The whole land is before you. You may freely go wherever you choose and select any places for settlement which please you," Brown said.

The chief explained that elections would be held the following July, and all Cherokees were eligible to seek office. In the meantime, Brown said, "it is expected that you will be subject to our government and laws."

Brown had quickly validated Ross's fears. The western chief insinuated that the eastern Cherokee government was dissolved, that he had the ultimate power. Still, Ross recognized what Brown naively overlooked. If all the Cherokees had voting rights, Ross would soon be in control. But that might not happen soon enough. The United States government had not yet paid the Cherokees for their land in the east. And Ross did not want that money delivered to the western chiefs. Already, Ross's people were requesting their share of the treaty money, and he knew they alone deserved it. They had suffered enough to earn all of it, and more.

To Ross, it must have seemed the move had solved nothing. The Cherokees were again threatened, not by white men but by their own people. It frustrated Ross, but when he finally was allowed to speak on June 10 he was diplomatic and conciliatory, yet firm. Standing beneath the council shed at Takatoka, he proclaimed, "We are all of the household of the Cherokee family and of one blood" and he asked that they take steps to cement their reunion.

The Indians of the Cherokee Nation East, Ross said, had "emigrated in their National Character," yet had not trespassed or infringed on any of the rights or privileges of those who came first. He noted that the eastern band constituted an overwhelming majority but had no intention or desires to impose its will beyond what was "equitable and just, satisfactory to the people." He said he hoped there would soon be "joint deliberations" for a permanent reunion.

"Let us never forget this self evident truth—that a house divided against itself cannot stand, or united we stand and divided we fall," Ross said.

Ross's eloquence may have excited his own people but the western chief was unmoved. Later, speaking in private, Brown told Ross he was free to settle the removal, but "with the name and style of the Eastern Cherokee Nation." He had no interest in a merger, whether Ross called it a "reunion or not." While publicly magnanimous Brown was blunt in private. He asked Ross to tell him "what you really wish," and he wanted it in writing.

Ross and George Lowrey did as they were asked and proposed appointing a committee to draft laws for a new government—three members from the west, three from the east, and three selected by the first six. The two bands would merge when the committee reached an agreement. Brown rejected the plan. As far as he was concerned the tribe had already been united.

"Our chiefs have met their brother emigrants, and made them welcome in the country; they are thereby made partakers of all the existing laws in the country, enjoy all its benefits; and are, in every respect, the same as ourselves," Brown, Looney, and Rogers wrote in a formal reply.

The original laws of the Cherokees, Brown said, are not valid here, and he would not let Ross "protract a debate."

Ross had to realize the threat he posed. To Brown, it must have appeared Ross had no more arrived than he wanted to take over their tribe. The western Cherokees had good reason to be territorial. They had settled the land decades earlier and, after surviving alone for years, were now forced to share it with newcomers. Ross understood this, and might not have pushed so forcefully had he not suspected conspiracy. The same day Brown rejected Ross's offer, the Ridges were spotted on the outskirts of the campgrounds.

The members of the Treaty Party had tried to stay out of sight since arriving in the new country. They had detected a certain animosity among some of the western Cherokees and realized the eastern Cherokees would soon arrive; they did not want to tempt fate. Of course, the Ridges' isolation also betrayed their motives. Given the remote location of their homes, nearly fifty miles away, their appearance at Takatoka that day could not be a coincidence. Everyone knew the Ridges would not have made such a long journey without a reason.

Several of Ross's men saw them that day—Major Ridge and his son, Boudinot and his brother Stand Watie—talking quietly with Brown and

Rogers. No one overheard their conversation, or knew the purpose of these conferences, but Ross suspected that the younger Ridge and Boudinot were trying to sabotage his efforts. Ross heard Major Ridge had been invited to address council and supposed the younger Ridge had ingratiated himself with the western chiefs, either to stop him or to promote himself for some high office. As soon as the Ridges realized they had been discovered by Ross's men they quickly slipped away.

The two sides argued for another week. Ross offered several alternative plans, but Brown dismissed every suggestion. C. Washburn, a missionary at the council, went away unimpressed by Ross. He could not understand why the eastern chief seemed so intent on pushing reunion and, in the process, agitating Brown. The missionary said that, for a man known as the model of tact and patience, Ross's performance was unimpressive. But even Washburn could see these were not the workings of a power-mad dictator. If Ross's sole interest was in being principal chief, the missionary noted, he had only to wait until the next election.

Ross had good reason to worry about the $5 million owed to his people. The same day Brown met with the Ridges, he sent the Indian agent Montfort Stokes a letter stating that all annuities should be paid to the western band of the government. John Ross would not learn about Brown's efforts for a week, until a day after Brown declared the council over.

On June 20 the western chiefs attempted to clear the Takatoka campground but the gathered Cherokees would hear one last plea for unity from an unlikely source. Sequoyah, the famous Cherokee who created the tribe's written language, had lived among the western band for fifteen years. He was the one Indian respected equally by every member of the tribe, immune to tribal politics. Sequoyah generally stayed out of such dealings, choosing to live quietly in a small cabin near the Arkansas border. Although he was now considered an Old Settler, he had been on good terms with Ross for years. The chief even traveled across the country once just to visit him.

Sequoyah was so disturbed by the recent events he was compelled to speak out. He urged them to shun the divisive rhetoric they had heard. Apparently without any prompting from Ross, Sequoyah asked every Cherokee

Brian Hicks

present to return to the campground in ten days—on July 1—to complete, once and for all, the reunion of the two bands.

By an impromptu voice vote the old-timers and new arrivals agreed. Despite their emotional outpouring and respect for Sequoyah, however, they would find it difficult to grant his wish.

The next day the survivors planned their revenge.

There were more than a hundred of them, men of the Light Horse Guard, tribal elders, even members of the General Council. These eastern Cherokees had decided it was time to collect all they were due. The Treaty of New Echota had cost them their homes, their families. They had suffered for more than a year, forced from their land and corralled like animals, robbed of their dignity at gunpoint. They had been made to march eight hundred miles and watch their brothers, wives, and children die on the trail. Now they faced the prospect of losing their money—their only hope for survival —to men in their own tribe. For all of these hardships and more they blamed the Ridges.

Earlier in the day, Ross had learned of Brown's attempt to claim the treaty money. Word of this ploy spread quickly and was what finally sent these Cherokees into a rage. One of the men had seen the Ridges at Takatoka, and that was all the proof required. They did not tell Ross of their plans, both for his own protection and because he would not approve. But they had heard enough of his pleas for peace and passivity. The time for all that had long since passed.

There was no debate on their course of action; they knew what to do. They started with a list of the people who signed the Treaty of New Echota and agreed they all should die. There would be no clan revenge for their actions because every clan was represented at the meeting, and none of them objected. To justify their actions they invoked the "law of blood." It was an old Cherokee tradition, one that had been updated and approved in the council just a decade earlier. It allowed the tribe to kill any Indian who sold Cherokee land. Ironically enough, the rule had been written into law by John Ridge to dissuade chiefs from signing unauthorized land deals with white men. Now

his own words condemned him. John Ridge's name went on the top of the
list, followed by his father and his cousins Elias Boudinot and Stand Watie.

The 1829 law of blood technically called for the accused to stand trial
before the General Council, but these vigilantes had little interest in formalities. They instead chose to send out large parties of multiple assassins, making it impossible to say who actually did the killing. They drew secret ballots
to determine who would hunt down each man on the list, and decided the
first four targets would be hit the next morning.

Years later, Allen Ross, the chief's son, would admit he was one of the
conspirators. It was no surprise the young Ross would want to take part in
the plot. He felt the Ridges had betrayed not only the tribe but also his father, and that was something he could not abide. Even though he knew his
father would not approve of such violence, Allen was ready to take some
small measure of revenge for all his family had been put through. But he
later recalled that, when he tried to draw a name out of the hat, one of the
Cherokees grabbed his wrist and stopped him.

"We have another job for you," the man had told the young Ross. "Go
to your father's house this evening and stay the night with him, the next day
too. If possible, keep him from finding out what is being done."

Allen Ross accepted his role without question, pleased to have an important part to play. He rode to Park Hill that afternoon. Although he likely
struggled with conflicted feelings, worried that he was somehow being disloyal
to his father, Allen carried out this mission as well as any man involved in the
plot. By the time John Ross found out what was happening it was too late.

They came at daybreak.

It took them several hours to reach Honey Creek on the dark trail. Once
there, they crept into the woods and undulating fields that surrounded the
house. There were more than two dozen Indians and none of them made
a sound—these were men accustomed to stalking prey in silence. In a few
minutes they had staked out their positions: some hid behind trees, while
others lay flat on the cool ground. And for a moment they sat still, listening,
waiting.

The house sat in a clearing on a rise of land. It was large and well built, a farmhouse, the home of a man with money. The Indians could see no light coming from its windows or any sign that anyone inside was yet awake. Then, just before dawn on Saturday, June 22, as the sky slowly faded from black to gray, the leader motioned for his men to move. While most of the Cherokees climbed atop their horses, rifles in hand, three Indians slowly walked up to the house. They climbed the steps onto the porch and stood together in front of the door. And then one of them kicked it in.

Surprisingly, no one stirred when the door flew open. The assassins cautiously stepped inside, prowling through the house with their knives and guns drawn. They paused briefly at each door, ignoring the children in one room and Sarah's sister and brother-in-law in another. Finally they found the master bedroom. There they saw John Ridge, asleep in his bed beside Sarah. They moved toward him slowly, then one man put his gun to Ridge's head and pulled the trigger. The gun misfired.

The click of the hammer woke Ridge. He tried to jump to his feet but the Indians were on him immediately. Ridge kicked and fought while Sarah, startled, recoiled from the violence. Her husband struggled with his attackers but he was no match for three Cherokees. Two of the men half-carried, half-dragged Ridge out of the bed and through the house while the third warned Sarah and the others, awakened by the noise, to stay back. They lugged him through the front door, down the steps, and into the yard, Ridge kicking the entire way.

John Ridge had long feared it would come to this. A few months earlier he had told Schermerhorn, "I may yet die by the hand of some poor, infatuated Indian, deluded by the counsel of Ross and his minions." It was for that reason he had tried to avoid politics in the West, why he chose to live so far from the rest of the tribe. His appearance at Takatoka a few days earlier had been out of character. It may have been that Ridge had come to despise Ross so much he could not help it, or maybe he thought he was doing the right thing for the tribe. He would never have the chance to explain. But as the Indians dragged him across his own yard, Ridge realized he was about to die, and he likely blamed John Ross.

The other Cherokees had moved closer to the house, and two of them pointed long rifles at the family, forcing the horrified Sarah to watch from the doorway. Her screams were drowned out in a wave of war cries from her husband's attackers. The Indians had been ordered to do whatever necessary to avoid listening to Ridge, for fear he might talk them out of finishing their job. They chose to yell, a fitting reminder of the tribe's violent past.

Two Indians stood Ridge up and held his arms while another pulled his knife. The Cherokee then stabbed Ridge in the chest once, then again. He did not stop until he had plunged the blade into Ridge twenty-five times, taking out several years of frustration in a matter of seconds. This was the man who had sold their homes, a man responsible for thousands of Cherokee deaths. These executioners did not believe their actions a crime. To their thinking, this was justice.

When the Cherokee had finished he sliced Ridge's jugular vein with a single flick of his knife, then the men threw him to the ground. Ridge lay bleeding in the grass as the Indians gathered around him. One by one, all of the two dozen Cherokees stomped on his body before mounting their horses and riding off. The entire incident lasted only a few minutes.

As the Cherokees retreated Sarah ran to her husband. Ridge managed to sit up on his elbows and weakly look at her a final time. He tried to speak but the only thing that came out of his mouth was blood.

As he lay there dying, Ridge's young son, John Rollin Ridge, watched his mother screaming in agony as she held her husband. The boy would later wonder if these Indians had once been friends. But at that moment he was frozen in shock, his heart breaking as he watched his father try to say one last word to the woman he loved.

"In a few moments more he died," John Ridge's son later wrote.

Elias Boudinot emerged from Samuel Worcester's house at about nine that morning. He and his wife, Delight, were staying with the missionary in Park Hill while their own home was under construction. It was an ideal situation. Boudinot and Worcester had been close since their days in New Echota and now worked together on a mission they had opened just a few miles from John Ross's new cabin. The two men planned once again to live nearly within seeing distance of each other.

Boudinot was on his way to check the progress of the carpenters working on his house, a daily ritual. Although he had worried about assassination back east, Boudinot did not hesitate to live among the western Cherokees. He believed, or at least hoped, that trouble was behind him. He likely gave it little thought that morning, enjoying the view of the rolling hills he would soon have from his own home. In some ways, this land was much more inviting than the cramped lot he'd had at New Echota. Here, the sky opened up and the world seemed somehow bigger.

The men came out of the woods while Boudinot was talking with his builders. There were four of them, Cherokees whom the carpenters—and, apparently, Boudinot—did not recognize. The men asked if he could spare some medicine, explaining that their families had taken ill. It was not an unusual request; Boudinot dispensed all medicine from the mission and a day rarely passed without someone asking for some tonic or other. He offered to fetch it for them and the four men followed along.

The Indians said little as they walked. About halfway to the mission, when the group was as far away as possible from the carpenters, Worcester's house, and the school, one of the Cherokees slowed and fell out of step with the others. Boudinot did not notice the man lagging slightly behind the group. Then the Indian behind him lunged, plunging a knife into his back.

Boudinot let out a single cry as he fell to the ground. The Cherokees quickly swarmed over him. While the others watched, one Cherokee beat Boudinot's skull with a tomahawk, striking hard enough to split his head open in half a dozen places. The beating continued until one of the executioners saw the carpenters running toward them. Before anyone could reach them the Indians disappeared into the woods.

Boudinot's scream had been loud enough to alert not only his builders but also his wife and Worcester. They came running out of the missionary's house just in time to see the retreating assassins. It took them less than a minute to reach Boudinot, lying in tall grass still wet from the morning dew. Delight screamed.

"Elias!"

Boudinot opened his eyes briefly but he never said a word. For a moment, he lay there staring at his wife. He died with his eyes open.

By then Worcester had reached the scene and was heartbroken by the sight of his friend, bloodied, broken, the great promise of this young man spilling out onto the wet morning grass.

"They have cut off my right hand," he said.

Stand Watie was not home when the Cherokees came for him.

A Choctaw Indian clearing land near the mission heard the screams of Delight Boudinot and rushed over to see what had happened. When the Indian realized Boudinot had been murdered, he feared Stand Watie might be next. After explaining his concerns, the Choctaw borrowed Worcester's horse—known as one of the quickest in the nation—and rode toward Watie's store, about a mile away.

The trading post was busy that morning, filled with Cherokees buying stock for their new homes. The Choctaw recognized some of the Indians as Ross loyalists and wondered if these men had come to kill Stand Watie. He feared the group might act more quickly if he made a scene, so he acted as if he were browsing through stacks of dry goods. He called Watie over and pretended to barter with him over sugar. As they talked the Indian whispered the news. He did not have to explain what that meant. Watie showed no emotion, no reaction of any kind. He simply stopped talking, quietly slipped out the back door, and disappeared. If his assassins thought to look at his store they could not track him; Watie was as good as or better than anyone else at avoiding detection.

Later that day, Watie showed up at Worcester's house, where they had moved Boudinot's body. For a moment he said nothing. He walked slowly over to the corpse, pulled back the sheet, and stared quietly at his brother. When he finally spoke, it was with a barely controlled rage. Stand Watie offered a thousand dollars for anyone who brought the murderers to him.

Delight Boudinot begged her brother-in-law to run away. She asked Watie not to become consumed by hate or to seek revenge. He should save himself. But he would not listen. Although the identity of Boudinot's killers would remain secret for years, Stand Watie would never give up his hunt for them. On that day, however, he believed he already knew who'd sent them.

The first target of his revenge would be John Ross.

That same day, Major Ridge stopped at a creek near the Line Road around ten a.m. He'd been traveling since Friday, when he was called away to check on one of his slaves in Van Buren, Arkansas, just north of Fort Smith. The slave had fallen ill and could not travel. Ridge hurried to his side, accompanied by a young slave boy, and spent several hours with the man. Finally deciding that the man could not travel, and that he could do nothing for him, Ridge set out for home. But he and his companion could not make it all the way back to Honey Creek and stopped for the night at the home of a man he knew from Cincinnati.

The Cherokee assassins had tracked Ridge to that house. For several hours they staked out the home, which belonged to Ambrose Harnage, to make sure they were in the right place. When they were convinced the old chief was indeed there, they rode north, anticipating his route home. They wanted to ambush him far from anyone who might interfere or help the aged chief.

Major Ridge and the slave boy set out at daybreak, following the Line Road, a path so named because it followed the western state line of Arkansas all the way to Missouri. It would lead Ridge home—he did not yet know the area well enough to veer off the trail. The ride took Ridge to the edge of the Ozarks and through a few small villages and towns. It looked a lot like northern Georgia, he likely noted. He mostly rode in silence, many things weighing on his mind.

He was an old man, nearly seventy, and had little use for politics anymore. Ridge no doubt had visited the western chiefs only at the request of his son. He did not want to get involved but John thought it important. He had not spoken to Ross since his old friend's arrival, for he knew there was nothing left to say. Their paths had split long ago. Now the tribe was in Ross's hands. Major Ridge wanted only to pass his final years in peace with his wife at Honey Creek.

He stopped to let his horse drink at White Rock Creek, a shallow stream with a sandstone beach surrounded by large, flat rocks. Here the creek was shaded by so many leafy trees that only the barest amount of sunlight shimmered on the water. It was a quiet, peaceful place and he lingered for a moment, resting. He was still several hours of slow riding from home.

The Cherokees were waiting for him on a hill near the creek, realizing he would likely stop at the water to allow his horse a drink, if nothing else. It was an ideal spot, hiding their presence while at the same time affording them a fair view of the stream. Unlike the other executioners, they would not get too close to their quarry. Even at his age Major Ridge was an imposing figure. He was a legend, the last of the great chiefs. Rumors of his constant sickness mattered little. If there was a man who could fight off a handful of Indians, they believed it was Ridge. He was such a skilled tracker that some of the men feared he'd already sensed their presence.

As the horse drank the Cherokees saw their opportunity. From their perch, they aimed their rifles at the old chief and, all at once, fired. The sharp sound of their shots echoed through the hills and off the rocks below.

Five bullets hit their mark. Major Ridge never said a word, did not let out a yell or make any discernible noise. He simply slumped over in his saddle. The report of the rifles scared his horse, however, and it bucked, throwing Ridge to the ground. He fell next to the silent water, his face only a few feet from the stream. The men who killed him would not venture closer to make sure they had done their job. They slipped away without making sure he was dead.

The young boy traveling with Ridge rode off for help, alerting some settlers in the nearby village of Dutchtown. A few men responded immediately, hooking up a wagon to collect the old Cherokee. They found his body in the same spot where he had fallen. Major Ridge had died alone.

Soon the villagers were met by a messenger from Honey Creek, sent by Sarah Ridge to tell the old chief of his son's death. By then the June 22 executions were over.

John Ross learned of Elias Boudinot's death later that afternoon. He had spent much of the day at home, planning for the July 1 council, but news of Boudinot's assassination—delivered by a passing Indian—disturbed him so much he couldn't work. He had not gotten along with the former newspaper editor, and could no longer trust him, but he did not wish the young man dead.

Ross sent his brother-in-law John Golden Ross to Worcester's home, and he returned little more than an hour later with a note from Delight Boudinot. She confirmed her husband had been killed and urged Ross to leave his house and seek shelter. Neither she nor Worcester believed Ross had been involved, but she allowed that Stand Watie blamed him for the death of his brother. Delight Boudinot warned Ross that Watie was recruiting a band of men to kill him.

Ross should have foreseen that one day there would be a reckoning. His people had been robbed of their land, humiliated, sent out ill-prepared on a journey that killed thousands of their family members. They had to blame someone. He had seen the hate in too many eyes, knew the Cherokees could not forever sit quietly and let go all that had happened. Now that blood had been shed he feared it would lead to a terrible conflict. That afternoon, he sent a soldier to Fort Gibson with a note to Arbuckle, asking him to send in troops to prevent further violence. He explained that these killings would be answered with revenge, beginning an unholy cycle that could quickly lead to an intratribal war. He mentioned that Watie was already plotting to kill him.

"Why I am thus to be murdered without guilt of any crime—I cannot conceive," the chief wrote.

Ross had to realize that, as the leader of these Cherokees, he would be held responsible. For anyone who did not know the chief it would have been a natural assumption. For centuries, Indians had killed for far lesser crimes than the deeds these Cherokees blamed on the members of the Treaty Party. But that was not the way John Ross thought. Later that evening, when he had heard John Ridge had been killed, too, Ross feared what might come next. And that night it came. Long after he had retired, an Indian stopped by his cabin to wake him with the news that Major Ridge had been shot to death.

On Sunday, Arbuckle offered Ross protection at Fort Gibson or a security detail if he chose to remain at his home. Ross declined both. He was more concerned about his people killing one another and, besides, he had no reason to fear for his own safety. When the news of Watie's threat spread, dozens of Cherokees rushed to Ross's cabin. By Monday there were several hundred Indians camped on his lawn; by Friday as many as five hundred. So many of them had assembled—more than enough to protect Ross—they soon organized a posse to hunt down and kill Watie and his men.

By the end of the week it was Stand Watie who showed up at Fort Gibson seeking asylum.

Ross remained sequestered in his home at Park Hill until the July 1 council. He tried to focus on his plans for uniting the two factions but could not keep his mind off the murders. In conversation, he referred to the assassinations as "unfortunate circumstances" and wondered if the killings would ruin any chance for a merger of the two bands. It was a low point for the chief. He had lost his nation, his home, and his wife. Now, his oldest adviser, his mentor, was gone as well.

Some visitors to his home later recalled that Ross spoke of his old friend several times, lamenting, "Once I saved Major Ridge at Red Clay, and would have done so again had I known of this plot." Although the men had become estranged, and Ross believed he had a right to blame Ridge for some of the tribe's problems, it did not extinguish his affection for the old man. Ridge had taught him much over the years, and the bond they had formed could not be broken by a disagreement, even one as serious as theirs. The loss of Ridge severed Ross's last ties to the old country, to his political beginnings. His family was a shambles, his tribe was in turmoil, and there were few men left he could turn to for help. He had suddenly become a middle-aged man who felt more alone than he ever had.

Despite his mixed feelings, Ross did not pursue any inquiries about the death of his old friend. He knew it was better for him, and for his tribe, if he did not have any information that could harm his own people. As was his way, he pushed those feelings out of his mind. Ross would not allow himself to dwell on any troubles for long, not when there was so much at stake.

The western chiefs did not show up for the July 1 council and convinced most of their people to stay away as well. Of the two thousand or so Indians who gathered at the Illinois campground, all but about two hundred were eastern Cherokees. Not even Sequoyah could persuade Brown to participate in this "general convention." Despite that setback, momentum slowly began to swing in Ross's direction.

The Old Settlers who attended the meeting felt Brown, Rogers, and Looney had shunned unity at the June council in favor of politics. Their standing was further eroded when they enlisted Arbuckle's aid, injecting the U.S. government—white men—into the negotiations. Brown had asked Ross to meet privately at Fort Gibson but he refused, arguing that reunification should be done by the people, not a committee of chiefs. In the eyes of many Cherokees, the clandestine efforts of the western chiefs made Ross seem much more reasonable by comparison.

The two bands began to find common ground. The Indians appointed a steering committee to guide the merger, and the group's first act was to pardon the murderers of the Ridges and Boudinot. Anyone who sought revenge for the killings would be considered an outlaw. The committee voted to grant amnesty to those who had threatened retribution or revenge for the deaths of Treaty Party members, provided they would appear before the council and apologize. Stand Watie, now the leader of the Treaty Party, said he would rather die than accept such terms.

On July 12, the convention adopted the "Act of Union." John Looney appeared and signed the document along with Sequoyah. Ross used their signatures as proof the plan had support of both bands, which was only a slight exaggeration. Brown countered with his own meeting but Ross had everything working in his favor. In September the committee drafted a new constitution that was nearly identical to the one Ross had composed years earlier.

The constitution included a declaration that the Treaty of New Echota was illegal, which would give them standing to try to negotiate a new deal with the United States. Some of the Old Settlers, who correctly gauged the emerging sentiment, held their own council to remove Brown and Rogers from office. The two chiefs were accused of conspiring with the Treaty Party to keep the tribe divided. Brown was so incensed he left the country, taking his family to Mexico.

A few weeks later, the new government was elected by popular vote of the entire tribe. The Old Settlers were guaranteed one-third of the seats in the new legislative body. William Shorey Coodey, Ross's nephew, was named president of the new National Committee, the Cherokee version of a senate. Young Wolf, an Old Settler, was chosen as speaker of the National Council. Lewis Ross, who had managed much of the removal, was appointed treasurer and Joseph Vann—another Old Settler—was appointed second principal chief by the General Council. John Ross was elected principal chief by an overwhelming margin.

The election did not end the Cherokees' troubles. John Rogers and some other western chiefs tried to take back the tribe several times. At the same time, Stand Watie and members of the Treaty Party traveled to Washington to convince the government not to recognize Ross's leadership. For a time, Secretary of War Joel Poinsett tried to have Ross arrested for the murder of the Ridges and Boudinot. These machinations would continue for more than six years.

Through the fall of 1839, Ross deftly avoided arrest, fought for federal recognition, and bought food and livestock to nurse his people back to health. He soon felt confident enough to leave his new nation for several months. Before the end of the year, Ross traveled to Washington to claim the money owed his people. The trip included a detour to New Jersey, where he enrolled Silas at Lawrenceville Classical and Commercial High School. In those days, it was a prep school for children poised to enter Princeton

University. Ross would make sure his sons, and their cousins, got a better education than most of the white settlers who had called them savages.

When Ross returned to the new Cherokee Nation in early 1840 he began to build a new Indian empire. He pushed forward an ambitious agenda, opening new schools, suppressing the flow of alcohol and gambling, and promoting the health of his people. In this new land he wanted to create the nation he had dreamed of long ago, a tribe that would stand equal to any state in the union. And now he had the power and support to do so. The Cherokees still seemed more than willing to do whatever he asked.

Slowly, the chief was remaking his tribe stronger than it had been before. In the decades to come, he would fend off a new wave of settlers, fight the United States government, and squash all attempts by his enemies to take over the tribe. He would lead his people into a new golden age of prosperity.

Led by John Ross the Cherokee Nation would rise from the ashes and reclaim its position as the most modern, the most civilized of Native American tribes.

The Way of the West

It took years for the Cherokees to find any peace in the West.

Some Indians refused to accept John Ross as chief, and their resentment festered until, periodically, someone was killed. These murders were always followed by an act of retribution. It seemed the mutual distrust between eastern Cherokees, the Treaty Party, and the Old Settlers would never end. According to tribal legend, even the chief's own brother Andrew was eventually shot for his role in the removal. No Cherokee was guaranteed immunity in the days after removal, not even a Ross.

The violence peaked in 1840, when Archilla Smith—one of the men who signed the Treaty of New Echota—got into a frivolous dispute with John McIntosh. In his fury, Smith stabbed the man to death. His arrest and subsequent trial were a test of the new Cherokee constitution, and divided the Treaty Party and the eastern Indians even more. Stand Watie defended Smith for the nine-day trial. When his client was pronounced guilty on December 26, 1840, the Treaty Party leader would not accept the verdict. He protested, then drew up a petition asking John Ross to pardon Smith, "with a desire that peace and harmony may prevail." The implied threat was that Smith's execution would lead to even more trouble for the Cherokees.

Ross ignored the request and was forced to deny charges that his refusal was due to lingering animosity against Watie. He instead claimed a chief had no power to grant pardons or undo the will of the court. Smith was hanged shortly thereafter. One by one, the Indians associated with the Treaty Party were slowly disappearing.

John Howard Payne, who was visiting Ross at the time, wrote a long account of the Smith trial for the *New York Journal of Commerce*. His narrative portrayed a tribe struggling to find its way in the changing world, still trying to adapt to the laws and customs of white men. Payne made it clear he considered these Indians as civilized, as humane, and more just than the men who had banished them to the Great Plains.

The Treaty Party stoked the fires of discontent for years. In 1842 Watie shot James Foreman, who he believed had been party to the murder of his brother. He went on trial in Arkansas but was acquitted—he claimed to have killed Foreman in self-defense. The next year, Isaac Bushyhead, David Vann, and Elijah Hicks were attacked in the Saline district, where opposition to Ross was strongest. Hicks and Vann survived but Bushyhead was killed. The murderers escaped into Arkansas, pulling the chief into an extradition fight. Critics said he was bent on revenge, but Ross knew if tribal law was not respected in its early years it never would be.

Ross could neither stop the fighting nor win over his harshest critics. After Bushyhead was killed, the rhetoric against Ross reached its peak. There were rumors that assassins would soon kill the chief. The General Council took the threat seriously enough to post several dozen Cherokees around his home. The warriors remained there for weeks but no one ever came.

Two years later, in 1845, someone burned the home of Ross's daughter. The arson was attributed to looters but many Indians believed it was a warning, or an attempt by the chief's enemies to hurt him. Jane claimed the men had tried to kill her husband, John Meigs. She feared this conflict would never end, Jane wrote in a frantic note to her father, who was in Washington at the time.

"The country is in such a state just now that there seems little encouragement for people to build good houses or make anything—for fear of being
robbed & murdered by these barbarous fellows," Jane wrote. "John said he
would go back & live there again, but I do not think it safe & will never
consent to go back again . . . I am so nervous I can scarce write at all. I hope
it will not be long you'll be at home but I hope the country will be settled by
that time too."

The chief and his family remained targets for years. Some believed Stand
Watie watched him constantly, waiting for the chance to strike. When Ross
traveled, which was often, Lewis urged him not to go out alone. It felt as if he
was a prisoner in his own country. Eventually, the council hired six full-time
guards to watch over the chief and the Cherokee papers at Park Hill.

Even in exile John Ross could not avoid the white man's politics. He
spent much of the early 1840s trying to get the $5 million the tribe was owed
as part of the Treaty of New Echota. The United States government refused
to live up to its end of the bargain, officials inventing any number of excuses.
Some refused to recognize the tribe so long as Ross was chief. At times, they
even threatened Ross, but he did not care. What could they do that they had
not already done?

Finally, in 1846, the federal government agreed to pay. Some of the
money, it was decided, would go to the Old Settlers because they had been
forced to share their homes. That gesture tempered many of the lingering
hard feelings. Even the heirs of the Ridges and Boudinot received some
money. According to some accounts, Ross and Stand Watie shook hands
when the agreement was signed, but others dispute that as legend. Either
way, the payments ultimately did little to extinguish the long-standing animosity between the Treaty Party and Ross.

Another four years passed before Congress eventually approved the payment. By then the Cherokees had suffered in poverty for nearly a decade.

Change came slowly to the Cherokee Nation through the 1840s. Just north
of Park Hill the tribe established its new capital. They called it Tahlequah, a
corruption of Tellico, the ancient Cherokee capital in Tennessee. Some had

wanted to name their new town Echota in honor of their great capital, but the council eventually decided against it, as the name reminded too many people of the treaty and all that happened afterward. At first, Tahlequah was not even as modern a city as New Echota; there was not enough money for the grand building program Ross envisioned. The Cherokees invested what little money they had in schools and, in 1843, a newspaper. Ross installed his nephew William Potter Ross as editor of the *Cherokee Advocate*.

A semblance of unity slowly took hold. Indians built log cabins and plank-sided homes in Tahlequah and eventually the factions began to mingle more easily. The eastern Cherokees found the new land not so different from the old. It took more patience to grow crops, and rain would wash away entire gardens if the seeds were not planted deep enough, but the Indians adapted well. For a while, they allowed themselves to believe their greatest troubles had passed.

By then the business of governing had grown tiresome to Ross. He had ruled in times of crisis for nearly two decades, and mundane decisions on issues such as teacher pay must have seemed hopelessly trivial by comparison. But he never showed any inclination to step down. The tribe's finances worried him constantly and, in truth, he did not trust anyone else to manage Cherokee affairs. He learned to delegate his duties, usually to family members.

Ross passed some days writing long notes of advice to his boys at their boarding school in New Jersey. He spent time with Jane's children, his grandchildren, Henry Clay Meigs and Elizabeth Grace Meigs. He also doted on the children of his brothers and sisters, an old tradition in Cherokee culture. He paid for the education of many nieces and nephews and became particularly close to William Potter Ross, the son of his sister Elizabeth.

It soon became apparent to everyone around Ross that he was, more than anything, lonely. He hid it as best he could, and slowly allowed himself a semblance of normal life. He replaced his modest cabin with one of the finest homes in the Cherokee Nation. The large house sat on a small hill shaded by oaks and elms, and its yellow siding and massive porch columns were reminiscent of a Georgia mansion. The driveway was lined with several species of roses, which gave the Ross home its name: Rose Cottage.

It was a larger, even more spectacular house than the one he'd designed at Head of Coosa, complete with an ornate parlor, a large library, and a number of guest rooms. He filled his home with books and china that carried a detailed blue pattern, and furnished it in mahogany and rosewood. Ross had built a mansion but he had no one to share it with save for strangers.

Rose Cottage became a mandatory stop for both visiting dignitaries and poor Indians who had no place else to go, and most nights Ross's large dining room was filled with guests. His servants always prepared large meals because they had no idea how many people the forlorn chief might invite to join him. John Howard Payne, who had resumed his research of the Cherokees, became a frequent guest, once staying nearly four months. Ross was delighted by the company of his old friend, and likely joked to Payne that no one would come to arrest them now.

Ross amassed a fortune through business dealings and land speculation. He turned his home into a huge plantation with numerous head of cattle and more than ninety sheep. This farm was run by more than fifty slaves, most of whom Ross had inherited from his grandfather. The time and attention he gave these workers suggests he considered them part of his family. After the Civil War, when his slaves were set free, many of them remained close to the chief.

Ross became a good friend of George Murrell, a wealthy Virginian who had married Lewis's oldest daughter, Minerva. The Murrells lived close to Ross in a house that rivaled the chief's in both size and decor. It was called Hunters' Home after Murrell's love of foxhunting. The neighborhood that grew up around Hunter's Home and Rose Cottage became the heart of the Park Hill social scene. In some ways the upper-class Cherokees mirrored the class system of the American South.

These society Indians were far different from the rest of the tribe, both in wealth and in learning. They largely kept to themselves, socializing and marrying from within the same group. Visitors found it hard to distinguish Park Hill from antebellum Georgia. There were Sunday barbecues and dances as well as traditional ceremonies that reflected their distinctly Indian heritage. The annual holiday party at Rose Cottage became the most popular social event of the year. Ross enjoyed playing host, but it often reminded him he had no wife with which to share this tradition.

John Ross met the Stapler family of Brandywine Springs, Delaware, in 1841. He was on an extended summer vacation that included stays in Cape May, New Jersey, and Saratoga Springs, New York. Some said he had a brief romantic interlude with a woman he had met in Philadelphia. He said little of the relationship to his family, although some would later claim he proposed to the woman. It's unclear whether she declined or Ross had second thoughts.

Thomas McKenney likely introduced Ross and the Staplers. The former Indian commissioner had kept in touch with Ross over the years, and even included him in his exhaustive history of the Native American tribes. Ross often dined with McKenney on his visits to the East. It was during one of these diplomatic trips that Ross met John Stapler, a Wilmington merchant who had much in common with the chief: both were businessmen by trade; both had lost a wife.

Before Ann Stapler died in 1838 she'd left the care of her three youngest children to her eldest daughter, Sarah. Ross became friends with John but found a true confidante in Sarah. She was a quick-witted, wise young lady and Ross addressed her as "sister" in letters. Although the two became constant pen pals, there was never anything more than a familial fondness for each other. In fact Ross was more interested in another of the Stapler girls.

Not yet sixteen, Mary Bryan Stapler made no secret of her attraction to the chief. After their first meeting she began writing flirtatious letters to Ross, complaining of her "imprisonment" at the Moravian Female Academy in Bethlehem, Pennsylvania, and calling him "Kooweskowe, the Chief of a generous and noble race." Ross was amused, but he restricted himself to sending regards to Mary through Sarah. He worried it was inappropriate to write directly to the girl at her school, and he may have been concerned that he was infatuated with someone several years younger than his own daughter, even if such age differences were not all that unusual for the era.

It was two years later that the actual courtship began, and again it was initiated by Mary. In May 1844 she wrote Ross a short note from Delaware, asking if "time and absence quite obliterated from thy memory" the girl he had once called his "niece." She invited him to visit her family in Wilmington, where the walks along the Brandywine River were "truly romantic."

As part of her flirting she teased Ross about his possible interest in another woman. A friend of the Stapler family was apparently infatuated with the chief and Mary noted that "a second person interested in the welfare of both parties can often work wonders. Will thee trust me with thy secrets?" It seemed she was testing Ross's affections. For months, they danced around their blossoming love, but soon there was a sharp change in the tone of their letters.

Mary not only distracted Ross from the tribe's problems; she made the middle-aged man feel young again, soothed his loneliness. When he was in Washington, he would drop tribal business to immediately respond to Mary's letters—and she chastised him if he didn't. By the middle of summer they had begun to write openly of their love. When Mary made a point of mentioning that no women had given away their hand in his absence from Wilmington, Ross pointedly asked if that included hers. She became coy.

"When I started in life I determined never to give my *hand* without *my heart,* until I can yield both," Mary wrote, "I remain as I am, although I am by no means invincible."

Ross, as blunt as ever, eventually told Mary he loved her. But she was not convinced, asking why they had not seen each other in two years. Ross was often in the Northeast on business yet did not stop in Wilmington to visit her. She suspected he was playing with her. At that point, she did not fully realize his devotion to the Cherokees. He tried to make it up to her by writing more often, addressing her as "My Beloved Mary," and talking of marriage.

"Why then should we longer be separated, if our hearts do not deceive us, and our affections for each other be really formed?" Ross said. "As to mine—they are pure sincere and ardent—and once united with yours in the solemn ties of matrimony, I am sure that nothing but the cold hand of death could ever extinguish them from my bosom."

Mary was somewhat put off by Ross's businesslike approach to romance. She longed for a lengthy courtship. She wanted Ross to visit her in Delaware, to woo her, win over her family. They both recognized that their age difference—thirty-six years—would be an issue for some people, and Mary had no desire to become a subject of idle gossip. But the idea of Ross returning to the Cherokee Nation halfway across the country scared her, and she realized she loved him too much to risk losing him. In August, Mary told Ross that she could not wait until the next spring to marry. She could not bear the thought of him traveling west without her.

"My very dear Friend I think I have investigated into the feelings of my heart and under all circumstances in life, they could not change *when Woman Loves she loves forever.*"

That short note prompted Ross to write letters to Sarah and John Stapler, asking both for Mary's hand. Sarah offered her blessing immediately—she must have suspected something of the romance—but John had to be convinced. Mary's father thought Ross a fine man, and if he worried about the age difference he said nothing of it. Instead, John Stapler's greatest fear was his daughter moving so far from the rest of the family. But Mary convinced him she could not be happy without John Ross in her life and Stapler consented.

They married in Philadelphia on September 2, 1844, an extravagant event covered by a local newspaper. After a honeymoon in New York, John and Mary Ross set out for the long journey to Park Hill, and Sarah moved with them. John Stapler had lost two daughters to the chief.

At the age of fifty-four, John Ross was a happy newlywed, and his contentment coincided with the Cherokees' first prolonged period of peace in more than three decades. Shortly after his wedding, Ross settled his dispute with the federal government and began efforts to retire the tribe's debt by selling off the "neutral lands"—500,000 acres between Tahlequah and the Kansas territory the Cherokees had been forced to buy as part of the Treaty of New

Echota. Settlers had begun to move onto the land and Ross no longer had the stomach to fight them.

What trouble the chief encountered he dispatched quickly. To curb the influx of squatters, Ross convinced the government to abandon nearby Fort Gibson, a source of protection for white settlers. And when the Treaty Party petitioned the United States to divide the Cherokees' land so they could form their own nation, Ross quashed their efforts. By then the Treaty Party and Old Settlers had given up on overthrowing Ross. A few eventually left the nation, settling in Mexico. Watie, however, remained. It seemed he was simply waiting for his moment.

By the late 1850s Ross had served longer than any principal chief in memory. Some white politicians complained that John and Lewis Ross ran the Cherokee Nation like their own empire, but most of the Indians did not mind. They did not impose term limits. They reelected Ross in 1847, 1851, 1855, and again in 1859. There was rarely a challenger, and when the council suggested an alternative candidate it was always someone close to the chief, such as his brother Lewis, his nephew William Shorey Coodey, his friend David Vann. Apparently, the council was offering to appoint a palatable successor if the chief wanted to step down.

There were always some troubles. In 1850 Ross was left to console his daughter, Jane, when her husband died. Meigs had gotten caught up in the California gold rush and disappeared. Some said he was shot before he could return. The chief could do little more to help his daughter than manage his dead son-in-law's mercantile business. His two favorite nephews, William Potter Ross and Daniel Hicks Ross, took over when the chief lost interest. Two years later, Jane married a Tahlequah merchant with the unlikely name Andrew Ross Nave.

John Ross was becoming an old man very much aware of his mortality. Short and growing pudgy, his face creased with deep lines, Ross buried many of his contemporaries, as well as some younger men. His brother-in-law Elijah Hicks passed away in 1856; John Golden Ross and John Stapler followed in 1858. Ross was left with only Lewis to advise him. The chief increasingly relied on his son Allen, who he appointed auditor of the Cherokee

Nation. Few Indians grumbled about the chief patronage. For Ross, it was
never about money but always about trust.

Ross soon turned his attention to improving Indian education. He built
more schools, hired more teachers—even some white ones. For a while,
Sarah taught at one of the schools in Tahlequah. Ross realized the world was
changing still and the Cherokees would need more education to survive. He
had no illusions the white men would stay away forever.

Soon, Ross and Mary had two children of their own, Annie and John
Jr. One of Mary's cousin's, Mary F. Stapler, came to tutor the children. It
was not an indictment of Cherokee schools as much as familial charity; the
young girl seemed eager to strike out on her own. But she died under bizarre
circumstances two years later. The young Mary sat too close to the hearth in
Rose Cottage one day and her dress caught fire. She ran out of the house,
where slave women helped Ross put out the fire, but the shock killed her a
few days later.

In the wake of that misfortune, Ross made his first trip to Washington
in years. He had long ago left these missions to younger men such as his
nephew William Potter Ross, and he'd agreed to go only because he wanted
to take Mary and the children to visit family in Delaware. While Mary spent
time at her old home, Ross tried to sell the neutral lands and win permission
to tax white traders on Indian land in order to make money. As usual, Congress was less than accommodating.

The trip served other purposes for Ross, however. Along the way he
stopped in Tennessee to show Mary his childhood home, the true land of
the Cherokees. The white-haired old chief was comforted to see the sloping profile of Lookout Mountain unchanged in the winter of 1860, yet he
could not help being surprised by the modern city that had grown up around
Ross's Landing.

Storefronts lined streets that stretched from the waterfront to the
mountain, and railroad tracks crossed near the spot where his father's house
once stood. On the banks of the river, huge storage sheds housed supplies
that were barged in daily. Fine homes overlooked the river, and a large iron
furnace had been built very near the site of his old trading post. In the center

of town, the Crutchfield House rivaled any hotel in Washington. His old home was now one of the largest cities in the South. But he was pleased to see that not everything had changed. His grandfather's house had survived.

The white men had renamed the outpost "Chattanooga," a word of undetermined Indian origin. Some said it referred to the rock that came to a point—Lookout Mountain—while others insisted it had to do with the good fishing in the area. Still others claimed it was incorporated from the name of a small Indian village that once stood at the base of the mountain. Ross was likely not amused the whites had appropriated not only Indian land but also their words. At least they still called the waterfront Ross's Landing.

Ross toured the town for several days, then left Mary and the children in the city while he rode south to visit his father's grave at Head of Coosa. It had been more than twenty years since he'd last walked those grounds and the place could only have stirred painful memories. When he returned to Chattanooga he gathered his family and left town, taking one last opportunity to admire the handsome profile of Lookout Mountain. He would never see it again.

Ultimately, the trip left Ross troubled. Throughout the South, there was talk of war and he worried that the Cherokees, even as far away as they were, would be pulled into another conflict. Already politicians in Arkansas were urging the tribe to align with the South. Ross warned his people, as well as the other tribes, to remain neutral. Let the white men kill each other all they want, Ross said; it was not the Cherokees' fight. He was finished with white man's politics.

The divide between North and South had been building since before removal. Ross was familiar with states' rights—he'd tried to use the idea to the tribe's advantage years before—and the controversial nature of slavery. In the 1850s, the tribe had found itself divided almost evenly on slavery: full-blooded Cherokees opposed it, while the mixed-bloods favored the peculiar institution. The difference of opinion came about honestly. Some full-blooded Indians had relatives who had been abducted into slavery generations before and therefore recognized its evils. Only wealthy mixed-blood Cherokees, like Ross, still held slaves. Ross carefully kept his opinions out of the debate, but he made no secret of his disdain for the War Between the States.

Although the Cherokees were surrounded by southern states, he feared that siding with them—and against the Union—would void the tribe's treaties. He wrote to U.S. officials for protection but his letters went unanswered. Four months after the first shots were fired on Fort Sumter, Confederate troops surrounded Tahlequah. The tribe had no choice but to align itself with the rebels. If they remained loyal to the Union, Ross knew, the southerners would likely attack.

The Confederates had courted the Cherokees shamelessly, offering protection and money in return for Indian soldiers. Ross could barely stand the thought of such an alliance—after all, it was southerners who had forced them from their homes—but eventually he was forced to sign an agreement. Stand Watie, for once, applauded Ross's decision. Watie had sided with the Confederacy long before the war started, in part because of rumors that President Lincoln would give white settlers Indian land. Most Cherokees would eventually choose sides. Even Ross's sons James, Allen, Silas, and George chose to fight, although they joined the Union forces.

The deal with the Confederates was, as Ross feared, a mistake. The rebels kept their promises no better than the politicians in Washington; the southerners fled the area as soon as Union troops marched on Tahlequah. Fortunately, the northern generals recognized the chief's predicament—and it did not hurt his position that his own family fought for the Union. Less than a year after the council signed a treaty with the Confederates, Ross welcomed federal commander Colonel William Weer into his home at Park Hill to negotiate a settlement. By August Ross and hundreds of Cherokee refugees had left Tahlequah. They would spend the remainder of the war at Fort Leavenworth, Kansas.

Ross did not remain in Kansas for long. Brigadier General James G. Blunt suggested Ross travel to Washington to explain the tribe's predicament to the president. Ross heeded his advice, taking Mary and the children to her family's boardinghouse in Philadelphia. Ross would not see them again for some time. He spent the rest of the war in Washington.

Stand Watie and the "southern" Cherokees briefly took over the tribe in Ross's absence. In February 1863, the Treaty Party claimed to depose Ross and, with most of the council members hundreds of miles away, elected Watie principal chief. One of his first, and only, acts as chief was to loot Rose Cottage and burn it to the ground. Ross lost all his belongings except some furniture and dishes that Mary had carried to Kansas. Watie's reign did not last long. Within a week the rightful Cherokee council gathered at Camp John Ross and reinstalled their chief in absentia.

Ross did not learn of this subterfuge until much later. He spent most of his days debating Abraham Lincoln and his cabinet. The president was initially cautious in his dealings with the Cherokees but soon Lincoln came to trust Ross. He even agreed to buy the neutral lands at a time when the government had decidedly more pressing matters. Like his military leaders, President Lincoln realized Ross had had no choice but to sign the Confederates' treaty.

Ross's time in the city was torturous. He wrote to Mary that he could no longer stand "this wearisome city," but his family and the Cherokee council refused to allow him to leave. It was too dangerous for him to travel during the war, they argued, and some feared that Watie would kill him if given the chance. And, they noted, Ross would have been even more miserable with his exiled tribe in Kansas. There was little food and they were freezing through the Great Plains winter. Ross directed Lewis to send what supplies he could gather, but there were precious few blankets and food to spare with a war raging.

The war had other costs for Ross. His son James was captured by Confederate forces while trying to carry supplies to Park Hill for his family. Ross's oldest boy was remanded to a prison camp, where he soon died, most likely from disease or starvation. And Stand Watie's troops killed Ross's son-in-law Andrew Ross Nave, leaving Jane twice widowed. In her grief, Jane took in her brother's children and raised them as her own.

John Ross finally left Washington in the spring of 1865, shortly after attending President Lincoln's second inauguration and receiving word the war had ended. But when he arrived in Philadelphia to collect his family there was no happy reunion. He found Mary gravely ill.

She had kept the severity of her condition a secret from Ross lest he worry. Mary was suffering from lung congestion, a diagnosis that covered a great many illnesses in those days. She could not travel and Ross refused to leave without her. She lingered for more than a month and Ross spent his days at her side. Mary finally passed away on July 20, 1865. She was only forty years old. Ross buried his "little wife" in Delaware and set off for home. His heart was broken.

John Ross was never the same after he lost Mary. He was nearing seventy-five, his health was poor, and he knew his end was near. On the voyage west he wrote to his sister-in-law Sarah that he had little desire to see Park Hill again. He had lost everything and nothing mattered to him anymore.

"I know that I am fast approaching my country & my people, and that I shall soon meet with my Dear children, relatives & friends who will greet me with joyful hearts—but, where is that delightful Home & the matron of the once happy family who so kindly & hospitably entertained our guests? Alas, I shall see them no more on earth. The loved wife and mother is at last in the Heavenly mansions prepared for the redeemed—and the family Homestead ruthlessly reduced to ashes by the hands of rebel incendiaries."

Ross might have been inclined to resign his position and leave governing to younger men, but he had one last fight in him, a struggle that would consume the rest of his days. In that final year stubbornness and willpower kept him going. They were all he had left.

Shortly after he returned home, Ross was called to Fort Smith, Arkansas, an imposing federal outpost on the edge of the Indian country. The fort had been established to keep the peace on Indian land and now served as a diplomatic outpost for the government. Federal officials had gathered there to force the tribes that sided with the Confederacy to renegotiate their treaties; the war had given the government another opportunity to take advantage of the Indians. Ross quickly recognized the farce—he was the target of these hearings.

Stand Watie and his nephew Elias Cornelius Boudinot accused Ross of conspiring to align the Cherokees with the Confederates so as to profit from it. Despite Watie's arrogant duplicity, the commissioner of Indian Affairs Dennis N. Cooley was inclined to believe the charges, or at least use them to his advantage. The two men urged Cooley to jail Ross as a traitor, or simply refuse to recognize him as chief. Boudinot claimed Ross ruled the tribe through lies and deception, but then he still blamed the chief for his father's death. Cooley was eager to go along with Watie's ludicrous claims, but when the meeting ended nothing had been settled. Ross did not go to jail.

John Ross spent the next two months at his niece's home near the ruins of Rose Cottage, growing sicker every day. He was in and out of bed with serious colds and relied on Lewis to handle much of the tribe's business. Despite the protests of Jane and his other children, Ross decided to travel to Washington for a continuation of his hearings with Cooley. He left Park Hill on November 9, 1865, riding with his nephew Daniel Hicks Ross. The trip left Ross weak but by February he had recovered enough to meet with the new president, Andrew Johnson.

Johnson was not duped as easily as Cooley. He remembered Ross's predicament during the war, just as he recalled it was Watie who had fought for the South until the conflict ended. Although the debate lingered into the summer Watie was beaten. When Cooley drew up a treaty to divide the Cherokee Nation into two governments, the president refused to sign it. He forced Cooley to write a new treaty that kept the tribe intact and ordered him to deal only with Ross's council. Those Cherokees, sensing they had the upper hand, made one final demand. They insisted Cooley leave a prominent spot on the treaty for Ross, who had scarcely participated in the negotiations, to sign.

John Ross would sign one final treaty but he did not live to see it ratified by Congress. He was growing sicker by the week and spent those final months writing letters and composing a will that divided his property evenly among his surviving children. He left no final words for his tribe but composed a fitting epitaph in his testimony with Cooley earlier that spring. Ross had been so sick the commissioner was forced to visit the chief's hotel room to take a statement for the ongoing investigation. During their discussion the principal chief of the Cherokee Nation summed up his life succinctly and elegantly.

"I am an old man, and have served my people and the Govt. of the United States a long time, over fifty years. My people have kept me in the harness, not of my seeking, but of their own choice. I have never deceived them, and now I look back, not one act of my public life rises up to upbraid me. I have done the best I could, and today, upon this bed of sickness, my heart approves all I have done. And still I am, John Ross, the same John Ross of former years, unchanged."

On August 1, 1866, at about seven p.m., John Ross died in his Washington hotel room, two months before his seventy-sixth birthday.

Initially, Ross was buried in Delaware with his wife's family, but the Cherokees would not allow their chief to rest anywhere other than Cherokee soil. That fall, they sent William Potter Ross to collect his uncle's body and carry it back to Park Hill. Ross was laid to rest on a hillside near the remains of his former home, a cemetery that would eventually hold nearly all of his family.

It was fitting that William Potter Ross accompanied his uncle to the grave, for he was the chief's handpicked successor. John Ross had spent years grooming the boy for leadership—paying his tuition at Princeton, naming him editor of the *Cherokee Advocate,* appointing him to Washington delegations. The son of John Ross's sister Elizabeth and John Golden Ross, the boy had been born in the shadow of Lookout Mountain and raised much as Ross had been. For his entire life, Will Ross had been his uncle's greatest defender.

The passing of the Cherokee chief—the only leader many in the tribe had ever known—brought a great deal of uncertainty. Many men had waited years for their chance to gain control of the tribe, and some Indians feared that the power struggle to replace John Ross might start an intratribal war. General Council ignored the political maneuvering and appointed William Potter Ross as principal chief, passing over the second principal chief, Lewis Downing. Some believed the honor was meant for John Ross as much as his nephew, although there was little doubt the younger Ross was suited to the job.

At forty-six, the tall, lanky William Ross was as businesslike and stoic as his famous uncle. He had a sharp mind, a keen sense of justice. Unfortunately, he lacked his uncle's common touch with Indians and proved to be vindictive against John Ross's enemies. He shut out the "southern Cherokees"—as Stand Watie's followers were called after the war—from all positions of prominence. His lack of diplomacy enraged many members of the tribe and speeded along a shift in the various Cherokee factions. Downing built a coalition between John Ross's old supporters and Watie's followers to defeat William Potter Ross in his campaign for reelection.

For a while, it seemed John Ross's legacy would end with Will Ross's defeat. Slowly, the last embers of that great Cherokee generation were dying out. Lewis Ross, the chief's brother and best friend, had retired years earlier and passed away in 1870 at the age of seventy-eight. None of Ross's surviving children ever rose to prominence. George Washington Ross served as the clerk of Tahlequah district court for a time, but he died in 1870 at the age of forty. Silas Dinsmore Ross passed away in 1872 at the age of forty-three. Allen Ross served as the tribe's auditor until his father's death, and then sat on various committees in the tribe. He was, at most, a minor politician.

John Ross Jr. returned to Park Hill after he finished school but never took an interest in politics. Annie Brian Ross married Leonidas Dobson the year her father died, but she passed away unexpectedly before she was thirty. Jane Ross Meigs Nave lived a quiet life, never bothering to talk about tribal business. It reminded her too much of her father. Jane died in 1894. She was seventy-three.

Several of Ross's nieces and nephews followed him into a life of public service. Eliza Jane Ross taught at the Cherokee Female Seminary. Henry Clay Ross became sheriff of the Saline District. Daniel Hicks Ross, who was with his uncle when he died, served on the council for a bit but never rose through the ranks. Henry Clay Meigs, Jane's daughter and Ross's grandson, eventually sat on the bench as a judge in the Cherokee court.

Although the Ross family contributed mightily to Cherokee life, and traded modestly on their name, they could not duplicate their patriarch's success. No one in his immediate family was considered a true heir to the

Ross political legacy. Only William Potter Ross held that distinction. Even in defeat, however, he was not finished with public life.

Just as many Cherokees had feared, the tribe was adrift without John Ross's leadership. By 1871 Chief Downing had lost much of his support, in part because of the considerable concessions he made to Stand Watie. Whether out of respect or just nostalgia, William Ross was nominated as chief once again. Downing managed a narrow win but died a year later. Ross was appointed to fill out the term.

As a principal chief William Ross found tribal unity as elusive for him as it had been for John Ross. For much of his term, serious debates on who qualified as a Cherokee citizen and who did not preoccupied him. As homesteaders began creeping onto the tribe's land—just as the settlers in the East had done generations earlier—it fell to Ross to keep the peace. He did not succeed. By 1875 there had been at least two gun battles between Cherokee sheriffs and U.S. marshals, one of which occurred in Tahlequah. Later that year the tribe elected Oochalata as principal chief, turning William Potter Ross out of the job for a second time.

Before the end of the nineteenth century Ross's dream for a state of Cherokee would finally die. In the mid-1880s Henry L. Dawes of Massachusetts, chairman of the U.S. Senate's committee on Indian Affairs, devised a plan for assimilating Indians into the white man's culture. By then the last of the western Indians, who fought behind the legendary Geronimo, had been defeated, opening up the country for expansion from coast to coast. The consensus among whites was to establish a single government over the more than sixty tribes in the West. Dawes seized on the idea, claiming the tribes could not progress so long as they held common land. He convinced Congress to pass a law called the Dawes Severalty Act (1887), which broke up Indian reservations and gave the head of each Indian household 160 acres. Critics said this was not enough land to cultivate profitably but it resulted in a lot of spare land for white settlers.

The Cherokees and the other Five Civilized Tribes were initially exempt from the law, but by 1898 the United States declared it would no longer recognize tribal jurisdiction over Indian land. Congress justified this by declaring the United States "one nation."

The Cherokees continued to fight and, in 1905, revived John Ross's dream, asking Congress for an Indian state. They proposed calling it Sequoyah. Instead Congress took the land given to the Five Civilized Tribes and named it "Oklahoma," the Choctaw word for the red man. By the time Oklahoma was admitted to the Union in 1907 it was controlled by white men.

The Cherokees would not be evicted but the new settlers took over once again. In that year, John Ross Jr.—the last of the chief's children—passed away. Not yet sixty, the youngest Ross had lived long enough to see his father's dream finally, irrevocably, extinguished. More than two decades later a government panel would determine the Dawes Act had been an illegal intrusion on the rights of Indians, a land grab that violated U.S. law. But by then the damage had been done.

John Ross would come to be known as the Cherokee Moses. Such biblical praise was not unwarranted or hyperbolic. Ross had saved his people, led them out of the wilderness. He was the architect of the tribe's greatest period of advancement; he made the Cherokees the most civilized of American Indian tribes. His legacy would be one of peace, of equality for Indians, of self-sufficiency and independence.

Some scholars of Native America would later second-guess many of Ross's decisions. They would speculate that his stubborn refusal to concede defeat in the days leading up to removal contributed to his tribe's suffering on the Trail of Tears. In truth, most tribes fared as poorly as the Cherokees on the trail. And even Ross's detractors, who criticized him for the subterfuge he employed during the dark days of removal, could hardly question his motives. There is little proof Ross was ever motivated by greed, personal gain, or anything other than an abiding desire to protect his people. Shortly after he died the Cherokee council praised him in a memorial.

"He never sacrificed the interests of this nation to expediency. He never lost sight of the welfare of the people. For them he labored for a long life, and upon them he bestowed his last expressed thoughts."

In his time Ross never gave the vast majority of Cherokees any reason to doubt his leadership. In the nearly forty years he served as chief, he never failed to get at least two-thirds of the vote in any campaign, and many elections were near unanimous. More than a century after his death he would still be the longest-serving chief in Cherokee history—and, many would argue, the greatest. Well into the twenty-first century, Cherokee leaders would study Ross's life and times for guidance. Monuments to the chief would rise across Oklahoma, Tennessee, and even Georgia.

His life was filled with triumphs and personal joy as well as great tragedy. He outlived two wives and one of his sons and saw many of his friends and mentors die or be killed. For all the things that weighed on him, all the regrets he kept to himself, there was only one true disappointment in his life. Ross ultimately lost the greatest battle of his life. Late in life he accepted that he would never see his dream of a "state of Cherokee" realized.

John Ross was never a man who believed in compromise, so it is likely he never considered himself a successful chief. He looked at all things in the broadest terms. To his mind, he had failed to keep his people safe in their homes, the original land of the Cherokees. But in those final days in Washington it's possible he had time to reflect on his long life. If he did, Ross had to realize he had done far more to help his people than anyone before him. He had saved his people, and his nation, ensuring both would survive into the coming centuries.

It may be that the most amazing thing about Ross is that he did all of this not because he was Cherokee by birth, but because he was a Cherokee by choice. The final irony of his life is that this man, who barely had any Indian blood coursing through his veins, would go down in history as perhaps the greatest Cherokee.

Notes and Sources

In Tennessee and Georgia there are dozens of parks, bridges, houses, boat landings—even a town—named after John Ross. Yet few people who pass through Rossville or visit Ross's Landing (near the Market Street Bridge, which is officially the John Ross Bridge) know much about him, other than the fact that he was an old Cherokee of some note. For most of my life I was one of those people.

I grew up in Cleveland, Tennessee, Ross's last home in the East. It is family lore that we are descended from the tribe (my father is at least one-eighth Cherokee, the same as Ross), but as a child I had little interest in that history. My school classes often took field trips to Red Clay, a state park my grandfather helped build, and I remember it primarily for how boring it was. There's not much there to hold the attention of elementary school kids—a small museum, a replica of the council shed, and a few cabins. When I took my own children there in 2007, they found Red Clay remarkable mostly for the wide-open spaces that gave them a chance to run off some car fatigue. By then I held a far higher regard for those grounds, and for the Cherokees.

The idea for this book was born at Christmastime in 2006. My family was visiting relatives in Chattanooga and we took a walk on Ross's Landing one cold December afternoon. The state of Tennessee has erected a historical marker near the site of the trading post John and Lewis Ross operated for years (now a magnificent park) and I stopped to read it. My wife, Beth, suggested Ross would make a fascinating book. A native of Georgia, she had learned about the great Cherokee chief in school. Curiously, I could remember almost nothing about him from Tennessee's history curriculum. When I began to make up for lost time I was hooked.

The story of John Ross and the Cherokees is an American epic. I describe it to friends only half-jokingly as a Native American *Gone with the Wind*, or as *The Godfather* on the old frontier. The golden age of the Cherokees was the end of an era. It is, in many ways, the oldest sort of story: it involves treachery, deceit, and pride, men who cross their own families for personal gain. At its core, the story is a power struggle that decided the fate of an entire people.

I felt that, in many histories, Ross's role in Cherokee history and Indian removal had been minimized, or at least glossed over. Some people I talked to in the course of researching this book told me there is a theory about this (there's always a theory). Some people claim the men who wrote the first drafts of the tribe's history more closely identified with, or were even related to, the Ridges and Boudinots. Ross, they said indelicately, was the hero of those Indians least likely to write histories of the tribe. I don't know if there is any truth to that, and I certainly don't think it's a fair depiction, but clearly there has not been enough scholarship on the chief.

The historian Gary E. Moulton, who wrote a biography of Ross in the 1970s, deserves the most credit for making Ross research possible. In the 1980s Moulton collected a two-volume set of the chief's letters, memorials, and other papers. Those documents and letters—and there are a surprising number of them that survive, some in private hands—not only tell John Ross's story; they also offer tremendous insight about what he thought, how he felt. Ross left a long trail, filled with the sorts of details that make it possible to put together a narrative history of his times.

Although much of the story plays out in official state and federal papers, the documents that brought this narrative to life were the unpublished papers of John Howard Payne. Payne had a writer's eye—and ear—and spent months observing Ross during the Cherokees' most desperate time.

His account helped this narrative nearly as much as Ross's own writing, and Payne's papers, held by the Newberry Library in Chicago, include copies of tribe history most likely written by Charles Hicks, Ross's mentor and predecessor.

Another vital source of information survives, again, because of Ross. The *Cherokee Phoenix,* the tribe's newspaper during its final years in the East, offered contemporary accounts of what the Cherokees endured. Amazingly, nearly entire runs of the paper survive in the archives of North Carolina and Georgia universities. Those stories, selected by Elias Boudinot—and, later, Elijah Hicks—tell much more about how things happened than any history book. Some of the clearest details in this book were taken from the pages of the first Native American newspaper.

Much of what is known about the Ridge family is available in the National Archives, and most of that was compiled by Thurman Wilkins, whose *Cherokee Tragedy* is one of the better books about this time in the tribe's history. I was drawn to Major Ridge as perhaps the most tragic figure in this story. It is up to the reader to pass judgment on his actions; I will not do so, because I suspect there is some of his story lost to history.

Researching the early nineteenth century can sometimes be an inexact science, but it is particularly troublesome to find credible information on Native American tribes. The Cherokees themselves kept only some documentation, and then primarily from the time of Ross forward. To add the details that bring the story to life, every detail, no matter how small, had to be extracted from notes, letters, or earlier accounts. Anything in quotation marks comes from letters or government documents—I have not invented dialogue.

Likewise, I have used the contemporary names of most places. In the narrative, Chattanooga is sometimes called Chickamauga, sometimes Ross's Landing; Head of Coosa is today Rome, Georgia; and Washington City is what the Cherokees called Washington, D.C. Officially, the White House was called the Executive Mansion in the early nineteenth century, and that is the designation I give it (there's a debate about whether it was called the White House unofficially even then, but Ross used the official term). The descriptions of the people, places, and land in the narrative are taken from historical sources or extracted from photographs or personal visits, taking into account what things have probably changed over the past two centuries. Any mistakes in interpretation are my own. The Cherokees and other Native Americans are called "Indians" throughout the narrative, even though that it somewhat politically incorrect these days, for one simple reason: it is how they referred to themselves back then.

There is one more thing. While working on this book, I occasionally found people who—once I mentioned the Cherokees—remarked about "savages" attacking poor, defenseless settlers. It is true that the victors write the first draft of history, but later generations attempt to correct this. What happened to the Cherokees, and other natives of this country, is one of the greatest sins ever perpetuated by the United States, second only to slavery. The story to a great extent has been ignored for years.

Since I began researching the Cherokees, I have become more sensitive to the ironies that continue to this day. Take *Gone with the Wind*. There is a scene early in Margaret Mitchell's novel in which Gerald O'Hara tells his headstrong daughter, Scarlett, "Land is the only thing in the world that amounts to anything." He calls it "the only thing worth working for, worth fighting for—worth dying for." These days, I find the rantings of a fictional Georgian (who probably stole his land from the Creeks) a fitting epigraph for this story.

The following notes refer to facts used in constructing the narrative. When quoting the letters of John Ross, in most instances I used Moulton's *Papers of Chief John Ross* as reference. Although that two-volume set is difficult to find, it is infinitely more accessible, and less fragile, than the actual letters. In some cases, I note where the original document resides, particularly if I inspected it as well.

Prologue: The Time of the Fall

1   *A gray dusk*: The narrative of John Ross's encounter with the assassin named Harris is taken entirely from the chief's own account, published in the *Cherokee Phoenix*, January 21, 1832, 1–2.

Chapter 1: An Old Prophecy

11   *The object of*: The description, rules, and legend of ballplay come from Marion L. Starkey, *The Cherokee Nation* (New York: Knopf, 1946), 75–76; the John Howard Payne Papers, vol. IV, 61–64, 87–88. The pagination of the Payne Papers throughout these notes refers to the typescript version, not the original, handwritten manuscript.

13   *In October of*: John P. Brown, *Old Frontiers* (Kingsport, Tenn.: Southern Publishers, 1938), 451.

14   *Meigs served as*: Henry T. Malone, "Return Jonathan Meigs: Indian Agent Extraordinary," *The East Tennessee Historical Society's Publications*, no. 28, 1956, 3–22.

15   *Doublehead walked with*: Brown, *Old Frontiers*, 451.

15   *"Sam, you are"*: Ibid.

16   *Doublehead was speaker*: Payne Papers, vol. II, 26–27.

16   *"When in white"*: Brown, *Old Frontiers*, 452.

17   *"You have betrayed"*: Ibid.

18   *"More than two dozen"*: Payne Papers, vol. II, 29.

19   *Vann was no*: Ibid., 28.

19   *At thirty-six*: Thomas L. McKenney and James Hall, *History of the Indian Tribes of North America* (Philadelphia: Edward C. Biddle, 1836), 181.

20   *When he was*: Ibid.

20   *In 1793*: Ibid., 185; Thurman Wilkins, *Cherokee Tragedy* (Norman: University of Oklahoma Press, 1896), 25.

20   *The hour grew*: The account of the attack on Doublehead comes from two sources, primarily Payne Papers, vol. II, 29; Brown, *Old Frontiers*, 452.

21   *"You live among"*: Brown, *Old Frontiers*, 452.

22   *As the Cherokees*: Wilkins, *Cherokee Tragedy*, 40; Payne Papers, vol. II, 29.

23   *Soon, Ridge quietly*: This account is originally from the spoliation records in the Office of Indian Affairs held by the National Archives. Apparently, the claim of the heirs of Doublehead is now missing. Much of the information from that record is reprinted in Wilkins, *Cherokee Tragedy*, 40.

23   *They stormed the*: The account of Doublehead's killing comes from two sources, Payne Papers, vol. II, 30; Brown, *Old Frontiers*, 452–53.

25   *When Doublehead was*: Payne Papers, vol. II, 30.

25 *According to legend*: "Remarkable Fulfillment of Indian Prophecy," *Cherokee Phoenix,* January 28, 1832, 3.

26 *The Cherokee called*: The brief summation of early Cherokee history was compiled from various sources, most notably James Mooney, *Myths of the Cherokee* (Nashville: Elder Booksellers, 1982), 15–61; Starkey, *The Cherokee Nation,* 4–20.

27 *Dragging Canoe killed*: Zella Armstrong, *The History of Hamilton County and Chattanooga, Tennessee,* vol. I (Johnson City, Tenn.: Overmountain Press, 1993), 25; Brown, *Old Frontiers, 163.*

28 *McDonald had traveled*: Gary E. Moulton, *John Ross: Cherokee Chief* (Athens: University of Georgia Press, 1978), 3–4; Gertrude McDaris Ruskin, *John Ross: Chief of an Eagle Race* (Chattanooga, Tenn.: John Ross House Association, 1963), 12.

29 *Before long McDonald:* Ibid.

29 *The Tennessee governor*: Gilbert E. Govan and James W. Livingood, *The Chattanooga Country 1540–1951: From Tomahawks to TVA* (New York: E. P. Dutton, 1952), 58.

30 *Lookout Mountain rose*: Robert Sparks Walker, *Lookout* (Kingsport, Tenn.: Southern Publishers, 1941), 238.

30 *In 1785, a man*: Moulton, *John Ross,* 5; Armstrong, *History of Hamilton County and Chattanooga, Tennessee,* vol. I, 54.

30 *When the boat*: Rachel Caroline Eaton, *John Ross and the Cherokee Indians* (Chicago: University of Chicago Libraries, 1921), 2.

30 *The chief was*: Ibid.

31 *McDonald gave Ross*: Ruskin, *John Ross,* 14.

31 *Daniel and Mollie*: Ibid., 15; Armstrong, *History of Hamilton County and Chattanooga, Tennessee,* vol. I, 57.

32 *The Cherokees had*: McKenney and Hall, *History of the Indian Tribes of North America,* 186–87.

32 *The Ridge was*: Ibid., 188.

32 *While hunting turkey*: Wilkins, *Cherokee Tragedy,* 42.

33 *Tell our Great*: McKenney and Hall, *History of the Indian Tribes of North America,* 186–89.

34 *"My friends, you"*: Ibid., 189.

35   *Thomas Jefferson met*: Wilkins, *Cherokee Tragedy*, 49.

36   *Someone had shot*: Payne Papers, vol. II, 43–46.

37   *The tribe debated*: Eaton, *John Ross and the Cherokee Indians*, 19; Wilkins, *Cherokee Tragedy*, 51.

Chapter 2: Little John

39   *He had been*: Letter of John Ross to Return J. Meigs, December 15, 1812, reprinted in Moulton (ed.), *The Papers of Chief John Ross* (Norman: University of Oklahoma, 1985), vol. I, 15–16.

40   *Other tribes had*: Eaton, *John Ross and the Cherokee Indians*, 20.

40   *He hoped to*: Moulton, *The Papers of Chief John Ross*, vol. I, 15–16.

41   *After a "disagreeable"*: Ibid.; Moulton, *John Ross*, 9.

41   *A better boat*: Letter of John Ross to Return J. Meigs, December 31, 1812. The Penelope Johnson Allen collection, series II, box 15, file 5, Chattanooga–Hamilton County Bicentennial Library (reprinted in Moulton, *The Papers of Chief John Ross*, vol. I, 16–17).

42   *On the first*: Letter of John Ross to Return J. Meigs, January 3, 1813, ibid., 17–18.

43   *The Rosses and*: Eaton, *John Ross and the Cherokee Indians*, 3.

43   *In most of*: Armstrong, *History of Hamilton County and Chattanooga, Tennessee, Vol. I*, 21.

44   *In 1797 Daniel*: Ibid., 52; Govan and Livingood, *Chattanooga Country 1540–1951*, 54.

44   *According to Cherokee*: Mooney, *Myths of the Cherokee*, 281–84.

45   *One day, his*: Eaton, *John Ross and the Cherokee Indians*, 3.

46   *Education was very*: Moulton, *John Ross*, 6.

46   *As resistance to*: Eaton, *John Ross and the Cherokee Indians*, 16.

46   *They "had no"*: Ruskin, *John Ross*, 25.

47   *John was away*: Letter of Daniel Ross to Return J. Meigs, March 24, 1806. The Penelope Johnson Allen collection, series II, box 15, file 5, Chattanooga–Hamilton County Bicentennial Library.

48   *He kept his*: Moulton, *John Ross*, 8.

48   *When he returned*: Notes of Penelope Johnson Allen, the Allen collection, series II, box 15, file 8, Chattanooga–Hamilton County Bicentennial Library.

49 *His eldest sister*: The Ross family tree is outlined in great detail in Ruskin, *John Ross*, 10.

50 *After making another*: Armstrong, *History of Hamilton County and Chattanooga, Tennessee*, vol. I, 60.

50 *Meigs had established*: Ruskin, *John Ross*, 20.

50 *It was around*: Ibid., 18; Moulton, *John Ross*, 12–13. The story of Ross and Quatie's honeymoon is local legend in Chattanooga. It is included in the narrative with qualifications.

51 *In 1809 General*: The story of Tecumseh and the Prophet, and their conflict with General William Henry Harrison, is well known and details were culled from several sources, including Brown, *Old Frontiers*, 455–60.

53 *The Ridge was*: Wilkins, *Cherokee Tragedy*, 52.

54 *"Your blood is"*: Brown, *Old Frontiers*, 458.

56 *While visiting the*: Letter of John Ross to Return J. Meigs, July 30, 1813. The Penelope Johnson Allen collection, series II, box 15, file 5, reprinted in Moulton, *The Papers of Chief John Ross*, vol. I, 19.

57 *"The intelligence received"*: Ibid.

58 *Shortly after the*: The description of the attack on Fort Mims comes from several books and Internet sites. One particularly gruesome account is found in John Ehle, *Trail of Tears* (New York: Anchor Books, 1989), 105.

58 *On August 30*: Wilkins, *Cherokee Tragedy*, 62–63.

59 *After night fell*: McKenney and Hall, *History of the Indian Tribes of North America*, 191–92.

59 *"My friends, the"*: Ibid. McKenney and Hall's accounts are considered more credible than most, because they actually interviewed the participants in these events in the years afterward. McKenney, a former U.S. Indian commissioner, had good relations with many tribal chiefs.

60 *General William McIntosh*: Ibid., 193.

61 *By October he*: Moulton, *John Ross*, 11.

Chapter 3: Horseshoe Bend

62 *The bodies were*: The description of what John Ross found at Tallushatchee comes from Davy Crockett's own account of the battle. David Crockett, *The Life of Col. David Crockett* (Philadelphia: G. G. Evans, 1859), 75–76.

62 *Ross rode into*: Moulton, *John Ross*, 11.

63 *"I flatter myself"*: Wilkins, *Cherokee Tragedy*, 67.

64 *"His death so"*: Crockett, *Life of Col. David Crockett*, 75–76.

64 *It was the*: The statistics of the Tallushatchee battle vary, but these numbers come from Andrew Jackson's report, as quoted in James W. Holland, *Victory at the Horseshoe: Andrew Jackson and the Creek War* (Tuscaloosa: University of Alabama Press, 2004), 14.

65 *Shortly after Tallushatchee*: The events at Talladega and Hillabee are recounted in Robert Vincent Remini, *Andrew Jackson and His Indian Wars* (New York: Viking, 2001), 58; Wilkins, *Cherokee Tragedy*, 69–70.

67 *However, Ridge did*: Joyce B. Phillips and Paul Gary Phillips, *The Brainerd Journal: A Mission to the Cherokees, 1817–1823* (Lincoln: University of Nebraska Press, 1998), 37.

68 *As 1814 began*: John Spencer Bassett, *The Life of Andrew Jackson* (New York: Doubleday, Page, 1911), vol. 1, 109.

68 *"It is as"*: Reprinted in Holland, *Victory at the Horseshoe*, 16.

69 *Before they disbanded*: Wilkins, *Cherokee Tragedy*, 71.

69 *By mid-January*: Remini, *Andrew Jackson and His Indian Wars*, 60.

70 *In anticipation of*: Letter of Ross to Return J. Meigs, March 2, 1814, reprinted in Moulton, *The Papers of Chief John Ross*, vol. I, 19–20.

70 *Ross collected a*: Ibid.

70 *Normally, Jackson would*: Bassett, *Life of Andrew Jackson*, 115.

71 *It took two*: Payne Papers, vol. II, 33.

72 *"Me crow like"*: Ibid.

73 *"Any officer or"*: From Jackson's general orders, March 24, as quoted in Holland, *Victory at the Horseshoe*, 22.

74 *At 10:30 a.m.*: Ibid., 23.

74 *Across the river*: The Cherokees' actions in the battle at Horseshoe Bend were reconstructed from McKenney and Hall, *History of the Indian Tribes of North America*, 194–95.

75 *The Thirty-ninth Regiment:* The battle of Horseshoe Bend is recreated here from a number of sources, including a study of the Horseshoe Bend National Park, near Dadeville, Alabama, and several secondary sources, including Bassett, *Life of Andrew Jackson*, vol. 1,

116–19; Remini, *Andrew Jackson and His Indian Wars,* 61; McKenney
and Hall, *History of the Indian Tribes of North America,* 195; Holland,
Victory at the Horseshoe, 24–28; and the John Howard Payne Papers,
vol. II, 33–34.

76   *According to Cherokee*: Mooney, *Myths of the Cherokee,* 97.
77   *Ridge jumped into*: McKenney and Hall, *History of the Indian Tribes of
     North America,* 195; Wilkins, *Cherokee Tragedy,* 78.
78   *John Ross reported*: Ross's casualty report to Return J. Meigs is held by the
     Newberry Library in Chicago, reprinted in Moulton, *The Papers of Chief
     John Ross,* vol. I, 20–21.
78   *In mid-April*: Remini, *Andrew Jackson and His Indian Wars,* 61–62.
79   *After Junaluska saved*: "Junaluska, the Tar Heel a President Betrayed," by
     Chester Davis, undated issue of the *Chattanooga News–Free Press,* the
     Allen collection, Chattanooga–Hamilton County Bicentennial Library,
     series II, box 15, file 9.

Chapter 4: A Sharp Knife

81   *By the end*: The genealogy of John Ross's family was compiled by Jennie
     Ross Cobb, former curator of the Murrell House, reprinted in Ruskin,
     John Ross, 10.
81   *Not even the*: Moulton, *John Ross,* 8.
81   *In the late*: Ibid.
82   *Pathkiller had waited*: Order of Pathkiller to the 1816 Cherokee delega-
     tion to Washington, on file at the Thomas Gilcrease Institute of American
     History and Art, Tulsa, Oklahoma, reprinted in Moulton, *The Papers of
     Chief John Ross,* vol. I, 22–24.
83   *"The multiplied Intrusions"*: Ibid.
84   *At one fete*: *Niles' Weekly Register,* March 2, 1816, reprinted in Wilkins,
     Cherokee Tragedy, 88.
85   *They met Madison*: Wilkins, *Cherokee Tragedy,* 90–91.
86   *"We are also"*: Letter of John Ross to George Graham, March 4, 1816, on
     file at the Thomas Gilcrease Institute of American History and Art, re-
     printed in Moulton, *The Papers of Chief John Ross,* vol. I, 24–26.

86   *"It is foreign"*: Letter of John Ross to William H. Crawford, March 12, 1816, National Archives, reprinted in Moulton, *The Papers of Chief John Ross,* vol. I, 26–27.

87   *News of the:* Remini, *Andrew Jackson and His Indians Wars,* 104.

88   *An irate Jackson:* Wilkins, *Cherokee Tragedy,* 93.

88   *Although Crawford repeatedly*: Letter of William H. Crawford to Andrew Jackson, June 19, 1816, *American State Papers 1789–1838, Indian Affairs, Vol. II,* 112

88   *That September, a*: Jackson's exploits that summer are explained in a letter of Return J. Meigs to William H. Crawford, August 8, 1816, ibid., 113–14.

89   *Jackson thought he*: Remini, *Andrew Jackson and His Indian Wars,* 111.

89   *At Turkeytown, most*: Moulton, *John Ross,* 19.

90   *Kingsbury had no*: Cyrus Kingsbury's introduction to the Cherokee council is recounted in a letter he wrote to Return J. Meigs on October 15, 1816, reprinted in Robert Sparks Walker, *Torchlights to the Cherokees: The Brainerd Mission* (New York: Macmillan, 1931), 17–21.

90   *"I told them"*: Ibid.

91   *John Ross played*: Letter of Cyrus Kingsbury to Samuel Worcester, November 25, 1816, reprinted ibid., 22–24.

91   *Major Ridge enrolled*: From an entry dated May 14, 1817, in the Brainerd Mission journals, reprinted in Phillips, *The Brainerd Journal,* 34.

92   *John Ridge would*: From an entry dated July 4, 1817, in the Brainerd Mission journals. reprinted ibid., 36.

92   *Just two days*: Ibid., 37.

93   *John Ross spent*: Letter of Ross to Return J. Meigs, April 11, 1817, reprinted in Moulton, *The Papers of Chief John Ross,* vol. I, 30.

93   *Meigs convinced him*: Ross to Meigs, April 11, 1817 (second letter with that date), reprinted ibid.

94   *A day before*: The story of Ross's ride to Amohe and his introduction to appointed office is recounted in McKenney and Hall, *History of the Indian Tribes of North America,* and quoted here from Eaton, *John Ross and the Cherokee Indians,* 25.

96   *A large crowd*: The account of Jackson's meeting with the Cherokees in
      June 1817 is recounted in the Payne Papers, vol. VII, part 1, 25–35.
97   *Nancy Ward, the*: Pat Alderman, *Nancy Ward / Dragging Canoe* (Johnson
      City, Tenn.: Overmountain Press, 1978), 80.
98   *"Brothers, we wish"*: Remini, *Andrew Jackson and His Indian Wars*, 125.
99   *The Indians who*: Eaton, *John Ross and the Cherokee Indians*, 26.
100   *The offer was*: Letter of Thomas L. McKenney to Ross, September 14, 1818,
      held in the National Archives, reprinted in Moulton, *The Papers of Chief
      John Ross*, vol. I, 31.
100   *Ross proved to*: Moulton, *John Ross*, 20.
101   *Later, Ross sent*: Ibid.
101   *In early 1819*: Orders from Pathkiller to Charles Hicks and John Ross, Na-
      tional Archives, Record Group 75, M 208, roll 7, reprinted in Moulton,
      The Papers of Chief John Ross, vol. I, 31–32.
102   *"So long as"*: Letter of John C. Calhoun to the Cherokee delegation,
      American State Papers, Indian Affairs, vol. II, 190.
103   *The government estimated*: Treaty with the Cherokees, March 2, 1819,
      ibid., 187–89.
104   *The Tennessee senator*: Moulton, *John Ross*, 21.
104   *Was this, Ross*: Ross's confrontation and subsequent fight with John
      Walker in 1819 are recounted in the Payne Papers, vol. II, 143–44.
105   *The night before*: Ibid.

Chapter 5: A Traitor in All Nations

111   *He stepped lightly*: The account of Ross's rescue of the Osage child comes
      from a missionary who wrote of it just a few years after it happened. The
      account was published to great acclaim six years before Ross was elected
      chief of the Cherokee Nation. Elias Cornelius, *The Little Osage Captive*
      (Boston: Armstrong, Crocker and Brewster, 1822), 42–47.
113   *He was at*: Letter of John Ross to Calvin Jones, July 3, 1819, reprinted in
      Moulton, *The Papers of Chief John Ross*, vol. I, 36–37.
114   *Despite the work*: Ibid.
114   *There were still*: Letter of John Ross to James Monroe, November 2, 1819,
      reprinted ibid., 38–40.

114   *The incident that*: Letter of John Ross to Andrew Jackson, June 19, 1820, reprinted in ibid., 40–41.

115   *When Ross returned*: Ibid.

115   *He had been*: Ruskin, *John Ross*, 20.

116   *By the early*: Moulton, *John Ross*, 23.

116   *These grandiose plans*: The biography of Sequoyah is pulled primarily from two sources: Brown, *Old Frontiers*, 478–85; Mooney, *Myths of the Cherokee*, 108–10.

118   *Jackson and McMinn*: Letter of John Ross to Return J. Meigs, October 26, 1822, reprinted in Moulton, *The Papers of Chief John Ross*, vol. I, 46–47.

118   "*If we had*": Letter of John Ross to John C. Calhoun, October 24, 1822, reprinted ibid., 44–45.

118   "*It will not*": Letter of Return J. Meigs to Charles Hicks, December 5, 1822, quoted in Moulton, *John Ross*, 24.

119   *Major Ridge spent*: The account of John Ridge's time in Cornwall is related extensively in Wilkins, *Cherokee Tragedy*, 119–37.

120   *On a cold*: Return J. Meigs's death is recounted in Henry T. Malone, "Return J. Meigs: Indian Agent Extraordinary," *The East Tennessee Historical Society's Publications*, no. 28, 1956, 3–22.

121   *The Cherokees realized*: Letter of John Ross to Joseph McMinn, April 26, 1823, National Archives, Record Group 75, M 208, roll 9, reprinted in Moulton, *The Papers of Chief John Ross*, vol. I, 47–48.

121   *At Pathkiller's insistence*: Ibid.

121   *In 1802 the*: Mooney, *Myths of the Cherokee*, 114.

122   *Ross was unsurprised*: Letter of John Ross to Joseph McMinn, July 22, 1823, National Archives, Record Group 75, M 208, roll 9, reprinted in Moulton, *The Papers of Chief John Ross*, vol. I, 48–49.

122   *Heavy spring rains*: Ibid.

123   *Campbell and Meriwether*: Letter of John Ross to Joseph McMinn, October 8, 1823, reprinted in Moulton, *The Papers of Chief John Ross*, vol. I, 50.

124   "*The difference is*": Letter of John Ross to Duncan G. Campbell and James Meriwether, October 20, 1823, reprinted ibid., 52.

124   *The Indians who*: Ibid.

125   "*Brothers, we cannot*": Ibid.

125   *The Creek ambassador*: The story of William McIntosh's attempt to bribe
       John Ross at the 1823 council is recounted in the Payne Papers, vol. II,
       158–64. Most likely, Ross told Payne this story, and Major Ridge's reac-
       tion, personally; it's unlikely Hicks added it to his own history.

128   *"My friends, five"*: Address of John Ross to General Council, ibid.

129   *"But all affection"*: Payne Papers, vol. II, 161.

130   *"You have stained"*: Ibid., 162.

Chapter 6: One Generation Passeth

132   *The Cherokees planned*: Letter of John Ross to John C. Calhoun, January
       13, 1824, National Archives, Records Group 107, M 221, roll 98, reprinted
       in Moulton, *The Papers of Chief John Ross,* vol. I, 56–57.

133   *Even Congress could*: Peter Tompkins, *The Magic of Obelisks* (New York:
       Harper and Row, 1981), 315.

134   *Along with the*: Charles Francis Adams, ed., *The Memoirs of John Quincy
       Adams,* vol. VI (Philadelphia: J. B. Lippincott and Co., 1874), 229.

134   *The Cherokees got*: Ibid.

135   *Adams later proclaimed*: Ibid.

135   *Ross finally appealed*: Letter of John Ross to James Monroe, January 19,
       1824, reprinted in Moulton, *The Papers of Chief John Ross,* vol. I, 59–61.

135   *"The state of"*: Letter of John C. Calhoun to John Ross et al., January 30,
       1824, National Archives, Records Group 75, M 15, roll 6, reprinted
       ibid., 62.

135   *"We beg leave"*: Letter of John Ross to John C. Calhoun, February 11, 1824,
       National Archives, Records Group 75, M 234, roll 71, reprinted ibid.,
       64–66.

136   *Playing to his*: Wilkins, *Cherokee Tragedy,* 158.

136   *A few nights*: Ibid.

137   *Adams was charmed*: Adams, *Memoirs of John Quincy Adams,* vol. VI, 373.

137   *On March 12*: Ibid., 254.

138   *"I have no"*: James Monroe to Congress, March 30, 1824. His full remarks
       are reprinted at the American Presidency Project, www.presidency.ucsb.
       edu/ws/index.php?pid=66392.

138   *Within a few*: Eaton, *John Ross and the Cherokee Indians,* 40.

139   *While Ross spent*: Ibid.

139   *On April 15*: *American State Papers, Indian Affairs,* vol. II, 502.

139   *This was a*: John Ross Memorial to the House and Senate, reprinted in Moulton, *The Papers of Chief John Ross,* vol. I, 76–78.

140   *John Quincy Adams*: Adams, *Memoirs of John Quincy Adams,* vol. VI, 373.

141   *He used even*: Letter of John Ross to Joseph Gales and William Seaton, April 20, 1824, on file in the Ross papers at the Thomas Gilcrease Institute of American History and Art, reprinted in Moulton, *The Papers of Chief John Ross,* vol. I, 78–80.

141   *John Ross returned*: Walker, *Torchlights to the Cherokees,* 36.

142   *John McDonald died*: Govan and Livingood, *Chattanooga Country 1540–1951,* 78.

143   *When his grandmother*: Ibid.

143   *Still, Ross found*: Moulton, *John Ross,* 9.

143   *More than with*: Starkey, *Cherokee Nation,* 51. In 1826, Hicks wrote several letters to Ross outlining the tribe's history and passing on fatherly advice. Those notes are collected in Moulton, *The Papers of Chief John Ross,* vol. I, 111–16.

144   *This new generation*: Wilkins, *Cherokee Tragedy,* 161.

144   *The 1824 vote*: Bassett, *The Life of Andrew Jackson,* vol. 1, 349.

145   *Ross turned to*: Letter of John Ross to Thomas L. McKenney, February 28, 1825, reprinted in Moulton, *The Papers of Chief John Ross,* vol. I, 99–101.

145   *Upon his appointment*: Moulton, *John Ross,* 27.

145   *"My heart is"*: Wilkins, *Cherokee Tragedy,* 163.

146   *He composed a*: Letter of John Ross to James Monroe, March 2, 1825, National Archives, Records Group 75, M 234, roll 71, reprinted in Moulton, *The Papers of Chief Ross,* vol. I, 102.

146–147   *The short, congratulatory*: Letter of John Ross to John Quincy Adams, March 12, 1825, reprinted ibid., 104–5.

147   *"The Cherokees if"*: Ibid.

148   *"It's like Baltimore"*: Chamberlin's account of his tour of Newtown with Ridge is from his own personal diary, as quoted in Starkey, *Cherokee Nation,* 61.

148   *Just as this*: Pathkiller's death is recounted in the Payne Papers, vol. II, 85.

149   *Charles Hicks would*: Ibid.

149   *At the fall*: Ehle, *Trail of Tears*, 205.

149   *They took Hicks's*: Walker, *Torchlights to the Cherokees*, 37.

149   *The state of Georgia*: *Georgia Journal*, May 22, 1827, as quoted in Wilkins, *Cherokee Tragedy*, 202.

150   *Ross took his*: Armstrong, *The History of Hamilton County and Chattanooga, Tennessee*, vol. I, 60.

150   *He sold the*: Ruskin, *John Ross*, 30; Moulton, *John Ross*, 30.

150   *John Ross built*: Eaton, *John Ross and the Cherokee Indians*, 45.

151   *Perhaps owing to*: Moulton, *John Ross*, 30.

151   *The General Council*: Letter of John Ross to James Barbour, August 1, 1827, reprinted in Moulton, *The Papers of Chief John Ross*, vol. I, 129–30.

152   *One old chief*: Starkey, *Cherokee Nation*, 104–5.

152   *"A noise which"*: Ibid.

152   *Many of them*: Payne Papers, vol. II, 85.

153   *John Cocke and*: Letter of John Ross to John Cocke et al., reprinted in Moulton, *The Papers of Chief John Ross*, vol. I, 135.

153   *With little fanfare*: Payne Papers, vol. II, 85.

153   *John Ross was*: Ibid.

Chapter 7: The Reins of Power

156   *As second principal*: Letter of William Hicks and John Ross to Alex Garvick, June 10, 1828, *Cherokee Phoenix*, June 18, 1828, 3; letter of Hicks and Ross to Francis W. Armstrong, July 19, 1828, *Cherokee Phoenix*, July 30, 1828, 2.

156   *Lately, most of*: Payne Papers, vol. II, 85. As Payne wrote, "William Hicks soon forfeited the confidence of the people."

157   *John Ridge had*: *Cherokee Phoenix*, June 25, 1828, 2–3.

157   *This list of*: *Cherokee Phoenix*, June 11, 1828, 3.

158   *As the summer*: *Cherokee Phoenix*, July 2, 1828, 3.

158   *"I know that"*: Ibid.

160   *On Monday, October*: *Cherokee Phoenix*, October 22, 1828, 1.

160   *After Hicks finished*: Ibid., 1–2.

160   *William Hicks believed*: Payne Papers, vol. II, 85–86.

161 *On Friday morning*: *Cherokee Phoenix,* October 22, 1828, 2.

162 *When the first*: Ibid.

163 *Soon after he*: Ibid.

164 *The 1828 presidential*: This account of the contest between President John Quincy Adams and Andrew Jackson is culled from a number of sources, including Bassett, *Life of Andrew Jackson,* vol. II, 375–407; Remini, *Andrew Jackson and His Indian Wars,* 222–25.

165 *This legislation required*: Eaton, *John Ross and the Cherokee Indians,* 48.

165 *The Indian agent*: Letter of John Ross to Hugh Montgomery, December 24, 1828, printed in the *Cherokee Phoenix,* January 14, 1829, 2–3.

166 *"I hope you"*: Ibid.

166 *"It will be"*: Andrew Jackson et al., *The Papers of Andrew Jackson,* vol. VII (Knoxville: University of Tennessee Press, 2007), 79.

167 *Ross waited a*: Letter of John Ross to Andrew Jackson, March 6, 1829, in the Ross papers at the Thomas Gilcrease Institute of American History and Art, and reprinted in Moulton, *The Papers of Chief John Ross,* vol. I, 157–58.

167 *Eaton proved every*: Letter of John H. Eaton to John Ross et al., April 18, 1829, National Archives, Records Group 75, M 21, roll 5, and summarized ibid., 162–63.

167 *Ross would not*: Letter of John Ross to Jeremiah Evarts, May 6, 1829, reprinted ibid., 164–65.

168 *"What will be"*: Ibid.

168 *Those who stayed*: Letter of Thomas McKenney to Hugh Montgomery, July 22, 1828, reprinted in the *Cherokee Phoenix,* March 11, 1829, 2.

168 *"But in case"*: Letter of an anonymous Cherokee farmer February 29, 1829, printed in the *Cherokee Phoenix,* March 18, 1829, 2.

169 *At Turkeytown, just*: Major Ridge delivered this speech on February 9, 1829, and it was later transcribed by John Ridge and printed in the *Cherokee Phoenix,* March 4, 1829, 2–3.

169 *"It is too"*: Ibid.

170 *"If Georgia was"*: Letter of John Ross to the Cherokee people, published in the July 1, 1829, edition of the *Cherokee Phoenix,* reprinted in Moulton, *The Papers of Chief John Ross,* vol. I, 166.

170   *Over the years*: Biographer Gary E. Moulton talks about the "fallibility"
      Ross found in Washington politicians over the years. It was a recurring
      theme in the chief's life. Moulton, *John Ross,* 33.

170   *For thirty years*: Starkey, *Cherokee Nation,* 111.

171   *In the summer*: Frank Logan is credited with the discovery of the gold
      that led to the Dahlonega rush on; see the Georgia history Web site http://
      ngeorgia .com/history/goldrush.html.

171   *The prospectors were*: Eaton, *John Ross and the Cherokee Indians,* 51.

171   *Within a year*: Letter of John Ross to Hugh Montgomery, November 25,
      1830, reprinted in Moulton, *The Papers of Chief John Ross,* vol. I, 208.

172   *The state also*: The concept behind public land states is described in Theda
      Perdue and Michael D. Green, *The Cherokee Nation and the Trail of Tears*
      (New York: Viking/Penguin, 2007), 79.

172   *With a fellow*: Andrew Jackson's conflict is described vividly in Remini,
      Andrew Jackson and His Indian Wars, 227–28.

173   *"No proposition could"*: Letter of John Ross to William Carroll, August 29,
      1829, reprinted in Moulton, *The Papers of Chief John Ross,* vol. I, 166–68.

173   *At New Echota*: Annual message of John Ross, October 1, 1829, reprinted
      ibid., 169–72.

174   *"A crisis seems"*: Ibid.

174   *In his first*: Jackson's 1829 annual message is available from any number
      of sources, including *The Statesmanship of Andrew Jackson as Told in His
      Writings and Speeches,* ed. Francis Newton Thorpe (New York: Tandy-
      Thomas Company, 1909), 35–65.

Chapter 8: A Dangerous Game

177   *They were led*: Wilkins, *Cherokee Tragedy,* 212.

177   *As they approached*: John Ross gave Major Ridge detailed instructions
      about how he wanted squatters removed. The chief recounted his orders
      and Ridge's actions in a letter to editor Elias Boudinot published in the
      Cherokee Phoenix, February 17, 1830, 2–3.

178   *The Cherokees had*: Letter of John Ross to Hugh Montgomery, February
      6, 1830, National Archives, Record Group 75, M 234, roll 74, reprinted in
      Moulton, *The Papers of Chief John Ross,* vol. I, 182–84.

179 *None of those*: Wilkins, *Cherokee Tragedy*, 212.

179 *On the afternoon*: Ross to Boudinot, *Cherokee Phoenix*, February 17, 1830.

180 *The assault set*: Ibid.

181 *In late February*: The Indian Removal Act debate is recounted here from several sources, including Remini, *Andrew Jackson and His Indians Wars*, 231–38; *Cherokee Phoenix*, June 12, July 3, July 10, and July 17, 1830. Elias Boudinot understandably reported on most of the speeches out of Congress, particularly those in favor of the tribes.

182 *As the argument*: Moulton, *John Ross*, 42.

183 *Lumpkin, who had*: Lumpkin's thoughts and comments in the House are taken from Wilson Lumpkin, *The Removal of the Cherokee Indians from Georgia*, vol. I (Wormsloe, Ga.: Dodd, Mead, 1907), 57–88.

183 *Lumpkin, a large*: Ibid., 9–11.

184 *Crockett had broken*: Jeremiah Evarts, *Speeches on the Passage of the Bill for the Removal of the Indians* (Boston: Perkins and Marvin, 1830), 251.

185 *Later, Crockett would*: Crockett, *Life of Col. David Crockett*, 167.

185 *President Jackson abandoned*: Remini, *Andrew Jackson and His Indians Wars*, 240.

185 *In August, Jackson*: Robert Vincent Remini, *Andrew Jackson and the Course of American Freedom*, 1822–1832 (New York: Harper and Row, 1981), 271.

186 *The principal chief*: Armstrong, *History of Hamilton County and Chattanooga, Tennessee*, vol. I, 57.

186–187 *Ross, Lumpkin said*: Lumpkin, *Removal of the Cherokee Indians from Georgia*, vol. I, 186.

187 *"My earliest and warmest"*: Letter of John Ross to David Crockett, January 13, 1831, reprinted in Moulton, *The Papers of Chief John Ross*, vol. I, 210–12.

187 *Ross first solicited*: Letter of John Ross to Jeremiah Evarts, July 24, 1830, reprinted ibid., 195–96.

187 *When Webster politely*: Letter of William Wirt to John Ross, August 9, 1830, reprinted ibid., 196.

188 *By the summer*: Annual address by John Ross, October 11, 1830, reprinted ibid., 201–3.

188 *Tassel, who had*: George, or Corn, Tassel is sometimes called by the name "Tassels"; his name here is presented as Ross spelled it at the time of the

events. This account is taken primarily from Jill Norgren, *The Cherokee Cases: Two Landmark Federal Decisions in the Fight for Sovereignty* (Norman: University of Oklahoma Press, 2004), 61.

188 *William Wirt believed*: Letter of Wirt to Ross, September 22, 1830, reprinted in Moulton, *The Papers of Chief John Ross,* vol. I, 199–200.

188 *Going Snake made*: Starkey, *Cherokee Nation,* 147.

189 *John Lowrey watched*: Lowrey recounted his visit with the Cherokees in letters to Secretary of War John Eaton, reprinted in 23rd Congress, Senate Documents, no. 512, II (Serial 245), 179–80.

190 *"What then," Lowrey*: Starkey, *Cherokee Nation,* 149.

190 *Most Cherokees were*: Wilkins, *Cherokee Tragedy,* 217.

190 *"The offer of"*: Letter of John Ross to John Lowrey, printed in the *Cherokee Phoenix,* October 30, 1830, 3.

190 *John Ross awoke*: Letter of John Ross to William Wirt, January 1, 1831, reprinted in Moulton, *The Papers of Chief John Ross,* vol. I, 209–10.

191 *Wirt had been*: Letter of William Wirt to John Ross, November 15, 1830, reprinted ibid., 205–6.

191 *It took Ross*: Letter of John Ross to William Wirt, January 1, 1831, reprinted ibid., 209–10.

192 *Marshall was both*: Norgren, *Cherokee Cases,* 98.

193 *While the Georgians*: Wilkins, *Cherokee Tragedy,* 219.

193 *On March 11*: This account of the Supreme Court hearing is from several sources, most notably Norgren, *Cherokee Cases,* 98–111.

194 *Historians would later*: Ibid., 102.

194 *In his order*: Ibid., 101.

194 *The president was*: John Ridge's encounter with Jackson was recounted in a letter of Ridge to Elias Boudinot, printed in the *Cherokee Phoenix,* May 21, 1831, 2–3.

194 *"I am glad"*: Ibid.

194 *"As a statesman"*: Ibid.

195 *"You can live"*: Ibid.

195 *The Georgia Guard*: Starkey, *Cherokee Nation,* 136–37.

196 *The men spent*: Ibid., 138.

196 *The Georgia Guard*: Ibid., 139

197 *That summer, Governor*: Perdue and Green, *The Cherokee Nation and the Trail of Tears*, 72.

197 *At first, Ross*: Letter of John Ross to the Cherokees, April 14, 1831, reprinted in Moulton, *The Papers of Chief John Ross*, vol. I, 215–19.

198 *"The busy tattlers"*: Ibid.

198 *In August, Colonel*: Editorial of Elias Boudinot in the *Cherokee Phoenix*, August 27, 1831, 2.

199 *By the middle*: Moulton, *John Ross*, 45.

199 *John Ross offered*: Ibid., 46.

199 *As the time*: Payne Papers, vol. II, 109.

200 *The meeting was*: Ibid.

200 *Ross thought the*: The meeting between Ross, Boudinot, and the Ridges is recounted by John Howard Payne, most likely as related to him by the chief. Payne Papers, vol. II, 110.

201 *"Suppose the members"*: Ibid., 111.

201 *"As mine is"*: Ibid.

201 *On Wednesday, October*: Ibid., 111–13.

203 *In his annual*: *Cherokee Phoenix*, November 19, 1831, 2–3.

203 *These men used*: Letter of John Ross to William Wirt, November 11, 1831, reprinted in Moulton, *The Papers of Chief John Ross*, vol. I, 231.

203 *"It would be"*: Ibid.

204 *That afternoon Ross*: This is a slightly different version of the incident recounted in the prologue, offering details left out of the first version for the sake of clarity. This truncated version is meant to put that story in context. The details were taken from Ross's own account, *Cherokee Phoenix*, January 21, 1832, 1–2.

Chapter 9: Turning Point

209 *On January 26*: The speaking tour of John Ridge and Elias Boudinot is recounted in the *Cherokee Phoenix*, February 18, 1832, 1.

210 *"You asked us"*: Ibid.

210 *"Your people," Cass*: Letter of Lewis Cass to John Ridge and the Cherokee delegation, 23rd Congress, 1st session, Senate Document 512 (Serial 245) 737–39.

210 *He explained that*: Ibid.

210 *Ridge was defiant*: Letter of John Ridge to Stand Watie, April 6, 1832, re-printed in Edward Everett Dale and Gaston Litton, *Cherokee Cavaliers: Forty Years of Cherokee Hisory as Told in the Correspondence of the Ridge-Watie-Boudinot Family* (Norman: University of Oklahoma Press, 1940) 7–10.

211 *When Boudinot stopped*: Letter of John Ridge to John Ross, January 12 and 13, 1832, reprinted in Moulton, *The Papers of Chief John Ross*, vol. I, 235–36.

211 *In Philadelphia Ridge*: Ibid.

211 *In February, their*: "Cherokee Meeting in New Haven," *Cherokee Phoenix*, March 24, 1832, 2.

211 *The* New Haven: Ibid.

212 *By early March*: Letter of John Ridge to John Ross, April 3, 1832, reprinted in Moulton, *The Papers of Chief John Ross*, vol. I, 241–42.

212 *"No," Ridge said*: Letter of Elias Boudinot to Stand Watie, March 7, 1832, reprinted in Dale and Litton, *Cherokee Cavaliers*, 4–7.

212 *The U.S. Supreme*: The account of the *Worcester v. Georgia* hearings is drawn from letters between Ross and Wirt, *Cherokee Phoenix*; Norgren, *Cherokee Cases*, 114–22.

214 *"Protection," Marshall wrote*: Norgren, *Cherokee Cases*, 119.

214 *"Our adversaries are"*: Letter of John Ross to John Ridge, John Martin, and William Shorey Coodey, March 30, 1832, reprinted in Moulton, *The Papers of Chief John Ross*, vol. I, 241.

214 *When the court's*: Norgren, *Cherokee Cases*, 122.

214 *Despite the court*: Wilkins, *Cherokee Tragedy*, 237.

214 *In fact, Jackson*: Marquis James, *The Life of Andrew Jackson Complete in One Volume* (New York: Bobbs-Merrill, 1938), 603.

214 *John Ridge soon*: Letter of John Ridge to John Ross, April 3, 1832, reprinted in Moulton, *The Papers of Chief John Ross*, vol. I, 241–42.

215 *That meeting went*: Wilkins, *Cherokee Tragedy*, 236.

215 *"Advise them that"*: Ibid.

215 *He later told*: Letter of John Ridge to Stand Watie April 6, 1832, reprinted in Dale and Litton, *Cherokee Cavaliers*, 7–10.

216 *Ridge said nothing*: Wilkins, *Cherokee Tragedy,* 236.

216 *"It makes me"*: Ibid., 240.

216 *On the street*: "Treaty with the Cherokees," *Cherokee Phoenix,* May 12, 1832, 2.

216 *There is not*: Ibid., 2–3.

217 *A week later*: 23rd Congress, Senate Documents, no. 512, III (Serial 246), 303–4.

217 *The surveyors arrived*: Starkey, *Cherokee Nation,* 180.

218 *"It is surprising"*: *Cherokee Phoenix,* April 21, 1832, 3.

218 *He even took*: Ibid.

218 *In May, Elias*: "Treaty with the Cherokees," *Cherokee Phoenix,* May 12, 1832, 2–3.

218 *Solely on the*: Payne Papers, vol. II, 88; Starkey, *Cherokee Nation,* 229.

219 *Ross suspected Newnan*: Letter of John Ridge to John Ross, April 3, 1832, reprinted in Moulton, *The Papers of Chief John Ross,* vol. I, 241–42.

219 *Ross feared that*: Letter of John Ross to Elias Boudinot, May 17, 1832, reprinted in ibid., 244.

219 *By early June*: Letter of John Ross to William Wirt, June 8, 1832, National Archives, Record Group 75, M 21, roll 8, reprinted ibid., I, 245–46.

220 *A week later*: Ibid.

220 *Chester seemed genuinely*: Letter of Elisha Chester to Lewis Cass, June 9, 1832, 23rd Congress, Senate Documents, no. 512, III (Serial 246), 372–73.

220 *He sat in*: Starkey, *Cherokee Nation,* 184–85.

220 *Ridge underestimated his*: Wilkins, *Cherokee Tragedy,* 241.

221 *For weeks after*: Ibid., 240.

221 *John Ross was*: *Cherokee Phoenix,* July 14, 1832, 2.

222 *John Ridge pushed*: Payne Papers, vol. II, 114.

222 *A generation earlier*: Letter of Elisha Chester to Lewis Cass, August 11, 1832, 23rd Congress, Senate Documents, no. 512, III (Serial 246), 421–24.

223 *But Boudinot, still*: "To the Readers of the Cherokee Phoenix," *Cherokee Phoenix,* August 11, 1832, 2–3.

223 *"I do conscientiously"*: Ibid.

223 *"The toleration of"*: Ross's response was printed on the same page, ibid.

224 *Ross appointed his*: Starkey, *Cherokee Nation,* 193.

224 *The commissioner had*: Ibid., 189.

224 *"Shut your eyes"*: Ibid.

224 *They immediately dismissed*: Letter of John Ross to Elisha Chester, August 3, 1832, reprinted in Moulton, *The Papers of Chief John Ross*, vol. I, 249.

225 *But some members*: Eaton, *John Ross and the Cherokee Indians*, 58.

225 *Heavy rains kept*: *Cherokee Phoenix*, October 27, 1832, 2.

226 *"Here then is"*: John Ross's address to the council, October 10, 1832, reprinted in the *Cherokee Phoenix*, October 27, 1832, 2–3.

226 *As Montgomery listened*: Letter of Hugh Montgomery to Lewis Cass, October 31, 1832, 23rd Congress, Senate Documents, no. 512, III (Serial 246), 513.

227 *In the final*: Ibid.

227 *The Cherokees voted*: Letter of Elisha Chester to Lewis Cass, October 27, 1832, ibid., 510–11.

227 *If . . . the present*: Letter of Hugh Montgomery to Lewis Cass, October 31, 1832, in ibid., 513.

Chapter 10: The Schemes of Traitors

228 *The news came*: Letter of John Ridge to John Ross, February 2, 1833, reprinted in Moulton, *The Papers of Chief John Ross*, vol. I, 259–60.

228 *"General Jackson did"*: Ibid.

229 *"I hope we"*: Ibid.

229 *For weeks, he*: Letter of John Ross to Lewis Cass, February 14, 1833, *Cherokee Phoenix*, August 10, 1833, 3.

229 *Eventually Ross managed*: Starkey, *Cherokee Nation*, 225–26.

230 *The president offered*: Ibid.

231 *The violence started*: Wilkins, *Cherokee Tragedy*, 256.

231 *Even the former*: Payne Papers, vol. II, 87.

232 *Hicks had initially*: Eaton, *John Ross and the Cherokee Indians*, 57.

232 *At the same*: Starkey, *Cherokee Nation*, 227.

232 *John Vann claimed*: Letter of John Walker Jr. to Hugh Montgomery, April 4, 1833, 23rd Congress, Senate Documents, no. 512, IV (Serial 247), 169.

232 *To bolster his*: Letter of Elbert Herring to John Ross, March 14, 1833, reprinted in the *Cherokee Phoenix*, July 20, 1833, 2.

233   *"Should it become"*: *Cherokee Phoenix,* August 10, 1833, 3.

233   *Ridge had learned*: Letter of John Ridge to Lewis Cass, April 5, 1833, 23rd Congress, Senate Documents, no. 512, IV (Serial 247), 169–70.

233   *When Ridge revealed*: *Cherokee Phoenix,* July 20, 1833, 3.

234   *These men secretly*: Letter of William S. Coodey et al. to General Council, May 15, 1833, 23rd Congress, Senate Documents, no. 512, IV (Serial 247), 415.

234   *"It must be"*: Ibid.

234   *Ross was shocked*: Letter of Benjamin Currey to Elbert Herring, May 23, 1833, ibid., 411–15.

235   *The resolution said*: Ibid.

236   *They considered Texas*: Moulton, *John Ross,* 61.

236   *John Ridge believed*: Ibid.

236   *"In case we"*: Ibid.

237   *One man even*: Ruskin, *John Ross,* 30.

237   *By the fall*: Starkey, *Cherokee Nation,* 231.

237   *Elijah Hicks, acting*: *Cherokee Phoenix,* July 20, 1833, 3.

237   *Hicks called Ridge's*: Ibid.

238   *He spent the*: Letter of R. G. Dunlap to Andrew Jackson, August 25, 1833, in the National Archives, Records Group 75, reprinted in Wilkins, *Cherokee Tragedy,* 257.

238   *Ross remained sequestered*: *Cherokee Phoenix,* November 23, 1833, 1.

239   *"On all important"*: Ibid.

239   *General Council remained*: Ibid., 1–2.

239   *The council even*: Letter of Benjamin Currey to Elbert Herring, November 4, 1833, 23rd Congress, Senate Documents, no. 512, IV (Serial 247), 644–45.

240   *The men set*: *Cherokee Phoenix,* April 5, 1834, 3.

240   *The bumbling cabal*: Wilkins, *Cherokee Tragedy,* 259.

241   *Despite their unofficial*: Eaton, *John Ross and the Cherokee Indians,* 64.

242   *At his own*: Robert V. Remini, *Andrew Jackson and the Course of American Democracy, 1833–1834* (New York: Harper and Row, 1984), 293.

242   *In a series*: Letters of John Ross to Andrew Jackson, March 12, March 17, and March 28, 1834, reprinted in Moulton, *The Papers of Chief John Ross,* vol. I, 277–84.

242   *The white men*: Wilkins, *Cherokee Tragedy*, 260.

243   *On this visit*: The description of Major Ridge comes from the portrait of the chief in McKenney and Hall, *History of the Indian Tribes of North America*, 181.

243   *Once he reached*: Ibid., 261.

244   *Andrew Ross eventually*: Moulton, *John Ross*, 56; Memorial to the Senate, June 24, 1834, reprinted in Moulton, *The Papers of Chief John Ross*, vol. I, 298–99.

244   *At the chief's*: Payne Papers, vol. II, 21.

244   *"The whole nation"*: Ibid.

245   *The Georgians were*: This incident is recounted in Lumpkin, *Removal of the Cherokee Indians from Georgia*, vol. I, 277–79.

245   *"But that anything"*: Ibid.

246   *That month, he*: Perdue and Green, *The Cherokee Nation and the Trail of Tears*, 104.

246   *Ross may have*: Letter of John Ross to William H. Underwood, August 12, 1834, Moulton, *The Papers of Chief John Ross*, vol. I, 300–1.

247   *Foreman called the*: This account of the summer 1834 council, and Foreman's call to lynch the Ridges, is reconstructed from several sources, including Moulton, *John Ross*, 57; Wilkins, *Cherokee Tragedy*, 262–63; and Ehle, *Trail of Tears*, 268–70.

248   *John Walker Jr.*: Wilkins, *Cherokee Tragedy*, 263; Ehle, *Trail of Tears*, 271.

249   *On Wednesday, September*: Letter of John Ross to John Ridge, September 12, 1834, reprinted in Moulton, *The Papers of Chief John Ross*, vol. I, 302–4.

249   *"With the utmost"*: Ibid.

249   *The tentative peace*: Ehle, *Trail of Tears*, 272.

250   *Over three days*: Wilkins, *Cherokee Tragedy*, 265.

Chapter 11: 1835

251   *It was a*: This account of Ross on the night he discovered he had lost his home to the Georgia land lottery was recounted by the chief himself as part of a memorial to Congress, June 21, 1836, reprinted in Moulton, *The Papers of Chief John Ross*, vol. I, 427–44.

254   *John Ridge returned*: Wilkins, *Cherokee Tragedy*, 269.

254 *"The poor Indian"*: Letter of John Ridge to Major Ridge, March 10, 1835, reprinted in Dale and Litton, *Cherokee Cavaliers,* 12–14.

254 *While Ross's home*: Governor Wilson Lumpkin's efforts to aid and appease the Ridges is outlined in his letter to Colonel William Bishop, May 28, 1835, reprinted in Lumpkin, *Removal of the Cherokee Indians from Georgia,* vol. I, 343–46.

254 *Ridge's elation soon*: Starkey, *Cherokee Nation,* 253.

255 *Benjamin Currey sent*: Wilkins, *Cherokee Tragedy,* 270.

255 *Even though he*: Starkey, *Cherokee Nation,* 256.

255 *General Council officially*: William R. Snell, *The Councils at Red Clay Council Grounds* (Cleveland, Tenn.: Lee University, 2002), 7.

255 *While the chiefs*: Moulton, *John Ross,* 62.

256 *Ross finally appeared*: John Ross's address to the General Council, May 18, 1835, reprinted in Moulton, *The Papers of Chief John Ross,* vol. I, 337–38.

256 *"You must break"*: Letter of John Ridge to Wilson Lumpkin, May 18, 1835, reprinted in Wilkins, *Cherokee Tragedy,* 271–72.

256 *Within two weeks*: Letter of Wilson Lumpkin to Colonel William N. Bishop, June 17, 1835, reprinted in Wilson, *Removal of the Cherokee Indians from Georgia,* vol. I, 353–56.

257 *Soon after he*: Payne Papers, vol. II, 127.

258 *Ross first considered*: Ibid.

258 *In a pouring*: The account of the July 1835 meeting at Running Waters was reconstructed from a number of sources, primarily the Payne Papers, vol. II, 132–40. A few of John Ridge's comments come from Wilkins, *Cherokee Tragedy,* 273; Moulton, *John Ross,* 64–65; and Starkey, *Cherokee Nation,* 257.

261 *John Ross had*: The account of Ross's meetings with the Ridges comes from various references, including the Payne Papers, vol. VII (part 2), 284; Moulton, *John Ross,* 65; and Wilkins, *Cherokee Tragedy,* 276.

262 *"We have no"*: Letter of Major Ridge and John Ridge to John Ross, July 31, 1835, reprinted in Moulton, *The Papers of Chief John Ross,* vol. I, 349–50.

263 *"Ho! Martin! Rouse"*: The account of John Martin's argument with the Treaty Party Cherokees is taken from the Payne Papers, vol. II, 40–43.

264 *"No," Ross told*: Payne Papers, vol. VII (part 2), 287.

264 *In mid-August, the*: Letter of John Ross to J. F. Schermerhorn and Benjamin Currey, August 22, 1835, included in the Payne Papers, vol. VII (part 2), 287–88.

264 *In late August*: This long account of John Howard Payne's months-long visit with John Ross and his experiences at the fall council of 1835 are taken from Payne's own account, originally published in the Knoxville, Tennessee, *Register,* December 2, 1835, as reprinted in George Magruder Battey Jr., *A History of Rome and Floyd County* (Atlanta: Webb and Vary Company, 1922), 55–74.

266 *The writer met*: Ibid.

267 *John Ross delivered*: Annual message of John Ross to the Cherokees at Red Clay, October 12, 1835, reprinted in Moulton, *The Papers of Chief John Ross,* vol. I, 354–59.

267 *"And, should it"*: Ibid.

268 *During the council*: Wilkins, *Cherokee Tragedy,* 279.

268 *"The question was"*: Ibid, 280.

269 *He announced that*: Starkey, *Cherokee Nation,* 264–65; Wilkins, *Cherokee Tragedy,* 281.

269 *On Saturday evening*: The account of Ross and Payne's arrest by the Georgia Guard is taken almost entirely from Payne's own newspaper account as reprinted in Battey, *A History of Rome and Floyd County,* 55–74.

273 *"This delegation has"*: Letter of John Ross to George Gilmer, November 13, 1835, as reprinted in Moulton, *The Papers of Chief John Ross,* vol. I, 372–73.

273 *John Ridge was*: Wilkins, *Cherokee Tragedy,* 283–84.

274 *When the men*: Battey, *A History of Rome and Floyd County,* 55–74.

275 *"You have never"*: Ibid.

276 *But when Ross*: Letter of Elias Boudinot to John Ross, November 25, 1835, reprinted in Moulton, *The Papers of Chief John Ross,* vol. I, 376.

276 *Two days before*: Letter of John Ross to John Ridge, November 30, 1835, reprinted ibid., 376.

276 *No sooner had*: Battey, *A History of Rome and Floyd County,* 55.

276 *John Ridge believed*: Letter of John Ridge to John Ross, December 4, 1835, reprinted in Moulton, *The Papers of Chief John Ross,* vol. I, 377.

277 *"I trust that"*: Ibid.

277   *Ross pleaded with*: Letter of John Ross to John Ridge, December 4, 1835, ibid., 378.

277   *New Echota was*: This account of the Schermerhorn council that resulted in the Treaty of New Echota is taken from a number of sources, primarily a letter of James J. Trott to John Ross, January 6, 1836, reprinted in Moulton, *The Papers of Chief John Ross*, vol. I, 379–80; the Payne Papers, vol. XIII, 55–64; Starkey, *Cherokee Nation*, 266–67.

280   *"I am one"*: Major Ridge's speech at New Echota is from the *Cartersville* (Ga.) *Courant*, March 26, 1885 quoted in Wilkins, *Cherokee Tragedy*, 286–87.

282   *"I have signed"*: Starkey, *Cherokee Nation*, 267.

Chapter 12: Where They Cried

283   *There were rules*: The account of Ross's meeting with Andrew Jackson comes from two sources: letter of Ross to John Payne, January 7, 1836, and a Memorial to the U.S. Senate, March 8, 1836. Both are reprinted in Moulton, *The Papers of Chief John Ross*, vol. I, 381–82, 394–413.

284   *Reverend James J. Trott*: Letter of James Trott to John Ross, January 6, 1836, ibid., 379–80.

285   *When he reached*: Letter of Major Ridge et al. to John Ross, February 6, 1836, reprinted in Moulton, *The Papers of Chief John Ross*, vol. I, 385.

286   *Within a day*: Wilkins, *Cherokee Tragedy*, 291.

286   *At one point*: Moulton, *John Ross*, 74.

286   *Schermerhorn claimed that*: Starkey, *Cherokee Nation*, 268–69.

286   *Major William M. Davis*: Moulton, *John Ross*, 76.

286   *The deception was*: Starkey, *Cherokee Nation*, 271–72.

287   *On March 8*: Memorial to the U.S. Senate, as reprinted in Moulton, *The Papers of Chief John Ross*, vol. I, 394–413.

287   *He addressed Congress*: Moulton, *The Papers of Chief John Ross*, vol. I, 427–44.

288   *John Ridge and*: From the Treaty of New Echota, as printed in Lumpkin, *Removal of the Cherokee Indians from Georgia*, vol. II, 17–27.

288   *"They intend to"*: Ibid., 112.

288   *The Ridges called*: Wilkins, *Cherokee Tragedy*, 296.

288 *The Red Clay*: Letter of Ross to John E. Wool, September 30, 1836, reprinted in Moulton, *The Papers of Chief John Ross,* vol. I, 461–62.

289 *Indian agents in*: John Ross, address to General Council, August 3, 1837, ibid., 507–12.

289 *The western Cherokees*: Eaton, *John Ross and the Cherokee Indians,* 74.

290 *"I do think"*: Letter of Lewis Ross to John Ross, January 16, 1837, reprinted in Moulton, *The Papers of Chief John Ross,* vol. I, 467.

290 *Ross avoided the*: John Ross, address to General Council, August 3, 1837, ibid., 507–12.

290 *Van Buren had*: Moulton, *John Ross,* 82.

290 *One committee promised*: Letter of John Ross to Henry A. Wise, February 25, 1837, reprinted in Moulton, *The Papers of Chief John Ross,* vol. I, 474–78.

291 *Before Ross checked*: "Letter from John Ross . . . to a Gentleman from Philadelphia," from McKenney and Hall, *History of the Indian Tribes of North America,* as reprinted ibid., 490–503.

291 *In Ross's absence*: Moulton, *John Ross,* 80.

291 *Ross left no*: John Ross, address to General Council, August 3, 1837, Moulton, *The Papers of Chief John Ross,* vol. I, 507–12.

292 *A few days*: Eaton, *John Ross and the Cherokee Indians,* 76.

292 *Featherstonhaugh was impressed*: Moulton, *John Ross,* 84–85.

293 *"There, Cherokees, in"*: Snell, *Councils at Red Clay Council Grounds,* 11.

293 *Shortly after John*: Wilkins, *Cherokee Tragedy,* 308.

294 *On March 3, 1837*: Ibid., 304.

295 *John Ridge and*: Ibid., 309.

295 *For much of*: Letter of John Ross to John H. Sherburne, Moulton, *The Papers of Chief John Ross,* vol. I, 518–19.

295 *He dispatched Cherokee*: Letter of John Ross to the chiefs of the Seminole Nation, October 18, 1837, ibid., 523–26.

296 *Lewis wrote to*: Letter of Lewis Ross to John Ross, October 25, 1837, ibid., 532–33; letter of Lewis Ross to John Ross, March 22, 1838, ibid., 615.

296 *Ross promised Poinsett*: Letter of John Ross to Lewis Ross, April 5, 1838, ibid., 622–24.

296 *Wilson Lumpkin, who*: Lumpkin, *Removal of the Cherokee Indians from Georgia,* vol. II, 183–88, 216.

297 *Not another moon*: Starkey, *Cherokee Nation,* 286.

297 *"Will you, then"*: Ibid.

298 *In late May*: Payne Papers, vol. IX, 67.

298 *Over the final*: These sad anecdotes from the roundup of Cherokees are taken from various sources, predominately the Payne Papers, vol. IX, 67–69; Starkey, *Cherokee Nation,* 267–68; and Mooney, *Myths of the Cherokee,* 130–35.

299 *One morning, Scott's*: The story of Tsali is perhaps the most famous, and most often repeated, of all the stories to come from the days before the Cherokees were sent west. This account comes from several sources, mainly Brown, *Old Frontiers,* 520–21.

301 *Later, some would*: "New Light on the Tsali Affair" by William Martin Jurgelski, printed in Thomas J. Pluckhahn and Robbie Ethridge, eds., *Light on the Path: The Anthropology and History of the Southeastern Indians* (Tuscaloosa: University of Alabama Press, 2006), 133–64.

301 *These stockades were*: The descriptions of the Cherokee holding areas, and the incidents that occurred in them, are taken largely from the descriptions of the missionary Daniel S. Butrick, as recounted in the Payne Papers, vol. IX, 67–97.

302 *"The poor captive"*: Walker, *Torchlights to the Cherokees,* 325.

302 *Butrick watched six*: Payne Papers, vol. IX, 67–97.

303 *The first group*: Starkey, *Cherokee Nation,* 291–92.

303 *In the midst*: Perdue and Green, *Cherokee Nation and the Trail of Tears,* 128.

304 *Ross was so*: Letter of John Ross to John Howard Payne, July 5 and 9, 1838, reprinted in Moulton, *The Papers of Chief John Ross,* vol. I, 648.

304 *She had left*: Moulton, *John Ross,* 97.

304 *Ross had sent*: Perdue and Green, *Cherokee Nation and the Trail of Tears,* 130; Letter of John Ross to Winfield Scott, July 23, 1838, Moulton, *The Papers of Chief John Ross,* vol. I, 650–51.

305 *The chief got*: Articles of Agreement between John Ross and Lewis Ross, August 10, 1838, Moulton, *The Papers of Chief John Ross,* vol., 657–58.

305 *"What madness and"*: Ehle, *Trail of Tears,* 349.

306 *On July 21*: Address of John Ross to the Cherokees, July 21, 1838, reprinted in Moulton, *The Papers of Chief John Ross,* vol. I, 649–50.

306 *"When the strong"*: Ibid.

307 *He organized the*: Letter from Winfield Scott to John Ross, October 3, 1838, Moulton, *The Papers of Chief John Ross,* vol. I, 676–77. The description of the routes comes largely from Starkey, *Cherokee Nation,* 297, and the maps on display at the Cherokee National Museum in Park Hill, Oklahoma. The museum's Trail of Tears exhibit is an impressive display that gets to the pain and misery the Cherokees encountered along their route.

308 *The first group*: The order and leadership of the detachments are recounted well in Conley, *Cherokee Nation,* 154–57.

308 *"At length the"*: Letter of William Shorey Coodey to John Howard Payne, August 13, 1840, Payne Papers, vol. XIII, 179–80. Also reprinted in Vicki Rozema, *Voices from the Trail of Tears* (Winston-Salem, N.C.: John F. Blair, 2003), 133–35.

308 *Wagons could not*: Letter of Jesse Bushyhead to John Ross, October 21, 1838, reprinted in Moulton, *The Papers of Chief John Ross,* vol. I, 683.

309 *"Necowee has given"*: Letter of Elijah Hicks to John Ross, October 24, 1838, ibid., 684–85.

309 *A few Indians*: The descriptions of hardships along the route throughout this section are taken from a variety of sources, including Starkey, *Cherokee Nation,* 297–301; Ehle, *Trail of Tears,* 352–62; Brown, *Old Frontiers,* 506–19; and the Cherokee National Museum Trail of Tears exhibit.

310 *"The forward part"*: Ehle, *Trail of Tears,* 358.

311 *In Illinois, a*: Perdue and Green, *Cherokee Nation and the Trail of Tears,* 135.

311 *"The agents for"*: Letter of Thomas N. Clark to John Ross, December 17, 1838, reprinted in Moulton, *The Papers of Chief John Ross,* vol. I, 685–96.

311 *"I have waited"*: Letter of Thomas N. Clark to John Ross, January 22, 1839, ibid., 697–98.

312 *"Long time we"*: Ehle, *Trail of Tears,* 358.

312 *It was December 4*: Moulton, *John Ross,* 100.

312   *In the town*: The account of Jane Ross's marriage comes from the Meigs family genealogy at www.meigs.org.

313   *As he loaded*: The description of what Ross saw as he left Ross's Landing comes in part from Govan and Livingood, *Chattanooga Country 1540–1951*, 99.

313   *The steamboat* Victoria: The account of John Ross's journey to the West comes from a number of sources, including Conley, *Cherokee Nation*, 100; Ruskin, *John Ross*, 35; and Moulton, *John Ross*, 100–101.

Chapter 13: Retribution

316   *Not only had*: Letter of Elijah Hicks to John Ross, March 6, 1839, reprinted in Moulton, *The Papers of Chief John Ross*, vol. I, 699–700.

316   *He secured a*: Moulton, *John Ross*, 144.

317   *"The health and"*: Letter of John Ross to Matthew Arbuckle, April 23, 1839, Moulton, *The Papers of Chief John Ross*, vol. I, 704–5.

317   *John Jolly, principal*: Eaton, *John Ross and the Cherokee Indians*, 94.

317   *The western tribe*: Starkey, *Cherokee Nation*, 305–6.

318   *Less than two*: Eaton, *John Ross and the Cherokee Indians*, 94.

318   *He was diplomatic*: Starkey, *Cherokee Nation*, 307.

318   *More than six thousand*: William G. McLoughlin, *After the Trail of Tears: The Cherokees' Struggle for Sovereignty 1839–1880* (Chapel Hill: University of North Carolina Press, 1993), 10.

319   *"We joyfully welcome"*: Ibid.

319   *Standing beneath the*: Address of John Ross to General Council of the Cherokees, June 10, 1839, reprinted in Moulton, *The Papers of Chief John Ross*, vol. I, 712–13.

319   *"Let us never"*: Ibid.

319   *Later, speaking in*: McLouglin, *After the Trail of Tears*, 11.

320   *Ross and George*: Letter of John Ross to John Brown, John Looney, and John Rogers, June 13, 1839, Thomas Gilcrease Institute of American History and Art, reprinted in Moulton, *The Papers of Chief John Ross*, vol. I, 713–14.

320   *"Our chiefs have"*: Letter of John Brown, John Looney, and John Rogers, June 14, 1839, ibid., 714–15.

320 *The members of*: This account of the Ridges' appearance at the Takatota council comes from a letter of the missionary Evan Jones to John Howard Payne, July 22, 1839, found in the Payne Papers, vol. V, 77–79.

321 *C. Washburn, a*: Starkey, *Cherokee Nation*, 308–9.

321 *Ross had good*: McLoughlin, *After the Trail of Tears*, 13.

321 *On June 20*: Ibid., 14–15.

322 *By an impromptu*: Letter of the missionary Evan Jones to John Howard Payne, July 22, 1839, found in the Payne Papers, vol. V, 77–79.

322 *The next day*: Ibid.

322 *There was no*: Ibid. The account of this secret meeting is also culled from various other sources, including Wilkins, *Cherokee Tragedy*, 334; McLoughlin, *After the Trail of Tears*, 16; Eaton, *John Ross and the Cherokee Indians*, 96.

323 *Years later, Allen*: Moulton, *Ross*, 113.

323 *But he later*: "The Murder of Elias Boudinot," *Chronicles of Oklahoma*, vol. 12, no. 1, March 1934, 19–24.

323 *They came at*: The account of John Ridge's death is compiled from various sources, including Starkey, *Cherokee Nation*, 311–12; Wilkins, *Cherokee Tragedy*, 335; Ehle, *Trail of Tears*, 375–76; the preface of John Rollin Ridge, *Poems* (San Francisco: Henry Payot & Company, 1868); and a letter of the missionary Evan Jones to John Howard Payne, July 22, 1839, found in the Payne Papers, vol. V, 77–79.

325 *In a few*: Ridge, *Poems*, 7.

325 *Elias Boudinot emerged*: Eaton, *John Ross and the Cherokees Indians*, 97.

326 *The men came*: Ibid. The account of Boudinot's murder also comes from "The Murder of Elias Boudinot"; Wilkins, *Cherokee Tragedy*, 376.

327 *"They have cut"*: Eaton, *John Ross and the Cherokee Indians*, 97.

327 *A Choctaw Indian*: Wilkins, *Cherokee Tragedy*, 336–37.

327 *When he finally*: McLoughlin, *After the Trail of Tears*, 16.

327 *Delight Boudinot begged*: Starkey, *Cherokee Nation*, 313.

328 *That same day*: The account of Major Ridge's assassination comes from a letter of the missionary Evan Jones to John Howard Payne, July 22, 1839, found in the Payne Papers, vol. V, 77-79; Eaton, *John Ross and the Cherokee Indians*, 96–97; and Wilkins, *Cherokee Tragedy*, 338–39.

330 *Ross sent his*: Moulton, *John Ross*, 113.

330   *She confirmed her*: Starkey, *Cherokee Nation*, 313.

330   *That afternoon, he*: Letter of John Ross to Matthew Arbuckle, June 22, 1839, reprinted in Moulton, *The Papers of Chief John Ross*, vol. I, 717.

330   *"Why I am"*: Ibid.

331   *On Sunday, Arbuckle*: This offer is mentioned in a letter Ross wrote to Arbuckle, June 23, 1839, ibid., 717–18.

331   *By Monday there*: Ibid.

331   *By the end*: Starkey, *Cherokee Nation*, 313.

331   *Some visitors to*: Deborah L. Duvall, *An Oral History of Tahlequah and the Cherokee Nation* (Charleston, S.C.: Arcadia Publishing, 2000), 32.

332   *The western chiefs*: McLoughlin, *After the Trail of Tears*, 17.

332   *Their standing was*: Ibid., 18; letter of John Ross to John Brown, John Looney, and John Rogers, June 30, 1839, reprinted in Moulton, *The Papers of Chief John Ross*, vol. I, 724.

332   *Brown had asked*: Letter of John Brown, John Looney, and John Rogers to John Ross, July 6, 1839, Thomas Gilcrease Institute of American History and Art, reprinted in Moulton, *The Papers of Chief John Ross*, vol. I, 730–71.

332   *The Indians appointed*: McLoughlin, *After the Trail of Tears*, 18.

332   *On July 12*: Moulton, *John Ross*, 116.

333   *The constitution included*: McLoughlin, *After the Trail of Tears*, 19.

333   *A few weeks*: Ibid., 21.

333   *The election did*: Eaton, *John Ross and the Cherokee Indians*, 100–101.

333   *At the same*: McLoughlin, *After the Trail of Tears*, 20.

333   *Before the end*: Moulton, *John Ross*, 119–22.

Epilogue: The Way of the West

335   *The violence peaked*: John Howard Payne, *Indian Justice: A Cherokee Murder Trial at Tahlequah in 1840* (Muskogee, Ga.: The Star Printery, 1962), 2.

335   *When his client*: Ibid., 91.

336   *Ross ignored the*: Ibid., 94–95.

336   *In 1842 Watie*: Conley, *Cherokee Nation*, 161.

336   *The next year*: Moulton, *John Ross*, 136.

336   *The arson was*: Perdue and Green, *Cherokee Nation and the Trail of Tears*, 156.

337   *"The country is"*: Letter of William P. Ross and Jane Ross Meigs to John
      Ross, November 5 and 7, 1845, reprinted in Moulton, *The Papers of Chief
      John Ross,* vol. II, 271–74.

337   *Eventually, the council*: Moulton, *John Ross,* 137.

337   *Finally, in 1846*: Eaton, *John Ross and the Cherokee Indians,* 108–9.

338   *Ross installed his*: Starkey, *Cherokee Nation,* 317.

338   *The large house*: The description of Ross's new home comes from drawings
      and several contemporary descriptions, as well as Eaton, *John Ross and
      the Cherokee Indians,* 114–15. The mention of his furnishings and dishes is
      taken from the chief's belongings that survive at the George M. Murrell
      House in Park Hill, Oklahoma.

339   *John Howard Payne*: Moulton, *John Ross,* 144.

339   *He turned his*: Ibid., 155.

340   *John Ross met*: Ibid., 139. Ross's early visits with the Stapler family are also
      recounted in several letters.

340   *After their first*: Letter of Mary Bryan Stapler and Sarah Stapler to John
      Ross, August 10, 1841, reprinted in Moulton, *The Papers of Chief John Ross,*
      vol. II, 94–95.

341   *It was two*: Letter of Mary B. Stapler to John Ross, May 3, 1844, ibid., 197.

341   *"When I started"*: Letter of Mary B. Stapler to John Ross, June 26, 1844,
      ibid., 211–12.

341   *Ross, as blunt*: Letter of John Ross to Mary B. Stapler, June 16, 1844, ibid.,
      208.

341   *"Why then should"*: Letter of John Ross to Mary B. Stapler, July 30, 1844,
      ibid., 230–31.

342   *"My very dear"*: Letter of Mary B. Stapler to John Ross, August 1, 1844,
      ibid., 231–32.

342   *That short note*: Ross wrote separate letters to John Stapler and Sarah F.
      Stapler on August 14, 1844. Both are reprinted in Moulton, *The Papers of
      Chief John Ross,* vol. II, 238–39.

342   *They married in*: Letter of John Ross to Thomas L. McKenney, September
      6, 1844, ibid., 243–44.

342   *Shortly after his*: McLoughlin, *After the Trail of Tears,* 64.

343   *To curb the*: Ibid., 84–85.

343   *And when the*: Eaton, *John Ross and the Cherokee Indians*, 107–8.

343   *There was rarely*: Moulton, *John Ross*, 161–62.

343   *In 1850 Ross*: Ibid., 154–55.

344   *He built more*: Eaton, *John Ross and the Cherokee Indians*, 117–18.

344   *The young Mary*: Letters of John Ross to Maria B. Stapler, December 31, 1860 and January 18, 1861, reprinted in Moulton, *The Papers of Chief John Ross*, vol. II, 453–56.

344   *The trip served*: Letter of John Ross to James M. Ross, February 12, 1860, ibid., 432; Moulton, *John Ross*, 163.

344   *Storefronts lined streets*: The description of Chattanooga as Ross saw it in the winter of 1860 comes from Govan and Livingood, *Chattanooga Country 1540–1951*, 159–75, and is based on photographs in Rob Clifton, *Chattanooga Then and Now* (Chattanooga: Clifton, 2006).

345   *Ross toured the*: Moulton, *John Ross*, 163.

345   *The difference of*: Eaton, *John Ross and the Cherokee Indians*, 123.

346   *Although the Cherokees*: Starkey, *Cherokee Nation*, 320.

346   *The Confederates had*: Ibid., 131.

346   *Less than a*: Conley, *Cherokee Nation*, 175–76.

346   *Brigadier General James*: Moulton, *John Ross*, 175.

347   *Stand Watie and*: McLoughlin, *After the Trail of Tears*, 207.

347   *One of his*: Eaton, *John Ross and the Cherokee Indians*, 139.

347   *He wrote to*: Letter of John Ross to Mary B. Ross, June 6, 1864, reprinted in Moulton, *The Papers of Chief John Ross*, vol. II, 583.

347   *The war had*: Ibid., 733.

348   *She had kept*: Moulton, *John Ross*, 182.

348   *"I know that"*: Letter of John Ross to Sarah F. Stapler, August 31, 1865, reprinted in Moulton, *The Papers of Chief John Ross*, vol. II, 645–46.

348   *Shortly after he*: Eaton, *John Ross and the Cherokee Indians*, 143–45; McLouglin, *After the Trail of Tears*, 219–21.

349   *Boudinot claimed Ross*: Moulton, *John Ross*, 187.

349   *He left Park*: Ibid., 188.

349   *Johnson was not*: Ibid., 194.

350   *"I am an"*: Ibid., 1.

350   *That fall, they*: Eaton, *John Ross and the Cherokee Indians*, 148–49.

351 *He shut out*: Ibid., 231.
351 *Slowly, the last*: The biographies of the Ross children were culled from various letters; genealogical searches; Ruskin, *John Ross;* and Moulton, *The Papers of Chief John Ross,* vol. II, 715–39.
352 *By 1871 Chief*: McLoughlin, *After the Trail of Tears,* 288.
352 *Ross was appointed*: Conley, *Cherokee Nation,* 185.
352 *By 1875 there*: Ibid., 186–87.
352 *Dawes seized on*: Ibid., 193.
353 *The Cherokees continued*: Ibid., 201.

Selected Bibliography

Alderman, Pat. *Nancy Ward/Dragging Canoe: Cherokee Chieftainess/Cherokee-Chickamauga War Chief.* Johnson City, Tenn.: Overmountain Press, 1978.

Armstrong, Zella. *The History of Hamilton County and Chattanooga, Tennessee, Vol. I.* Johnson City, Tenn.: Overmountain Press, 1993.

Bass, Althea. *Cherokee Messenger.* Norman: University of Oklahoma Press, 1996.

Bassett, John Spencer. *The Life of Andrew Jackson.* New York: Doubleday, Page, 1911.

Battey, George Magruder, Jr. *A History of Rome and Floyd County.* Atlanta: The Webb and Vary Company, 1922.

Brown, John P. *Old Frontiers: The Story of the Cherokee Indians from Earliest Times to the Date of Their Removal to the West, 1838.* Kingsport, Tenn.: Southern Publishers, 1938.

Conley, Robert J. *The Cherokee Nation: A History.* Albuquerque: University of New Mexico Press, 2005.

Cornelius, Elias. *The Little Osage Captive: An Authentic Narrative.* Boston: Armstrong, Crocker and Brewster, 1822.

Crockett, David. *The Life of Col. David Crockett.* Philadelphia: G. G. Evans, 1859.

Dale, Edward Everett, and Gaston Litton. *Cherokee Cavaliers: Forty Years of Cherokee Hisory as Told in the Correspondence of the Ridge-Watie-Boudinot Family.* Norman: University of Oklahoma Press, 1940.

Eaton, Rachel Caroline. *John Ross and the Cherokee Indians*. Chicago: University of Chicago Libraries, 1921.

Ehle, John. *Trail of Tears: The Rise and Fall of the Cherokee Nation*. New York: Anchor Books, 1989.

Evarts, Jeremiah. *Speeches on the Passage of the Bill for the Removal of the Indians*. Boston: Perkins and Marvin, 1830.

Foreman, Grant. *Indian Removal: The Emigration of the Five Civilized Tribes of Indians*. Norman: University of Oklahoma Press, 1972.

Govan, Gilbert E., and James W. Livingood. *The Chattanooga Country 1540–1951: From Tomahawks to TVA*. New York: E. P. Dutton, 1952.

Holland, James W. *Victory at the Horseshoe: Andrew Jackson and the Creek War*. Tuscaloosa: University of Alabama Press, 2004.

King, Duane H. (ed.). *The Cherokee Indian Nation: A Troubled History*. Knoxville: University of Tennessee Press, 1979.

Lillard, Roy G. (ed.). *The History of Bradley County*. Cleveland, Tenn.: Bradley County Chapter, East Tennessee Historical Society, Cleveland-Bradley County American Revolution Bicentennial Commission, 1976.

Lumpkin, Wilson. *The Removal of the Cherokee Indians from Georgia*. Wormsloe, Ga.: Dodd, Mead, 1907.

McKenney, Thomas L., and James Hall. *History of the Indian Tribes of North America, with Biographical Sketches and Anecdotes of the Principal Chiefs*. Philadelphia: Edward C. Biddle, 1836.

McLoughlin, William G. *Cherokee Renascence in the New Republic*. Princeton, N.J.: Princeton University Press, 1986.

———. *After the Trail of Tears: The Cherokees' Struggle for Sovereignty, 1839–1880*. Chapel Hill: University of North Carolina Press, 1993.

Mooney, James. *Myths of the Cherokee and Sacred Formulas of the Cherokees*. Nashville: Charles and Randy Elder, Booksellers, 1982.

Moulton, Gary E. *John Ross: Cherokee Chief*. Athens: University of Georgia Press, 1978.

——— (ed.). *The Papers of Chief John Ross,* two volumes. Norman: University of Oklahoma Press, 1985.

Norgren, Jill. *The Cherokee Cases: Two Landmark Federal Decisions in the Fight for Sovereignty*. Norman: University of Oklahoma Press, 2004.

Parker, Thomas Valentine. *The Cherokee Indians, with Special Referene to Their Relations with the United States Government*. New York: Grafton Press, 1907.

Payne, John Howard. *Indian Justice: A Cherokee Murder Trial at Tahlequah in 1840*. Muskogee, Ga.: The Star Printery, 1962.

Perdue, Theda (ed.). *Cherokee Editor: The Writings of Elias Boudinot*. Athens: University of Georgia Press, 1996.

Perdue, Theda, and Michael D. Green. *The Cherokee Nation and the Trail of Tears*. New York: Viking/Penguin Library of American Indian History 2007.

Phillips, Joyce B., and Paul Gary Phillips. *The Brainerd Journal: A Mission to the Cherokees, 1817–1823*. Lincoln: University of Nebraska Press, 1998.

Raulston, J. Leonard, and James W. Livingood. *Sequatchie: A Story of the Southern Cumberlands*. Knoxville: University of Tennessee Press, 1980.

Remini, Robert Vincent. *Andrew Jackson and the Course of American Freedom, 1822–1832*. New York: Harper and Row, 1981.

———. *Andrew Jackson and the Course of American Democracy, 1833–1845*. New York: Harper and Row, 1984.

———. *Andrew Jackson and His Indian Wars*. New York: Viking, 2001.

Royce, Charles C. *The Cherokee Nation of Indians*. Chicago: Aldine Publishing Company/Smithsonian Institution Press, 1975.

Rozema, Vicki. *Footsteps of the Cherokees: A Guide to the Eastern Homelands of the Cherokee Nation*. Winston-Salem, N.C.: John F. Blair, 1995.

———. *Voices from the Trail of Tears*. Winston-Salem, N.C.: John F. Blair, 2003.

Ruskin, Gertrude McDaris. *John Ross: Chief of an Eagle Race*. Chattanooga, Tenn.: John Ross House Association, 1963.

Snell, William R. *The Councils at Red Clay Council Grounds*. Cleveland, Tenn.: Lee University, 2002.

Starkey, Marion L. *The Cherokee Nation*. New York: Alfred A. Knopf, 1946.

Walker, Robert Sparks. *Torchlights to the Cherokees: The Brainerd Mission*. New York: Macmillan, 1931.

———. *Lookout, The Story of a Mountain*. Kingsport, Tenn.: Southern Publishers, 1941.

Whitmire, Mildred E. (ed.) *Noland's Cherokee Diary: A U.S. Soldier's Story from Inside the Cherokee Nation.* Spartanburg, S.C.: The Reprint Company, 1990.

Wilkins, Thurman. *Cherokee Tragedy: The Ridge Family and the Decimation of a People,* 2nd edition, revised. Norman: University of Oklahoma Press, 1986.

Acknowledgments

I owe a great deal of thanks to Joan Bingham, my editor at Grove/Atlantic. Joan was enthusiastic about this project from the beginning and had a clear vision of what I wanted to do before I did. Her thorough, thoughtful editing made this a much, much better book than I could have written on my own. It's rare to find an editor with an equally astute eye for the big picture and the smallest detail. At the same time, early reads by Alex Littlefield saved me on countless occasions. Emily Cunningham also gave me very helpful ideas and encouragement. Thanks also to the Grove production staff for making the book *look-and-read* great.

I am lucky to be represented by the Tracy Brown Literary Agency. Tracy has been the steady and sage guiding force behind my publishing career for ten years, and it's not an exaggeration to say I could not have written any of my books without him (it doesn't hurt that he is a fantastic editor too). Through it all, Tracy's advice has been invaluable. He is also a good friend.

I met many amazing people on my journey through Cherokee history. In Park Hill, Oklahoma, I spent a serene rainy afternoon talking with Shirley Pettengill on the front porch of the George Murrell House. Shirley, the longtime site manager at the house, offered me valuable insights on Cherokee culture and life in the tribe during the mid-1800s. Carey Tilley, the director of the Cherokee Heritage Center in Park Hill, also gave me a generous amount of time. His thoughts on Ross and Ridge convinced me I was on the right track, and he told me many things I didn't know. The people of Tahlequah made me feel right at home.

Thanks also to the staffs at Fort Smith National Historic Site in Arkansas; Horseshoe Bend National Military Park in Alabama; New Echota State Historic Site in Georgia; and Red Clay State Historic Area in Cleveland, Tennessee. I also picked up important details at the John Ross House in Rossville, Georgia, and Major Ridge's home, the Chieftains Museum, in Rome. Claudia M. Oakes, executive director at Chieftains, was particularly kind and helpful.

I'm indebted to the librarians and archivists at the Chattanooga–Hamilton County Bicentennial Library; the Newberry Library in Chicago; the National Archives in Washington, D.C.; and the Charleston, South Carolina, County Public Library. Barbara Fagen, manager of the History Branch and Archives at the Cleveland, Tennessee, Public Library, put me on the right course more than once, and Beverly Mosman at the Oklahoma Historical Society offered good advice.

Special thanks go to the Charleston Library Society, one of the oldest subscription libraries in the country, and my home base. In addition to its being a wonderful place to work, the society's Janice Knight, Carol Jones, executive director Anne Cleveland, and former director Eric Emerson provided some particularly difficult-to-find volumes. They not only had Wilson Lumpkin's scarce book, but also had in their vaults two copies—*two*—of the ultra-rare first edition of McKenney and Hall's *History of the Indian Tribes of North America.* Such is the luxury of having been around 260 years. As Eric joked, "We probably bought them new."

At my newspaper, the *Post and Courier,* I have always gotten great support and understanding from Bill Hawkins, Steve Mullins, and Rick Nelson. Finding time to write a book in this business is never easy, particularly now. But I've never had a problem getting the time to take off on a research trip—as long as my column was filed. A number of people at the paper contribute in other ways, including Schuyler, Tom, Fred, Ben, Steve, David, Bryce, Robert, Mic (who technically isn't there anymore, except in spirit), and my traveling buddy

Andy Lyons. Ben Morgan deserves extra thanks for reading the initial manuscript and offering valuable suggestions from a constant reader.

My family has been particularly supportive for the past few years, especially my in-laws, Alan and Donna Spears, who supplied some Cherokee materials for my research. My grandparents Hershel and Mildred Hicks provided me some details about Cleveland history, and my aunt Sandy Hughes sent along interesting details. My mother, Judy Hicks, still lives in Cleveland and helped more than she realizes.

Finally, I owe an unending amount of gratitude to my boys, Cole and Nate, who endured trips to middle-of-nowhere Alabama and more museums than kids care to see. They handled it all with good humor and made my travels enjoyable. My wife, Beth, to whom this book is dedicated, suffers more than anyone else while I'm off wandering through history, and it is a testament to her innate greatness and good nature that she actually suggested this book and read it any number of times to offer suggestions. I could do none of this without her and she'll never know how much I appreciate it, especially on this one.

Just a few weeks before this book was finished, Beth and I lost our seventeen-year-old cat Hemmy, who was with us from the day he was born until the day he died. He sat with me nearly every night as I worked on this book, and it will always remind me of him.

Brian Hicks
Charleston, South Carolina
January 3, 2010

Index

About the Author

Brian Hicks, a metro columnist with the *Post and Courier* in Charleston, South Carolina, is the author of *When the Dancing Stopped: The Real Story of the Morro Castle Disaster and Its Deadly Wake* and *Ghost Ship: The Mysterious True Story of the Mary Celeste and Her Missing Crew.* He is coauthor of *Raising the Hunley: The Remarkable History and Recovery of the Lost Confederate Submarine* and *Into the Wind: The Story of the World's Longest Race.* Hicks's journalism has been recognized with more than two dozen journalism awards, including the South Carolina Press Association's award for Journalist of the Year. A native of Tennessee, Hicks lives in Charleston with his wife and two sons.